THE STILLBIRTH OF CAPITAL

For Aneesha,
who made my entry
into the Gunaratne family
easier by reporting that
'I was a "good bugger."

With love and gratitude,

dilaj

THE STILLBIRTH
OF CAPITAL
Enlightenment Writing and Colonial India

SIRAJ AHMED

Stanford University Press
Stanford, California

Stanford University Press
Stanford, California

This book has been published with the assistance of the Mount Holyoke College
Dean of Faculty Office.

Printed in the United States of America on acid-free, archival-quality paper

Library of Congress Cataloging-in-Publication Data

Ahmed, Siraj Dean, author.
  The stillbirth of capital : Enlightenment writing and colonial India / Siraj Ahmed.
    pages cm
  Includes bibliographical references and index.
  ISBN 978-0-8047-7522-9 (cloth : alk. paper) — ISBN 978-0-8047-7523-6 (pbk. : alk. paper)
  1. English literature—18th century—History and criticism. 2. India—In literature. 3. Colonies
in literature. 4. Enlightenment. 5. Great Britain—Colonies—Asia—History. 6. India—History—
British occupation, 1765–1947. I. Title.
  PR448.I534A36 2012
  820.9'005—dc22

                          2011012292

Typeset by Bruce Lundquist in 10/15 Minion.

For Muthu Beevi Fathima and Syed Kader Ahmed

CONTENTS

ACKNOWLEDGMENTS

I have dedicated this book to my parents, whose lives have involved dislocations more painful than I can even imagine and sacrifices more profound than I could ever perform.

My oldest debt is to David McWhirter, whom I turn to still and admire more than ever.

David Kastan, Mike Seidel, and Jim Basker have been unfailingly generous and astute.

Because of its source, Jonathan Lamb's encouragement over the years has meant the world to me.

Sanjay Krishnan's brilliance and sensitivity provide models—which I recall almost daily—of how to think and live in this confused time.

Nigel Alderman and Stanford's readers, Suvir Kaul and Ala Alryyes, read a long manuscript with exceptional care and skill when their own obligations must have left them little time to do so.

Emily-Jane Cohen guided this book through the stages of publication with enthusiasm, kindness, and expert judgment. Carolyn Brown, Rob Ehle, Nick Koenig, Cynthia Lindlof, and Sarah Crane Newman were equally adept.

Yashi Ahmed's compassion, counsel, and gentle prodding have routinely saved me.

Many others have helped me, often with extraordinary selflessness, during the time I worked on this book: John Archer, Sulochana Asirvatham, Carlos Austin, Moustafa Bayoumi, Renee Bergland, Watson Brown, Eric Bulson, Daniel Carey, Ruchi Chaturvedi, Joan Cocks, Justin Crumbaugh, Iyko Day, Rohan Deb Roy, Frances Dickey, Michael Dodson, Susan Egenolf, Marian Eide, Margaret Ezell, Karen Fernandes, Lynn Festa, Durba Ghosh, Carol Howard, Steven Leslie, Vicki Mahaffey, Howard Marchitello, Pam Matthews, Susanne Mrozik, Ilaria Natali, Max Novak, Mary Ann O'Farrell, Suneeta Peres da Costa, Claudio Pikielny, Karen Remmler, Larry Reynolds, Victoria Rosner, Ahmed Salahuddin, Sejal Shah,

Bob Shandley, Shabnum Tejani, Robert Travers, Gauri Viswanathan, Milind Wakankar, Tim Watson, Ronaldo Wilson, and Wes Yu.

Three people who inspired me are no longer here. Edward Said treated every encounter as a challenge; I had hoped to write a book worth his precious time. Karl Kroeber died as fearlessly as he lived; I wish I could hear his voice again. Omar Azfar taught everyone around him how to play and in doing so lived as intensely as anyone I have known.

I have benefited from the opportunity to present my work at the University of London School of Advanced Study; the Yale University Paul Mellon Centre; University of California, Berkeley; University of California, Los Angeles; University of California, Santa Barbara; Indiana University; Vanderbilt University; Georgetown University; and University of Córdoba.

I could not have completed this book without fellowships from the National Endowment for the Humanities, the Mellon and the Whiting Foundations, the Huntington and the Clark Libraries, and the University of London Institutes of Commonwealth and of English Studies.

An earlier version of Chapter 5 was published in *Representations* 78 and reprinted in *Edmund Burke*, ed. Iain Hampsher-Monk (Ashgate, 2009). An earlier version of Chapter 6 was published in *The Postcolonial Enlightenment: Eighteenth-Century Colonialism and Postcolonial Theory*, ed. Daniel Carey and Lynn Festa (Oxford University Press, 2009). I thank the editors for permission to rework these articles.

From the moment I met her, Anjuli has made me feel part of a life much deeper than this one. The way she lives reminds me—in the words of the postcard above her desk—that "your heart is a muscle the size of your fist": in this world, love demands a fight.

THE STILLBIRTH OF CAPITAL

INTRODUCTION

The Enlightenment and Colonial India

For more than two decades, the main lines of scholarship in eighteenth-century and postcolonial studies have presupposed that the Enlightenment provided European imperialism its intellectual foundation. The widely accepted view in these fields is that eighteenth-century writers believed their political and social ideals to be universally valid and hence justified the imposition of European rule across the globe. An irony of this shared presupposition is that neither field has paid much attention to how eighteenth-century texts actually represent the material history of colonialism. This book examines a body of literature that no single study has yet considered: writing about the origins of British rule in India, ca. 1670–1815. It argues that far from justifying colonialism, this literature articulates a historical vision so deeply critical that it calls our own theoretical paradigms into question.

Recent works by Suleri, Teltscher, and Raman study British literary representations of the colonial encounter in order to delineate "the rhetoric of English India."[1] In contrast, equally commanding works by Muthu, Pitts, and Israel study eighteenth-century philosophical arguments for human diversity and equality in order to recover an "Enlightenment against empire."[2] But in either case, these works identify the texts they examine with versions of European modernity—whether imperial or emancipatory—that are already familiar to us. They do not explore how these texts force us to rethink our very concept of modernity. In fact, the Enlightenment understanding of colonial history not only differs from our own but also incriminates the world we inhabit even more profoundly than it does the eighteenth century. The subject of this study is, in short, neither British Orientalism nor Enlightenment anti-imperialism but rather the literary and philosophical consequences of this understanding.

The period in question here coincides not only with the Enlightenment but also with the mercantile era, and the texts I treat are correspondingly saturated with references to the historical constitution of the global economy. These references refute commonplace ideas about the Enlightenment; they represent European rule not in terms of historical progress but rather in terms of its antitheses: war, economic ruin, and political degeneration. They point, ultimately, to the alliance between militarized states and monopoly corporations that lies at the origins of the global economy, and they register in exceptionally precise ways the reorientation of Indian Ocean trade toward this alliance's spiraling military expenditures and war debts. Rather than suggest that British colonialism lifted non-European societies into a higher historical stage, these texts recognize that the Indian Ocean's already flourishing economies financed Europe's bankrupt form of sovereign power. They contain, therefore, a more heterodox sense of the global economy's origins than prevailing concepts of the Enlightenment acknowledge.

These texts do not merely invoke the eighteenth century's universal principles but also allude to the global history within which those principles emerged in the first place. Once we attend to how eighteenth-century authors understood the historical origins and limits of eighteenth-century discourse, their texts will reappear in forms quite different from what the scholarship has so far discerned. We will find ultimately that the characteristic procedure of contemporary theory—the calling into question of Enlightenment reason and European modernity—is at work in these texts already.

The first section of the Introduction analyzes the critique of the Enlightenment current not only in postcolonial studies but also in the humanities more broadly: Enlightenment thought is supposed to echo the logic of capital and by extension the dominant trajectory of modern history. The second and third sections contend that eighteenth-century texts concerning colonial history do not conform to the logic of capital but instead enable us to question whether modern history was ever a transition to capitalism in the first place. Their attention to colonial history recalls the material forces that the abstract category "capital" now obscures. The fourth section presents the overarching structure of the book and the notion of literariness at its core. The fifth returns to the concept of the Enlightenment in the work of its most searching critics, Horkheimer, Adorno, and Foucault, each of whom has inspired my own method. I aim to re-inhabit what they believed was the Enlightenment's essence: a "historicophilosophical" practice, a thinking that, no less than the literary, occurs at the very limits of conceptual thought.[3]

The Postcolonial Critique of the Enlightenment

A critique of the Enlightenment connects the origins of postcolonial studies to its current practice. This critique is implicit in postcolonial urtexts such as *The Wretched of the Earth* (1961), *A Rule of Property for Bengal* (1963), and *Orientalism*

(1978), all of which emphasize that the Enlightenment disclosed its dark side in the colonies. Fanon concluded the first by declaring that European humanism turned into an alibi for extermination in the colonies.[4] Guha commenced the second by explaining that eighteenth-century political economy, however progressive in France and Britain, became the instrument of East India Company despotism in Bengal.[5] And Said argued in the third that a discipline originating according to him in the late eighteenth century enabled Europeans to "produce" and so rule the Orient during what he referred to as "the post-Enlightenment period."[6]

This critique became explicit with the Subaltern Studies scholars, from Chatterjee's *Nationalist Thought and the Colonial World* (1986) to Guha's *History at the Limit of World-History* (2003) and beyond. Here "Enlightenment" is a synonym for "universalist critical thought," to cite a phrase Chatterjee uses elsewhere.[7] In other words, eighteenth-century intellectuals resisted political domination within Europe only by articulating principles they believed to be universal (e.g., human rights, citizenship, nationhood, empirical analysis).[8] According to Chakrabarty, the Enlightenment's "global heritage" is as a consequence a politics unable to recognize "life practices" that do not participate in its own ideals.[9] In response, the Subaltern Studies group has undertaken an equally far-reaching project: to document ways of life that exist outside those ideals.

Scholars such as Berman and Sarkar, concerned to defend their own version of the Enlightenment project, have claimed that the postcolonial critique of the Enlightenment rejects reason as such.[10] But Chakrabarty, Aravamudan, and Mufti, among others, have in fact called for a critical engagement with the Enlightenment.[11] Far from disavowing the Enlightenment, they have attempted instead to turn its emancipatory politics against its universalizing logic in order to discover the forms of thought this logic has suppressed. Their work suggests that the "Enlightenment project" depends on postcolonial studies for its fulfillment, and vice versa.

The importance of this work is beyond question. Yet, even as it claims to engage with the Enlightenment, it takes the form of Enlightenment thought for granted. In Chakrabarty's words, "Postcolonial scholarship is committed . . . to *engaging the universals* . . . that were forged in eighteenth-century Europe and that underlie the human sciences"; in Prakash's, a truly postcolonial thought must "fully *confront the universalism* of the post-Enlightenment order of reason."[12] In no way confined to the Subaltern Studies collective, the premise that Enlightenment thought was universalistic and hence imperialistic has now become axiomatic in the humanities, regardless of whether one pursues eighteenth-century studies, postcolonial studies, or even fields of study oblique to both.[13] Indeed, the Enlightenment now serves as the origin of all subsequent universalizing movements. Adorno and Horkheimer's declaration that "Enlightenment is totalitarian" inaugurated a long tradition of analogous claims: the Enlightenment has been called the origin of bourgeois ideology and the transcendental framework of modern thought (Hardt and Negri); the civilizing mission (Chakrabarty); Fascism and Stalinism (Nandy); both sides in the Cold War (Laclau); neoliberalism (Spivak); and globalization (Nussbaum).[14] This concept of the Enlightenment has become such a reflex in academic writing that it cries out now for its own critique.

The universalizing tendency these scholars locate in the Enlightenment corresponds less to the form of eighteenth-century texts than to the concept that most often subtends critical narratives of European and colonial history, "capital." To paraphrase the *Grundrisse*, it is capital—in contradistinction to all previous modes of production—that takes on a "universalizing role" in history.[15] Because it wants to reproduce itself everywhere, capital attempts to subsume all other modes of production into itself and needs as a consequence to draw everyone into a single mode of seeing, knowing, and speaking. It supposedly finds that universal structure in the Enlightenment. In Chakrabarty's words, "Capital . . . brings into every history some of the universal themes of the European Enlightenment."[16] As capital reorients all other modes of production to its own ceaseless expansion, it spreads Enlightenment categories across the globe.

The idea of "modernity" turns, then, on these three axioms: (1) its dominant trajectory conforms to the logic of capital; (2) capital depends on and disseminates universal discourses; and (3) these discourses originate in the Enlightenment. These axioms predetermine the form of both modernity and the Enlightenment. They are tacitly presupposed by the contemporary engagement with the Enlightenment and hence decide the very terms of that engagement before it takes place.

For example, Eagleton's discussion of the Enlightenment in *The Function of Criticism* is predetermined in precisely this way. Typically, the Enlightenment's historical context here is the rise of capitalism and hence of the bourgeoisie, whose overriding aim is "class consolidation" within Europe.[17] In pursuit of this aim, it produces "a style of enunciation"—which Eagleton calls "Enlightenment criticism"—that draws all particular forms of speech into a "universal" model apparently free of class interests.[18] *The Function of Criticism* turns Enlightenment writing, therefore, into an extension of the commodity-form: in the Enlightenment, "the bourgeois principle of abstract free and equal exchange is elevated from the market-place to the sphere of discourse, to mystify and idealize real bourgeois social relations."[19] In Eagleton's account, capital necessarily engenders a discursive structure that circumscribes the limits and possibilities of early eighteenth-century writing. This kind of argument—which seamlessly interweaves historical development, capitalism, and textual meaning—has now become so deeply ingrained in literary studies that it appears beyond question.

But it is precisely this logic that binds contemporary critical method, against its best intentions, to Marxist teleology. Chakrabarty explains that for Marx, "The coming of [capitalist society] gives rise for the first time to a history that can be apprehended through a . . . universal category, 'capital.'"[20] Marx considered all prior history meaningful only from the perspective of the historically necessary emergence and overcoming of capital. But if Marx was unable to see non-European worlds outside the trajectory of capitalism, postcolonial studies risks remaining within parameters set by capital in a different sense. To the extent that it sees subaltern consciousness as an interruption of capital's logic, postcolonial studies still depends on "capital" to make modernity intelligible. For postcolonial studies no less than for orthodox Marxism, "modernity" involves a transition to capitalism, and capitalism depends necessarily on Enlightenment categories. In his own synoptic account of the "transition to capitalism," Chakrabarty symptomatically collapses the three terms "modernity," "capitalism," and "Enlightenment" into one: "This transition is [a] translation of diverse life-worlds . . . into the categories of Enlightenment thought."[21] An engagement with the Enlightenment only on these terms reifies it no less than an absolute rejection would.

A genuine engagement with the Enlightenment entails, first of all, an openness to the vision of eighteenth-century texts and a corresponding willingness to unlearn our own paradigms—in particular, the common premise that capitalism is the basis of modernity. Both Wallerstein and Deleuze and Guattari have argued against that premise. For them, it is not the abstract logic of capital—that is, the freedom of markets from political intervention—but instead the alliance of corporations and states that lies at the origins of modernity. Because corporations make the highest rate of profit in monopoly conditions rather than in competitive ones, they "are structurally forced," Wallerstein explains, "to seek monopoly positions . . . via the principal agency that can make [them] enduringly possible, the state."[22] He notes that as a consequence of this alliance, our world "is topsy-turvy": "from the sixteenth century to the present . . . , there is more not less monopoly, . . . more rent and less profit, . . . more aristocracy and less bourgeoisie." Building on the work of Maurice Dobb, Deleuze and Guattari observe similarly that when European states granted monopolies to exclusive merchant corporations, they "promot[ed], not the rise of capitalist production, but the insertion of the bourgeoisie into . . . State feudalism."[23] They conclude that "capitalism does not lead to the dissolution of feudalism, but rather the contrary."[24] For Deleuze and Guattari as for Wallerstein, modernity is initiated not by the birth of capital but rather by its stillbirth in this sense: far from encouraging the free circulation of capital, the modern global economy has in fact suppressed it. They suggest that modern sovereigns may be even more opposed to the liberation of the economic from the political sphere than their feudal precursors had been.

Eighteenth-century representations of colonial history have more in common with these explanations than with the transition-to-capitalism paradigm. Enlightenment authors held that global commerce had failed to liberate humanity from feudal tyranny, because it had itself become a privilege dispensed by sovereign power to exclusive corporations. European states could not let the profits of global commerce circulate freely as "capital," because they needed to channel that profit toward their own militarization. After the seventeenth-century "military revolution," the unprecedented costs of securing national borders exceeded the revenue that European states had conventionally appropriated within those borders.[25] If we identify Western modernity with the logic of capital rather than the antiproductive exigencies of militarization, we will not be able to discern the eighteenth century's different historical vision.

Admittedly, when the postcolonial scholars I have cited refer to Enlightenment, they have in mind the political and scientific institutions of colonial modernity, not eighteenth-century texts. But by choosing the term "Enlightenment" as shorthand, they implicitly identify the former with the latter, nineteenth- and twentieth-century colonial history with eighteenth-century intellectual history. This identity implies that their work targets not simply the praxis of a specific colonial institution but rather an epochal episteme; not simply one instance of a knowledge-power nexus but rather the way in which disciplinary knowledge and institutional authority as such have become entangled in the modern world. But the straight line these scholars draw from the Enlightenment as a set of philosophical and literary texts to Enlightenment as the rationality of colonial rule has the effect of replacing the former with the latter. In other words, this concept of the Enlightenment detextualizes "Enlightenment reason," abstracting it from what was, after all, its original form. To this extent, the critique of the Enlightenment depends on an ontological confusion.

We could say then that the "Enlightenment" from a postcolonial perspective is analogous to the "Orient" from an Orientalist perspective. Said argued that the "Orient" Orientalism produced informed a wide array of disciplines, fields, and institutions. He emphasized that the discourse of the Orient had the effect of "settling" it, pun clearly intended: "by making statements about [the Orient], authorizing views of it, describing it, . . . teaching it," Orientalism enabled Europeans to settle the East without ever encountering it empirically.[26] The particularity of the East was rarely allowed to trouble either the settler's authority or the scholar's confidence.

If we altered each of these points only slightly, we could transfer them from the "Orient" to the "Enlightenment." As the Orient was the effect of Orientalism, the Enlightenment is now to a great extent the effect of contemporary critical theory. Although the current concept of Enlightenment reason as an intrinsically universalizing form of thought claims to be empirically valid, it in fact constitutes a discourse about the eighteenth century that has broad effects across the humanities. In particular, the lines we have drawn from Enlightenment intellectual history to post-Enlightenment colonial history militate against our capacity to appreciate the historical vision of the former on its own terms. This concept of the "Enlightenment" is analogous to the "Orient" in the sense finally, then, that it serves to render the difference of the entity to which it refers incapable of interrupting the reflexes of scholarly thought.

But to abuse a characteristic gesture of Subaltern Studies scholarship, I would insist that we cannot dispense with the postcolonial critique of the Enlightenment.[27] It has taught us that if we want to exit the tragedy of colonial modernity, we must first of all think outside its universal categories, regardless of where they originate. I would suggest then that rather than abandon the critique of the Enlightenment, we should inhabit it otherwise. The chapters that follow turn this critique on itself: they locate forms of representation that the critique of the Enlightenment cannot see. They attend, in other words, not only to the eighteenth century's "universal themes" but also to its particular understanding of European colonialism in the Indian Ocean. In the process, they reconsider the Enlightenment's relationship to the moment of danger in which we live now, when the military alliance of hegemonic states and private corporations has become even more far reaching than it was then.

The Enlightenment Critique of Colonialism I: The Stillbirth of Capital

In the nineteenth- and twentieth-century models of social development that still form the basis of academic knowledge, Europe tends to be the source of historical progress, the non-European world at best only its recipient, trying to catch up.[28] The European bourgeoisie liberates capitalist production and exchange from feudal tyranny, in the process turning itself into history's driving force. Such models have come under sustained criticism. Like Wallerstein, both Braudel and Arrighi have argued that the distinctive characteristic of European modernity is not the liberation of capital from sovereignty but their fusion.[29] They conceive the modern global economy in terms of three tiers: (1) a primordial layer of human labor, production, and exchange existing from time immemorial; (2) a world market economy in which small groups of capitalists scattered across Africa and Eurasia connected disparate production centers centuries, if not millennia, before the rise of European modernity; and (3) a level superimposed on the prior two, originating solely in early modern Europe, where capitalists suddenly came together, joined their wealth to state power, and created the state-form necessary to conquer the world market economy. According to Braudel, this third tier alone "is the real home of [modern European] capitalism."[30]

Other scholars, including Perlin, Chaudhuri, Abu-Lughod, Frank, and Washbrook, have provided a complementary account of the premodern Indian Ocean world, in which economic processes traditionally ascribed to the supposedly European rise of capitalism take place across Asia, from the Ottoman through the Safavid to the Qing empires, long before the European invasion.[31] In this account, commercialization, monetization, and even bulk commodity production precede the advent of European colonialism by centuries. Precolonial bureaucracies remain loosely articulated, making great symbolic claims to village wealth but extracting comparatively little. It is only under colonial rule that the Indian village, for example, finally begins to lose its connections to the world market economy. In the light of this research, Braudel's apparently paradoxical description of modern European "capitalism"—"the zone of the anti-market, where the great predators roam and the law of the jungle operates"—appears increasingly to have been apt.[32]

Against the commonplace association of the Enlightenment's historical vision with subsequent models of social development, I argue that eighteenth-century authors preceded us not only in questioning the origins of European modernity but also in recasting them in terms of the "anti-market" and "the law of the jungle."[33] See, for example, Denis Diderot's and Adam Ferguson's respective descriptions of European colonial settlers:

Beyond the Equator a man is neither English, Dutch, French, Spanish, nor Portuguese. [He is] capable of every crime which will lead him most quickly to his goals [*ses fins*]. He is a domestic tiger returning to the forest; the thirst for blood takes hold of him once more.[34]

Having found means to cross the Atlantic, and to double the cape of Good Hope, the inhabitants of one half the world were let loose on the other, and . . . wading in blood, and at the expence of every crime, and of every danger, [they] traversed the earth in search of gold.[35]

These quotations explicitly identify European colonialism with moral and social degeneration rather than political and economic progress. Here, colonialism depends not on new modes of production but rather on prehistoric ones, for example, savagery, nomadism, and rapine. The European discoveries of the New World and the Cape passage to India were supposed to inaugurate an international civil society, doux commerce extending from the Far East to the Americas. But in Diderot's and Ferguson's accounts, European corporations disseminate their own predatory behavior alone, subverting the very possibility of a global doux commerce. In these passages, French and Scottish Enlightenment thought prefigures the revisionary scholarship just discussed: it represents modernity's origins as the stillbirth of capital.

In contrast to nineteenth- and twentieth-century narratives of European-centered progress, eighteenth-century texts on empire generally acknowledge that the wealth circulating in metropolitan economies came to a great extent from elsewhere and that merchant corporations had used the most unprincipled means to acquire it. As Chapters 2 and 3 explain, news from the Indian colonies was of great interest in London, because it affected public and private finance alike, the former because of the East India Company's intimate financial relationship with the state, the latter because of its centrality to the stock market. Studies as early as Stephen's *English Literature and Society in the Eighteenth Century* (1904) and as recent as Rothschild's *Economic Sentiments* (2001) have observed how fundamental discussions of finance and economic policy were to the eighteenth-century British coffeehouse and French public sphere.[36] Eighteenth-century texts were as a consequence much more aware of the sophisticated Indian Ocean trading world that preceded European colonialism than the scholarship on eighteenth-century literature is now. For example, the eighteenth century's encyclopedia of imperialism, the *Histoire des deux Indes*, recognized that "there was a global commerce, from Africa to China, centred in the Indian Ocean before the Europeans came to seize it, [which was] largely the creation of a sea-borne Islam."[37] As far as the *Histoire* was concerned, European colonialists in the Indian Ocean were contemporary versions of the barbarians, Goths, Vikings, and conquistadors.[38]

The trade surplus between East and West was in fact still "massively" on Asia's side during the eighteenth century.[39] Producing not only spices, dyes, and textiles, but even iron and steel, South Asia in particular is thought to have been responsible for one-fourth of world manufactures.[40] Recognizing these circumstances, European statesmen and economists alike called for the conquest of Indian Ocean trade routes in order to staunch the flow of European precious metals east. For example, the balance-of-trade theorist Charles Davenant declared in 1696 that "whatever country can be in the full and undisputed possession of [the East-India trade] will give law to all the commercial world."[41] He correctly saw that if Europe was to undermine the Indian Ocean's commercial advantages, it would have to deal with it on a military footing.

Why has the eighteenth-century understanding of European modernity as the expropriation of global trade—not the origin of global progress—been overlooked? In part, the reason lies in the long shadow Hegel's more systematic philosophy of history has cast over the eighteenth century's own historical vision. But we need to keep in mind that Hegel's philosophy of history reacted *against* late Enlightenment historiography, which placed humanity's origins in the East. In response, Hegel claimed, inaccurately as it turns out, that the cultures responsible for ancient Indian civilization "scarcely formed a society, let alone a state," and he considered any society that failed to produce a state literally pointless and hence "prehistorical": "Peoples may have continued a long life before they reach their destination of becoming a state. They may even have attained considerable culture in certain directions. This *prehistory* . . . lies outside of our plan (*Diese* Vorgeschichte *liegt . . . ohnehin außer unserem Zwecke*).[42] If all non-European civilizations, cultures, and economies "lie outside of our plan," it follows that we can understand the origins and development of European history without reference to them. In Hegel's terms, the European state is, no less than Spirit, the "object of itself," responsible for "mak[ing] itself what it essentially is."[43] It is in Hegel's rendering that the state-form finally becomes, as Deleuze and Guattari would subsequently observe, the "sole quasi cause."[44]

The scholarship on the eighteenth century has tended to extend this Hegelian model backward in time, even when studying eighteenth-century texts that suggest otherwise. For example, both Mehta and Dirks present Burke's condemnation of East India Company rule as an isolated instance. Mehta observes that "the major British political thinkers did not write books that elaborated in any detail on the notion of empire or its cognate practices. . . . [They] were largely untroubled by the empire"; Dirks comments that "in the histories that played such an important role in the Enlightenment, . . . empire was always offstage, not a historical force that would dramatically change world history."[45] I would suggest instead that in such cases, the scholar has read selectively and then held the Enlightenment responsible for an omission that is in fact his own. The idea that the Enlightenment was untroubled by empire corresponds not to the eighteenth century itself but rather to our own critical traditions, which—having assumed that Europe is the origin of itself—still suppose that eighteenth-century authors saw their own history in this way. Rather than read Hegel back into the Enlightenment, we need to recognize that his philosophy aimed to solve problems to which the eighteenth century's own dialectical vision had called attention: where eighteenth-century texts represented the European state's expropriation of non-European production, the Hegelian dialectic made that history disappear.[46]

According to Jonathan Israel, the modern critique of imperialism, a part of the Enlightenment's broader critique of transcendental orders, originated precisely during the late seventeenth and eighteenth centuries. He notes that writers condemned European states' "unrestrained mercantilism" and "war-mongering," producing in the process "a fully fledged anti-colonial thesis."[47] And while the general assumption has been that the eighteenth-century critique of mercantilism led to nineteenth-century arguments for "free trade" imperialism, Bayly has argued that the latter vulgarize the "complex ethical and political argument[s]" of the former beyond recognition.[48] We need to reconsider eighteenth-century representations of the colonial encounter in light of the period's awareness of the Indian Ocean trading world and its deeply informed critique of European colonialism. Rather than inevitably subsume non-European "life-practices" into

European value systems, eighteenth-century texts often recognize the fundamental difference between the two. On one side, the Indian Ocean economies that preceded European modernity, that operated outside its terms, and that eventually became one of its primary sources of production; on the other, the European military-monopoly system: the texts we will explore register the discontinuity between these two economies in more subtle ways than we can easily appreciate, because we lack the historical sense they possessed.[49]

The Enlightenment Critique of Colonialism II: The Limits of the Universal

The postcolonial critique of the Enlightenment identifies European modernity with the transition to capitalism and assumes that this transition circumscribes the possibilities of Enlightenment thought. In contrast, figures as central to the Enlightenment as Diderot and Ferguson suggested that European states and corporations practiced feudalism on a global scale and attempted to dissociate their thought from this practice. The following discussion reconsiders the function of "Enlightenment universalism" in such thought. It argues that when universal principles—such as the idea, for example, of an international civil society—occur alongside colonial history in texts such as Diderot's and Ferguson's, they exist in tension with each other. These texts' critical power lies here, in how they represent the disjunction between the eighteenth century's universal principles, on one hand, and the actual course of global history, on the other.

Kant's exemplary Enlightenment essay "Idea for a Universal History from a Cosmopolitan Perspective" (1784), for instance, attributes an ideal telos to history: "a universal *cosmopolitan condition* [*ein allgemeiner weltbürgerlicher Zustand*], . . . the womb in which all the original predispositions of the human species can develop."[50] But Kant argues that the actual course of history has not encouraged the development of this ideal. He repeatedly emphasizes that in its ceaseless concern to augment its war-making capacity, the modern state retards progress: "Through the use of all of the commonwealth's resources to arm for war against others, through the ravages of war, but more still through the need to remain constantly prepared for war, progress toward the full development of our natural predispositions is hindered."[51] The global expansion of the modern state-form exists, in Kant's view, in a strictly antithetical relationship to the growth of reason and ethics: "As long as states use all their resources to realize their vain and violent goals of expansion [*Erweiterungsabsichten*] and thereby continue to hinder the slow efforts to cultivate their citizens' minds and even to withhold all support from them in this regard, then [no moral cultivation] can be expected."[52] Hence, Kant identifies European "world rule" not with "the best interests of the world" but rather with an endless investment in war.[53]

In other words, two centuries before historians would renarrate eighteenth-century British history in terms of the military-fiscal state, Kant suggested that the European state's "new invention" was its "ever-growing war debt [*immer anwachsenden Schuldenlast*]."[54] He recognized the fundamental contradiction in which Western history had become trapped: the military costs states paid in the pursuit of hegemonic power exhausted domestic revenue, producing as a consequence the very compulsion behind imperial expansion. If one wants to understand the logic of European modernity—and eighteenth-century representations of it—one cannot stress this historical contradiction enough. Its implication—that the logic of war shapes the global economy every bit as much as the logic of capital—has become increasingly hard to deny yet remains even harder to assimilate to current theoretical paradigms.[55] But this implication is common to the texts I treat. For them as for Kant, the modern state's effect on history—understood ideally as the full development of humanity—tends to be degenerative: the state exhausts human wealth.

In "Idea for a Universal History," "progress" is not a reality but solely a concept, the possibility of a different future. Kant speaks of it only in the subjunctive, within the register of "hoping" and "imagining." In regard to the universal cosmopolitan condition he describes as history's ideal end, Kant observes: "Does nature reveal anything of a path to this end? . . . something, but very little."[56] Kant describes history, rather than progressive, as "this idiotic course of things human" (*diesem widersinnigen Gange menschlicher Dinge*).[57] In fact, "Idea for a Universal History" set out the problem Hegel's dialectical theory aimed to solve: to find not idiocy but rather a rational order in history.[58] Hegel solved the problem, though, not by addressing what Kant suggests is its source—the fact that European states are so militarized they bankrupt the commonwealth—but rather, as mentioned, by making it disappear. In contrast, like "Idea for a Universal History," the texts I treat represent the opposition between the state and any ethical ideal.[59] In these texts, universal ideals tend to function as critical tools, not as historical realities or even as the telos toward which history necessarily tends.

To consider another example, Condorcet's equally emblematic Enlightenment inquiry, *Sketch for a Historical Picture of the Progress of the Human Mind* (1795), operates on many of the same premises as Kant's "Idea for a Universal History." Condorcet presents contemporary colonialism in terms of an "oppressive and avaricious system of monopoly" (*système oppresseur et mesquin d'un commerce de monopole*), not universal ideals.[60] Like Kant, Condorcet identifies this system with war rather than the liberation of capital. On one hand, monopoly commerce engenders violence: "a false sense of commercial interest . . . drench[es] the earth in blood and . . . ruin[s] nations under pretext of enriching them."[61] On the other hand, it finances violence: "monopolistic companies are nothing more than a tax imposed upon [the nations of Europe] in order to provide their governments with a new instrument of tyranny."[62] From the *Sketch*'s perspective, state monopolies on global trade are the precondition of its monopoly on violence, a source of revenue from outside the state that helps it resolve its internal contradiction: domestic revenues cannot meet the unprecedented cost of modern war. In Condorcet's *Sketch* as in Kant's "Idea for a Universal History," the European state leads not to the fulfillment of humanity's "organic perfectibility" but rather to an equally possible human tendency, "deterioration" (*la dégénera-tion*).[63] Here also, imperial history is the antithesis of progress.

Like "Idea for a Universal History," the *Sketch* refers to progress only in the future tense. Its realization entails a revolution against the global system: the nations of Europe will become "enlightened" only after they "finally learn" that "the monopoly [merchant companies] have sustained with so much treachery, persecution and crime" does not serve their interests.[64] This revolution points toward a universal ideal resembling Kant's cosmopolitan condition: "permanent confederations" standing above the state and ensuring that "foreigners . . . share equally in all . . . benefits."[65] But like Kant's ideal, Condorcet's is designed to criticize the global expansion of European states and corporations, not justify it. Kant and Condorcet emphasized the discrepancy between metropolitan ideals aspiring to a cosmopolitan order and colonial histories rooted in a military-corporate alliance. In texts such as theirs, universal ideals function less as ends in themselves than as critical principles targeted at that alliance.

The antithesis between the eighteenth century's universal ideals and its colonial history is no less present in fictional texts than in philosophical ones, though it operates differently there. Consider, for example, the author who is thought to have pioneered the capitalist form of the novel, Daniel Defoe. Immediately after the *Robinson Crusoe* series, Defoe wrote two narratives that represent primitive accumulation in terms not of Protestant ethics but rather of piracy. Saving *Cap-*

tain Singleton (1720) for a subsequent chapter, we turn now to *The King of Pirates* (1719). Like Defoe's subsequent *A General History of Pyrates* (1724), *The King of Pirates* treats the life of the infamous Englishman Henry Avery and details in particular his legendary capture of a treasure-laden Mughal fleet.[66] Its most recent editor claims that this novella lacks even the aspiration for form, but if we look more carefully at its allusions to the global economy, we will see that it in fact turns narrative form into a problem.[67] Although Avery's gang wants to end their adventure and go home, thereby giving their narrative proper form, they cannot easily return to England, because their Indian Ocean plunder is material evidence that they have violated merchant company monopolies and, by extension, interstate law.[68] Avery observes, "Here is one thing remarkable, viz. that the great mass of wealth I had gotten together was so far from forwarding my deliverance that it really was the only thing that hindered it most effectually."[69] This narrative refuses simply to return home and instead problematizes the very idea of "home": here it comprises a system of states whose raison d'être is to defend privately held monopolies on extra-European commodities with the threat of violence. *Pace* its own editor, this text not only contains form—the conceptual ideal of home that is supposed to be the aim of Defoe's novels—but also subtly takes this ideal apart.

Defoe set much of the novel in 1691, three years before the English state created the Bank of England to finance its war debts, a year coincidentally in which Defoe himself was imprisoned for his own debts. After taking the dowry of a princess aboard one of the Mughal ships, Avery immediately realizes that he has acquired the means to return home, a source of wealth large enough to help pay England's debts. He forces an encounter with English merchants in order to make the English state an offer: "*We know you want money in England* . . . [we] would not grudge to advance five or six million ducats to the government to give [us] leave to return in peace to England, and sit down quietly with the rest"; "if they would do this, . . . they can ask no reasonable sum but [we] might advance it."[70] The pirates' deal was widely rumored at the time. Avery's bargain promises to resolve two levels of form at once. On the level of narrative, it would enable the pirates to return home or, as Avery puts it, "to come in," thereby bringing their history to a proper conclusion. On the level of political economy, it would enable the English state finally to square its revenues with its military costs, thereby resolving its own internal contradiction. The bargain reveals at once the material reality concealed within the ideal form both of narrative and of the nation. It points to a global system literary scholars now have difficulty discerning, meant not to facilitate the circulation of capital but rather to circumscribe it within the economy of modern war.

Organizing Principles and Practices

The British Empire—and by extension the global context of British writing— underwent fundamental shifts during the course of the long eighteenth century. The three parts of this book mark these shifts, each the outcome of Europe's earliest colonial wars. In the wake of the Anglo-Dutch Wars, the East India Company first instituted a monopoly trading system across the Indian Ocean (1670–1760). After the Seven Years' War, the Company transformed this trading empire into a territorial one (1760–90). And during the Revolutionary and Napoleonic wars, the British state greatly expanded the Company's territorial conquests and finally justified them in terms of "progress" (1790–1815). As these wars turned Britain from a commercial to a territorial and finally to a world empire, its national debt increased almost exponentially at every turn.[71]

Each of the works I study invokes a universal principle that was supposed to govern the British Empire in one of these three phases. Each principle imagined a global economy subordinate to an ethical order, something other than war and monopoly commerce. Not coincidentally, each principle has subsequently become the ideology most closely identified with the author in question. For example, in Part I, the principle is aristocratic sovereignty (Dryden's *Amboyna* [1673]) for the first chapter; and Protestant ethics (Defoe's *Captain Singleton* [1720]) for the second. In Part II, the principle is sentimental ethics (Sterne's *Bramine's Journal* [1767] and Foote's *Nabob* [1772]) for the third chapter; the free market and universal law (Smith's *Wealth of Nations* [1776] and Bentham's "Essay on Time and Place" [1782], respectively) for the fourth; and national traditions (Edmund Burke's speeches in the Hastings impeachment [1786–94]) for the fifth. In Part III, the principle is Orientalist knowledge (Sir William Jones's legal codes [1792–97]) for the sixth chapter; and the progressive state (Sir Walter Scott's *Guy Mannering* [1815]) for the seventh.

But each text counterposes to these universal principles colonial practices that contradict them. These practices involved the capture of Indian Ocean commodities whose monopoly control promised the British state and the East India Company the superprofits they needed to finance their debts.[72] The commodities were, successively, spices (Chapter 1); silks and calicoes (Chapter 2); tea and salt

(Chapter 3); opium (Chapter 4); grain (Chapter 5); landed property (Chapter 6); and cotton textiles (Chapter 7). Each commodity contains an occulted history of Indian Ocean labor and its expropriation. Hence, these texts represent both the principles that were supposed to harmonize the British Empire *and* the global context within which these principles were originally articulated. The first term in each chapter title refers to a universal principle; the second, to a colonial practice. Each chapter explores how the material presence of the second term within the text overturns the abstract authority of the first.

If we can understand the extent to which, far from resolving the contradiction between abstract categories and material histories, literary texts hold it in permanent suspension, we will begin to escape the premises that now often program literary criticism. The text will no longer appear to be a mere manifestation of the commodity-form, capital's universalizing logic, or European imperial discourse. We will be able instead to identify the "literary" with forms of representation that are in excess of all such paradigms and that as a consequence call into question both the political ideologies of the past and the critical commonplaces of the present.

I register two caveats here. One: In the first part of this book, works by Dryden and Defoe represent a ninety-year span, because no other major author wrote about India during this period. Two: I focus on British authors, because colonial India was almost exclusively British after the middle of the eighteenth century.

Conclusion: Eccentric Enlightenment

The postcolonial critique of the Enlightenment conceives it in terms of what Spivak refers to as an "Enlightenment episteme," a single analytic and representational framework.[73] As a consequence, scholars such as Guha, Chatterjee, Bhabha, and Aravamudan have posited an opposition between Enlightenment reason as a homogenizing force, on one hand, and colonial or postcolonial society as a hybrid space, on the other.[74] This opposition implies that whereas the Enlightenment recognizes only the unilinear time of progress, the colony and postcolony comprise different temporalities.

But the concept of Enlightenment reason as a unitary episteme differs sharply from Frankfurt School and poststructural critiques of the Enlightenment, where it intrinsically contains difference within itself. For example, in Adorno and Horkheimer's account, Enlightenment reason reverts to myth only after it is forced to obey logical and mathematical formulas.[75] Before its formalization, Enlightenment reason's essential attitude toward universal principles is "determinate negativity" (*bestimmte Negation*): it denies their universality by revealing their discursive form and limits.[76] It does this, in turn, by treating such principles not as "absolute" or above all temporal determination, but rather as "mediated": the indirect expression of "social, historical, and human" processes.[77] Hence, Adorno and Horkheimer concluded in various works that only "Enlightenment . . . in possession of itself and coming to power can break through the bounds of Enlightenment [*die Grenzen der Aufklärung*]" superimposed by logical formalism.[78]

Similarly, if poststructuralism is founded on a critique of Western reason, that critique presupposes in turn that every work of art or philosophy contains heterogeneous rationalities within itself.[79] For example, although Foucault popularized the term "episteme," he did not see the Enlightenment as one. His essays on the Enlightenment describe it instead as an interrogation of modernity's epistemic limits, "a philosophical ethos consisting in a critique of what we are [thinking] through a historical ontology of ourselves."[80] The Enlightenment purposefully "depart[ed] from . . . the historic destiny of knowledge": where modern science buttresses the claims of a "state system that . . . presented itself as the . . . rationality of history," the Enlightenment asks, "for what excess of power . . . is this reason itself historically responsible?"[81] It consequently undertakes "a permanent critique of our historical era."[82]

According to Adorno, Horkheimer, and Foucault, therefore, the Enlightenment already contains what Chakrabarty suggests is characteristic of the colony, "a disjuncture of the present with itself."[83] In their view, Enlightenment thinking intrinsically opposes one time with another, the apparently suprahistorical time of modern conceptual thought with the specific histories within which such concepts evolved in the first place. My intention is not to oppose Adorno, Horkheimer, and Foucault's "true" accounts of the Enlightenment to postcolonial studies' "false" account. I am less interested in the former as empirically true descriptions than as programs for the work of critical thought. For each of these figures, "Enlightenment" is as much a trope as an objective event: it signifies the thought process that discloses our conceptual limits, by returning universal principles to their own particular histories.[84]

According to Adorno and Horkheimer, critical thinking must home in on the tension between singular lives and universal principles not to reconcile them but rather to emphasize their permanent discrepancy. Rather than accelerate historical progress, then, this peculiar kind of dialectical thought stops it in its tracks.[85] For

Adorno and Horkheimer, such thought is at the essence of both critical method and art: "the work of art . . . transcends reality [not] in achieved harmony, in the questionable unity of form and content, . . . but in those traits in which the discrepancy [between the two] emerges."[86] Adorno's *Aesthetic Theory* describes art as a fundamentally anti-epistemic and, by extension, counterhistorical practice: "The vortex of [the aesthetic] dialectic ultimately consumes the concept of meaning. When . . . the individual elements refuse to mold themselves to the . . . preconceived totality, the gaping divergence tears meaning apart."[87] Hence, Adorno aligned the artistic truth he valued with the Enlightenment: "Artworks participate in enlightenment because they do not lie: They do not feign the literalness of what speaks out of them."[88]

The chapters that follow are modeled on Adorno's approach, his belief that we begin to realize art's revolutionary potential only when we explore how it annuls what we know. To oppose the universalizing abstractions that have accompanied the global career of Western modernity, they appeal to the resources of literature itself. Each chapter attempts to perform a historically attentive reading that "disfigures" the text in Spivak's sense—negating the ideology we now identify with it by following metaphorical trains that lead away from the self-evident to the very edge of intelligibility.[89] Such tropes are, for Adorno, the elements that "refuse to mold themselves to the . . . preconceived totality"; Derrida refers to them alternatively as the text's "excentric center" (*centre excentré*).[90] He implies that to produce the ideology of the artwork, we make one of its elements central and marginalize all the others. But these other elements nonetheless remain; they are, Derrida notes, "at work [*au travail*] in the work [*à l'oeuvre*]." Their peripheral presence there not only is necessary to the construction of the artwork but also threatens to deconstruct it from within, revealing that the labor that constitutes the work is other than we have assumed. This dynamic is, Derrida suggests, "the very condition of deconstruction."[91] Every work in the sense of an aesthetic unity is ultimately work in the sense of labor, a complex product incorporating heterogeneous elements that are themselves the products of labor.

We need, finally, to recognize the Indian Ocean trading world as one of the Enlightenment's (excentric) centers. In participating in the construction of the eighteenth century's various ideological systems, the products of its labor left residues of difference therein. This difference subtly shifts the texts' frames of representation, turning them away from the universal values of the global market economy toward the trace of other systems of value. For example, after

Captain Avery seizes the Mughal bride's dowry in *The King of Pirates*, he confesses, "We did not know the value of [the costly things we took here,] . . . we
never knew how rich we were."[92] As he subsequently makes clear, the pirates do
not know the value of their plunder for two overlapping reasons. First, much of
the wealth is foreign to them, possessing value in Indian Ocean societies but not
necessarily in European markets: alongside the "calicoes" and "wrought silks"
with which any European trafficking in Indian Ocean commodities would have
been familiar, much of the rest of the plunder Avery cannot even specify, except
to recognize it as part of "the bride's portion."[93] Second, even when the goods
possess value in Europe, the pirates cannot market them because of merchant
corporation monopolies.

As pirate plunder caught between the diverse economies of the premodern
world and the monopolistic structure of the mercantile era, these goods resist
the universal equivalence to which the market economy subjects all commodities: "we could not bring *particular* things to a just valuation."[94] Irredeemably
"particular," these things refuse sublation to a higher realm. The "inestimable
value" of pirate wealth here marks modernity's limit, both the monopoly system
it imposed on non-European economies and the different forms of production and exchange that existed outside this system. Indian Ocean pirate wealth
performs the work of literature, alluding to histories that remain intransigently
foreign to our categories of value and knowledge; it points not to progress but
rather to other worlds. Eighteenth-century texts about European colonialism
in the Indian Ocean register the difference of those other worlds but are in no
position to define it. That difference exists at the edge of what they know, as
particular systems of production and value that their abstractions cannot subsume.[95] It corresponds, then, to what we call subalternity—"the memory of the
anonymous" to which Benjamin dedicated his own historical constructions.[96]

Every entity, "Enlightenment reason" no less than the colony, contains difference within itself, the heterogeneous forms of human labor that necessarily
compose it. Eighteenth-century texts are divided on more levels than we can
now easily comprehend by the different economies, geographies, and temporalities that inform them. It is our own critical premises that impose the seamless rationality we perceive there. Regardless of the universal principles that
eighteenth-century texts on the global economy advocate explicitly, they refer
in detail to a different history, in which the alliance of European states and monopoly corporations did not unleash global production but instead redirected

it toward their own militarization. Eighteenth-century representations of global antiproduction offer us the opportunity to read back into the principles that have shaped our understanding of the Enlightenment the eighteenth century's own historicophilosophical practice, which, documenting a global economy based on war and monopoly control, is even more pertinent to us now than it was then. Perhaps our critical method needs to recognize that precisely to the extent literature registers empire, it represents not the rise of capital—modernity's most intractable ideology—but rather, antithetically, its stillbirth.

PART I

Commerce (1670–1760)

1 SOVEREIGNTY AND MONOPOLY
Dryden's Amboyna

Perhaps now the most widely read piece of Restoration writing, Aphra Behn's masterful novella *Oroonoko* (1688) is an ideal starting point for almost any survey of the long eighteenth century. It presents, among much else, an ingeniously neat account of the interrelated rise of modern literature and the global economy. The narrative begins as a self-consciously stilted romance set, typically, in an Old World court. But when slave traders enter the court, lure the noble prince Oroonoko onto a slave ship headed for the New World, and imprison him in chains, the narrative undergoes as abrupt a transformation as its hero has. En route from Old World court to New World colony, it replaces romance conventions with the novel-form (*avant la lettre*): the fabulous with the scientific, a feudal economy with a commercial one, nobility with merchants, honor and fidelity with profit and duplicity, and sovereign character with private interest. Published in the year of the Glorious Revolution, *Oroonoko* not only reflects that rupture but also manages uncannily to capture its historical significance. For Anglo-American literary histories, *Oroonoko* could not be more exemplary.[1] They have assimilated its remarkably prescient narrative to a concept of modernity whose roots lie in Europe, where capitalist economics first gained the upper hand over feudal politics.[2]

Aravamudan opens his excellent study in this way: "A book on colonialism and eighteenth-century literature cannot begin without invoking *Oroonoko*."[3] And so I have. Yet, before *Oroonoko*, there was John Dryden's *Amboyna, or the Cruelty of the Dutch to the English Merchants* (1673), which dramatizes an event at the British Empire's very origins: the Dutch East India Company's execution of ten English East India Company servants at Ambon in 1623. Dryden returned to the massacre fifty years after the fact in order to provide the English state propaganda during the Third Anglo-Dutch War (1672–74). Though now little remembered and generally discredited when it is, *Amboyna* prefigures *Oroonoko* in essential ways. It represents a merchant colony contested by England and Holland, Europe's primary commercial empires; homes in on conflicts between feudal and merchant classes; and culminates in the merchant class's betrayal, abjection, and ultimate execution of a noble character who embodies the very idea of sovereignty. In both texts, the execution marks the historical chasm between feudal and mercantile worlds.[4]

But *Amboyna*'s salient difference from *Oroonoko* is that it takes place not in a New World supposedly bereft of long-distance trade before its European discovery but rather in the Spice Islands, the legendary archipelago near present-day Indonesia's far eastern boundary that had long been the focus of exceptionally wide-ranging and complicated exchange networks. This chapter asks a paradigmatic question: What would happen if we were to follow *Amboyna* and dislocate our narrative of modernity's commercial origins from the transatlantic world to the Indian Ocean?

First, we would need to rethink the very terms of this narrative. It would be careless to consider the first Europeans who arrived in the Indian Ocean by way of the Cape passage "merchants" or "traders" in any conventional sense. Unlike the merchants who had traded from time immemorial across what contemporary economic historians describe as a genuine *mare liberum*, or "free sea," these sailors came armed, using the backing of sovereign power to break preexisting trading arrangements and subject them to their own monopoly control. Portuguese sailors arrived on India's Malabar Coast at the turn of the sixteenth century, intending to replace Arab predominance in the spice trade by any means necessary; the Dutch and the English East India companies' first ventures were sent to India and the Spice Islands at the turn of the seventeenth century to prey on the Portuguese Empire with similar ruthlessness.[5] Hence, from an Indian Ocean perspective, European modernity originates not with the revolution of capitalist economics against feudal politics but with their collusion: merchant capitalists and absolutist rulers joined forces in the armed pursuit of trading monopolies. Dryden's description of *Amboyna*'s setting—the Dutch East India Company's colonial fort on Ambon—as a "Castle on the Sea" is, therefore, particularly apt.[6]

I would suggest that the essence of "modernity" lies here, in the difference between the trade that followed European colonialism in the Indian Ocean and the trade that preceded it there. Since at least the Roman Empire, European traders had offered precious metals in exchange for Asian commodities, since their goods did not interest Eastern consumers. In contrast, East Indies spices were the exotic commodities most desired in European markets.[7] By the time they arrived there—by way of "prahu, dhow, camel caravan, oared galley, wagon, pack-horse and river barge" across the countless exchanges that linked the Spice Islands to western Europe—they were literally thousands of times more expensive than they had been at the point of production, possibly the most profitable commodity anywhere on the globe.[8] European statesmen watched the spice trade exhaust their bullion reserves and understood that if they could wrest the trade from its Arab and Venetian intermediaries and control it all the way from production to consumption, they would acquire unheard-of profits and, by extension, the source of global hegemony. They foresaw, in other words, the interdependence of the military and administrative elaboration of the European state, on one hand, and the monopoly control of immemorial Indian Ocean networks, on the other—hence the pathbreaking voyages of Columbus, Gama, and Magellan.[9] Simply stated, what distinguishes European modernity is not the uniquely free circulation of commodities and capital but the unprecedented application of armed force to their circumscription: *not* merchant capital but rather the *monopoly state.*[10]

If we follow *Amboyna* and relocate modernity's commercial origins to the Indian Ocean, we will need to rethink literature's response to those origins accordingly. Literary scholars habitually discuss whether late seventeenth- and eighteenth-century texts took sides with the landed classes against the commercial classes, or the reverse.[11] But social scientists—Wallerstein and Wood among many others—have argued that capitalist modernity was in fact nowhere the outcome of this conflict: in England, capitalism's origins lay, ironically, with the landed aristocracy; in France, the bourgeoisie was a political and juridical class, not a particularly capitalist one. In both cases, aristocracy and bourgeoisie depended on each other and became increasingly hard to disentangle.[12] If the conflict between aristocracy and bourgeoisie was "in the last resort shadowboxing," as Hill argued, an analysis of early modern literature in terms of its alignment with one or the other can never delve very far into history.[13]

Superficially, *Amboyna* does present a conflict between aristocratic and bourgeois characters and, in line with Dryden's public position, sides with the former. But on a deeper level, the play alludes to the birth of the European interstate system and the parallel development of the East Indian colonial economy. This level registers the rise of a new state-form that aimed to monopolize global trade, rendered all other sovereign forms obsolete, and consequently created a vortex into which the aristocracy and the bourgeoisie alike were ineluctably drawn. *Amboyna* dissolves the conflict between aristocracy and bourgeoisie into the more historically compelling logic of mercantile state formation and global monopoly trade. In still more artful ways, the play insinuates that its own aristocratic values are merely a front for the material interests of English mercantilism. But *Amboyna*'s self-reflexive subtlety becomes apparent only when we understand its Indian Ocean context. Hence, this chapter first explores how *Amboyna* understands the birth of the modern state system; then how it represents the simultaneous elaboration of a colonial political economy; and finally, how it designs an aesthetic form to respond to these epochal events, one that attempts not to restore the sovereign but rather to partake in his execution.

The Conflict of Orders

Amboyna's plot turns on two explicitly tragic moments. The climax of the play is the execution of its hero, the English captain Towerson, by Ambon's Dutch governor Harman. But before that, the governor's son, Harman Junior, rapes Towerson's fiancée, the native noblewoman Ysabinda. However common rape has subsequently become as a metaphor of colonial expropriation, when we return this scene to its own history, the commonplace fades away. What comes into focus instead is a historically specific tenor: *Amboyna* uses the rape to capture the conflict of sovereign forms that seemed to define the period. Ysabinda stands for an increasingly obsolete feudal order; Harman Junior, for the mercantile state that brings a new political economy violently into being. Prefiguring the execution—in which Towerson will stand for the nobility and Harman Senior for the merchant classes—the rape crystallizes the plot's general tendency.

The rape also exemplifies the trope of degeneration, which will constantly recur in eighteenth-century writing about imperialism. Confessing his crime to the Dutch revenue officer, Harman Junior describes the rape in terms of his own degeneration:

Dutch Fiscal. Where have you left the Bride?

Harman Junior. Ty'd to a Tree and Gagg'd, and—

Dutch Fiscal. And what? Why do you stare and tremble? Answer me like a man.

Harman Junior. . . . I have nothing of Manhood in me; I am turn'd Beast or Devil; have I not Hornes, and Tayle, and Leathern wings? methinks I shou'd have by my Actions— . . . I have done a Deed so ill, I cannot name it. (4.4.35–42)

The Fiscal's final response to Harman Junior resituates his personal degeneration within European political history: "Those Fits of Conscience in another might be excusable; but, in you, a Dutchman, who are of a Race that are born Rebels, and live every where on Rapine; Wou'd you degenerate, and have remorse?" The Fiscal refers here to the United Provinces' eighty-year rebellion against the Spanish Habsburg monarchy, which gave birth not only to the Dutch state but also to the modern interstate system in the Peace of Westphalia (1648). To understand the significance of that rebellion—of which the rape, the Fiscal implies, is merely the logical extension—we need to return it to a *longue durée* that the play has continuously in mind.

In the late fifteenth century, Venice's and Genoa's respective monopolies on spices and silk enabled them to exert an influence within Europe out of all proportion to their size.[14] In response, European rulers attempted to appropriate the city-states' power by seizing their long-distance trade. All the participants in this contest—including Spain, Portugal, the United Provinces, France, and England—developed radically more expensive military and administrative apparatuses.[15] Spain was the most successful among these states and attempted to contain the others within a medieval system centered on the papacy and the Habsburg Empire. But the contest had unleashed forces much too powerful for any suprastate authority. Hence, when it rebelled against Spain, Holland led a revolution against the medieval system and its principle that there must be a sovereign entity above the state.[16]

The Fiscal encapsulates the historical significance of Holland's rebellion when he asks rhetorically, "What makes any thing a sin but Law?" (4.4.52). The Fiscal implies that with the medieval system's disintegration, sovereignty no longer expresses divine will but instead a wholly secular agreement *between* states. The Fiscal's rhetorical question becomes even more historically acute: "What law is there here against it? . . . If there be Hell, 'tis but for those that sin in *Europe*, not for us in *Asia*." The state system's international law applied only inside Europe, within the so-called lines of amity. The world outside Europe was "an internationally defined zone of anarchy," where Europeans could engage in violence against each other, as well as against natives, with impunity.[17] Even when European states signed a series of bilateral treaties during the 1680s, they placed limits only on the former violence, not on the latter. Westphalia officially replaced the idea of "Rome," as Foucault has observed, with the concept of "Europe": a system of states that relates to the outside world in terms of economic utility and hence violence without limit.[18] From *Amboyna*'s perspective, the Dutch rebellion against the feudal order turned "rapine"—capital accumulation outside the constraints of any preexisting religious or political principle—into the very basis of modern sovereignty. World-system theorists agree: Wallerstein has noted that the "Revolution liberated a force that could sustain the world-system"; Arrighi, that "this reorganization of political space in the interest of capital accumulation marks the birth not just of the modern inter-state system, but also of capitalism as a world system."[19] Marx referred to Holland simply as "the capitalist nation *par excellence.*"[20]

Amboyna locates in Holland's rebellion, most profoundly, the historical rupture that collapsed the theoretically separate spheres of politics and economics. Their conceptual segregation had been immemorial: the Lex Claudia, for example, denied Roman senators the right to engage in maritime commerce precisely in order to quarantine sovereignty from the corrupting influence of profit making.[21] The most insightful English character, Beamont, condemns the Dutch in a form that makes sense only within the terms of classical thought, referring to them as "an infamous Nation, that ought to have been slaves . . . [but] had cast off the Yoke of their lawful Soveraign" (5.1.166–68). He implies that because the merchant, like the slave, is incapable of thinking outside his own interests, he is bereft of public character and unfit to exercise sovereign powers. The Dutch inappropriately join the sovereign sphere of rule to the subordinated sphere of commodity exchange: "You shew'd your ambition, when you began to be a State: for not being Gentlemen, you have stollen the Arms of the best Families of *Europe* . . . and call'd your Selves the *HIGH and MIGHTY*" (2.1.370–74). Beamont's jibe critiques not merely the merchant's seizure of sovereign power but also, more provocatively, the very origins of the modern "state" in the sudden and unprecedented combination of trade ("not being Gentlemen") with the prerogatives of military power ("you have stollen the Arms of the best Families"). According to *Amboyna*, "Monarchys" (i.e., England) segregate commercial exchange and sovereign power; "states" (i.e., Holland) collapse the two.

In sum, *Amboyna* presents an account of modernity's origins that appears to resemble our own narrative of bourgeois revolution but is in fact fundamentally different. The play's opposition between England and Holland seems to correspond to the now conventional antithesis of aristocratic and bourgeois orders. But where we associate the bourgeoisie with the liberation of capital, late seventeenth-century writers instead identified Holland with global monopoly. For example, one of the pamphlets about the Amboyna massacre Dryden read insisted that the Dutch "will never be satisfied until they have subjected the

trade [of all] nations upon earth to their unlimited East-India arbitrary government."[22] *Amboyna* emphasizes, accordingly, that Holland's modern innovation is the conjunction of merchant capital and military power, and the play's
subversive force lies here: where our own narratives about the birth of capital
feed Eurocentric ideologies of progress, *Amboyna*'s allusions to the militarization of trade resist such ideologies. But the full extent of *Amboyna*'s heterodoxy
becomes visible when we study the play's allusions not only to the history of
state formation in Europe but also to colonialism in the East Indies. The next
section takes *Amboyna*'s historical vision to its limit, where it turns back on the
play itself, calling into question the play's own ideology.

The Monopoly State

The allegory that occurs in the rape plot recurs in a cuckoldry subplot, but here
it focuses on the birth not of the European state but of an East Indian colonial
economy. This history centers in turn not on the Dutch-led rebellion against the
Spanish Empire but on Holland and England's *shared* war against the Iberian
powers. In the cuckoldry subplot, the Dutch Fiscal and the English character
Beamont are both involved with a native woman, Julia, who is married to the
Spaniard don Perez. Augustin Perez was a Portuguese colonist executed alongside
the English on Ambon. Turning him Spanish, Dryden activates the broader history within which both the Dutch and the English overseas empires originated,
by preying alike on Iberian colonies.[23] In a historically acute way, this subplot
collapses the distinction on which the play's own ideology depends, implying
that Holland and England together embody the political economy of the future.

The Portuguese captured Ambon during the 1560s.[24] After Habsburg Spain
conquered Portugal in 1580, it used the profits of Portugal's East Indies empire,
the *Estado da Índia*, to finance its own military ventures. Hence, when the United
Provinces rebelled against Spain, they attacked Portugal's East Indian colonies.[25]
The first Dutch East India Company (VOC) fleets set sail under the directive to
destroy Portuguese trade wherever possible: Curtin claims that the VOC "was
less a capitalist trading firm than . . . a syndicate for piracy."[26] The VOC targeted
Ambon in particular, on which the Portuguese had only a tenuous hold, but
which was essential to Spain's revenue. The Dutch took it in 1605, making it their
very first colonial possession.

Meanwhile, from 1586 to 1604, England was also at war with Spain and likewise attacked colonial ships and factories: English merchants who had traded

with Spain before the war compensated for the loss of that trade during the war by turning to piracy instead.[27] It was more than adequate compensation, the annual value of pirated Spanish goods during the war surpassing the annual value of imported Spanish goods before it. The wealth English privateers acquired in the process constituted their primitive accumulation, transforming them into London's "great merchants" and enabling them to initiate large-scale English shipping. England's earliest planned New World settlements were designed as bases for pirate attacks on the Spanish, and England colonized the New World in earnest only after establishing peace with Spain, since English risk capital preferred piracy, whenever possible, to colonial settlement. Like Holland, England used the precious metals it pillaged from Iberian colonial America to organize monopoly commerce in the Indian Ocean.[28]

The cuckoldry subplot insinuates that though Holland and England are in competition with each other, they together constitute the shape of the future, replacing Iberian hegemony:

Jul. My [husband don Perez's] Plantation's like to thrive well betwixt you.

Beam. Horn him, he deserves not so much happiness as he enjoyes in you; he's jealous.

Jul. 'Tis no wonder if a *Spaniard* looks yellow.

Beam. Betwixt you and me; 'tis a little kind of venture, that we make in doing this Dons drudgery for him; for the whole Nation of 'em is generally so Pocky, that 'tis no longer a Disease, but a second nature. (2.1.288–95)

In the contest for the native woman, who stands for the Iberian empires' overseas territories, a character with an aristocratic title represents Spain, whereas merchants represent Holland and England. These characterizations catch at the material history of early modern colonialism. The conquistadors were in large part Andalusians of little social standing within Spain who aspired above all to turn themselves into dons. Once they arrived in the Americas, they typically took that title or cognate ones such as *gentilhombre* and *caballero*. Such titles reflect not only what Subrahmanyam calls the "landbound mentality" of the Spanish who emigrated but also, consequently, the very logic of the Spanish Empire in Asia as well as the Americas.[29] Contemporaries believed that because of its strict adherence to a feudal logic of power, the bullion Spain seized from American mines ended up rotting its own economy, devaluing and hence eroding its productive forces. By the turn of the sixteenth century, unable to compete with either the United Provinces or England, Spain had entered a period of economic decline.

To further appreciate Dryden's use of the title *don*, we should note that the Portuguese Crown mimicked the Spanish Empire: it also invested its imperial revenue not in trade but rather in largely ill-fated military efforts to expand its territories.[30] It eventually privatized its East Indian trading network and turned the *Estado da Índia* away from commerce toward the collection of customs instead: "The Portuguese," Braudel noted, "became tax-gatherers."[31] But because the cost of its forts and fleets surpassed its customs revenue, the *Estado da Índia* turned out to be a losing proposition. As the term "don" suggests, the *Estado da Índia* clung to economic practices that according to Steensgaard were "archaic," though the economic context in which it arose was novel.[32] It was the *Estado da Índia*'s obsolete economy that rendered it vulnerable in the first place and hence that drew the Dutch and English to the Indian Ocean at the turn of the seventeenth century.

When Beamont claims that "the whole Nation of [Spaniards] is . . . Pocky," he associates the New World bullion that supposedly corrupted the Spanish economy with the New World syphilis, or "pox," that the conquistadors supposedly imported home. Where Julia implies that don Perez's humors are responsible for his "yellow" skin, Beamont instead invokes the nascent realization that disease has exogenous causes.[33] The causal relationship between the creation of a global economy and the proliferation of syphilis was immediately recognized as such: the Dutch referred to syphilis as "the Spanish sickness," while East Indians held the Europeans they knew best responsible, referring to it as "the Portuguese sickness." Dryden built on such associations, insinuating that precisely because the Spanish and the Portuguese have allowed their colonial territories to become sources of corruption, the Dutch and the English must now take over the Iberian "venture," finally turning the East Indian fertility into European commercial hegemony.

But this scene gains its full historical resonance only in the context of Dutch colonial policy, whose general outline was described in another Amboyna pamphlet Dryden read, *A True Relation of the Unjust, Cruell, and Barbarous Proceedings against the English at Amboyna* (1772).[34] Before the VOC reorganized it, the Indian Ocean economy was, according to Das Gupta, a "multitudinous peddling trade," containing as many markets as it did ports and towns.[35] Although these markets employed sophisticated credit mechanisms and monetary instruments, no centralized entity coordinated the trade between them. Hence, East Indian and Middle Eastern markets were, in Steensgaard's words, "almost clinical example[s]" of the free market European modernity supposedly first brought into existence.[36] The *Estado da Índia* failed to control this trading world because the cash-strapped Portuguese Crown invested relatively little capital in it. In contrast, the United Provinces turned to private capital and endowed the exceptionally well-financed VOC with quasi-state powers, including the right to raise armies, make war, and conquer territory. Unlike the *Estado da Índia*, the VOC was able consequently to attack all the other participants in the East Indies trade. Only a small number of the *Estado da Índia*'s ships ever reached their final destinations during the first two decades of the seventeenth century, and the VOC effectively ruined Portuguese trade in the East Indies by the end of the second decade.

The VOC used its arms, though, not only against any trading entity that would compete with it but also against native producers: only by virtue of the latter violence was it able to monopolize the spice trade.[37] It aimed to control all the Spice Islands' production, determining how much nutmeg, mace, or cloves each island generated. To ensure that it would be the sole buyer of cloves in the Spice Islands, the VOC instituted a policy of destroying clove trees, sending expeditions for this purpose, a single one able to eliminate sixty-five thousand trees at a conservative estimate. The VOC's antiproductive measures were so successful that by midcentury clove supplies were insufficient to meet global demand. In the process, the VOC transformed the Spice Islands' economy: where local nobles had used peasant labor to produce goods for both local subsistence and the diverse buyers who called at Spice Islands ports, the VOC became the sole buyer and reoriented the Spice Islands' production to global markets alone.

The policy of destroying spice trees turned the famously productive Moluccas into a "wilderness," according to Davies.[38] The policy involved the destruction of villages, the removal of whole populations from one island to another (which severed them from their livelihoods and hence led sometimes to mass starvation), and their enslavement. Augustin Perez was in fact not a don but rather a VOC employee whose job was to oversee the native slave population on Ambon; Julia was actually a slave. The VOC's demands for slave labor led to native uprisings and, ultimately, to the three Dutch-Ambonese wars. When the VOC did not enslave native peasants, it placed them in dependent relationships: it gave them advances on their harvests, placing them in debt; and it made itself the only seller of the foodstuffs they lacked, producing widespread hunger and famine. *A True Relation* recounted the VOC's destruction of spice trees;

its transfer of spice production from one island to another, its depopulation of islands, its enslavement of native populations, and its eradication of whole towns and villages.[39]

The VOC took this "policy of frightfulness" far beyond its Spice Islands colonies.[40] Recognizing that spices were an essential element within both a bilateral Eurasian trade and a multilateral inter-Asian trade, it aimed to transform the whole pattern of Indian Ocean trade. The Indonesian markets where spices were sold demanded cloth and clothes from India's textile centers, while these areas wanted the gold, silver, and copper that were particularly abundant in Japan. With its historically unprecedented concentration of merchant capital and military power, the VOC was able, unlike any trader before it, to seize monopoly control or privileged access to each of these commodities. It set up factories in all the aforementioned regions and eliminated Asian shipping wherever possible, thereby coordinating a previously decentralized network. For the first time in history, Indians gave Europeans bullion for the spices Europeans purveyed.

Because the VOC came in the process to possess these goods in great quantities, it could function as a cartel all by itself, determining market prices so that its competition could not survive, as *A True Relation* observes at its outset.[41] Hence, in the first decades of the seventeenth century, the VOC destroyed the caravan trade that had supplied Europe with spices from time out of mind. The VOC's centralizing operations in Indian Ocean trade and Amsterdam's centrality to European commerce and finance were interdependent: the former ensured that Amsterdam would be Europe's chief entrepôt; the latter, that the VOC would have unrivaled access to markets and capital. With both its European and its Asian competition marginalized, the VOC succeeded where the *Estado da Índia* had failed: it subordinated East Indian labor to European markets—a moment of historical rupture that would become the shape of the future, as Julia and Beamont's repartee suggests.

But what is most striking about their dialogue is how completely it upends the play's aristocratic ideology: it not only acknowledges the landed order's vulnerability to the modern state but also revels in it. And when Beamont joins the Fiscal in humiliating the Spanish don, the play's representation of the English is turned on its head as well. Rather than stand for the segregation of sovereign power from commercial exchange, the English reassume their historical role: to give the Dutch military support in exchange for a share of the Dutch monopoly.

The banter between the Fiscal and Beamont alludes to the 1619 "Treaty of Defense" between the English East India Company and the VOC:

Beam. Now Mr. *Fiscall*, you are the happy Man with the Ladies, and have got the precedence of Traffick here too; you've the *Indies* in your Arms, yet I hope a poor *English* Man may come in for a third part of the Merchandise.

Fisc. Oh Sir, in these Commodities, here's enough for both, here's Mace for you, and Nutmegg for me in the same Fruit. (2.1.281–87)

By the terms of the treaty, the VOC and the English company divided the spice trade between them, two-thirds to the Dutch, one-third to the English, in exchange for which the latter paid one-third of the VOC's military costs.[42] In emphasizing the English willingness to support, participate in, and profit from Holland's armed monopoly, the scene focuses on the ethical equivalence of the English and the Dutch, contradicting the binary opposition that otherwise structures the play.

This equivalence reflects the economic thought of the quarter century that preceded *Amboyna*'s publication (1647–72), which happened to be the classic period of mercantilist theory.[43] During these decades of Anglo-Dutch conflict, English writers advised the English state to imitate Dutch colonial policy and the East India Company to model itself on the VOC. Heeding the advice, England passed its first comprehensive pieces of protective legislation (the Navigation Acts of 1651 and 1660), which undermined Amsterdam's entrepôt status and precipitated the First and Second Anglo-Dutch Wars. At the same time, the Company's 1657 charter gave it a permanent capital fund and enabled it to follow the VOC in constructing fortified military bases around the Indian Ocean. As a consequence, its trade increased dramatically: Chaudhuri and Israel note that "the rapidity with which the East India Company overhauled the VOC was a success story perhaps only equaled in our own times by the post-war record of Japanese industries."[44] If the Dutch conceived war as commerce's instrument, the English had taken note.

Seventeenth-century Holland and England, though, are part of a history that pertains not to them alone but rather to the modern state in general. Emerging out of the Holy Roman Empire's collapse, the Westphalian system presented the state as the highest form of human association.[45] *Raison d'État*, the political rationality that accompanied this system, was concerned above all to maximize the state's commercial possibilities within a suddenly expanded sphere of seaborne trade and colonial conquest. Henceforth, the aim of politics, far from liberating capital, was to circumscribe it within the state's interests and military ambitions: according to Foucault, this was "one of the most fundamental mutations in both the form of Western political life and the form of Western history."[46] With the rise of the state system, the traditional struggle against "universal empire"—whose rhetoric the English state invoked in its war against Holland—had come to conceal a different political reality, in which *all* states sought positions of dominance in global trade.[47] The degenerative collapsing of politics and economics that *Amboyna*'s aristocratic ideology ascribes to Holland was instead constitutive of the modern state-form as such.

Indeed, Stone and Clay, among others, have argued that the aristocracy participated in global monopoly trade no less than the bourgeoisie did: as the economic basis of aristocracy gradually shifted from property ownership to commerce, it had little choice but to do so.[48] Not merely in England but across western Europe, aristocracies were in fact more open to commercial risk—both more able and willing to take it on—than the middle classes were. Hence, the conflict between the English monarchy and the Dutch republic occurred not *between* aristocratic and bourgeois orders but rather *within* monopoly capital, part of a prototypically European struggle to control the most lucrative long-distance trade routes.

Although Dryden scholars have identified his politics with a defense of the landed against the commercial order, *Amboyna* recognizes that this conflict is already decided.[49] The play's first level—the apparent conflict of orders—dissolves on closer inspection into a deeper second level. Here, too powerful for any strictly feudal order, the mercantile state exerts a centripetal force on landed and commercial classes alike, drawing them into its all-encompassing logic, rendering other orders obsolete. As the Fiscal and Beamont's banter suggests, political dominion depends now not on tribute or customs but rather on monopoly profit. So, while aristocratic honor remained an influential discourse, the aristocracy was no longer historically viable, at least not as a relict of a feudal economy. Behind this discourse lies a history that had rendered landed orders in general, like don Perez in particular, absurd: in this scene, the aristocratic code reappears as nothing more than ideology. McKeon explains that "'aristocratic ideology' names the impulse . . . to conceal the perennial alteration in ruling elites . . . 'aristocracy' is itself the new term, the 'antithetical' simple abstraction, needed to announce the emergence of a new social organization."[50] What is remarkable about *Amboyna* is not, therefore, that it speaks in terms of the aristocratic world while thinking in terms of the mercantile but rather that it subtly acknowledges the hypocrisy of its own values.[51]

The Death of the Sovereign

While *Amboyna*'s attack on aristocratic honor is clearest in the cuckoldry scene, it also takes place elsewhere: the climax of the play, toward which it points from its first scenes, is the Dutch execution of Towerson, the English "captain." Although the play explicitly defends aristocratic honor against merchant capital's imperial ambitions, it implicitly repeats the Dutch *and* English attacks on the Iberian empires. Indeed, its plot corresponds to the seventeenth century's historical trajectory, manifest not only in the United Provinces' rebellion against the Habsburg monarchy and the Peace of Westphalia's consequent substitution of republican for monarchic hegemony but also in the English beheading of Charles I and the century's general "crisis of legitimacy." *Amboyna* moves not to the restoration of an earlier form of sovereignty but instead to its execution at the hands of the mercantile state.

The play emphasizes Towerson's sovereign character: he is "a Publick Person, intrusted by [his] King and [his] Employers" (2.1.111–12). The English merchant Collins explains that Towerson's aristocratic aura enables the English to compete against the Dutch without resorting to military intimidation: "though 'tis true, we have no Castle here, he has an aw upon 'em in his worth, which [the Dutch] both fear and reverence" (1.1.97–99). Towerson relates to his fiancée, Ysabinda, accordingly, as one noble to another: his aura naturally elicits her affection. Their relationship symbolically removes the English presence at Amboyna from the mercantile arena to an aristocratic order.

The English aura consequently stands in the way of the Dutch ambition to monopolize the spice trade and achieve universal empire. Whereas the play's first movement focuses on Harman Junior's attempt to wrest Ysabinda from Towerson and ends in Towerson killing Harman Junior, the play's second movement focuses on Harman Senior's attempt to assassinate Towerson and culminates with Harman Senior executing all of the English at Ambon. In the shift from the first to the second movement, the play translates Harman Junior's personal degeneracy into Harman Senior's drive for global monopoly. By the play's end, the Dutch have executed the sovereign and imposed a de facto monopoly on the spice trade. Mercantilism rules without opposition.

Although *Amboyna* called on the English to avenge this murder in the Third Anglo-Dutch War, it insinuates more subtly that the English cannot ultimately avenge the sovereign because his murder is historically necessary. Towerson's execution corresponds not only to Holland's recent political history but also to England's: they were the first two European states to eliminate monarchic sovereignty—however briefly in England's case.[52] Even after the English Restoration, English radicals were expected to start another revolution throughout the 1660s; revolutionary republicanism flashed up both in the Fifth Monarchists' insurrection (1661) and the "Bawdy House Riots" (1668). Republicanism was an accepted position in mainstream political debate throughout the Restoration, and when the revolution finally occurred, the 1688 settlement produced a "crowned republic," in which Parliament controlled the state's military and financial assets.

Harman Junior describes Towerson as "an *Englishman*, part Captain, and part Merchant; his Nation of declining interest here" (2.1.21–23). The relationship of the apposite clauses is not coincidental: England is of "declining interest" in the Spice Islands, precisely because Towerson—at best only "part Merchant"—wants to subordinate private interest to traditional sovereign principles and hence cannot compete with the Dutch, who have made "interest" autonomous. To the extent that Towerson—or any principle outside the pursuit of monopoly trade—governs England's imperial ventures, it will always be of declining interest in the Indies.

Amboyna emphasizes Towerson's complete incomprehension of mercantilism from his first words. He comments to Harman Senior: "[Amboyna] yields Spice enough for both [the English and the Dutch]; and *Europe*, Ports, and Chapmen, where to vend them" (1.1.215–17). Towerson's premise that one state can have "enough" of a commodity to share it with another makes no sense within mercantilist theory, which presupposes that trade must not be free, regardless of a commodity's abundance, because competition compromises profit. Hence, while Harman Senior appears to agree with Towerson, he adds an ominous qualification: "It does, it does, we have enough, if we can be contented." Where Harman Senior hints at his desire for global monopoly, Towerson invokes historically more esteemed principles:

Why shou'd we not [be contented], what mean these endless jars of Trading Nations? 'tis true, the World was never large enough for Avarice or Ambition; but those who can be pleas'd with moderate gain, may have the ends of Nature, not to want: nay, even its Luxuries may be supply'd from her o'erflowing bounties in these parts: from whence she yearly sends Spices, . . . the Food of Heaven in Sacrifice. And besides these, her Gems of richest value, for Ornament, more then necessity. (1.1.220–27)

Towerson thinks in the terms of aristocratic ideals: for him, exchange is meant to serve not "Avarice or Ambition" but rather "bounty," "luxury," and "ornament"; in other words, not the desire for profit and power but an ethical code rooted in gift giving and hence extravagance and inutility. His problem is that, like the Iberian empires, he does not pursue trading monopolies ruthlessly enough. Against a political economy based on monopoly and the concentration of wealth, he stands for one supposedly based on generosity and redistribution.

But though the play explicitly honors Towerson for his subordination of trade to traditional sovereignty, it insinuates that this priority is tragically out of step with the times. Here, *Amboyna* resembles Dryden's other plays in which the sovereign's failure to appreciate the necessity of raison d'État renders him obsolete. For example, even though Restoration drama is supposed symbolically to reverse England's still-recent regicide, *The Indian Emperour* reiterates it, ending with the execution of the king and the exile of the prince.[53] Its obedience to the code of honor is precisely what destroys the royal family. In *The Conquest of Granada*, the "restoration" of Christian sovereignty entails that it replace honor with a ruthless political calculus.

Amboyna likewise leaves its hero in the past and follows its villain into the future; it understands the value of trade not like Towerson in terms of aristocratic ideals but like Harman Senior in terms of raison d'État. In doing so, *Amboyna* merely invokes the political economy with which Dryden had already aligned his poetics. He had rehearsed Harman Senior's part, for example, in *Annus Mirabilis* (1667): in regard to the Second Anglo-Dutch War, he asked, "What peace can be where both to one pretend?"[54] Earlier, at the start of his career, Dryden had put himself at the service of an antimonarchical mercantile state. Having been a functionary in Cromwell's republic, Dryden wrote his first significant poem, *Heroic Stanzas* (1659), after Cromwell's death, celebrating him for leading England's original policy of aggressive mercantile expansion: "By his command we boldly cross'd the line / And bravely fought where southern stars arise, / We trac'd the far-fetch'd gold unto the mine / And that which brib'd our fathers made our prize."[55] Cromwell made available to Dryden a vision of what English sovereignty must become to be truly modern: under Cromwell, England expanded its naval power almost exponentially and first attempted to seize other states' colonies.[56] Dryden turned from supporter of regicide to "royalist" only after

Cromwell's death, in whose funeral procession he numbered and for which he wrote a eulogy. When the Stuarts were restored to the English throne, Dryden reused the vocabulary he had devised for Cromwell to celebrate Charles II's crowning. *Astraea Redux* ends with a paean to the English mercantile state's potential to form a universal empire: "Abroad your Empire shall no Limits know, / But like the Sea in boundless Circles flow. / Your much lov'd Fleet shall with a wide Command / Besiege the petty Monarchs of the Land: / And as Old Time his Off-spring swallow'd down / Our Ocean in its depths all Seas shall drown."[57] Dryden's mercantile rhetoric replaces sovereign character with raison d'État, encouraging the royal no less than the republican to pursue a mercantile logic, whose boundlessness now surpasses even the seas' own. Whereas the scholarship judges Dryden's writing to be royalist, the works I have cited suggest that for as long as he served the English state, his poetics were mercantilist instead.

The Cunning of Mercantilism

In short, though the scholarship on Dryden aligns his work with aristocratic values, the texts I have discussed consider such values obsolete. Even as it employs the rhetoric of aristocratic honor, *Amboyna* insinuates that this rhetoric is now nothing more than a disguise for mercantile interests. In other words, the play's duplicity in regard to aristocratic values inculcates a reading practice that recognizes, behind the political ideology of the aristocracy, the political economy of the monopoly state.

The tragic flaw that eventually leads Towerson to his own execution is a peculiarly aristocratic one: an ethical naïveté or credulity, a fidelity to the word, which conventionally characterizes the nobility and which the rise of merchant cunning throws into stark relief.[58] Always the voice of critical insight, Beamont describes Towerson before he enters the scene: "If he has any fault, 'tis only that . . . he thinks all honest, 'cause himself is so, and therefore none suspects" (1.1.132–34). When Towerson accepts Harman Junior's disingenuous apology for his pursuit of Ysabinda, Beamont is more blunt: "*Towerson* is easy, and too credulous. I fear 'tis all dissembl'd on their parts" (3.2.112–13). When it finally dawns on Towerson that the Dutch have always intended only to betray his trust, he exclaims: "Curse my fond credulity, to think there cou'd be Faith or Honor in the *Dutch*" (5.1.235–36). Towerson's credulousness prefigures Oroonoko's precisely. Oroonoko's "honour was such as he never had violated a word in his life": as a consequence he is betrayed successively by slave traders in Coramantien; the captain of the slave ship; and

Byam, the deputy governor of Surinam, if not his intimate friends Trefry, Colonel Martin, and the narrator herself.[59] Like Towerson, Oroonoko thinks in terms of an obsolete ethical code premised on honor, revenge, and justice rather than the covert calculations proper to mercantilism. And so like *Amboyna, Oroonoko* implies that the ultimate responsibility for the demise of the aristocratic code lies as much in its naïveté as in merchant capital's duplicity.[60]

If *Amboyna* mocks Towerson's credulity, it must advocate suspicion as the proper interpretive stance. In fact, the play repays suspicion with a surplus of meaning. For example, Towerson's last words cry out for a cynical read:

Tell my friends I dy'd so as became a Christian and a Man; give to my brave Employers of the *East India* Company, the last remembrance of my faithful service; tell 'em I Seal that Service with my Blood; and dying, wish to all their Factories, and all the famous Merchants of our Isle, that Wealth their gen'rous Industry deserves; but dare not hope it with *Dutch* partnership. (5.1.398–403)

Offering a "last remembrance," Towerson's words would dictate how we see English colonialism in the East Indies, by transfiguring the obviously private nature of his own and the Company's presence there. Towerson's noble equanimity in the face of death becomes his "seal," the sign of a public office, which the Company has presumably conferred on him, despite the fact that it is a private entity. His relationship with the Company ceases to be contractual and reverts to "faithful service," a feudal obligation. The Company is the appropriate guardian of this remembrance because it is itself "brave," possessing of all things an aristocratic character. Finally, the claim that the English disavow their partnership and wage war with the Dutch only because they want the just fruits of their "industry" transfigures the English state, concealing its actual motive, to usurp the United Provinces' global hegemony.

But what *Amboyna* transfigures points precisely to the material history the play's ideology needs to suppress. For example, in regard to Towerson's public character, one of the pamphlets Dryden read observed that Towerson had been party to the Spanish colonists' plan of robbing the Dutch factories.[61] Towerson's rebellion against civil authority parallels the Dutch rebellion against imperial Spain, and the equivalence between Towerson and the Dutch rebels could be extended to the English revolutionaries who executed Charles I, republicans whom Dryden claimed to detest, but with whom he had worked as a civil servant in Cromwell's republic.

Amboyna alludes, in short, to a history that exceeds its ideology. The East India Company's minutely detailed archives also suggest that our hero's history was more complicated than his dramatic persona. In a letter dated 11 March 1606, Company directors instruct Company merchants scheduled to depart for the East Indies to place Towerson under surveillance:

We vnderstand mr Towerson hast beene a lardge dealer for him self, haueing sould to the Hollenders att one tyme 300 sackes of pepp beside other thinge. . . . And yf vpon due examinacon thereof he doe not giue good satisfaccon to yor content, then we praye you to reduced the same to the Common stocke . . . for that the same is Contrarie to or expresse order.[62]

The play exalts the very character the archive suspects; rather than confident about his "faithful service," the Company was anxious that Towerson's pursuit of his private interests would compromise his ability to further their own. That Towerson actually cared whether or not "Dutch partnership" robbed English merchants of the wealth "their generous industry deserves" is doubtful, since he not only skimmed the Company's profits by trading illicitly on his own account but did so precisely with the Dutch.[63] The diametric opposite of his theatrical character, the historical Towerson instead resembles the Dutch merchants *Amboyna* portrays.

Towerson's renegade trade manifested a more basic problem, which the archives ceaselessly document: the potential autonomy of merchant capital from any sovereign order, particularly pronounced in colonies separated from the metropolis by half the globe. A 1611 East India Company letter to Towerson addresses the general problem directly:

Forasmuch as or ffactors att Bantam & elswhere haue . . . ymployed there in priuate tradeinge for their owne pticuler gaine wthe the greate neglect of ors, . . . wee doe therefore rsolue . . . that no ffactor or other ymployed in or said seruice shall be pmitted to receiue, or take in those partes such wages as shall growe due vnto them, but onlie soe much as shall be necessarie for their apprell.[64]

Even as *Amboyna* claims that English colonialism is subject to a higher principle, the play's historical allusions subtly give the lie to this claim. The historical Towerson's wayward actions suggest the truth: rather than subordinate to the commonwealth, English merchant capital relentlessly privatized global production, as private traders appropriated what the merchant company considered to be its profits and merchant companies appropriated what the state considered to be its own. The sovereign anxiety about trade documented in the preceding quotations betrays, above all, the absence of aristocratic values, which on principle considered sovereign power and market exchange to be separate spheres. The modernity that the superbly armed East India companies brought to the Indian Ocean collapsed this distinction, attempting to circumscribe forms of trade that had generally existed outside sovereign prerogative. The prototypically modern ingenuity of *Amboyna* is to register English mercantilism in all of its duplicity, both its ideology *and* its underlying political economy, thereby revealing the purely instrumental function of aristocratic rhetoric in Restoration literary culture and beyond.

The Public Treasury

Amboyna presents us a naïve character in Towerson but encourages us not to read him naïvely. If, following the play's own cues, we read it with a corresponding suspicion, it offers us even more vertiginous perspectives just beneath its surface. If the play's characters insinuate that merchant capital is every bit as sovereign in England as in Holland, the play's frame—its dedication, prologue, and epilogue—takes this insinuation to its logical conclusion, hinting that Dryden self-consciously designed the play itself to operate according to the tactics of the mercantile state rather than the ideals of feudal honor. The play suggests, therefore, that the death of Towerson and traditional sovereignty is not only historically inevitable but also aesthetically necessary. One of the play's deepest ironies emerges here: the murder of the sovereign is both the Netherlands' aim *and* Dryden's. *Pace* received wisdom, Dryden appropriates aristocratic forms not to mourn their loss but rather to profit from them in the mercantile system. Dryden's aesthetic was designed to have currency in this new economy.

The dedication prefigures the necessity of Towerson's death, suggesting that the sovereign's execution enables new practices in the realm of both political economy and aesthetic form. Dryden addressed the dedication to his patron, Lord Clifford, who resigned from his office as Lord Treasurer because of the 1673 Test Act, which made Anglicanism the prerequisite of public service: "'Tis the Interest of the World that Vertuous Men should attain to Greatness, because it gives them the power of doing good. But, when by the Iniquity of the Times they are brought to that extremity, that they must either quit their Vertue or their Fortune, they owe themselves so much, as to retire to the private exercise of their Honour" (4.24–30).[65] Clifford's "retirement" foretells Towerson's death (Clifford hanged himself two months after his resignation from public office). Both imply that sovereign character cannot master "the Iniquity of the Times," the private interests that govern the mercantile state. The dedication enacts a reversal that marks an epochal transformation: the noble becomes a private person, public character obtaining now only within the rural estate; in contrast, a vicious private logic governs the state. Like the play he dedicates to him, Dryden's praise of Clifford argues—with an irony typical of Dryden's dedications—that the patron's sovereign character is now powerless.[66]

But even as Dryden retires Clifford in the dedication, his tropes turn Clifford's patronage into his own personal monopoly, thereby replacing a feudal with a mercantile order: "You have been a Good so Universal, that almost every Man in three Nations may think me Injurious to his Propriety, that I invade your Praises, in undertaking to celebrate them alone. And, that have assum'd to my self a Patron, who was no more to be circumscrib'd than the Sun and Elements, which are of Publick benefit to humane kind" (3–4). As Lord Treasurer, Clifford benefited "three Nations," a term that refers of course to England, Scotland, and Wales but gestures toward the triangulated imperial contest between Spain, Holland, and England in the play. At the moment he was writing, Dryden literally possessed a monopoly on English public patronage, which all three nations had equal right to consider their property or "propriety." Before he resigned as Lord Treasurer, Clifford made sure that Dryden received his full government salaries both as Poet Laureate and as Historiographer Royal for 1672 and 1673, even though Clifford himself had insisted that all state expenditures save those that supported the war be suspended: during the Third Anglo-Dutch War, the English state refused even to service its debts.[67] Dryden's composition of *Amboyna*—which he designed as propaganda for a deeply unpopular war—appears to have been the act of obeisance he offered in exchange for the de facto monopoly he had been gifted.[68] Expropriating what had been of "Publick benefit," Dryden's "circumscription" of Clifford's patronage literally places one figure within another, a symbol of feudal relations within the shape of the mercantile state. While Clifford now operates only within the confines of the country estate, *Amboyna* takes Clifford's patronage into the much wider sphere of interstate competition.

Dryden claimed to detest this sphere—"To this Retirement of your Lordship, I wish I could bring a better Entertainment, than this *Play*; which, though it succeeded on the Stage, will scarcely bear a serious perusal, . . . the Subject barren, the Persons low, and the Writing not heightned with many laboured Scenes" (5)—but he knew all too well that it was the only one that could guarantee his professional success. While he sought aristocratic patronage, his income came primarily from the literary and theatrical markets: the sale of his books; his exclusive contract as the King's Company's house playwright; his share, as one of its partners, in its profits; and his government salaries as Poet Laureate and Historiographer Royal.[69] As a professional writer involved in the negotiation of contracts, Dryden understood that his economic position was defined no longer by patronage and feudal servility but rather by the market and modern legal and economic rights, and in his dedications he addressed his patrons brazenly as the bearer of such rights. Dryden was more than a merely *professional* writer though. He oriented himself toward the market as a shareholder, not as petty producer, and he colluded with the state in order to give his work a uniquely protected status. Dryden was a mercantilist in the strict sense of the word.

Contemporaries identified Dryden's writing with state positions.[70] But he was not simply—as the title pages of his own plays declared—"servant of his Majesty." His own sophisticated understanding of modern sovereignty entailed that neither "servant" nor "majesty" preserved its conventional sense when he invoked it.[71] By circumscribing sovereignty within the figure of mercantilism, he both represented sovereign ideology and betrayed it. The cunning of Dryden's dedication here and his poetics in general is that they work both codes—the rhetoric of the aristocracy and the tactics of mercantilism—simultaneously, using the former to serve the latter, thereby enacting a typically modern duplicity. Although Dryden's rhetoric explicitly opposes the commodification of art, his "retirement" of the patron implies the obsolescence of the aristocratic world's literary economy. In this way, *Amboyna* contains the contradiction between its ideology and its material history, and it is here that its richness—or duplicity—lies.

Sovereignty, Trade, War

Amboyna's epilogue represents this contradiction in still more sophisticated ways. It chooses Rome as a metaphor for England's nascent empire, a trope that first became pervasive during the Anglo-Dutch Wars: the correspondence between the three Punic Wars, which effectively cleared the field for Rome's imperial development, and the three Anglo-Dutch Wars, which were in their own way the precondition of the British Empire, seemed only too exact.[72] References to the Punic Wars became commonplace, because the invocation of Rome honored England's war efforts.[73] It is not surprising, then, that *Amboyna* alludes to Rome—its subtlety lies rather in how it empties this metaphor out.

The most provocative part of the play, the epilogue calls for England to crush Holland as Rome had Carthage. In particular, it quotes Shaftesbury, who as Lord Chancellor opened the 1673 session of Parliament by citing Cato the Elder's famous senatorial pronouncement, "Delenda est Carthago" (Carthage must be destroyed).[74] Cato's political career focused on the same binary opposition—between aristocratic honor and mercantile interest—that appears to shape *Amboyna*'s plot. Both as censor and as senator, Cato was concerned to punish Roman statesmen who threatened to turn their public office into private gain and hence to replace Roman sovereignty with tyranny. Dryden's own translation of Plutarch's *Life of Cato* explains that "everybody admired Cato, when they saw others . . . grow effeminate by pleasures; and yet beheld him unconquered . . . persevering in his exercise and maintaining his character to the very last. . . . All which was for the sake of the commonwealth, that so his body might be the hardier for the war."[75] Cato's embodiment of Roman agrarian-military virtue found its most extreme expression in his obsessive call for war with Carthage.

Among the reasons Carthage provided Cato a perfect enemy was its historical reputation as an almost purely mercantile state, ruled by a corrupt and venal oligarchy whose wealth stemmed from maritime commerce.[76] Carthage's economy, like seventeenth-century Holland's, was based on a carrying trade rather than its own production. And Carthage, like Holland again, made its fortune by shipping Indian Ocean goods to western ports. Finally, Carthage also possessed a monopoly—of western Mediterranean trade—that statesmen feared would become a universal empire. In Cato's pronouncement "Delenda est Carthago"—which supposedly concluded all of his senatorial pronouncements regardless of their subject—we see a central conflict of premodern economies: between aristocratic sovereignty and merchant capital, politics and economics, landed property and trade.[77] In Rome, aristocracy, politics, and property ownership prevailed for a time, but the proximity of Mediterranean trade always posed a threat to the aristocratic order.

The Third Punic War was among the most ruthless of classical wars.[78] Rome's aim was to destroy Carthage as a fortified city and a harbor so completely that it would have no value to any other regional power. Hence, Rome largely fabricated the violation on which it based the war. This is the background to the history many of us know by rote: Carthage's unconditional submission, in which it sent three hundred nobles as hostages to Rome and then surrendered all its arms and engines of war; Rome demanding yet another condition for peace, that all of Carthage's citizens leave their city, which Rome would destroy, and relocate at least ten miles from the Mediterranean; and finally, Rome reputedly burning and razing Carthage to the ground and sowing its soil with salt so that it would never rise again. The five-thousand-square-mile territory that Carthage had governed became a Roman province.

The United Provinces' breathtakingly rapid elaboration of the mercantile state-form appeared to reincarnate Carthage: by 1670, its long-distance trade surpassed the rest of western Europe's combined; the United Provinces carried practically all Eastern commodities to their European markets.[79] The allusion to Cato, then, enabled Dryden to celebrate England's war on Holland as an act full of honor. Dryden's translation tells us that "[Cato] thought it more honourable to conquer those who possessed the gold, than to possess the gold itself."[80] The capacity to make war is proof of sovereign character: conquest frees one from engaging directly in the denigrated sphere of trade. In *Annus Mirabilis*, England plays the part of Rome by destroying Dutch commercial property, burning VOC merchantmen carrying spice; honor resides in military, not commercial, power.[81] Hence, in Dryden's poetics—*An Essay of Dramatick Poesie* as well as *Annus Mirabilis*—English poetic and military greatness go hand in hand.[82]

Accordingly, the epilogue does not avert its gaze from Rome's ruthlessness but fixates on it: "*As* Cato *did his* Affricque *Fruits display*: / *So we before your Eies their* Indies *lay*: / *All Loyal* English *will like him conclude*, / *Let* Caesar *Live, and* Carthage *be subdu'd*." Dryden refers to the supposed fact that Cato once prefaced the declaration "Carthage must be destroyed" by holding a fig aloft and noting, "This was gathered at Carthage three days ago." The still-fresh fig, a symbol not only of the fruitfulness of the land under Carthage's rule but also of its proximity to Rome, appeals directly to the senators' aristocratic ethos: in the zero-sum game of territorial power, one must either relentlessly expand the revenue-producing land under one's dominion or become vulnerable to conquest.[83] Carthage always presented Rome a golden opportunity. Within the play's ideological register, Amboyner nutmegs repeat Carthaginian figs—if England seizes the former as Rome took the latter, even if it must destroy Holland as completely as Rome did Carthage, similar honor will redound to it.

The ideological work Dryden's invocation of Cato performs is to disavow the English state's basis in monopoly capital and hence private interest. The epilogue implies that like Cato's Rome, the English prove their sovereign character by going to war *against* the collusion of merchant capital and sovereign power. But if as propaganda, *Amboyna* reiterates Cato's logic precisely, as a historically acute literary text, it introduces a fundamental difference. Between Rome and England, the essential difference lies in the distinction between figs and nutmegs. The fig represents land and the revenue this land produces: by conquering Carthage, Rome expanded its territory, increasing its revenue primarily by means of rent. Nutmegs, on the other hand, represent the monopoly trade the East India companies brought to the Indian Ocean: the English state's aim in the Anglo-Dutch Wars was not to conquer Holland, nor even the Spice Islands, but the trade routes Holland controlled. England's part in the Anglo-Dutch Wars embraced the conjunction of monopoly capital and military power; its war effort expressed a thoroughly modern raison d'État rather than classical republican virtue.

Before *Amboyna* used the trope of the Punic Wars to propagandize for the Third Anglo-Dutch War and *Annus Mirabilis* used it for the Second, Marvell's "The Character of Holland" (1653) used it for the First, in support of Cromwell's aggressive mercantilism.[84] Cromwell's aim was not to eradicate the threat mercantile power posed to aristocratic sovereignty but rather to combine them. Likewise, the invocation of the Punic Wars appears to call forth classical republicanism, but more precisely empties it out and reorients it around raison d'État and mercantilism. The new Rome that England is about to become—in "The Character of Holland," "their Carthage overcome / Would render fain unto our better Rome"—is not simply the global emporium but itself the trader, not only the center toward which all traffic tends but the traffic itself and its monopoly profits.[85] The substance of the English state—what it shares with Rome—is decidedly not republican virtue but merely its shell: overwhelming military force, the precondition now of global monopoly trade.

Like Dryden, the East India Company directors saw its conflict with the VOC in terms of the Third Punic War, but they turned his analogy around. In the early 1660s, they wrote in official correspondence: "[The VOC] think themselves in the same condition as the ancient Romans were with the Carthaginians, when they told them they would treat of peace when they had removed their city ten miles further into the country."[86] The Company's directors give the VOC the role of Rome (an empire suffering no trade outside its purview); and the Company, the part of Carthage (traders bereft of wider territorial aspirations). In their account, sovereignty and trade occur in separate spheres.

Not surprisingly, Dryden's allusion to the Punic War is richer. The work it performs is explicitly to disavow, and hence implicitly to draw attention to, the corruption at the heart of the English state. For *Amboyna*, that corruption lies ultimately in the collapsing of spheres, sovereignty and trade, that classical political theory insists must be quarantined from each other. In this play, it is precisely the mutual interpenetration of these spheres that constitutes the logic at the core of the modern state, England every bit as much as Holland: the aristocratic pursuit of territorial aggrandizement suddenly depends on the profits of merchant capital, and—equally problematically—the merchant company's profits depend on the ever-present threat of military coercion. In its prototypically modern form—which simultaneously invokes the separation of economic and political spheres and collapses them—*Amboyna* subtly represents the inexorable rise of a modern sovereignty, which renders other social forms obsolete. When we lose sight of *Amboyna*'s historical vision and substitute in its place the narrative of bourgeois revolution, we risk playing, no less than the fictional Towerson, into the hands of colonial modernity. We accept the ideology that, with the birth of capital Europe liberated economics from politics and subsequently gifted this supposedly novel possibility to the rest of the world.[87]

2

CONVERSION AND PIRACY
Defoe's Captain Singleton

In histories of the novel ranging from Watt's *The Rise of the Novel* and Armstrong's *Desire and Domestic Fiction* to McKeon's *Origins of the English Novel* and Thompson's *Models of Value*, the novel not only follows the rise of capital but also always abets it. The early novel in these accounts is an element of bourgeois ideology: it touches not on the material base of human life but rather only on the mystified superstructure of bourgeois consciousness. To a great extent, these histories of the novel have their own origins in Lukács's utterly commanding *The Theory of the Novel* (1920), which argued that the novel belongs to a time in which the economy cannot be grasped empirically. "The novel," Lukács famously declared, "is the epic of an age in which the extensive totality of life is no longer directly given."[1]

The studies that have followed in Lukács's wake argue, accordingly, that the early novel constructs self-enclosed spaces—for example, Crusoe's island or Pamela's country house—that segregate the nascent individual from the primitive accumulation of capital.[2] The country house appears in Armstrong's words to be a "self-contained social unit," its "means of support . . . elsewhere, invisible, removed from the scene."[3] In *The Theory of the Novel*, as in these subsequent studies, the novel generally excludes economic exploitation, because it works outward from the "bourgeois individual" back to the world, reconstructing the concentric circles that circumscribe him or her—home, property ownership, the nation-state, and the global economy—so that they are whitewashed of their material history.[4] This representation of the individual fulfills literature's ideological function: to resolve aesthetically historical contradictions that capitalism cannot reconcile materially.[5]

In this regard, Defoe's novels serve as the prototype of the form. Though their heroes participate initially in what Thompson refers to as "primitive accumulation," their subjective development turns on the transition to legitimate trade. This "graduation," he observes, depends on "financial amnesia, as stolen treasure is turned into . . . capital."[6] *Robinson Crusoe* exemplifies this argument particularly well, since Crusoe's slave-trade origins are effaced by his spiritual conversion on the island, which resituates his labor within a providential frame-work.[7] Indeed, according to Armstrong, Crusoe's island may have provided the model of a "domain where money did not really matter," which the novel would subsequently make the basis of bourgeois domesticity.[8] Interpreting *Robinson Crusoe* as "a great exemplar . . . of progressive ideology," McKeon argues that, "like all ideology," *Robinson Crusoe* discloses social contradictions only in order to mediate and thereby rationalize them.[9] In our histories, then, the novel-form's triumphal celebration of economic individualism and the rise of the middle classes patterns itself on Defoe's novels in general and *Robinson Crusoe* in particular.[10]

This chapter presents a diametrically opposed narrative of the rise of the novel—or at least of one. I take as counterexample to *Robinson Crusoe* another work by Defoe: *Captain Singleton* (1720), the barely remembered pirate novel that he wrote immediately after his Crusoe narratives and that, long considered merely a rushed attempt to capitalize on their phenomenal success, has been consistently overlooked by our histories of the novel.[11] During the course of his narrative, Single-ton leads hundreds of pirates across the Indian Ocean and back again, tracing and retracing the trade routes European merchant corporations were integrating into increasingly coordinated imperial networks. In contrast to *Robinson Crusoe*'s al-leged celebration of economic individualism, *Captain Singleton* is a wide-ranging exploration of the global monopoly system European states had imposed on the circulation of capital. Where *Robinson Crusoe* supposedly aligns the bourgeois in-dividual, home, and economy with providential design, *Captain Singleton* describes their basis instead in this monopoly system. In the process, it touches on a mate-rial history of capitalism to which our histories of the novel are not yet attuned.

For example, Britain became Europe's preeminent commercial economy—between the end of the Restoration and the rise of the novel, not coinciden-tally—by means of war, and its war-making capacity depended in turn on monopoly capital from the East Indies. The Nine Years' War (1688–97) and the War of Spanish Succession (1701–14) enabled Britain to supersede Spain, Holland, and France as Europe's dominant colonial power.[12] By the end of the latter war, Britain possessed new colonies in the Americas and the Mediterranean, control over all commercial movement between the Atlantic and the Mediterranean, and, most lucrative of all, a monopoly on the New World slave trade. But it also faced cash shortages during both these wars and hence needed the East India Company to finance them. In the wake of the first war, the state gave a group of British merchants the right to establish the New East India Company and to operate in the East Indies on an exclusive basis in exchange for a £2 million loan. In the middle of the second, the state allowed the old Company to merge with the new in exchange for a loan exceeding £1 million. And near the end of that war, the state extended the united Company's monopoly for a three-year term in exchange for a loan exceeding £3 million.

In these deals, the British state and the East India Company entered into the same type of collusion that the Dutch state and the Dutch East India Company (VOC) had pioneered during the seventeenth century, in which the state's capacity to make war and the profits of monopoly trade—or, in other words, military power and global capital—depended on each other. Even though the 1695 parliamentary sessions had revealed the Company's widespread engagement in bribery, it was allowed to become an important lobby once again after the second war.[13] In virtue of its collusion with the British state, the English Company had surpassed the VOC as the dominant European power in the East Indies by the time of *Captain Singleton*'s publication. Its commodities, East Indian textiles in particular, became a major portion of British imports, and reexported to American and West Indian slave plantations, would tie together the two ends of primitive accumulation.

The novel emerges within the context of *this* global economy—not simply the rise of economic individualism and the middle classes, concepts that our accounts of the novel reflexively repeat and hence themselves reify. At least in the case of *Captain Singleton*, the novel, furthermore, responds to this global economy critically. Crusoe's conversion redeems his typically bourgeois sin—"a rash and immoderate desire of rising faster than the nature of the thing admitted"—by resituating it within not only providential design but also, once he has reinvested his wealth in British property, the national economy.[14] As *Captain Singleton* carefully explores the global monopoly system, it questions *Robinson Crusoe*'s conversion narrative. *Captain Singleton* refuses both facile conversions and the seamless incorporation of capital accumulated sinfully outside the nation back into it. Rather than spiritualize primitive accumulation, this novel carefully materializes it, tracing both the illicit origins of the wealth that invests the state's legitimate property and the precise networks in which it was converted from the one to the other along the way.

Captain Singleton's allusions to the monopoly system refute the widely accepted premise that European modernity *unleashed* capital globally, thereby first bringing the individual and socioeconomic mobility into history. These allusions point to a different history, in which European states and corporations together attempted, on the contrary, to subordinate the production of already flourishing non-European economies to their own war-making capacity. *Captain Singleton* therefore questions the narrative about capital's birth at the center of our histories of the novel and, by extension, those histories themselves.

This chapter's five parts argue that rather than segregate the individual from primitive accumulation, *Captain Singleton* represents their interpenetration. The first part discusses the novel's opening pages, an account of Singleton's origins that begins with theft: after child robbers kidnap Singleton in order to steal his clothes, he himself becomes the loot in a series of illicit exchanges. In this allegory, the modern individual, far from being autonomous of the market economy, is instead its product, and markets are based, in turn, on expropriation rather than free exchange. The second discusses this allegory's historical context, the seventeenth- and early eighteenth-century "golden age" of piracy. While theft originates the modern individual in this novel, piracy helped institute English mercantilism during the period. In fact, Defoe's pamphlets claimed that the metropolitan economy was little else but acts of piracy turned into legitimate commerce.

The third part studies Singleton's own conversion, in which his pirates launder their fortune through the East India Company. This conversion enables Singleton to buy an English country house and so return home. In this novel, therefore, the bourgeois individual and bourgeois property are effects of Indian Ocean exchanges between pirates and merchant capitalists—exchanges that were in fact central to England's commercial revolution. Singleton's conversion and country house index their own colonial preconditions, which Defoe understood but our histories of the novel do not.

The fourth part discusses Singleton's belief, *pace* Crusoe, that no conversion, material or spiritual, can redeem his ill-gotten gains and his consequent reluctance to return home. The fifth analyzes the home that Singleton does finally construct in England: rather than readopt clothes proper to his birth, he insists on disguising himself in robes of Asian silk. This strange conclusion makes sense only in light of the colonial history we will explore. It harks back not to a precapitalist past but rather to the pirate plunder that spurred English commerce. This novel does not abet the rise of capital, therefore, but traces its lost origins instead.[15]

Origins

Singleton begins his narrative by acknowledging the demand that he describe his genealogy: "As it is usual for great Persons . . . to insist much upon their Originals, give full Accounts of their Families, and the Histories of their Ancestors . . . , I shall do the same, tho' I can look but a very little Way into my Pedigree."[16] Even as he accedes to romance conventions, Singleton insists that his history must disappoint them.[17] Singleton cannot know his "Originals," because they have been lost—or more precisely, because they managed somehow to lose him. When he was an infant, his nursery maid left him outside a pub while having an assignation inside, thereby allowing child robbers to steal him for the clothes off his back. With a characteristic lack of self-pity, Singleton refers to the maid simply as "the careless Hussy . . . that lost me" (2). Singleton's loss effaces his origins from his memory and hence from his history: "as I never knew anything of . . . who my Father and Mother were, so it would make but a needless Digression to talk of [them] here" (2). A novelistic hero with an uncommon understanding of his place in the order of things, Singleton knows his origins lie in theft and loss.

Singleton's theft removes him from a past organized by birth and rank and deposits him willy-nilly into another time organized by exchange. His abrupt transition allegorizes, on a private level, the socioeconomic transformation that produced the novel-form itself. Devoid of genealogy and hence of an "Original," Singleton is free to become a different kind of protagonist. But whereas the novelistic hero's loss of origins would subsequently imply that an intrinsic nobility will govern his life until he recovers his social standing, in Defoe's fallen world, virtue belongs to a lost time.[18] Singleton is a private individual driven solely by private interest; though he operates in a global arena, he is obviously bereft of a public character. His surname captures his ontological condition, representing not filiation but rather alienation, the fact that the modern self inhabits an essentially atomized society.[19] Though they require only a few paragraphs, Singleton's origins contain in remarkably condensed form an allegory of the modern individual as such.

This allegory focuses less on trade than on robbery: channeled through markets that do not question the provenance of the goods they purvey, Singleton's clothes will return legal profits whose bases lie, however invisibly, in theft. His kidnapping turns Singleton into stolen goods as well. A female beggar takes him from the child robbers in order to make herself a more sympathetic figure to passing alms givers. When he outgrows this function, she converts him even more directly into a commodity, peddling him for "Twelve Shillings" to a gypsy woman who employs him in her own "strolling trade." After she is hanged for her crimes, Singleton becomes an apprentice on a ship that is captured first by Algerian pirates and then immediately recaptured by a Portuguese warship, one of whose merchants enslaves Singleton. He is, by this point, a form of plunder five removes from the propertied individual with whom we associate the novel's rise. His theft activates a chain of transactions that constitute the new market society, in which the illicit origins of things must be lost.

Singleton's personal story is also an allegory of global history: theft is originary here as well. The novel represents the commerce between English pirates and the East India Company that occurred at the very origins of the British Empire and, in doing so, alludes both to the Indian Ocean economies that preceded European mercantilism and to the histories of their expropriation and loss. If we follow these allusions, we will find that Defoe had a much more critical understanding of "capitalism" than we have attributed to him. In the process, we will study a different history of capitalism—and, by extension, a different context for the novel as well.

Piracy and the State

Singleton's theft serves as a new "original," since his future is fated to copy it. Made into plunder himself, he will spend the rest of the narrative repeating this originary event by plundering others: "I that was, as I have hinted before, an original Thief, and a Pyrate even by Inclination before, was now in my Element, and never undertook any Thing in my Life with more particular Satisfaction" (140). When Singleton becomes a pirate, he in effect chooses to be a gypsy outside the purview of the state, largely beyond the long arm of its law. Explaining the end of his gypsy life, Singleton notes laconically, "My good *Gypsey Mother*, for some of her worthy Actions *no doubt*, happened in Process of Time to be hang'd" (2). The gypsy woman, the only one of his owners Singleton calls "Mother," threatens to become the origin of his life in this way also, compelling his narrative to end in execution as well. Belying his brief mention of her execution, the prospect of hanging—the specter of his "mother"—haunts him throughout his life of piracy. When, still in his teens, Singleton advises fellow mutineers to turn pirate, one of them reads his palm and concludes, "Thou art born to do a world of Mischief; . . . but have a Care of the Gallows" (25).[20]

The threat of hanging that haunts *Captain Singleton* documents the novel-form's own historical origins. During the early eighteenth century, the English state began to hang pirates in unprecedented numbers, holding mass trials and then executing pirates en masse: for example, in 1700, fifty-two pirates were hung at one time; in 1722, more than fifty again.[21] The state turned the executions into elaborate ritual: after a procession through city streets, over London Bridge, and along the north bank of the Thames, the pirates were hanged at Wapping, which was inhabited by the sailors the state wanted to discipline. Located on the banks of the river where they committed many of their crimes, the gallows was known as "Execution Dock." The pirates were executed pendant over the river, their corpses left dangling for high tide to wash over them. The executions are thought to have been at least as popular as those that took place at Tyburn—in fact, Wapping held a larger audience.

The trials preceding the executions spawned a literary industry and, because of the trial transcripts' popularity, became equally public events. The transcripts engendered another genre, compendia of "dying confessions," a gallows literature that recorded the pirates' last words from the execution stage.[22] In addition, the first important collections of criminals' lives appeared immediately before the publication of *Captain Singleton* and were among the most marketable books.[23] Early novels, including *Robinson Crusoe*, tended to absorb their narrative structures, which led inexorably toward the criminal's repentance, confession, and, after his execution, supposed redemption. The early eighteenth century's inchoate preoccupation with the lives of private individuals focused first of all on criminals, the prototype of the novelistic hero. Singleton's conclusion had already been written for him: the state and the public sphere alike demanded his execution.

But though the world of pirates appears to define the limits of the state, one cannot study early modern state formation without discovering piracy's constitutive presence there.[24] Elizabeth licensed Francis Drake's and John Hawkins's late sixteenth-century privateering ventures against Spain in order to pay for the state's debt. Preying on Spanish galleons as he circumnavigated the globe, Drake is thought to have accumulated £600,000, returning more than half to Elizabeth, a quantity greater than the Exchequer's annual income.[25] As John Maynard Keynes noted, Drake's "booty . . . may fairly be considered the . . . origin of British Foreign Investment. Elizabeth paid off out of the proceeds the whole of her foreign debt and invested a part of the balance . . . in the Levant Company; largely out of the profits of the Levant Company . . . was formed the East India Company, the profits of which during the seventeenth and eighteenth centuries were the . . . foundation of England's foreign connections."[26] English and Dutch piracy led to the ruin of the Spanish Empire, a precondition of England's own imperial development. The English state joined Europe's overseas trading ventures only after its piracy convinced it of long-distance trade's profitability.[27] And so it was under state auspices that the intimacy—often verging on identity—between piracy and English overseas trade developed.

Even after the first era of English piracy came to a close in the early seventeenth century, English merchants and pirates remained entwined. In fact, commerce and piracy were often simply two aspects of the same English venture: when they encountered vulnerable ships, English "merchantmen" had the capacity to become pirates—turning their supposedly defensive weapons against the other ship and capturing its goods—and then just as suddenly to redisguise themselves as traders, continuing on their way.[28] During times of war throughout the seventeenth and early eighteenth centuries, the state would hire English pirate ships to fight their battles; during times of peace, suddenly demobilized sailors would retool their military skills for piracy. First in the late sixteenth and early seventeenth centuries and then again a century later, England was known internationally as "a nation of pirates," and the phrase "none make better pirates than the English" became proverbial.

British society traded with pirates at all levels, both indirectly, by means of Jews and Muslims in North Africa, and directly, by means of numerous coastal villages, particularly in Ireland, whose economies depended on this trade.[29] Emblematic of piracy's elaborate incorporation into the British economy, the most pirate-infested river in England, the Thames, was literally under the state's nose. Even more ironically, the Admiralty, the agency charged with policing piracy, engaged in it. Rather than sentence pirates, the Admiralty more often blackmailed them in order to appropriate their booty—one historian notes that "admiralty men were on first-name terms with pirates."[30]

Defoe had no illusions about this history; in his view, state formation begins with piracy: "The First Founders of Old *Rome*," he noted in one pamphlet, "were but a Company of Publick Robbers."[31] Entering a public debate about whether or not England should ally itself with pirates who had created a state on Madagascar, Defoe reminded his readers that England routinely converted piracy into "honest" commerce:

We are told ... the [Madagascar] Pyrates ... have made proposals, that if they may have their Pardon, they will return to [England], live quietly at home, and ceasing their old roving Trade, become honest Freeholders, as others of our *West-India* Pyrates, *Merchants I should have said*, have done before them. I hope, the Gentlemen won't be offended, that by a Slip, I ... have given some of them their true Names; I am not about to point them out, ... it would make a sad Chasm on the *Exchange* of London, if all the

Pyrates should be taken away from among the Merchants there, whether we be understood to speak of your Litteral or Allegorical Pyrates; whether . . . the Clandestine Trade Pyrates, who pyrate upon fair Trade at home; the Custom-Stealing Pyrates, who pyrate upon the Government; the [wool smuggling] Pyrates, who rob the Manufactures; the privateering Pyrates, who rob of Law [etc.].[32]

While this passage collapses the distinction between British merchants and pirates, its irony lies, more profoundly, in the fact that the violations it names were British capitalism's necessary precondition. They produced the wealth British merchants invested in the East India Company, the Bank of England, and the South Sea Company, which were, in turn, the British state's largest creditors. The salient conversion that accompanies capitalism, Defoe insinuates, is not spiritual but material, taking place at points of exchange like the stock market where illicit wealth reappears as legitimate property. In his vision of capitalism, the "true Name" of "pirate" belongs to the merchant, the property owner, and the state alike. Never vexed by the sum of two wrongs, Defoe proposed that England offer the Madagascar pirates citizenship in exchange for their wealth: "Let them offer their illgotten Money, then I am clear, it will be well gotten money to us."[33] Refusing to engage in the state's hypocrisy, he suggested that it make pirate trade official policy.

The seventeenth- and early eighteenth-century proliferation of piracy attests, above all, to the monopolistic structure of modern global trade. When states licensed corporate monopolies, they produced piracy automatically, since it was the only means available to excluded merchants who wanted to trade. When the novel follows Singleton across the Indian Ocean and back again, it provides a comprehensive description of the global monopoly system.[34] And when it details pirate wealth's itinerary back to the nation, it provides an account of capitalism's secret history. The one stop that this itinerary cannot avoid is the British Empire in India.

Empire and Conversion

Both the novel's action (the turn of the eighteenth century) and its publication (1720) occurred during piracy's golden age, which took place in the Indian Ocean and followed the establishment of English and Dutch East India Company monopoly trade there.[35] European privateers left the Atlantic for the Indian Ocean during the 1690s, European pirates such as Captain Kidd and Captain Avery following in their wake. From the outset of Singleton's pirate life, his "Design was always for the . . . *East Indies,*" because "[he] had heard some flaming Stories of ... the fine things [Captain *Avery*] had done in the *Indies*, ... doubled even Ten Thousand-fold ... from taking a great Prize in the Bay of Bengal" (154). The "fine things" Avery did in the Indian Ocean were to capture the treasure-laden *Ganj-i-Sawai*, one of the Mughal emperor's ships, and, according to popular rumor, "ravish" one of his daughters. Whereas the former nearly provoked the emperor to rescind the Company's trading privileges, the latter led to Avery's mythologization in English print culture. Defoe fanned these "flaming stories," writing multiple works about Avery.

Singleton's East Indies fantasies parallel those of his more famous seafaring contemporaries Crusoe and Gulliver, both of whom have an irrepressible, though largely unremarked, desire to go there. After twenty-seven shipwrecked years, whose raison d'être was to teach him that the settled life is the only path to grace, and seven years as an English property owner, Crusoe abandons his new family, set-ting sail "as a private trader to the East Indies," at the beginning of piracy's golden age.[36] In the second part of *Robinson Crusoe*, he plies the eastern seas in a ship for-merly owned by pirates. And all four of the trips Gulliver takes through the luna-tic spaces of his would-be merchant's mind begin with the supposed intention to visit or cross the East Indies, a fantasy he keeps regardless of how absurd it proves.

These observations suggest the extent to which early eighteenth-century Brit-ish writers were aware of the Indian Ocean trading world. The second half of *Captain Singleton* maps this world in precise detail. Learning like Arab, Indian, and Chinese traders from time immemorial to follow monsoon winds across the ocean's vast expanse (197–98), Singleton's pirates discover ancient and modern trading routes radiating from port towns on the Arabian peninsula, the Indian subcontinent, and the Spice Islands. They sail from Mocha at the Red Sea's mouth and Hormuz along the Persian Gulf to India's Malabar Coast, around Cape Co-morin and then along the Coromandel Coast, up and down the Bay of Bengal, through the Strait of Malacca, to Batavia, the coast of Sumatra, Mindanao, and the southern Philippines, going partway to Formosa, before returning via Ceylon.

Revealing an elaborate understanding of Indian Ocean trading patterns, Defoe describes European and Arab ships bringing bullion, European goods, and Gulf pearls to the East Indies and returning from there with spices and tex-tiles (186–87). Indian ships reverse this order, returning with bullion or taking it, along with pepper, farther east for spices (189). Chinese junks trade finely wrought silks and tea for spices, precious stones, and bullion. Japanese ships offer bullion for spices, textiles, and European goods (196). Journeying all the way across the Pacific from Acapulco, Spanish ships trade New World bullion and European goods in the Philippines for East Indian luxuries (196). Singleton's pirates acquire saltpeter, pepper, cinnamon, nutmegs, mace, cloves, calicoes, muslins, silk from different regions, diamonds, pearls, tea, and fifteen bales of a handkerchief called *Romall,* Urdu finding its way into Defoe's English (189). They accumulate precious metals in various forms and national currencies, the only one of these many commodities they will be able to bring across the European state-system's borders.

Sailing to the Spice Islands, Singleton seizes "sixteen Ton of Nutmegs" from Dutch merchantman near Ambon: "I had much ado to prevent our Men murthering all the Men, as soon as they heard them say, they belong to *Amboyna,* the Reason I suppose any one will guess" (191). They accumulate twelve more tons of nutmegs at Banda, which, Defoe recognized, the Dutch had attempted to make the sole point of nutmeg production in the decades after the massacre, uprooting trees elsewhere on a massive scale.[37] In search of cloves at Ternate, the pirates are stumped by the Spice Islands' labyrinthine navigational demands and finally leave (192).

Across these voyages, Singleton's pirates come into contact with a pattern of seaborne commerce so complicated they can barely comprehend its outline. At one point, they cross paths with "an *European* freighted for a Voyage from *Goa,* on the Coast of *Malabar,* to the Red Sea, . . . Manned with *Portuguese* Seamen, but under the Direction of five Merchant *Turks,* who had hired her on the Coast of *Malabar,* of some *Portugal* Merchants" (174–75). At another, "the Ship was of *Bengal,* belonging to the Great *Mogul*'s Country, but had on board a *Dutch* Pilot, . . . and several *European* Seamen, whereof three were *English.* . . . The rest of her Seamen were *Indians* of the *Mogul*'s Subjects, some *Malabars,* and some others. There were five *Indian* Merchants on board, and some *Armenian*" (176). Finally, they come across two ships sailing from Golconda to Malacca, "on whose Account," Singleton notes in passing, "we know not" (189).

Once they have made their fortune, Singleton's shipmate William the Quaker senses the time is ripe for a return. He asks Singleton "whether . . . thou hast any Thought of leaving off this Trade; . . . for no body trades for the sake of Trading, much less do any Men rob for the sake of Thieving"; "it is natural for most Men that are abroad," William observes, "to come Home again at last" (256). In a manner that would become typical of the eighteenth-century colonial novel, the protagonists have remedied the deficiencies that prevented them from being property owners in England, Singleton in particular finally capable of regaining the social identity lost when he was stolen and hence bringing both the voyage narrative and his own personal history to a proper conclusion.

But here, as in *Robinson Crusoe*, a conversion must precede the return home. Crusoe's spiritual conversion enables him to find the kind of subjective meaning that modernity supposedly exiles. It enables him to return "home" in this sense, to a realm where meaning is immanent.[38] *Captain Singleton* worries the process of conversion, describing it not in the spiritual terms of the individual psyche but rather in the material terms of the global economy. The obstacle this novel must confront before it reunites its heroes with their homes is the East India Company: everything in their booty besides their precious metals is *material* evidence that they have violated its monopoly. Goods such as spices, calico, and silk could not cross English borders because they were, obviously, plunder from a geographic sphere to which the Company possessed *all* commercial rights.[39] Hence, no less than the "Allegorical Pyrates" on London's stock exchange, Singleton's pirates must, as he notes, "*vert* our Treasure in Things proper to make us look like Merchants, as we were now to be, and not like Free-booters, as we really had been" (263, my emphasis). To return home, they must finally defer not to providential design but rather to the European state-system.

In fact, throughout their voyages, the pirates work carefully around this system. They avoid East India Company merchantmen of any nation as a matter of principle, because these ships were heavily armed (172). When the pirates do attack European merchantmen, they look for outgoing ships, loaded with bullion, rather than returning ones, loaded with East Indies commodities: "We had rather have taken one outward bound *East India* Ship, with her ready Cash on board ... than three homeward bound, though their Loading would at *London* be worth three times the Money; because, we knew not whither to go to dispose of the Cargo" (172–73). Singleton's pirates develop the habit of flying a Dutch national flag when they sail past English factories and an English one when they sail past Dutch (189), in order not to tip off either Company to their true nature, which would have led to their discovery throughout the network of European factories in the East Indies: "Being fully loaden with the Spices which we had in the Sense of their Trade plundered them of, it would soon have told them what we were, ... and they would, no doubt, ... have fallen upon us" (249).

British India itself enters the narrative, therefore, only at the point of conversion. Because the Company possessed monopoly rights on Indian Ocean commodities, it was one of the few entities that could turn Indian Ocean plunder into legitimate capital. Near the Company factory at Surat on India's northwest coast, the pirates encounter Englishmen who appear to be Company servants trading "upon their own accounts" (251). The pirates exchange the major portion of their loot with these merchants for seventy-eight thousand pieces of eight and diamonds worth hundreds of pounds more (251–54). William and Singleton are in a position to buy the English country house for which William pines only after this conversion: "We have sold so much of our Cargo here at *Surat*, that we have money enough," William notes (259). Their plunder returns home only after being laundered through the East India Company, and this conversion does not reconcile Protestantism and primitive accumulation but, on the contrary, points out the discrepancy between the two.

The next three sections study the conversion in detail: its time and place, the characters involved, and the objects of exchange. If we return these allusions to their historical contexts, we will find that they focus not on the bourgeois individual and middle classes but rather on the militarized expropriation of non-European production. In doing so, they trouble our narrative of capital's birth—and of the novel trailing faithfully behind.

SURAT, INDIA, CA. 1657–1720

Long before the English East India Company arrived there, Surat was the hub of an Asian world-system ranging from Africa to the Far East and consequently possessed sophisticated forms of capitalist production and exchange.[40] The late seventeenth-century Italian traveler Careri noted simply: "Surat is the prime mart of India, all nations in the world trading thither, no ship sailing the Indian Ocean, but what puts in there to buy, sell, or load."[41] When the Company made Surat the headquarters of its East Indies operations in 1657, its aim was to reorient Indian Ocean commerce away from Surat's markets toward its own factories instead. It hoped in this way to coordinate trading networks dispersed so widely across the Indian Ocean that they had remained outside centralized control.[42] The Company's militarized forts in Bombay, Madras, and Calcutta eventually undercut Surat's trade, using sovereign power to redraw the Indian Ocean world's lines of force. Maloni has observed in this regard that "English mercantile activities in Surat acquire significance as a phase in the effort of European merchant capital to engross world trade on the basis of monopolistic control wherever possible."[43]

As part of that effort, the Company launched its first war against the Mughal Empire in the years immediately before the novel's action. The Company was led at this time by Sir Josiah Child, who happened to be not only one of the leading economic theorists of the period but also James II's economic adviser.[44] During the years Child led the Company, it entered into a deeply collusive relationship with the English state: it financed James's Court, while James is thought to have invested at least £10,000 of his own wealth in Company shares. Attacking the collusion between Company and Court, metropolitan writers insisted that "Child's War" was an act of "military adventurism" that undermined the very possibility of legitimate trade and argued furthermore that the Company had used its profits not to expand English trade but rather to bribe Members of Parliament.[45] This criticism, Chaudhuri notes, targeted the Company's "policy of harnessing political power and privileges to commercial purpose."[46] According to Barber, the Company "was now perceived as the lynch-pin in a sinister 'military-mercantile complex.'"[47]

To Defoe, Child symbolized the original collapsing of corporate wealth and public office into one another or, in other words, the danger of stock market speculation replacing political deliberation as the state's basis. Referring perhaps to the relationship between Child, who has been listed as one of the richest men in British history, and his brother, who was president of the Surat Factory, Defoe wrote in 1719 that Child's "Methods laid the Foundation" merely "of an Opulent Family," not a "great Stone House."[48] Child's widely influential premise was that the joint-stock corporation was the only arrangement capable of financing the cost of fortified trade.[49] Defoe understood the logic of that arrangement precisely. The East India Company took advantage of the "degenerated" state's indebtedness by extracting monopoly privileges from it and hence undermining the very possibility of "fair" trade.[50] And it took advantage of public credulity by "cheating" the people of their investment capital and using it to finance the colonial wars monopoly trade provoked.[51] In short, Defoe's decision to place this narrative's conversion experience near Surat at the turn of the eighteenth century reflects histories of capitalism that he and his contemporaries understood, but that we no longer do.

EAST INDIA COMPANY MERCHANTS AND PRIVATE TRADE

Defoe's choice of characters to perform the conversion is no less historically dense than his choice of time and place. The status of the English merchants whom

Singleton's pirates encounter near the Surat Factory is not entirely clear: Singleton describes them as "some Englishmen, who though they[,] perhaps, were the Company's Servants at first, yet appeared then to be Traders for themselves" (251). The haziness of these merchants' position was in fact typical of those who operated in the early British India.[52] Though Company employees worked for a corporation to which the English Crown had granted sovereign powers, their reason for being in India was to pursue their own private trade and accumulate fortunes unavailable to them in Britain. During the period of this novel's action, half the British trade with India was private. Under pressure from its servants, the Company actually protected their trade, thereby incurring financial losses to defend a practice that only added to those losses. The Company hoped, by allowing private trade within its factories and forts, to attract a commercial population from which it could collect customs duties to offset its military costs. Hence, while the Company appears at first glance to have been a corporate entity, it dissolves under analysis into a congeries of atomized individuals who used the backing of sovereign power to subject Asian production to private control.

But the exchange between the English merchants and Singleton's pirates registers the history of the Surat Factory in even more precise ways, since it was widely rumored to be involved in "secret dealings" with pirates at the time.[53] Singleton alludes to the fact that Company factories used "Letters of mart . . . from the Government" (249). By interstate law, European sovereigns could grant their subjects a letter of marque, thereby authorizing them to engage on behalf of the sovereign in what would otherwise be considered piracy, seizing the merchant ships of any other nation deemed to be "hostile." Invoking this principle, the Surat Factory arrogated to itself the right to dictate which ships could sail in the seas around Surat, granting licenses only to some, claiming the right to seize all others.[54] As a consequence, the Mughal Empire imprisoned Factory officials on charges of piracy at the end of the seventeenth century.

The Factory nonetheless made piracy general policy in the early eighteenth century, allowing any English ship that seized an Indian vessel to keep a portion of its capture, the Factory appropriating the rest, as the East India Company archives attest: "The Mallabars that you may encounter, we desire you if possible not to let escape. . . . For your so doing, 1/6th part is yours."[55] The Surat Factory's alliance with English pirates, including its own factors, during the late seventeenth century inflicted incalculable costs on Indian Ocean commerce, in the loss of merchandise, shipping delays, and increased insurance charges. As a consequence, the state-pirate alliance helped ensure that trading routes centered on the Company's forts would supersede the Indian Ocean's precolonial pattern of commerce.

Kincaid and Maloni have referred to the English as both the "worst" and the "most notorious" pirates in the Indian Ocean at the end of the seventeenth century.[56] They converged around Surat (the Mughal Empire's Arabian Sea entrepôt), because of the high-volume routes between it and Mocha (the Ottoman Empire's Red Sea entrepôt), along which treasure-laden, Asian-owned ships sailed. The English pirates needed the English East India Company, on one hand, because they recruited men from it: Defoe alludes to this fact, when Singleton's pirates meet an East India Company crew who ask to join the pirates (169–71). Company servants were in a particularly good position to buy pirate goods, on the other hand, because they traded under the purview of the Company's monopoly privileges. About the Company servants at Surat, Singleton notes: "The Merchants were as fond of the Bargain as our Men were of the Merchants" (251). Company servants and English pirates mirror each other, enabling one another to cross and recross the line between piracy and commerce to their own endless profit.

So, in their duplicity, the "Company's Servants [who] appeared to be Traders for themselves" capture the East India Company's own double nature. The Company operated in two economies simultaneously, taking the goods its servants had acquired illicitly and recirculating them within the supposedly law-governed markets of the interstate system. Against the principle that the pirates must find the best market for their cargo, Singleton insists instead that they take advantage of the fact that the Company servants were "not at all inquisitive" (254): "It was much better for us to sell all our Cargoe here, though we made but half Price for them, than to go with them to the Gulph of *Persia*, . . . where People would be much more curious and inquisitive into Things than they were here" (253). The servants need not ask questions, because in the East India Company's irregularly administered spaces, no one would ask them questions in turn.[57] Without questions that probe the provenance of commercial goods, the border between licit and illicit becomes porous. British India's borders were exceptionally porous, because they were governed not by a state but rather by the mere veneer of one, individuals who used the backing of sovereign power to operate privately. In this novel, it is precisely the permeability of British India's borders that ensures the fluid movement of plunder from origin through conversion to the national economy.

SILKS AND CALICOES

Singleton converts not only silk but also different types of cotton, including muslin and calico, both printed (chintz) and plain. Textiles passed spices as the Company's most valuable export just before the time of the novel's action: silk became England's largest raw material import in the late seventeenth century, while Indian calico along with American tobacco and Caribbean sugar constituted two-thirds of all English reexports during the same period.[58] As Defoe himself observed, "*England* not only receives all the Manufacturers of *India*, . . . but is the Center of the Consumptions of *East-India* Goods [for all] of *Europe*."[59] Responsible for England's economic growth during the late seventeenth century, the reexport of Asian silk and cotton provided the stimulus, according to Barber, for England's Commercial Revolution.[60]

Company servants were particularly drawn to the illicit trade in these textiles and in Persian silk, because of extraordinary profit margins.[61] After laundering enough of their plunder with the English merchants to return home, Singleton's men take their remaining goods to the Persian Gulf. Their cargo contains "Fifteen Bales of very fine *China* Silks" and "two and Forty Bales of *Indian* Stuffs of sundry Sorts, Silk, Muslins, and fine Chints" (271), which they could not have sold at Surat, since its own hinterland was a center of textile production. Avoiding the Company factory on Hormuz Island, where they "may be laid hold of" as interlopers on the Company's monopoly (259–60), they take their cargo to the Persian Gulf port of Basra, planning to trade with the English and Dutch merchants who operate privately there.

In the year before and the year of *Captain Singleton's* publication, Defoe wrote multiple pamphlets arguing that "East India rags" undercut England's own textile industry, which he considered the heart of Britain's economy: "the so general wearing and using *East-India* printed Callicoes, &c. had been the Ruin of our Trade, had put a stop to the Employment of the Weavers, and, in a word, had *starv'd our Poor*."[62] Just after the turn of the century, Defoe had proposed that England create its own calico industry; near the end of that decade, he called on Parliament to ban the importation of Asian silk; and just before the publication of *Captain Singleton*, he called for a ban even on the wearing of calico.[63] While Defoe argued that the Company's monopoly on Asian textiles enabled it to undersell English labor, the laborers turned their anger on the textiles themselves: during the Spitalfields Riots of 1719 and 1720, angry crowds of silk weavers tore Indian garments from women's bodies, giving vent to widespread industrial discontent.[64]

When he criticized silk and calico importation, Defoe emphasized that much of it was private trade, though it entered England on East India Company ships.[65] Claiming it "impossible . . . to make exact Calculations of the Value of Things . . . done *by Stealth*, and *in private*," he nonetheless determined the national cost of the East Indian textile trade with admirable precision: "one Million eight Hundred and sixty five Thousand four Hundred and nineteen Pounds a Year dead Loss to the Nation"—"Deny it they that can."[66] For Defoe, these imports represented the interrelationship of Indian Ocean theft (or primitive accumulation), on one hand, and metropolitan political corruption (or state formation), on the other. About the origins of the smuggled textiles, he asked, "Whence can [this trade] be supply'd but by foul Practices?"[67] And about the lobby of cloth merchants, Company servants, and stock market speculators who kept the trade alive, he commented sarcastically, "I can never imagine, that any Cabals of Drapers, *East-India*-Men, Brokers, and Jobbers shall be able to biass the Members of a British Parliament . . . in a Case so clear as this, that wearing a foreign Manufacture, and despising our own, is . . . the most certain Method of starving us all, that can possibly be invented."[68] In fact, he understood that state-corporate collusion was much more advanced than this, commenting in *The Anatomy of Exchange-Alley* that Company members had already used "Trick, Artifice, Cunning and Corruption" to become MPs.[69] The premise of Defoe's many pamphlets against the East India Company's textiles was that their importation converted Indian Ocean piracy into English private interests.

Though it occupies only a few pages, *Captain Singleton*'s conversion of pirate plunder into merchant capital near the East India Company factory at Surat, mediated by Englishmen trading privately, is not trivial. The details of the conversion point to the material forces that transformed the Indian Ocean's precolonial trading world, a transformation that involved not the global dissemination of capitalist exchange but its militarization. These textual details confound our narratives of modernity, the ones we critique and the ones we cherish alike.[70]

Home

If Gulliver's problem is reaching the East Indies, Singleton's is returning. In *Robinson Crusoe* and *Captain Singleton*, Defoe dramatizes a similar problem in different ways: How can one return from the practices of empire to the principles of civil society? Singleton's conversion complete, he should be ready to go home. But Singleton trusts neither the conversion nor the idea of "home." He doubts that the material conversion of pirate wealth entails the spiritual conversion of the pirate. He responds to William's request that they return home: "Do you think if [God] be a righteous Judge, he will let us escape thus with the Plunder . . . of so many innocent . . . Nations[?]" (266).

Because of his faith, William is concerned only about the material conversion of their wealth, confident that once he and Singleton accomplish that conversion, their own moral conversion will be unproblematic. William reinterprets their plunder, remarkably, as an instrument of God's will and hence an element in their own providential trajectories: "We ought to keep [our wealth] carefully together, . . . who knows what Opportunity Providence may put into our Hands, to do Justice at least to some of those we have injured" (267). However perverse his logic, it is closely related to one that would pervade eighteenth-century thought, the logic of charity: the acquisition of wealth is always potentially moral regardless of its means, because when one possesses wealth, one can redistribute it and hence do justice. William's logic echoes Crusoe's belief that if one reinvests one's wealth providently, one's avarice redounds to God's benefit.

Singleton buys neither William's logic nor Protestant ethics. About their wealth, William says simply, "By whatsoever Way it has been gotten, that is not the Question" (256). For Singleton, *that* is precisely the question: "I look'd upon [my Wealth] as a Hoard of other Mens Goods, which I had robbed the innocent Owners of, and which I ought, in a Word, to be hanged for here, and damned for hereafter; . . . I began sincerely to hate my self for . . . a Thief" (267). A "Hoard of other Mens Goods": the origins of English merchant capital trouble Singleton and, more generally, the narrative of his life; this text refuses to hide the trouble. Though he claims that he "can look but a very little Way" into his own origins, Singleton cannot forget the origin of his wealth, which in fact repeats the original trauma of his own expropriation. Knowing himself *only* as the product of theft, he lacks civil society's capacity to deny the crimes at its basis. The origins of the wealth Crusoe invests in English property lie in the sale of his faithful Muslim companion, Xury, to New World slave owners for sixty pieces of eight, twice Judas's sum; his subsequent purchase of a Brazilian slave plantation, which makes him fabulously wealthy; and his slaving expeditions, which end finally in shipwreck.[71] The material reality of Singleton's narrative disavows the ideology of Crusoe's: here there is no providential framework that can undo, deny, or conceal the corrupt origins of the mercantile economy.

To explain his failure to escape despair, Singleton points to his ignorance of Christianity: "As for my Knowledge of Religion, you have heard my History; you may suppose I had not much" (268). But in fact Singleton's supposed ignorance casts doubt on Christianity. It leads him to believe that genuine penance should involve undoing the consequences of one's crimes: "Tho' I had the Wealth by me, yet it was impossible that I should ever make any Restitution; and upon this Account it run in my Head, that I could never repent, for that Repentence could not be sincere without Restitution" (267). Though William and Singleton convert and reconvert their pirate wealth into legitimate forms of property in Aleppo, the Levant, Venice, and Naples while traveling from Basra to London, Singleton is unable to see the private possession of that wealth as anything other than immoral: "I thought, as it was got by a general Plunder, ... which I could make no Satisfaction for, it was due to the Community, and I ought to distribute it for the general Good" (276).

Singleton's problem, though, is that he conceives "Home" as a den of thieves, not a commonwealth. In regard to redistributing his wealth, he concludes, "Still I was at a Loss how, ... not daring to go Home to my own Country, lest some of my Comrades stroled Home should ..., for the very Spoil of my Money, or the Purchase of his own Pardon, betray and expose me to an untimely End" (276). Hence, he responds to William's argument that "it is natural for most Men ... to come Home again at last" by rejecting William's premises: "You have not explained what you mean by Home. ... I am at Home, [the open sea] is my Habitation, I never had any other in my Life time" (256). The following dialogue between William and Singleton ensues:

> Art not thou an *Englishman*? ...
>
> I came out of *England* a Child, and never was in it but once since ... and then I was cheated and imposed upon, and used so ill, that I care not if I never see it more.
>
> Why hast thou no Relations or Friends there[?]
>
> Not I ... not one, no more than I have in the Court of the Great *Mogul*.
>
> Nor any Kindness for the Country, where thou wast born[?]
>
> Not I, any more than for the Island of *Madagascar*, nor so much neither, for that has been a fortunate Island to me more than once. (256–57)

This dialogue encapsulates the novel's argument, testifying to the historical transformation of the nation that the novel represents. William's use of the word *kindness* is most telling in this regard. One of the meanings of the Old English etymon of *kindness* is in fact "nation," a concept of the nation apparently linked to kinship and the affections that grow therefrom.[72] William's use of the word activates modern connotations of "tenderness" but ties them to a now obsolete social structure. His anxious questions suppose the nation to provide a refuge from the mercenary social relations that characterize the global economy, which was rendering this "kind" of nation obsolete.

Singleton's responses deftly translate William's nation into a modern economy and genealogical filiation into civil alienation. In Singleton's narrative, the only experience the nation provides is theft: "I . . . never was in [*England*] but . . . I was cheated and imposed upon." Singleton's subsequent responses are equally subversive, replacing England with its putative opposites, the Mughal Court (a prominent example of "Asiatic Despotism") and Madagascar (infamous as the pirate state). But Mughal India and Madagascar—a royal court and an island, both engaged in empire building—appear here as England's mirror images. The mirror Singleton's responses hold up to England display the image it needs to deny, the theft its kindness conceals, the insinuation that this home is premised on an endemic singleness that resembles his own.

Singleton's emphatic disavowal of home defeats William's arguments that they should return. William responds in amazement, "Thou hast put me to Silence, and all I had to say is over-thrown; all my projects are come to nothing, and gone" (257). William's silence expresses a narrative aporia the novel refuses to resolve. A voyage epic that has no legitimate origin, whose origin is lost: to what can such a narrative return?

Conclusion

In fact, this early novel responds in the prototypical way to the "transcendental homelessness" Lukács considered the novel's ontological condition: it turns its protagonists into English property owners.[73] Equally typically, their home is a country house that pretends to be founded on a moral economy exterior to the market. William's widowed sister, a London shopkeeper, buys the estate with part of their fortune without disclosing its origin to anyone else or even questioning it herself. Singleton comments, "This was opening the very Door for us, that we thought had been effectually shut for this Life" (275). William and Singleton retire there, Singleton marrying William's sister, confident that in this arrangement no one will inquire about them.

But the country house is only part of an elaborately constructed surrogate home. Having begun to retrace an ancient trade route when they sail from Surat to Basra, William and Singleton continue overland on its way, taking a caravan from Baghdad through Aleppo to the Levantine port city Alexandria, a two-month journey. From there, they embark for Venice, where, in the timeworn way, they convert what remains of their spices and textiles into currency. With this, they purchase commodities at Naples—ironically, textiles again—that can pass British customs since they come directly from the Mediterranean rather than the Indian Ocean. Throughout the journey from Basra to Naples, William and Singleton "pas[s] for Merchants of *Persia*" (263) or Armenians (272–73)—both groups famously involved in Indian Ocean trade—in order to conceal their pirate histories.

But even after all these conversions Singleton's fear of hanging remains. He refuses to leave Venice for two years, because his "Heart failed [him]" (275), and agrees finally to go home only on the paradoxical condition that he and William preserve their alienation by maintaining their Persian personae. They agree never to speak English in front of anyone except William's sister, using instead "the *Persian* and *Armenian* Jargon" (272) they had picked up along the way from Basra to Venice, and to keep the disguise they had adopted in Basra, "after the *Persian* Manner, in long Vests of Silk" (264). Even after purchasing landed property, Singleton refuses, therefore, to revert to the aristocratic clothes stolen from him at his origins. He enshrouds his wealth in a remote and occulted past.

We should recall here that the Spitalfields workers who rioted in the year before and year of *Captain Singleton*'s publication were silk weavers and furthermore that Persian silk was one of the most lucrative commodities Company servants traded privately—facts Defoe recognized, as his pamphlet writing makes clear. William's and Singleton's costumed selves are elaborate artifices meant to ensure that no one discovers their pirate histories. But ironically the Persian silk robes conceal the provenance of their wealth—which lies to a great extent in Asian textiles—by displaying it in the most ostentatious manner. Here, Persian silk stands for the stolen goods at the origins of European modernity and hence the forgotten histories that constitute the European individual. William's and Singleton's costume slyly reverses the conversion, preserving the trace of other worlds.

Armstrong has claimed that "the good country life" at the heart of domestic fiction "no longer revealed one's origins."[74] In contrast, *Captain Singleton* returns home only to question it, interrogating the country house so thoroughly that it can no longer screen the constitutive presence of empire, the nascent global system, and piracy. While "the new country house harked back to an . . . agrarian world where the household was a . . . self-contained social unit," *Captain Singleton* does not conceal the country house's foreign sources but *dramatizes* their concealment.[75] It charts the global transactions that generate the novel's prerequisites (the individual, private property, and the nation-state) in terms of violence and theft rather than providentially designed commerce. What does *Captain Singleton* have to teach us, then, about the novel's origins?

Aligning the novel with its supposedly intrinsic aspiration for totality, Lukács managed to expunge from the novel-form any detail that disturbs either the hero's subjectivity or the work's ideology.[76] If it does not conform to the total-ity, it by definition does not belong for Lukács to the form of the novel. It fol-lows logically—or rather tautologically—from Lukács's premises that the novel always consolidates the "bourgeois separation of spheres," segregating the aes-thetic from the economic.

Thompson argues, more subtly, that "Defoe's novels aim at th[e] moment . . . when the protagonist can conceal the origins of his property."[77] Like *Captain Singleton*, novels such as *Moll Flanders* and *Roxanna* do not conceal their hero's origins but instead dramatize the act of concealment. The moment Singleton begins the story of his own loss, theft, and sale, he draws suspicion to it by not-ing that it was told him by a gypsy, herself a thief, who had somehow gained possession of him; he begins the history, "If I may believe the Woman, whom I was taught to call Mother" (1). It is of course possible that the gypsy did not buy but stole Singleton and concealed this transaction with her narrative—the gypsy woman who snatched children was an eighteenth-century commonplace. Singleton concludes his own narrative by suggesting that like his "mother" he also has reason to be unreliable: "'Tis Time to leave off, and say no more for the present, lest some should be willing to inquire too nicely after" (277). *Captain Singleton*'s dramatization of the disguises that mask the individual's origins goes to the source of civil society itself. About that, David Hume would subsequently remark: "There is no property in durable objects, such as lands or houses, when carefully examined in passing from hand to hand, but must . . . have been founded on fraud and injustice. The necessities of human society, neither in private nor public life, will allow of such an accurate enquiry."[78]

Even after their conversion, stolen goods in *Captain Singleton* carry the mark of their own secret histories, the chain of exchanges whereby primitive accu-mulation is converted into the legal forms of the interstate system. Like *Captain Singleton*, early novels in general allude to material processes that exceed their own supposedly self-enclosed spaces.[79] Whenever they do so, they contain the trace of modernity's lost origins, giving us the chance to locate the discrepancy between the novel-form's abstract totalities and capitalism's actual history.[80] In *Captain Singleton*, at any rate, the foundations of the novel dissolve back into their own silenced histories. The capital that originates modernity in this narrative has its roots, before all the conversions and border crossings, in "fraud and injustice," in the collusion of European pirates, corporations, and states. Like *Captain Singleton*, the literature I explore in the chapters to follow is profoundly aware of this collusion. Its awareness troubles any attempt to produce narrative or ideological closure, to bring its story to a happy end. Once we have recovered this awareness, we can return to the supposedly self-enclosed spaces of other eighteenth-century texts, which we have assumed underwrite progress, and recognize that like Singleton they know much more than they are willing to say.

3

SENTIMENT AND DEBT
Sterne's Bramine's Journal
and Foote's Nabob

As a period of literary history, the late eighteenth century is conventionally demarcated by sentimentalism's sudden rise and equally sudden decline. Intellectually, sentimentalism appears now little more than an embarrassment, a historical aberration in which bourgeois culture went badly out of kilter. But however bizarre it may seem to us, the rise of overwrought sentiment in the late eighteenth century was in fact seminal for modern ethics. Of a piece with Kant's most influential formulation of the "Categorical Imperative"—treat each human not as a means to an end outside of himself but rather as an end in himself—sentimentalism argued that one's humanity is directly proportional to one's concern with the other's rights, will, and affective life, an essential redefinition for a world increasingly determined by horizontal social structures.[1] As a consequence of sentimentalism, to be moral in our world is not simply to accept but indeed to inhabit subjective differences, and we could say by extension that the modern category of "ethics" merely elaborates sentimental morality.

Typically, the rise of market society provides our studies of sentimentalism their historical context.[2] Yet market society was not new in the late eighteenth century; it does not distinguish this period from those that immediately preceded it. "The market" serves so well—or at least so frequently—as the catch-all context for sentimental literature precisely because it is an ahistorical abstraction. When scholars of sentimentalism invoke the market, they accept the obscurity in which sentimental ethics enshrouded the material history of the global economy—and in which it still does.

This chapter thinks about literary sentimentalism differently. It argues that sentiment's context is not an abstract market but rather the credit economy that emerged out of the first truly global conflict, the Seven Years' War (1756–63). In its wake, Britain appeared to be an empire founded no longer on commerce but on conquest. As even casual observers could see, the state now needed wealth from outside its borders to service its dramatically increased military debt: colonial expropriation had become the state's manifest precondition. The postwar years

witnessed, in other words, the interrelated development of a metropolitan ethics based on recognition of the other's sovereignty and a global economy based
contrariwise on its eradication.

This chapter studies three sentimental texts that span the late eighteenth
century and represent global economic history in precise though different ways.[3]
The anonymously published three-volume novel *The Disinterested Nabob* (1787)
sentimentalizes colonial capital, claiming that it frees metropolitan society from
debt. But in the process the novel alludes to the very history of colonial expropriation its sentimentalism is supposed to obscure. Samuel Foote's comedy *The
Nabob* (1772) sentimentalizes metropolitan capital instead, claiming that it frees
metropolitan society from debt *without* colonial entanglements. But the play
implies more subtly that colonial *and* metropolitan capital are equally part of a
single corrupt system. Laurence Sterne's memoir *The Continuation of the Bramine's Journal* (1767) sentimentalizes writing itself, claiming that it is a refuge
precisely from that system. But the memoir acknowledges more profoundly that
the global economy is the precondition of sentimental writing: on its most heterodox level, it embraces the former as wholeheartedly as the latter.

The scholarship generally assumes that literary sentimentalism was oblivi-
ous to the structure of the global economy.[4] In fact, though, it had no choice
but to be aware, since Britain's dependence on colonial finance capital was common knowledge. Hence, whether they underscore what they know about that
economy or attempt to deny it, the texts this chapter explores enable us to write
a sentimental history of the global economy, finally rejoining modern ethics to
the colonial histories that gave them rise.

Continuation of the Bramine's Journal

Word first arrived in London that the Mughal emperor had vested the East India
Company with the title of *diwan*—or collector of all revenues—for the Indian
provinces of Bengal, Bihar, and Orissa in April 1766.[5] A logical outcome of the
de facto regional sovereignty the Company had obtained with Robert Clive's
victories in battles ranging from Plassey (1757) to Buxar (1764), the *diwani* gave
the Company all the rent from an unusually fertile swath of territory thought to
contain twenty million inhabitants. The acquisition of the diwani—from which
we conventionally date the beginning of British colonial rule in India—appeared
to be a gift from heaven for the Company and the British state, both of whom
desperately needed to service their war debts. News of the diwani inspired three

years of intense speculation in Company shares, making them the most popular ones on the London exchange. Company stock sold at record prices—investors hoping that, with a previously unimagined and practically unimaginable source of surplus revenue, the Company would increase its dividends. One of many prominent figures who invested in the Company, Edmund Burke told the House of Commons: "The Orient sun never laid more glorious expectations before us."[6]

Soon after news of the diwani shook London's money markets, Laurence Sterne, who was about to become the century's most influential sentimentalist, suddenly gained the acquaintance of numerous individuals at the forefront of British imperial expansion.[7] In January 1767, the Soho home of Commodore William James became the center of Sterne's social life. The former commander-in-chief of the Company's marine force, James had become famous for taking the supposedly impregnable island fortresses from which the pirate chief Angria operated south of Bombay. James—who would subsequently serve as a director of the Company for fifteen years and as an MP for nine—used his share of Angria's booty to buy two adjoining houses on Gerrard Street, which became London's most important salon for Company servants. While visiting the Jameses, Sterne met, among many other British imperialists, George Macartney, who would become governor of the Caribbean Islands, governor of Madras, ambassador to China, and governor of the Cape of Good Hope; and George Pigot, who had been and would again be governor of Madras, the eventual target of a coup known famously as the Lord Pigot Affair.

In this salon for sometime and soon-to-be imperialists, the sentimentalist fell immediately in love. Elizabeth Draper was the offspring of two significant Anglo-Indian families: her father had been the assistant secretary of Bombay Factory and the secretary of Anjengo Factory, where Draper was born; her maternal grandfather was the chief at Anjengo.[8] Just turned fourteen, she married an infamously ambitious Company servant, Daniel Draper. The son of Bombay's mayor, he was the Company's marine paymaster and well on his way to a lucrative career. When Daniel needed to convalesce from "a nervous malady," Elizabeth left with him to England. Though he soon returned to Bombay, where he was appointed accountant-general, she spent winter 1766–67 at Gerrard Street. In the spring, she received word from her husband instructing her to return to him—a prospect that, apparently, made her fall violently ill.

Before Draper began her voyage back to Bombay in April 1767, Sterne exacted a pledge from her that they would keep journals for each other. Invoking his pet name for Draper, Sterne entitled the text he composed for her from April to November 1767 *Continuation of the Bramine's Journal.*[9] Sterne wrote it simultaneously with *A Sentimental Journey*, which more than any other single text popularized literary sentimentalism across Europe, and he emphasized the sentimental nature of his writings for Draper as well: "Sew them together under a cover . . . they will be a perpetual refuge to thee[; and] thou wilt (when weary of fools, and uninteresting discourse) retire, and converse an hour with them, and me."[10] The writings constitute a memoir of London's sentimental life—which Draper's imperialist husband had forced her to abandon—and hence provide her "a perpetual refuge" from the immediate world that surrounds her, whether along the seaborne route that connected the Company's various forts and factories from London to Bombay or within the fort at Bombay itself. To protect her from a global economy constructed in terms of mercantilism, they offer her a literary space composed in terms of sentimentalism instead.

CONQUEST

The difference between mercantilism and sentimentalism was particularly stark in the wake of the Seven Years' War. As mentioned, the war precipitated the transformation of the "First British Empire," based supposedly on purely commercial relations and hence reciprocity, into the Second, based instead on territorial conquest and the imposition of colonial rule. As an outcome of the war, the British Empire grew to encompass Bengal, a territory much larger and more populous than Britain itself, and the primary source of the Company's wealth shifted from profit to rent.

The month before Sterne began writing *The Bramine's Journal*, a parliamentary Select Committee began public hearings into Company affairs, motivated by concerns with private and public finance alike.[11] In regard to the former, the Company had failed to increase its dividend, though the diwani was supposed to have added nearly £2 million to its annual revenue. In regard to the latter, the British state hoped to acquire a legal right to the Company's new revenue: the Seven Years' War had made Britain not only the most extensive empire but also the greatest debtor state in history—the national debt more than £130 million; the annual interest on it £4–£5 million. Financial experts feared that unless the state skimmed the Company's revenue, it would default on its payments and have to declare bankruptcy. Bengal's ultimate value lay in its capacity to help service the national debt.

The Select Committee came to focus on a single question: Had the Company gained its territories by means of conquest—"through the terror of military force . . . over a naked and defenceless possessor"—or by means of purchase?[12] If the former, the territories and all their revenue were in fact the property of the Crown, the only power in Britain invested with the right to conquer. If the latter, the Company had a right to the territories. During the following month, while Sterne began *The Bramine's Journal,* the committee brought forward overwhelming evidence that the Company had gained its territories by conquest.

Ironically, though, the committee's position posed the state an insuperable dilemma because it lacked the resources necessary to administer such a large colony.[13] Hence, while Prime Minister Chatham insisted that the Company acquired its territories through conquest in order to validate the state's claims on Company revenue, Treasury Secretary Townshend argued instead that the state should simply strike a deal with the Company. In the event, Townshend's position prevailed, and without articulating any principle that could legitimize the Company's conquests, the committee negotiated an annual £400,000 grant from the Company—no coincidence, perhaps, that this figure counterbalanced precisely the revenue the state had just sacrificed in lowering the British land tax from four shillings to three.[14] The outcome of the parliamentary hearings that coincided with Sterne's first entries in *The Bramine's Journal* was, in sum, overwhelming evidence of an empire that practically everyone understood must remain illegitimate. Parliament had aired the paradox of the period's new global economy exactly.

The Bramine's Journal registers the conquest of Bengal and the postwar imperial economy on various levels. The language of the hearings, for example, entered directly into Sterne's and Draper's rhetoric when they described Company servants. Draper wrote to Sterne: "As to Nabobs, I despise them all. . . . Have they not depopulated towns—laid waste villages, and desolated the plains of my native country—Alas! they have fertilized the immense fields of India, with the blood of its inhabitants—they have sacrificed the lives of millions of my countrymen to their insatiable avarice . . . [and] have waded through blood, to gain riches and power."[15] About Draper's husband, Sterne wrote to her in turn, "sunk my heart wth an infamous Acc^t of Draper & his detested Character at Bombay" (324); "for What a wretch are thou now hazarding thy life, my dear friend, & what thanks is his nature capable of returning? . . . thou wilt be repaid with Injuries & Insults!" (368).

In fact, *The Bramine's Journal* turns colonial conquest into a metaphor for interpersonal relations: Sterne used this trope to describe both Draper's and his own marriages. Addressing Draper as if she were her husband's slave, Sterne asked, "What Impression can you make upon Mr Draper, towards setting You at Liberty—& leaving you to pursue the best measures for Y^r preservation[?]" (367). Likewise, referring to his detested wife's pending trip to England from across the Channel, Sterne explained to Draper: "'Tis a visit, such as I know you will never make me,—of pure Interest—to . . . pillage What [she] can from me" (347); "she is coming, every one says, to flea poor Yorick or slay him—& I am spirited up by every friend I have to sell my Life dear, & fight valiantly in defence both of my property & Life" (373). Once she finally arrives, Sterne explains that there is no time to write because he has "a Wife to receive & . . . make Treaties with" (376). When she is about to return to France, Sterne notes that "[she has] entered upon a new plan of . . . waging War with me, a thousand miles off" (378).

The Bramine's Journal presents sentimental relationships as the antithesis of colonial conquest. Consider, for example, the contrast between the imperial portrait Draper's Anglo-Indian friends ordered and the sentimental one Sterne commissioned: "In the one, you are dressed in . . . all the advantages of silks, pearls, and ermine;—in the other, simple as a vestal—appearing the good girl nature made you;—which, to me, conveys an idea of more unaffected sweetness, than Mrs. Draper, habited for conquest" (312). Here Sterne opposes sentimental affect to imperial luxury ("silks, pearls, and ermine"). Elsewhere he implies that his sentimental feelings for Draper resist the very terms of the modern credit economy, which drove Britain to its initial conquests in the first place: "[Your husband's] repugnance to your living in England, arises only from the dread which has entered his brain, that thou mayest run him in debt. . . . Oh! my child, that I could, with propriety indemnify him for every charge, even to the last mite, that thou hast been of to him! With joy would I give him my whole subsistence" (317–18). If the imperialist values his wife only for the wealth she represents, Sterne claims to value wealth only for the sentimental functions it serves.

Yet the language of credit and debt continually interrupts Sterne's sentimental rhetoric. In fact, it is less Draper's husband than Sterne himself who describes her in the former terms: "Thou owest me much Eliza!—& . . . thou wilt pay me all—But the Demand is equal: . . . much I owe thee, & with much shalt thou be requited" (323); "'tis cruel to dun thee when thou are not in a condition to pay—I think Eliza has not run off in her Yoricks debt" (377). Sterne's rhetoric is of course ironic, meant to imply that the terms of the credit economy are inappropriate to his sentimental relationship with Draper. But as such terms multiply within the text, they insinuate unmistakably that the credit economy has infected even this relationship. Sterne's decision to court an imperialist's wife is particularly ambiguous in this regard. It is never completely clear whether Sterne aims to liberate her from mercantilism's fetters or use her to acquire a mercantile fortune: "sent for a Chart of the Atlantic Ocean, to make conjectures upon what part of it my Treasure was floating—O! tis but a little way off—and I could venture after it in a Boat, methinks" (323).

Sterne never loses sight, in any case, of Draper's financial potential: "[I hope] to see [Eliza] eclipse all other nabobesses as much in wealth, as she does already . . . in interior merit" (304). The term "nabob"—an anglicization of "nawab," the title of a provincial ruler within the Mughal Empire—was applied to Company servants who became fabulously wealthy in the wake of Bengal's conquest, investing them with the despotic qualities that supposedly characterized Muslim rulers. Its use in metropolitan circles reflected the widespread understanding of the forms of corruption—including bribery, usury, and the private appropriation of the Company's trading privileges—that servants practiced after the conquest. Sterne's wish that Draper become the richest "nabobess" expresses, therefore, a shameless attitude toward colonial capital. Elsewhere, alluding to his inability to consummate their relationship because of age and infirmity, Sterne's double entendre implies that he desires only Draper's fortune anyway: "What say You, Eliza! shall we join our *little Capitals together*?—will Mʳ Draper give us leave?— he may safely—if yʳ *Virtue* & Honour are only concerned,—'twould be safe in Yoricks hands, as in a Brothers" (348).[16]

Sterne invented a literary style whose aim was to complicate—if not to contradict—sentiment's moral claims, a paradoxical form that would become characteristic of sentimental writing.[17] On its most profound level, this style returned to consciousness what sentiment was supposed to conceal, the economic context that made sentimental culture possible in the first place. This level—which shamelessly represents the interdependence of sentimental affect and colonial expropriation—is not only sentiment's most rhetorically sophisticated but also its most historically acute. The precondition of sentimental society was that the roles of creditor and debtor had come to define social relations as such, in both private and public realms.

MILITARY AND FINANCIAL REVOLUTIONS

During the course of the Seven Years' War, the British national debt more than doubled.[18] But the war and the debt were, in turn, part of a longer *durée*. In the sixteenth and seventeenth centuries, European states revolutionized the technology of war, inventing the gunboat, infantry firepower, the artillery fortress, and national standing armies and, in the process, increasing the cost of war tremendously.[19] The "military revolution" compelled European states to augment their revenue accordingly, whether they aimed to extend their hegemony or merely defend their sovereignty. Domestic sources of revenue became insufficient to states' military needs: the more states extracted domestically, the more people rioted. National debts solved the problem.

A bit player on the world stage throughout the military revolution, Britain reentered the scene only during the Anglo-Dutch Wars. When its revenue fell short of its military ambitions during the Third Anglo-Dutch War (1672–74), the British state created its first modern debt and, turning to the East India Company, its first modern credit mechanism. Even after it created the permanent national debt two decades later, global capitalists remained its major creditors: not only the Company, whose establishment predated the national debt but whose real importance to the state lay therein, but also the Bank of England (est. 1694), which received its capital overwhelmingly from imperial merchants; and finally, the South Sea Company (est. 1711).[20] The capital that the British state invested in its war-making capacity came, in other words, from elsewhere.

But the national debt depended on ordinary members of the British public as well as global capitalists. The East India Company, the Bank of England, and the South Sea Company not only were the state's major creditors but also constituted the largest part of the stock market.[21] When they purchased these corporations' shares, the middle classes were indirectly buying the national debt. It was precisely these corporations' financial liquidity—made possible by the ceaseless exchange of their shares—that enabled them to serve so well as the state's creditors.

If we believe the modern state and individual to be essentially capitalist, the responsibility lies not with "the market" in some abstract sense but rather with these two deeply interwoven credit mechanisms, national debts and stock exchanges. The former enable states to operate on a previously unimagined scale, constructing the national and international infrastructures we associate with progress and modernization. The latter give "the individual" previously unavailable types of social currency and mobility, as he or she receives dividends from revenue yet to be collected or, in many cases, even found.[22] To remain debt-free in this economy, one has little choice but to turn to the stock market and its extranational modes of accumulation.

The stock market made Britain "a nation of creditors" who lent not only to their own state and traders but even to those outside its borders: the Bank of England became the "Bank of the universe."[23] Observers across Europe noted that borrowing had become second nature in Britain; they pinpointed its unrivaled capacity to mobilize credit as the basis of its newfound commercial hegemony. For their part, British observers had recognized the financial revolution long before: for example, Defoe wrote in 1711, "At this Time, *The Credit of the Nation is ... its Politick Life*—Money is the sinews of War; Credit is Money."[24] As Pocock has observed, the financial revolution made credit fundamental to politics.[25]

In a real sense, then, the British debt crisis during the Third Anglo-Dutch War—the starting point of this study—marks the modern emergence of the British state. War constituted the modern state, spurring the simultaneous and interdependent growth of its military and financial apparatuses. This claim— "war makes the state; the state makes war"—is a commonplace now.[26] But precisely to the extent that it is true, debt must be scarcely less constitutive. It is at the origins of European modernity and the epoch of global devastation it has unleashed.

SENTIMENTAL SURPLUS

Sterne himself lived and died deeply in debt, his "livings" inadequate to his sentimental expenses.[27] In fact, it was debt that forced him to end *Tristram Shandy* and begin his sentimental writing in the first place: when the novel's sales flagged, readers encouraged him to mine its sentimental vein.[28] In the novel's penultimate book (1765), Tristram addresses himself: "Is it not enough that thou are in debt, and ... hast ten cart-loads of thy fifth and sixth volumes ... still unsold, and art almost at thy wit's end, how to get them off thy hands[?]"[29] Referring to *A Sentimental Journey* two years later, Sterne noted privately, "Till my Sentimental Work is published, I shall not have a single Sous more than will Indemnify People for my immediate Expences" (387). In private correspondence with the African-British writer Ignatius Sancho, Sterne leaves aside all pleasantries quickly and gets to the bottom line: "I was very sorry, my good Sancho, that I was not at home to return my compliments ... for the great courtesy of the Duke of

M[onta]g[u]'s family to me, in honouring [*A Sentimental Journey*'s] list of sub-
scribers with their names.... But you have something to add, Sancho,... and
that is to send me the subscription money, which I find a necessity of dunning
my best friends for" (340).

Subscription lists reflected the fact that the merchant classes had become the
largest part of the reading public. With these lists, literary patronage took on a
joint-stock form, as Leslie Stephen noted: they enabled Sterne to turn his sentimental imagination into a joint-stock company in order to service his debts.[30] As
a consequence, the capital that underwrote Sterne's creativity came in large part
from the colonies: the subscription lists for *A Sentimental Journey* contained many
of the British imperialists he met on Gerrard Street, including such prominent
Anglo-Indians as Pigot; Luke Scrafton, Company director and the author of the
widely read *Reflections on the Government of Indostan*; and most famously, Laurence Sullivan, chairman of the Company directors, known as "the autocrat of
the India House."[31] The lists also included people involved in the British Empire
outside India, such as Nathaniel Newnham, South Sea Company director, and
members of his merchant family.

Sterne was shameless about the economy of sentimental writing, dream-
ing, for example, of renting Draper from her husband in order to increase the
value of his work: "Were your husband in England, I would freely give him five
hundred pounds (if money could purchase the acquisition) to let you only sit
by me two hours in a day, while I wrote my Sentimental Journey ... the work
would sell so much the better for it, that I should be reimbursed the sum more
than seven times told" (313). Imagining India's toxic climate and Draper's own
infirmity finishing her off before his tuberculosis did him, he considers marketing her writing after her death: "When I am in want of ready cash, ... I shall
print your letters, as finished essays, 'by an unfortunate Indian lady.' The style
is new; and would almost be sufficient recommendation for their selling well,
without merit" (320–21). Sterne's shamelessness about his desire to commodify
sentiment is at the essence of his sentimental style. His writing takes pleasure
in *exchange*—whether mortality, sexuality, or desire of *any* kind—as the true
substance of being alive. It was, presumably, the pleasure Sterne took in these
forms of exchange that enabled him to maintain his irrepressible exuberance
throughout the composition of *The Bramine's Journal*, despite the daily futility
of his struggle with tuberculosis: he possessed an endless capacity to celebrate
the material world without idealizing it.[32]

For Sterne, therefore, markets were hardly the problem: in themselves, they increase the opportunity for exchange. He understood that they have existed time out of mind—and in much more richly complicated forms before the mercantile state. He imagined his letters to Draper following the circuits that preceded mercantilism, the ancient overland routes radiating from Rome, Byzantium, and Venice, which no single entity had been able to conquer or monopolize: "May. 4. Writing by way of Vienna & Bussorah [Basra] to My Eliza. May 6th . . . writing to thee over Land—all day" (338); "May 13th Could not get the Genl post Office to take charg[e] of my Letters to You—so gave thirty shilling to a Merchant to further them to Aleppo & from thence to [Basra]" (338). Sterne's letters reconstruct the geography that separates him from Draper: where she traveled from London to Bombay along a passage defined by the East India Company's fortified factories in a merchantman she referred to as "my floating prison," his letters pretend to trace an economy where profit was so dispersed that it could not be subsumed by any single economic or political entity.[33] The intention behind his sentimental writing is to liberate its sentimental reader in no sense from the market but rather from the mercantile state's grasp.

Sterne invented a literary style for an epoch founded on war, debt, and colonial finance capital. By bringing the debtor-creditor relationship explicitly into the sentimental one, he suggested how the two could be reconciled: not by mutually exclusive spheres of European sentiment and colonial conquest but rather in one sphere that embraces both the desire to recognize and the desire to profit from the other. In its ceaseless oscillation from sentimental affections to profit seeking and back again, Sterne's style literally contains both ends of the paradoxical and otherwise contradictory ethics of European modernity. Life for Sterne necessarily involved exchange: it was only the desire to conquer and hence immobilize such processes, turning them toward one's own gain alone, that Sterne considered aberrant. Against a mercantile system based on conquest and ruin, Sterne explicitly offered a literary and libidinal economy that continuously multiplies possibilities for exchange, endlessly generating surpluses of value and meaning.[34] At its most exuberant and heterodox level, Sterne's writing shamelessly insinuates that the modern world's signal and supposedly antithetical modes of interconnection—the affective and the economic, sentiment and debt—are mutually constitutive, indeed now inescapably so. His sensitivity to the material world ensured that despite its purportedly intimate nature, *The Bramine's Journal* nonetheless marks its moment in imperial history.

CODA: COLONIAL SURPLUS

Like his sentimental style, Sterne's actual debts also outlived him. And as he imagined, it was colonial capital that eventually paid them, thereby preserving his sentimental reputation intact. In 1768, after Draper had returned to Bombay, her husband was transferred to Tellicherry, a pepper and cardamom port on the Malabar Coast, where he served as chief of the factory.[35] While in Tellicherry, Sterne recently deceased, Draper began to receive letters from Sterne's wife, who had discovered Draper's letters to her husband and who no less than her husband—though with much less good humor—understood the relationship of colonial capital and metropolitan debt. Angry that he had lavished gifts on Draper, while leaving her supposedly penniless, his wife threatened to publish the letters. Draper immediately wrote to Sterne's publisher, Becket, offering to compensate him for the profits he would lose by not publishing the letters. She also sought financial help from Colonel Campbell, a friend in Bengal, who gathered contributions from Company servants to create a six hundred–rupee fund for Sterne's widow and daughter.

Draper's subsequent letter to Campbell describes his donation as a sentimental expenditure in the most paradigmatic terms imaginable: "Educated Women of Talents, and Sensibility, are, I believe of all Others, the most serious objects of a Generous Compassion, when obliged to Descend . . . to the Mortifying Vicissitudes of Neglect & pecuniary Embarrassments."[36] In fact, Draper saw Sterne's wife otherwise; to a different correspondent, she wrote: "Her violence of Temper . . . and the hatefulness of her Character are strongly urged to me, as the Cause of his Indifferent Health, the whole of his Misfortunes, and the Evils that . . . Shorten[ed] his Life"; elsewhere she described Sterne's wife as "a Drinker, a Swearer . . . & Unchaste."[37] Colonial wealth paid metropolitan debt, not because of its inherently sentimental tendencies but rather because that was its raison d'être. When it failed to do so, metropolitan investors inevitably called the morality of the colonists and the whole colonial enterprise into question.

The Nabob

Whereas news in April 1766 concerning the diwani generated feverish buying of Company shares and a stock market bubble, reports in May 1769 concerning the sultan of Mysore's victories over the Company precipitated even more feverish selling of Company shares, precipitating a stock market crash.[38] Contemporaries compared the crash to the South Sea Bubble; Edmund Burke, who had expected so much from East Indian wealth, numbered among the many who were ruined or nearly ruined. In the years immediately following, the Company's military and administrative expenditures exhausted its surplus revenue and led to the collapse of its credit, which in turn catalyzed new crises in private and public finance. By 1772, with the Company close to ruin, the House of Commons brought metropolitan criticism to a head by establishing another Select Committee to investigate the Company.

As part of the investigation, the committee put Robert Clive—who had led the conquest of Bengal in the late 1750s and returned there as governor in 1765—on trial for misgovernment. Lord Clive from 1762, he had acquired nearly £500,000 in India in addition to a £26,000 yearly income (or *jaghire*) that he had coerced the nawab of Bengal into paying him for life; Burke referred to him in the *Annual Register* as "the richest subject in the three kingdoms."[39] Though George III had initially hailed Clive, metropolitan print culture made him the embodiment of imperial corruption during the credit crisis. Clive used the parliamentary seat he had bought during the 1768 elections as a forum from which to defend himself and his Company colleagues. Referring to Britain's most influential satirist during one such defense in March 1772, Clive proclaimed, "There has not yet been one character found amongst [the Company servants] sufficiently flagitious for Mr. Foote to exhibit on the theatre in the Haymarket."[40] Samuel Foote's comedy *The Nabob* was performed for the first time three months later.

Foote was not only one of the period's most subversive figures but also one of its most famously indebted; he was, as one biographer notes, "the most notorious wit and prodigal of his day."[41] In regard to the former quality, Johnson commented that Foote is "the most incompressible fellow that I ever knew; when you have driven him into a corner, and think you are sure of him, he runs through between your legs, or jumps over your head, and makes his escape."[42] In regard to the latter, Foote allegedly responded to the one-sentence epistle from his mother "I am in prison for debt; come and assist your loving mother": "Dear Mother, So am I; which prevents his duty being paid to his loving mother by her affectionate son, Sam. Foote."[43] Whether that anecdote is accurate or apocryphal, we know that his mother numbered among "a small army" of creditors who sued Foote for nonpayment of his debts, leading to his imprisonment from November 1742 until September 1743.[44] The first play he composed after *The Nabob* was *The Bankrupt*.

Born a gentleman, Foote completely exhausted his large inheritance on a single tour of the Continent and subsequently squandered his wife's dowry with equal efficiency.[45] His indebtedness forced him to become a professional dramatist; only when the British state gave him monopoly privileges—a lifetime royal patent for summer theater in London—was he able to remain (relatively) debt-free. Once he received the patent, he bought the Little Theatre at the Haymarket, which then became one of London's three royal theaters, presenting a season of comedy and satire every summer.

UNION

The Nabob represents the epochal transformation of Britain's economic basis from landed property to colonial finance capital.[46] It concerns a traditional aristocratic family (the appropriately named Oldhams) now encumbered by debt. Unbeknown to them, one of the loans they have received comes from a nabob, Matthew Mite, recently returned from India. The play opens with a letter from Mite informing Sir John Oldham that because of his failure to repay the loan, Mite will imprison him and seize his property if he does not allow Mite to marry his only child, Sophy.

The play turns on the question of whether Sophy will marry the nabob or a suitor uncorrupted by colonial wealth. The marriage plot is an allegory that operates on the level of private and public finance alike: in its indebtedness and consequent dependence on colonial capital, the landed family corresponded precisely to the state. In the same year as *The Nabob*'s first edition, Thomas Pownall, a widely read expert on colonial political economy, observed that the marriage of national and colonial economies had already taken place: "People ... begin to view [Indian] revenues being wrought into the very composition and frame of our finances. [They] begin to see such an *union* of interest ... that they tremble with horror [at] the downfall of this Indian part of our system; knowing that it must necessarily involve ... the ruin of the whole edifice of the British Empire."[47] As mentioned previously, the Company had begun to increase the dividend on its shares after the 1767 parliamentary investigation and to give the Treasury £400,000 annually at the same time.

But Pownall referred to the "union" of colonial and national finance only to emphasize that as its consequence, the "downfall" of the former necessarily portended the "ruin" of the latter. After the Europe-wide credit crises of 1763 and 1771–72, there was a widespread belief that ruin was intrinsic to the system of public credit that had developed over the previous century.[48] As a consequence of its private and public financial commitments, the Company was running a £2 million deficit in London alone by early 1773: Pownall was concerned its insolvency would send tremors throughout London's financial markets. The Company's acquisition of the diwani had, ironically, made British finance even more precarious than before.

In *The Nabob*, Mite imports the Company's conquest economy back to England. He presents his marriage proposal to the Oldhams, for example, in the form of a treaty: "'*Imprimis:* Upon a matrimonial union between the young lady and him, all hostilities and contention shall cease, and Sir John be suffered to take his seat in security.'"[49] Mite's treaty pointedly recalls the *firmans* the Mughal emperor signed at Allahabad in August 1765, which first recognized the Company's supremacy in Bengal: the Select Committee's initial point of business when it began its hearings in April 1772 was to read these treaties.[50] Offering the Oldhams a "jagghire" for their mortgaged estate, Mite's treaty alludes to both the *jaghire* Clive wrested from the nawab of Bengal and the 2.6 million rupee annual payment the Company promised the emperor in exchange for sovereignty over Bengal. Allahabad was the culmination of nearly a decade of Company intervention in Bengali affairs, including the deposition of one nawab, Mir Jafar, in favor of his supposedly more pliable son-in-law Mir Kasim, against whom the Company fought a series battles only to reinstate Mir Jafar in February 1765. In response to the treaty, Sir John Oldham's younger brother Thomas notes, "His style is a little oriental, . . . but most exceedingly clear," a comment to which Lady Oldham quips, "Yes, to Cossim Ali-Khan, or Mihir Jaffier."

The precarious state of the Company's finances stemmed from its financial commitments in London, but only in part. As *The Nabob*'s allusion to the Company's habit of deposing local rulers suggests, the primary cause of its financial crisis was its conquest economy. From the time of its first battles against the nawab of Bengal in 1757, the Company had engaged in "warfare on a massive . . . scale," with its troop numbers in Bengal increasing more than eightfold in the decade following 1756.[51] But like European states during the previous century's military revolution, the Company employed military technology it could not afford. It responded to its debts, perversely, by conquering more territory, hoping in this way to increase its revenue. The deposition of Mir Jafar was one move within this strategy, which the Company soon extended elsewhere. In each case, the Company imposed a military protectorate over a princely state—which the state itself was obligated to finance—and deposed the prince, when he failed to meet its revenue demands. The strategy became a vicious cycle, as the costs of the conquest and domination of territory always overwhelmed the revenue it provided. The news of Hyder Ali's victories, which precipitated the free fall of the Company's shares in 1769, also included reports of a monetary crisis produced by the Company's rapacity. In the space of only a few years, the Company's conquest economy had devastated a region that had been bullion rich for centuries and had enjoyed a favorable balance of trade with Europe from time out of mind.

It is this conquest economy that Mite imports to England: Lady Oldham observes that "sir Matthew Mite, from the Indies, came thundering amongst us, and, profusely scattering the spoils of ruined provinces, corrupted the virtue and alienated the affections of all the old friends to the family" (84). The play therefore dramatizes both the "union" of colonial and national finance and the widespread belief that this union corrupted England. To "Touchit"—the spokesmen for "Bribe'em," a borough that offers to sell him its two MPs—Mite responds: "I accept their offer with pleasure, and am happy to find . . . that the union still subsists between Bengal and the ancient corporation of Bribe'em" (100). Mite plans to use his colonial fortune to buy off the electors and take Sir John Oldham's parliamentary seat from him. The 1768 parliamentary elections did in fact return an unprecedented number of Company servants, often associated with rotten boroughs.[52]

Explicitly, then, the play follows the general discourse that the nabobs are a source of civil degeneration—in fact, it carefully documents their corrupt practices. In a scene that would otherwise be completely random, Mite talks to two Jewish characters—"Moses Mendoza" and "Nathan"—whom he uses to control the stock market. He asks them if they have followed his instructions to "split" his East India stock (99), a strategy by which the Company's largest shareholders would divide their investment into £500 blocks that they would give to friends, thereby qualifying each of them to vote in the Company's General Court of Proprietors. The aim was to ensure the election of directors who represented the same interests as the original owner did: Clive used the ploy when he was under investigation.[53] The value of "stock splitting" lay in the fact that Parliament generally rubber-stamped the directors' proposals, because MPs and directors were overlapping populations. As a consequence, the General Court became a subject of public interest from 1769 forward, with the daily press reporting on its proceedings.

Mite's second directive to the Jews is to sink East India share prices "two and a half" (99). During these years, Company servants would place reports in the papers in order to raise or lower Company share prices; Clive and his confederates, in particular, were accused of using insider information to manipulate the stock market.[54] A parliamentary Secret Committee discovered that a group of Company servants had kept share prices artificially high during autumn 1771 in order to conceal the Company's acute financial distress and avoid the widespread selling off of Company stock. The servants' corruption in the colonies became associated with "stock fixing" in London, whether they wanted, like Mite, to purchase devalued shares or, like this group, to prevent devaluation.

Finally, Mite tells Nathan and Moses that he has yet to decide whether the market in Company shares is to be bullish or bearish by the "next settlement" (100). In leaving that choice undecided, Foote revealed his subtle understanding of the East Indian interest. If the market was bullish at the next quarterly meeting of the General Court, the Company would be obligated to increase the dividend or at least maintain it; if bearish, it could decrease the dividend. The decision was tricky: on one hand, the state was obligated to release the Company from its £400,000 annual payment if the dividend fell to 6 percent; on the other, if the Company reduced the dividend to any extent, it would disclose its financial distress and incite panic among its shareholders. Hence, the directors put the decision off in September 1771.[55] The Company needed carefully to construct the appearance of good credit, precisely because its conquest economy had undermined its creditworthiness.

The play also dramatizes the widespread claim that the nabobs' corrupt practices reflected their oriental degeneration. Here Foote toes the Company line—though with subtle irony. In response to the parliamentary investigations, the Company directors undertook a secret campaign to scapegoat their own servants for the credit crisis.[56] In April 1772—as debate raged in Parliament and Foote began *The Nabob*—the *London Magazine* and the *London Evening Post* ran excerpts from books recently authored by former Company servants detailing their colleagues' crimes in India. Building on such reports, the directors' print campaign—involving countless periodicals, pamphlets, and books—argued that nabobs conspired to use the profit they had expropriated from the Company to bribe, influence, and control the British state.

The Nabob's representation of colonial wealth subverting civil society also dramatizes Enlightenment theories about imperial expansion. French and Scottish philosophers alike considered the mutation of republic into empire the main problem of ancient history.[57] For them, the republic is intrinsically unstable, because its very success leads to colonies in the lands it has conquered, which in turn unleash its citizens from all restraint. Referring to Company servants, *The Nabob* claims that "these new gentlemen, who . . . have acquired immoderate wealth, and rose to uncontrolled power abroad, find it difficult to descend from their dignity, and admit of any equal at home" (90). Gibbon in particular gleaned from Rome the lesson that "empire had absorbed the city and destroyed its virtue" or, in other words, that the despotism republics license in their colonies comes back to haunt them.[58] During the late 1760s and early 1770s, as he composed the first volume of *The Decline and Fall,* the returned nabob must have brought this lesson home, with British India in the role of the imperial provinces. Gibbon likely attended *The Nabob*: explaining his reluctance to leave London during the summer, he noted privately that "when I am tired of the Roman Empire I can laugh away the Evening at Foote's Theatre."[59]

DESPOTISM

If comedy's ideological function is to mediate social contradictions, *The Nabob* appears to resolve the conflict between the nation-state's public ideals and colonial capital's private interests. The resolution arrives in the form of Thomas Oldham, the honorable English tradesman, a second son bereft of inheritance rights. At the moment of crisis, when Sir John must respond to the nabob's proposal, Thomas suddenly pays off Sir John's debts, restores his estate to him, and enables Sophy to follow the dictates of her heart, which lead her to a union with Thomas's son. This resolution implies that, in contrast to imperial wealth, domestic capital can be trusted to lead the nation out of debt. The play's final words are Thomas Oldham's: "However praiseworthy the spirit of adventure may be, whoever keeps his post, and does his duty at home, will be found to render his country best service at last!" (111). The play's conclusion appears to reiterate its general argument: empire is responsible for the state's problems.

But the conclusion's sentimental excess is hard to miss—in fact, it contains Foote's signature.[60] Often described as the most innovative British dramatist between Fielding and Sheridan and admired by his peers as "one of the major talents of his generation," Foote began his dramatic career as a kind of jongleur, forced into unorthodox modes of performance by the 1737 Licensing Act, which gave Covent Garden and Drury Lane a monopoly on metropolitan drama.[61] While those theaters colluded with the Licensing Act to empty themselves of political content, Foote's early performances were political critiques, using his exceptional talent for mimicry to parody not only the playwrights and actors who worked at the two Royal Theatres but also London's most prominent statesmen. Often improvising, he would make pointedly topical jibes that targeted current hypocrisies, reportedly keeping adoring audiences in stitches.

Throughout his period at the Haymarket (1762–76), when sentimental comedy was the fashionable genre, Foote restaged the comic plot to reveal its absurdity.[62] Merely by parodying the sentimental maxim—as at *The Nabob*'s conclusion— Foote could make its platitudinous and hypocritical quality self-evident. Joshua Reynolds claimed that as a consequence of Foote's attack on sentiment, "private friendship, public decency, and everything estimable among men were trod under foot."[63] With friends like these: along with Burke, Reynolds served as Foote's character witness during the sodomy trial that, though he was acquitted, effectively ended his career. But Foote's aim was, merely, to teach his audience a lesson: his theater was, he explained, "a faithful Imitation of singular Absurdities, . . . which are openly produced, as Criminals are publickly punished, for the Correction of Individuals, and as an Example to the whole Community."[64]

Hence, even as *The Nabob* exemplifies sentimental comedy, it forestalls naïve approaches to the genre. In fact, the play helps us read its sentimental resolution properly: even as it moves predictably toward that conclusion, it continuously alludes to another history that renders sentimental resolutions absurd. The Mayor of Bribe'em must decide to whom he should "sell" himself. Since he has "never been beyond the sea," he asks Touchit, "where do these [nabobs] get all their wealth?" The following dialogue ensues:

Touchit: I will explain that in a moment. Why, here are a body of merchants that beg to be admitted as friends, and take possession of a small spot in a country, and carry on a beneficial commerce with the inoffensive and innocent people, to which their chiefs kindly gave their consent.

Mayor: Don't you think now, that is very civil of them?

Touchit: Doubtless. Upon which, Mr Mayor, we cunningly encroach, and fortify by little and little, till at length, growing too strong for the natives, we turn them out of their lands and take possession of their money and jewels.

Mayor: And don't you think, Master Touchit, that is a little uncivil in us?

Touchit: Oh, nothing at all. These people are but a little better than Tartars or Turks.

Mayor: No, no, Master Touchit, just the reverse: it is they have caught the Tartar in us. (99)

This dialogue rehearses eighteenth-century political theory, wherein the circulation of merchant capital originally promises *doux commerce*, creating sympathetic exchange relationships between different cultures, "friends" carrying on "a beneficial commerce." *Doux commerce* would by definition have been "very civil," the construction of an international civil society. But while imperial merchants present themselves as agents of civil progress, they leave the confines of the European nation-state only in order to escape its laws, as Diderot explained in the *Histoire des deux Indes*.[65] They travel to nations of "Tartars and Turks"— that is, people ruled by Asiatic despotism, barbarism, and nomadism—precisely because such nations were thought not to safeguard property.

While Touchit offers the commonplace that the climate of Asiatic despotism is responsible for the imperial merchant's moral degeneration, it is the idiot, "revers[ing]" the commonplace, who possesses insight. "It is they have caught the Tartar in us": the tropics merely give license to a disregard for property inherent in the European body politic. From the perspective of eighteenth-century historical writing, someone akin to the Tartar lies at Europe's origin, since the barbarian invasions that brought Rome to an end gave birth to "Europe." War and conquest were the barbarians' essential economic strategy. The logic they introduced into Europe at its very origin warped its development away from *doux commerce*. The play's sentimental conclusion encounters the most disturbing strands of Enlightenment historiography: the origins of European states lie in a barbarism that has persisted across the ages. For this play, in contrast to the print campaign against the Company servants, the significance of the nabob lies not in any new threat that he poses but rather in the ease with which he enters the British state and economy, thereby revealing the indistinction between European progress and "Asiatic despotism."

The Select Committee held its first hearings from April 27 to May 26 (a month before *The Nabob* was first performed), receiving publicity commensurate with the intensity of public outrage at the nabobs' alleged crimes.[66] The hearings quickly degenerated from their mandate—investigating the Company's "corporate activities"—to hurling accusations at individual servants. After describing one such hearing to his correspondent, Gibbon concluded, "The hounds go out again on Friday."[67] To see *The Nabob* as a satire on the Company servant—as the critical literature almost universally does—is, therefore, to render the play superfluous: the attack on the nabob pervaded political discourse and dominated the literary representation of India during the period (and beyond). It is also to do little justice to Foote, who would not have let his own audience escape so easily.

To understand the play's significance, we need to look beyond its unremarkable satire of "the nabob" to its much more subtle dramatization of the ideological work this figure performed: displacing public corruption onto the servant's private activities. Rather than succumb to this ideology, Foote's play thinks through the implications of the nabob's easy insertion into national politics: not that empire imports barbarism but that barbarism is already there, at the origins of European state formation itself. *Pace* French and Scottish Enlightenment analyses of the contemporary state in light of classical history, *The Nabob* insinuates that there never was a (modern) republic for empire to destroy in the first place. One of Foote's critics referred to his work as a "court of inquiry."[68] If so, it was diametrically opposed to the one established by Parliament: it resolutely refused to shift the source of British corruption from the metropolis to the colony.

As a result, Foote's court of inquiry teaches us much more about the 1771–72 credit crisis than the Select Committee's own hearings do. The Company had devised a system in the 1760s that enabled its servants to transfer their fortunes back to England and the Company to increase its cash reserves in India. The servants could deposit their cash with the Company in Calcutta, receive bills of exchange in return, and subsequently draw these bills on the Company in London.[69] Though its directors restricted the number of bills the Company could issue in Calcutta, the Company ignored the instructions. The bills the Company received between March 1771 and March 1772 depleted its currency reserves in London, preventing it from paying out dividends or making its annual grant to the Treasury. By focusing metropolitan attention on its servants' alleged crimes, the Company implied that it suffered from financial problems only because its servants expropriated its profits.

In fact, it was the Company that had exhausted its servants' fortunes, not the other way around. And it was the British state that had encouraged the Company to conquer Indian territory in the first place, thereby pushing the Company into debt.[70] Both Company and state desperately needed to transfer wealth from the servants' pockets to their own coffers, because their military expenditures exceeded their revenue: the 1773 Regulating Act would subsequently bring the servants' private trade increasingly under the Company's purview and the Company's under the state's. In these attempts to profit from the nabobs' crimes, both Company and state operated like nomad castes—as the mayor insinuates—unable to think of economy outside of war and conquest.

The Company could not receive the loans it needed to cover its cash shortage because its crisis coincided, tellingly, with a more general collapse throughout the City, in which ten banking firms declared bankruptcy within a two-week span, straining the Bank of England's resources.[71] The City's problems were in turn part of a Europe-wide crisis that hit London, Glasgow, and Amsterdam equally. It was not colonial capital that had corrupted European civil society but the military and financial revolutions; new credit instruments such as the national debt and the stock market; and the expansionist forces European states unleashed to service their debts.

The nabob's final pronouncement observes that the circulation of finance capital effaces the origins of modern wealth: "This is not Sparta, nor are these the chaste times of the Roman republic. Nowadays, riches possess . . . one magical power, that, being rightly dispensed, they closely conceal the source from whence they proceeded" (111). Sentimental discourse can make moral claims on capital's behalf precisely to the extent that its source remains invisible. But Thomas's fortune originates in war no less than the nabob's does and is, as a consequence, every bit as suspect.[72] If sentimentalism attempted to displace the history of conquest to the colony, Foote, like Sterne, returned it to the heart of the metropolis. Their sentimental works comprehend the discrepancy between modernity's ethical claims and its global history.

CODA: TEA

The Nabob asks the Jews a final question: "Has my advice been followed for burning the tea?" Brief though it is, the allusion could not be richer. The Company suffered declining sales during the early 1770s because smugglers undersold Company tea, which traded at monopoly prices.[73] In the American colonies, for example, tea imported from Britain, rather than smuggled from Europe, accounted for less than 5 percent of consumption. By 1772, more than £3 million of tea filled Company warehouses, representing more capital than the Company needed to escape its cash crisis.

Rather than burn its tea, the Company dumped it on the American colonies, obtaining special tax exemptions from the British state to that end.[74] The colonies of course had different ideas and sided with their own smugglers against the British state's attempt to extend the Company's tea monopoly to the New World, which they considered a harbinger of future monopolies. In the wake of the Boston Tea Party, other colonists followed Mite's counsel after a fashion, burning tea cargoes in ports from Greenwich to Charleston. The policy that provoked the American Revolution originated, in other words, in the Company's strategy to finance its debt.

Dumping its tea on the colonies could only be a quick fix, because it was the tea trade itself that had impoverished Bengal, as even Company officials argued in writing.[75] From the moment the Company acquired the diwani, it saw Bengali territorial revenue as a means to acquire Chinese tea. Even as the Select Committee noted Bengal's sudden lack of cash reserves, the Company continued to transfer Bengal's surplus revenue to Canton, whose tea was a lucrative commodity in European and American markets. It was this remarkably shortsighted practice that had helped precipitate the Company's cash crisis in the first place.

The Disinterested Nabob

East Indian affairs receded to the background after 1773, while Britain focused on the American colonies. The national debt proliferated again at an unprecedented rate during the war, totaling £243 million by its end.[76] Astonishingly, the British state paid £9 million merely to service its debts in 1783 alone, three-quarters of its annual budget. After the war, the loss of the colonies, and the growth of the national debt, Britain reoriented its empire around India, which became even more fundamental to public finance, remaining at the center of foreign policy from 1784 to 1787. The 1784 Commutation Act lowered the import duty on tea from 119 percent to 12.5 percent, finally enabling the Company to outcompete smugglers and to realize superprofits from the tea trade. London became the global tea entrepôt, and tea became central to British economic development. While British shipping exploded around it, increased tea consumption spurred sugar sales, the two articles on which the state placed its highest taxes. In contrast to the early 1770s, there was a general belief in the necessity of the Company's territorial expansion, though ambivalence toward its servants nonetheless remained.

These events provide the immediate context for *The Disinterested Nabob* (1787). Making the Company servant the hero of its narrative, the novel represents the renascent fantasy of a capital that despite its colonial origins is truly public. As the title emphasizes, its nabob is the archetypal sentimentalist who never pursues his self-interest because he only expends his wealth philanthropically, paying the debts of other characters and hence enabling them to enjoy property and, by extension, "liberty" within the terms of a credit economy.[77] His philanthropy enacts on a private level what British statesmen hoped Indian wealth would perform on the level of public finance. Responding to the critique of the Company Edmund Burke had articulated in his 1786 parliamentary motion to impeach Governor-General of India Warren Hastings, *The Disinterested*

Nabob identifies the Company servant with the social functions his wealth supposedly serves in the nation, dissociating him from the conditions in which he accumulated that wealth in the colony.

The novel incorporates the satire on the nabob only to displace it now onto British colonial merchants who operate outside the Company's purview. The narrative's single traditional nabob is Mr. Smith, "a free merchant," not a Company servant.[78] Smith asks for the hand of Caroline Selwyn, who along with her sister Sophy, is one of the two female protagonists in this epistolary novel's double marriage plot. Finding the private trader "every thing that is disagreeable, mean . . . , narrow minded, and selfish" (2:70), Caroline repeatedly refuses him, finally responding, "I had rather be wrapped in my winding sheet, than as your bride be arrayed, with all the pomp of asiatic grandeur" (2:79). But Caroline's father—like Sir John Oldham, an indebted landowner—has come to India "in hopes to repair his shattered fortune" (1:163–64): he cannot afford to refuse Smith's £20,000 settlement. Only the intercession of Company servant Frederic Douglas (the "Disinterested Nabob")—who threatens to expose Smith's dishonest financial dealings—puts an end to the marriage. Giving the marriage plot a false start, Mr. Smith helps the novel rewrite the allegory about national finance and colonial wealth.

The eighteenth-century marriage plot highlights the fact that for the landed classes, ethics (traditionally rooted in the principle of "disinterestedness") and economics (now based on "interest"-bearing credit mechanisms) have become disjunct. For example, when her father first calls Caroline to India, she quickly reconciles herself to her fate, though she will have to separate herself from her lover, Charles Danvers, himself the son of a bankrupt landowner. She explains to Charles that once in India she may have to marry against her own wishes: "You and you alone will have my heart, though my person may be the sacrifice of duty" (1:26–27). In her obedience to her parents' concerns about income, Caroline has little choice but to subject herself to the modern economy, sacrificing the freedom to make her "heart" the guide of her behavior.

The Disinterested Nabob must, then, resolve a tension everywhere implicit in the marriage plot: How can the text reconcile the aristocratic family's economic requirements with its moral values, when it is finance capital, not property, that produces wealth? This novel eliminates the first obstacle to Caroline and Danvers's marriage when it kills off her father in the third volume, the victim of a sudden, fatal, and unaccountable "*Paaka* [Pucka] fever" (3:159), thereby obviating the necessity that she marry a nabob. It eliminates the second obstacle with another opportune death, that of Danvers's aunt, which enables him finally to support a family. About her, Danvers announces: "She is dead, and has made me heir to five hundred a year, to render me . . . independent of my mother" (3:114). But Danvers's mother continues to see her son as if he were heir to £4,000 a year and hence wants him to marry someone of similar wealth. At this point, Douglas, also back in England, steps in again, surreptitiously adding £5,000 to Caroline's fortune and telling Mrs. Danvers, "Ladies with ten thousand pounds, might not every day be offered" (3:209). Caroline concludes, "Never surely was there a man, . . . who acted on such refined principles of generosity, for he seems to have no idea of the value of money, but as it will contribute to the happiness of those he loves" (3:220–21).

Caroline's use of the term "generosity" recalls an earlier letter recounting the colonial community's charity toward a widow with two sons. Noting that the subscription the community started in her name is common practice when a servant's wife is widowed, Caroline concludes: "There is a generosity in such actions, unknown in the colder regions of Europe" (2:65). Her comment performs the novel's primary ideological task, to argue that colonial wealth operates sentimentally—or, in other words, that it will return from the servants' accounts to the national economy. This act of charity recalls not only the subscription British settlers in Calcutta created for Sterne's wife and child after his death—albeit only under the threat of extortion—but also the insistence of Foote's nabob that "riches . . . rightly dispensed . . . closely conceal the source from whence they proceeded." The nabob's dictum explains the logic of this novel's structure, which always returns to scenes of charity. If the novel is to sentimentalize colonial wealth, it must insist on the nabob's capacity to rise above private interest, because it was precisely with this that he remained associated.[79]

INTEREST

In 1783, as a decade earlier, the Company confronted a cash crisis produced by its inability to honor the bills of exchange its servants had drawn on it, in this case, worth more than £2 million.[80] Parliament investigated the Company yet again and, blaming the servants' illicit activities, placed them under stricter supervision. Prime Minister Fox noted that the state's creditworthiness depended on the Company's and argued, furthermore, that its servants had extorted the native elite, beggared and starved native peasants, and ruined what had been a

land of abundance in their pursuit of private gain.[81] Pitt's 1784 India Act banned
all private trading among Company servants.

The disinterested nabob is, accordingly, free of *all* private interest: he expends
his colonial fortune only in acts of philanthropy, referring to it as "a fund, I no
longer regard as my own property, it having for years been appropriated to the
use of merit in distress" (3:75). The novel displays Douglas's wealth only in the
form of property he refuses on principle to consider private. He explains that
he created his philanthropic fund because he had "the power to lend . . . money
. . . without extracting interest" (3:77). "Interest" is obviously polysemous here: if
the money he lends does not collect "interest," it cannot serve his private interest to any extent. Douglas's "fund for the aid of merit in distress" is a synecdoche for colonial capital as such. The 1784 Commutation Act not only increased
the revenue the British state acquired by taxing the tea trade but also enabled
the Company to make its £400,000 annual grant to the state.[82] In contrast to
their late seventeenth-century financial arrangements, this grant demanded no
repayment and extracted no interest; one could see it, like Douglas's fund, as
inherently benevolent.

But the novel's argument depends ultimately on offering Douglas's sentimental expenditures as proof that the Company obtained its wealth fairly. In
the process, however, the novel cannot avoid alluding to the Company's actual
methods. In response to "the torrents of abuse poured on [Company servants]
in all publications" claiming they are "rapacious wretches, who commit every
act of injustice" (2:156), Douglas provides the following argument: "I can never
think, that he, whose purse is always open to the wants of his friends, without
bestowing a thought, whether it will ever be returned, would the next hour cut
the throats of those people, you immaculate Englishmen stile the innocent, un-
offending natives, though God knows, there are not a greater set of rascals in the
universe" (2:160). If one gives one's wealth away sentimentally, one surely would
not have acquired it immorally in the first place.

But Douglas's racism—"there are not a greater set of rascals in the universe"—
hints at the Company's violence. His comment here, alongside the novel's earlier
reference to Indians as "grotesque blacks" (1:175), is meant in fact precisely to
justify that violence. If the natives are not civilized, the Company has no choice
but despotism: "It can surely be of little importance to men who are born under
such a despotic government as that of *Indostan*, who are their masters—to men
who from their birth are in a state of actual, if not nominal slavery, what matters

it whether under the East-India company, or the Great Mogul" (2:161). Douglas's apology recalls Touchit's: "These people are but a little better than Tartars and Turks." Having acknowledged Company despotism, Douglas backtracks even further, this time admitting torture: "Would you in *England* believe that it is a common practice here, when the people are called on, to refuse paying their rents, and in order to avoid payment, suffer themselves to be punished, and after receiving the punishment, and possibly orders for a second, that they will then produce the money they have had in their pockets all the time[?]" (2:161–62). The following year, Edmund Burke would describe to the visibly horrified audience of the Hastings impeachment the various forms of torture, including genital mutilation, Company agents used to extract rent from Bengali peasants. Unable to deny that colonial wealth involves violence, the novel argues instead that the native is responsible.

But the very necessity of such an apology testifies to how disturbed the nation's fantasies about colonial capital were. Whereas the narrative is devoted to the sentimental expenditure of colonial wealth from beginning to end, it touches on primitive accumulation only in this single passage. While the novel argues that sentiment is the antithesis of expropriation, it also insinuates—with profound insight—that the function of sentiment is to legitimize colonial violence. Hence, even this sentimental text records the global history sentimentalism was supposed to disavow.

SALT

With somewhat less irony than Sterne, Caroline's sister Sophy dreams about the life of a nabobess while still in England: "Sleeping or waking I can think nothing but diamonds, pearls, gold muslins, palanquins, and all the charming paraphernalia of a nabob's lady" (1:2). She explains that her excitement is occasioned by "the pleasure I shall not only enjoy there, but on my return, when *my* carriage, the first for elegance and magnificence, rolls along the town, and myself a very queen of diamonds" (1:3). Although she hopes to marry a servant at the top of the Company hierarchy, her marriage proposal comes from a decidedly less fashionable sphere. Her fiancé, she confesses to her correspondent, "is—how shall I relate it—A SALT AGENT" (2:229). The novel intends Sophy's acceptance of his proposal to signal the victory of her sentimental over her fashionable tendencies. But no less than its reference to torture, the novel's allusion to the salt agent betrays an all-too-intimate awareness of the history it needs to erase.

The Company's monopoly on Bengali salt was its second-largest source of revenue, trailing only property tax.[83] Its servants had purchased salt from Bengali peasants known as *malangis* throughout the 1760s and marketed it without the Company's sanction in regions far outside its jurisdiction, extending the geography of the British Empire in the process. Though Company officials acknowledged that these incursions into the salt trade were not only illicit but also potentially incendiary, they themselves followed the servants when given a chance. For example, before returning to Bengal in 1764, Clive advised the Company directors to ban the private salt trade: he called the servants' "intrusion" into Bengal's internal commerce "the foundation of all the Bloodshed, Massacres, and confusion which have happened of late."[84] But once in Bengal, he drew up a plan that took the salt trade away from lower servants and gave it to officers instead, though the profits remained no less private. Hastings similarly declared the trade illegal in 1759 but also eventually became involved in it.[85] William Bolts, one of the Company officials who had the largest share of the trade, later singled it out in his widely read critique of the Company, *Considerations on Indian Affairs* (1772), as "in the highest degree injurious to the population and manufactures of the country."[86] The Company's own Secret Select Committee found in 1775 that "[the malangis] are defrauded of not less than 29 rupees [of every 50 rupees of their salt's value]" as well as being "in a state of vassalage[,] compelled to work at whatever price the master imposes on them."[87]

In response to the committee's findings, Hastings devised the "Agency System" in 1780. It divided the salt fields into six districts, each supervised by a British "salt agent" who single-handedly replaced all the native property owners, farmers, and merchants traditionally involved in the marketing of salt.[88] As a consequence of the Agency System, the Company finally ensured that the profits of the salt trade returned to it rather than its servants. The salt trade by itself generated significantly more wealth for the Company in 1785 than the Treasury demanded from it by the terms of the 1784 India Act.

But for the malangis, the Agency System was no improvement.[89] As the sole figure who organized the trade, the salt agent was in a position to extend both the hours of the malangi's workday and the months of the season in which he panned salt, thereby making it difficult for him to undertake agricultural labor. Because the salt agent effectively set prices, he had no compulsion to offer the malangis fair value. Eventually, the British would destroy an industry that had been present in Bengal from time immemorial by importing foreign-made salt into India—and in the process inspire Gandhi to make the native production and control of salt one of his movement's primary aspirations. Long before that, the Agency System had rendered the malangis uniquely abject: one colonial official claimed that "they were the most pitiable of the 'native subjects, from [the] nature of their work.'"[90]

Sophy assuages whatever discomfort she feels about the origins of her marital wealth by emphasizing, like the novel in general, the functions it will serve when it reaches Britain: "when your Sophia . . . is driving a smart equipage about town, no one will ask whether her husband was a *chief*, or a *salt agent*" (3:132). By novel's end, all its characters have returned to the land from which their debts had originally exiled them, but now with colonial fortunes that free their property from encumbrance. The disinterested nabob plans to buy an estate near his much admired correspondent and follow his example of "possessing" an "amiable" woman and a delightful "domestic œconomy" (3:205). He ironizes himself as a typical nabob who "with asiatic folly, sport[s] a few thousands in the purchase of [the estate]," implying that his expenditure should be read not as extravagance but rather as an investment in the nation's sentimental values. This was, of course, always the narrative telos: the reinvestment of colonial wealth in a realm where its constitutive violence is no longer visible.[91]

In the critique that concludes Foote's play—"This is not Sparta, nor . . . the chaste times of the Roman republic. Nowadays, riches . . . rightly dispensed . . . closely conceal the source from whence they proceeded"—the British public's failure to question the origins of its wealth manifests the fact that it has reached the downward spiral of imperial degeneration. Though it hardly applied in the context of Parliament's sensational vetting of colonial violence during the early 1770s, Foote's critique must have been more apt when the corrupt nabob's virtual disappearance from popular discourse in the late 1780s marked the apparently successful union of Company wealth and public finance.[92] To celebrate that union, *The Disinterested Nabob* needed to conceal the troubling legacy of the Seven Years' War, when a conquest economy became the foundation of a distinctively modern ethics. Before this novel, sentimental texts joined the colonial and the domestic, the global and the affective, in much more subtle forms. It is left for us to discern in sentimental expression the now practically inescapable cycle of war, debt, and empire.

4 FREE TRADE AND FAMINE
The Wealth of Nations
and Bentham's "Essay"

Except among specialists, the universally accepted view is that Adam Smith was the prophet of free trade and presented it as the solution to the problems of modern commercial society.[1] But as Frank, Arrighi, and Copley each observed, these claims depend on a selective reading of *The Wealth of Nations* that focuses almost entirely on certain passages from its first two books alone.[2] These books famously extol the division of labor, arguing that from the perspective of a labor theory of value, the clothes of the poorest European pauper are more valuable than those of the richest African king. By reducing *The Wealth of Nations'* five books to quotations from these two, the classical economists who followed Smith during the nineteenth century and the neoclassical economists who in turn succeeded them during the twentieth were able to remake Smith as a purely theoretical economist as well.[3] His importance came to lie in the formulation of concepts—such as the theories of value, distribution, and the price mechanism—seminal for the field.

This chapter shares in the effort of scholars such as Winch, Pocock, Fleischacker, and Rothschild to provide a fuller picture of Smith's thought than classical and neoclassical economics have allowed.[4] But it focuses on a series of historical arguments within *The Wealth of Nations* that even these scholars have underplayed. The first is Smith's startling assertion in Book 3 that European economic history has been "retrograde," *not* progressive, from its origins to the present. In Smith's view, Europe uniquely reversed the natural order of things, participating in transnational commerce before it experienced agricultural development. Because of Europe's retrograde history, capital became the possession not of people in general but instead, Smith emphasizes, of exclusive groups of merchants and manufacturers alone. Second, Smith claims in Book 4 that these exclusive groups have made monopoly the organizing principle of modern trade. Their state-sanctioned monopolies displace Europe's ancient prejudices against agricultural labor and free exchange from its own history to the global economy. This fusion of sovereign power and corporate wealth against the free operation of the market is what defines the global economy for Smith. Third, Smith concludes—perhaps most surprisingly of all—that because of the merchant and manufacturing stranglehold on European states, free trade will *never* entirely come to pass. The collusion of monopoly capital and sovereign power is, in sum, a problem intrinsic to European history that deforms the global economy.

This chapter focuses, finally, on Smith's discussions of British India, which the scholarship on Smith has also overlooked, parts of recent articles by Muthu and Travers excepted.[5] Indeed, the neglect of the arguments just listed follows from the neglect of British India, because the former converge in Smith's analysis of the latter. Focusing on its date of publication (1776), the scholarship has taken Britain's failing policies in America to be *The Wealth of Nations'* immediate context. But the composition of the text, which Smith began in 1764, coincides with the rise of the English East India Company to sovereign power in India from 1765 forward.[6] Not coincidentally, then, the European destruction of Indian Ocean economies is a leitmotif in *The Wealth of Nations*. Smith references, in particular, the 1770–71 Bengal famine, when the number of natives who had starved to death under Company rule was estimated to be in the millions. These references illustrate the link between the respective histories of Book 3 and Book 4: as an exclusive group of merchants who could think of trade only in terms of monopoly, the Company encouraged neither agricultural production nor commercial exchange but instead created the conditions in which famine became possible. The Company's economic system in Bengal exemplified the problems intrinsic to European economic development much more profoundly for Smith than British policy in the Americas did.

Hence, while Books 1 and 2 provide largely theoretical accounts of capitalism's logic, Books 3 and 4 document the historical forces that have militated against that logic from Europe's origins until the present. If Smith insisted free trade would never come to pass, we need to rethink his use of this principle. This chapter argues, in short, that in *The Wealth of Nations* the ideal of free trade operates critically rather than ideologically: it does not justify European and global history but points out their defects. It does so because this history's distinguishing feature is not progress toward free trade but state-corporate collusion. For Smith, therefore, free trade is the principle not of European development but rather its interruption. Because this principle calls the co-optation of markets into question, it serves for Smith as the fulcrum on which a *permanent* critique of modern political economy can pivot.

I am not denying that *The Wealth of Nations* also attributes progressive tendencies to European history, whether the aforementioned early modern division of labor in Book 1 or the late medieval rise of towns and decline of feudalism in Book 3.[7] Nor do I mean to present *The Wealth of Nations* as an attack on modernity and empire *tout court*. Indeed, the text comprises a series of policy proposals meant not to dissolve the British Empire nor even transform it fundamentally but rather merely to reform it. But our focus on *The Wealth of Nations'* celebrations of progress and its engagement with the British Empire, such as they are, has obscured a very different undercurrent in the text: its profoundly critical understanding of European rule in the East Indies, which targets the very constitution of European history and of the global economy. We need to consider how this understanding inflects *The Wealth of Nations'* project. Smith offered his account of European and global history's progressive potential and his policy proposals to the British state within the context of a political economy whose flaws were so deep that he believed they could only be ameliorated, not solved.

The chapter's first section treats *The Wealth of Nations'* idea of progress, arguing that it functions critically. The second and third discuss Smith's accounts of European history and the global economy, respectively, arguing that the retrograde order of the former leads to state-corporate collusion in the latter. The fourth and fifth focus on Smith's analyses of British rule in India and the Bengal famine, where the negative consequences of that collusion were most evident. The sixth argues that this collusion was Smith's central concern. The final section extends the chapter's argument to Jeremy Bentham's contemporaneous analysis of British rule and the Bengal famine.

Progress

To understand why Smith believed that European history and the global economy work against progress, we need first to recognize the goal of progress for him. When he described the prototypically progressive moment in modern history, the European discovery of the New World, then frequently paired with the discovery of the Cape route, he declared: "The discovery of America, and . . . a passage to the East Indies by the Cape of Good Hope, are the two greatest and most important events recorded in the history of mankind."[8] But where did the discoveries' greatness lie for Smith? We conventionally infer that Smith identified progress with the growth of national wealth. The discoveries were progressive because they founded new markets, which encouraged surplus production and in turn specialization and technical innovation. Such innovation increases labor productivity and, along with it, national wealth. Brenner has described this cause-effect chain—from the expansion of markets through the division of labor to the increase of national wealth—as the essence of Smith's model of capitalist development, "Smith's fundamental proposition," which, Brenner has claimed, exerts a baleful influence even on Marxist theories of capitalism.[9]

But as Brenner has himself acknowledged, his account of "Smith's model" ignores Smith's various analyses of European history.[10] Once we resituate Smith's concept of progress within these analyses, we will find that its goal is not to increase national wealth per se but rather to redress the European peasant's economic exclusion. In fact, contemporaries considered Smith's thought dangerous, precisely because its premise was, in the words of *The Lectures on Jurisprudence*, that the poor laborer "supports the whole frame of society" but is "himself possessed of a very small share and . . . buried in obscurity."[11] Such comments targeted the previously axiomatic claim that an impoverished working class was the necessary precondition of economic growth. Smith argued instead that the "liberal reward of labour" is always the "necessary effect and cause of the greatest public prosperity" (99).[12] He believed that European peasants had lost access to capital during the earliest stages of feudalism and hoped that the global economy would enable them to turn their wages into capital and so experience economic and social mobility. The end of progress for Smith is this mobility, not the mere increase of national wealth.

Hence, Smith criticizes European history and the global economy whenever they immobilize labor: each of the following sections explores such criticism at length. For now we can observe that even when Smith explains the discoveries' progressive potential, he does so to preface his wider claim that Europe has squandered the greater part of that potential. To capital's promise, *The Wealth of Nations* rarely fails to counterpose its history. For example, the celebration of the discoveries' infinite potential turns immediately into a lament for their lost possibilities: "To the natives, however, both of the East and West Indies, all the commercial benefits which can have resulted from those events have been sunk and lost in the dreadful misfortunes which they have occasioned" (626). Similarly, a paragraph claiming that the "discovery of America . . . made a most essential [change in the state of Europe]" emphasizes that it had the opposite effect on native economies: "The savage injustice of the Europeans rendered an event, which ought to have been beneficial to all, ruinous and destructive to several of those unfortunate countries" (448).

If the early modern discoveries had initiated a truly global history promising universal liberty, this promise culminated for Smith not in progress but rather in extreme degeneration.[13] "Dreadful misfortunes" refer to what Smith considered the starkest form of that degeneration, a historical phenomenon *The Wealth of Nations* explores in detail across its five books: the collapse of native economies around the Indian Ocean under the weight of European mercantilism. *The Wealth of Nations'* progressive vision occurs, therefore, largely on the level of capital's potential and serves to underscore capital's actual failure.[14]

European History: The Barbarian Invasions

The respective analyses in Book 3 and Book 4 of premodern European history and the modern global economy explain this failure in depth. Scholars who have used *The Wealth of Nations* to authorize free-market ideology avoid these books, Coats speculated, because "they have been embarrassed by its decidedly polemical tone and orientation."[15] Reiterating Brenner's attitude, one recent study begins, emblematically, "Smith's sociological analysis of the rise of capitalism . . . has been strangely neglected, and will, unfortunately, also be neglected here."[16] Because both those who praise and those who condemn *The Wealth of Nations* as an apology for the present global order study these two books only in passing, they assume that Smith held mercantilism *alone* responsible for the problems of commercial society.[17] Such approaches to *The Wealth of Nations* cannot cope with these parts of the work because they locate the roots of capital's failure much more deeply in European history than the rise of mercantilism. The following discussion returns Smith's free-trade arguments to their historical matrices, in line with his own description of *The Wealth of Nations* as a "theory *and* History of Law and Government."[18]

My argument is that *The Wealth of Nations* represents European rule in the Indian Ocean in terms of degeneration, not progress, in order to call European history and the global economy alike into question. In fact, Smith explicitly referred to European economic development as "retrograde" and "unnatural" (380), arguing—in a claim whose importance to his historical vision we cannot overstate—that "progress" occurred, paradoxically, in reverse. As he took great pains to explain, it was not "the natural course of things"—"the greater part of the capital of every growing society . . . first, directed to agriculture, afterwards to manufactures, and last of all to foreign commerce"—but rather the inverse that occurred throughout feudal and early modern Europe. According to Smith, "This natural order of things . . . has, in all the modern states of Europe, been . . . entirely inverted. The foreign commerce of their cities has introduced all their finer manufactures . . . ; and manufactures and foreign commerce together, have given birth to the principal improvements of agriculture" (380). Smith noted that English merchants established the domestic manufacture of fine commodities only after they had tired of buying them from "more civilized nations" (407, 408, 410). This process of imitation provided the impetus for urbanization. Agricultural growth followed only afterward, to feed those cities alone: "Through the greater part of Europe the commerce and manufactures of cities, instead of being the effect, have been the cause and occasion of the improvement and cultivation of the country" (422).

First question: Why is the former order alone "natural"?[19] If agriculture had developed first, its growth would have required the employment of more people, thereby placing labor at a premium.[20] If landowners had wanted to attract laborers under such circumstances, they would have had to compensate them with part of the surplus value the laborers had produced. Hence, if the development of agriculture had preceded the rise of international commerce, this order would have ensured that people in general, rather than an exclusive merchant class alone, would have gained access to capital. As Arrighi has explained at length in *Adam Smith in Beijing*, only this order of development "mobilize[s] human rather than non-human resources," labor rather than merchant capital.[21] This course of economic development is "natural" for Smith precisely to the extent that it mobilizes labor.

In contrast, when international commerce precedes agricultural development, economic growth tends to immobilize labor: "The capital . . . that is acquired in any country by commerce and manufactures, is all a very precarious and uncertain possession. . . . A merchant . . . is not necessarily the citizen of any particular country. It is in a great measure indifferent to him from what place he carries on his trade; and a very trifling disgust will make him remove his capital, and together with it all the industry which it supports, from one country to another" (426). Hence, when capital began to circulate in Europe, it reflected the sudden mobility of exclusive groups of merchants, not people in general. In short, the discoveries increased production *within* Europe alone, according to Smith, and even then only unnaturally, following an inverted order that did not serve the people. As a consequence of this order, cities might well "grow up to great wealth and splendour, while not only the country in its neighborhood, but all those to which it traded, were in poverty and wretchedness" (405). In Smith's view, merchant capital read the script of progress backward, entering the scene of history too early, before agricultural capital had been properly introduced. If capital's revolutionary potential lies in the mobilization of labor, that potential was largely stillborn in Europe.

Second question: Why did this unnatural order replace the natural course of development in Europe? Smith's explanation returns to the origins of feudalism—to the birth of "Europe" from the ashes of Rome. One part of the explanation lies in the barbarian invasions that overran Rome's western provinces, when Germanic and Scythian tribes "usurped to themselves . . . the lands," all of which "were engrossed, and the greater part by a few great proprietors" (382). Smith notes that "this original engrossing" turned a flourishing economy of peasant proprietors and town-country trade into a barren landscape, the towns depopulated, the countryside uncultivated, and culture "sunk into the lowest state of poverty and barbarism" (381).[22] The invasions dispossessed and enserfed western Europe's peasantry, making it a slave population that far from having any right to property became an extension of the property it farmed, as immobile as the estate was: "The occupiers of land . . . were supposed to belong more directly to the land than to their master. They could . . . be sold with it, but not separately. . . . Whatever they acquired was acquired to their master, and he could take it from them at pleasure" (386–87).[23] Smith noted that the barbarians' original expropriation "might have been but a transitory evil" (382), if the lands had been divided once again into smaller estates in the process of inheritance, but the laws of primogeniture and entail only consolidated the engrossment.[24] Here we begin to see how deep-seated and intractable Europe's antiproductive tendencies are. Segregating labor from capital, the invasions sowed the seeds of a "barbarism" that in Smith's view has never ceased to shape European development.[25]

The other reason for Europe's retrograde history lies in its immemorial distrust of the merchant. Smith observed that from antiquity to feudalism, "trade was disgraceful to a gentleman" (907–8) and "merchants, like all the other inhabitants of burghs, were considered as little better than emancipated bondmen, whose persons were despised" (878–79).[26] Sovereigns supposed that merchants made profit only by engrossing commodities and raising prices. Consequently, medieval laws limited the grain trade to those with official licenses.[27] But the effect of these laws was to block the development not only of the merchant class but also of agricultural markets and agricultural capital as such (396, 532). Alongside the European distrust of the merchant, there also lies a distaste for agricultural labor that Smith dated at least to Rome. Indeed, since the peasant's disgrace surpassed the trader's, those with capital would rarely invest it in agriculture (395). Even those who accumulated capital in the country were more likely to shelter it in the city, which provided it greater safeguards (405).

In sum, Smith identified a series of ancient European processes that had precipitated agricultural degeneration and culminated in the rise of the corporations: the barbarian conquests, the consequent engrossment of territory, the laws of primogeniture and entail, the restrictions on the grain trade, and premature urbanization.[28] His vision of European development suggests that far from being Eurocentric, Smith considered Europe to be congenitally abnormal. As Arrighi and Frank have noted, Smith deemed China more economically advanced than Europe and did not expect Europe to catch up.[29] We can summarize his argument about Europe's unnatural order in this way: since Rome, but even more intensely after the barbarian invasions that brought its western empire to an end, European political economy has been based on conquest, not production or trade.[30] The scholarship on Smith associates Book 3 with its famous narrative of progress: the early modern rise of international commerce, European cities, and city-countryside trade, all of which led to feudalism's decline. But we must keep in mind that an earlier history shapes—and distorts—*The Wealth of Nations*' progress narrative. As a consequence, European "progress" only reinforces the exclusion of the people from capital.

The Global Economy

Book 3's account of European history's unnatural development is, at least formally, the prelude to Book 4's analysis of global political economy. Turning from one to the other, we find that the barbarian invasions' conquest economy not only defined feudalism but also survived it. The problem of European history is that it suppressed agriculture, enabling foreign trade to precede agricultural development and international merchants to separate the peasantry from capital. The problem of the global economy is that these merchants use their differential access to capital to control the British state, determine its laws, and impose monopolies on all lucrative sectors of domestic and global commerce. These monopolies suppressed production not only within Britain, according to

Smith, but also worldwide: they projected Europe's ancient prejudices against free exchange onto a truly global economy. Book 4's critique of mercantilism is, therefore, part of a broader historical analysis, targeting not the mercantile system alone but European and global development as such.

In regard to the two ends of the British Empire, Smith declares, "Monopoly is the great engine of both" (630). For Smith and his contemporaries, in contrast to much recent historiography, the British Empire had a systematic character: the construction and defense of monopoly commerce.[31] Book 4 repeatedly emphasizes that the elite merchant and manufacturing groups to whom the state has accorded monopoly privileges have a stranglehold on national politics. Smith referred, for example, to wool manufacturers' capacity to "extort" laws "for the support of their own absurd and oppressive monopolies" (348) and described the threat of violence that hung over the enforcement of such laws: "By the 8th of Elizabeth, chap. 3.34 the exporter of sheep, lambs or rams, was for the first offence to forfeit all his goods for ever, to suffer a year's imprisonment, and then to have his left hand cut off in a market town upon a market day, to be there nailed up; and for the second offence to be adjudged a felon, and to suffer death accordingly" (648). Smith observed tersely: "Like the laws of Draco, these laws [are] written in blood." English commercial laws were designed in his view to suppress the production and trade of those who lacked capital, in order to enable those who already possessed it to market their goods without competition: "It is the industry which is carried on for the benefit of the rich and the powerful, that is principally encouraged by our mercantile system. That which is carried on for the benefit of the poor and the indigent, is too often, either neglected, or oppressed" (644).

Bearing such claims in mind, we might wonder at Hont and Ignatieff's confident assertion that for Smith, "modern commercial society was unequal and unvirtuous but it was not unjust. . . . However unequal men might be, in property and citizenship, they could be equal in access to the means to satisfy basic need."[32] In contrast, Smith commented, "It is unnecessary . . . to observe how contrary [modern commercial] regulations are to the boasted liberty of the subject, of which we affect to be so very jealous; but which . . . is so plainly sacrificed to the futile interests of our merchants and manufacturers" (660). Such comments do not prefigure liberal ideology but instead recall a tradition of protest older than *The Wealth of Nations*, evident, for example, in *Darcy v. Allein* (1603, a.k.a. "The Case of Monopolies") and Civil War–era Leveller tracts.[33] Where the liberal tradition presents modern commerce as a vehicle of justice and liberty, this radical strain saw it in diametric contrast as an instrument of tyranny by which the state privileged corporate entities, thereby violating the individual's sacred right to labor as he saw fit.[34]

The liberal presupposition that Smith's free-trade arguments target "political intervention" (to invoke an often-repeated phrase) tacitly recasts his thought so that it opposes state interference in markets alone.[35] Such misappropriations of Smith's thought reduce its critical force, turning it into a simple attack on mercantile policy. In fact, Book 4's target is the collusion of sovereign power and corporate wealth. When Smith criticized laws that prevented the free flow of labor, he declared, for example: "Let the . . . natural liberty of exercising what species of industry they please be restored to all his majesty's subjects . . . ; that is, break down the exclusive privileges of corporations, . . . which are real encroachments upon natural liberty" (470). He insisted, moreover, that Britain would *never* fully reverse these policies: "To expect . . . that the freedom of trade should ever be entirely restored in Great Britain, is as absurd as to expect that an Oceana or Utopia should ever be established in it" (471).

Hence, while the liberal reading of Smith fastens onto his argument that free markets would be an instrument in the struggle for freedom, it overlooks the fact that for Smith the free market is, as Coats noted, "an unattainable ideal": "The policy of Europe," Smith emphasized, "nowhere leaves things at perfect liberty" (151).[36] The late eighteenth-century term "policy" still carried the connotations of its etymon, "civil administration." The "policy" of Europe—in this sense not of specific political actions but of political organization as such—is designed to co-opt the circulation of labor, commodities, and capital. Smith's critique of modern commercial society is therefore much more fundamental than either the classical economists or Smith scholars have observed. Mercantilism for Smith was the logical extension of Europe's "retrograde" history; its degenerative effect on production and exchange had ancient roots therein. The barbarian prejudice against agriculture and trade is not merely Europe's prehistory but also its fate, a wraith it ignores at its own peril.[37] My point corresponds to Arrighi's too-brief argument in *The Long Twentieth Century* that what distinguishes the European capitalist system for Smith is a layer above and *against* the market in which the state and corporate wealth are fused together. Arrighi claims that only this layer, where sovereign power backs monopoly commerce, enables exclusive groups of capitalists in Smith's view to acquire superprofits over an extended time.[38]

Smith not only advocated free trade but also claimed that it would never come to pass. It follows from this apparent contradiction that free trade cannot be the telos of history, except in an ideal sense: *The Wealth of Nations* offers free trade less as a historical possibility than as a critical principle that will *always* possess oppositional force, because European policy ensures state-corporate collusion. The distinguishing feature of capitalism for him was not free trade but, in diametric opposition, precisely this collusion, which Braudel and Arrighi would call the *contre-marché* (the "anti-market").[39]

When Smith aligned the idea of free trade with More's *Utopia* and Harrington's *Oceana*, he implied that his ultimate aim, in contrast to theirs, was not to imagine an ideal condition in the place of an actual order. He explained that

not only the prejudices of the publick, but what is much more unconquerable, the private interests of many individuals, irresistibly oppose [freedom of trade]. . . . The monopoly which our manufacturers have obtained against us . . . has so much increased [their] number . . . , that, like an overgrown standing army, they have become formidable to the government, and . . . intimidate the legislature. . . . If [an MP] opposes them, [nothing] can protect him . . . from real danger, arising from the insolent outrage of furious and disappointed monopolists. (471)[40]

The Wealth of Nations invokes the ideal of free trade here only to underscore the complexity and intransigence of the forces arrayed against it. Smith never suggested that his philosophy could transcend the developmental trajectory European policy had set in motion so long ago. The economic and political advantages monopoly corporations enjoy enable them to turn any reform meant to serve the commonwealth toward their own private interests instead. Smith hoped only to put obstacles in their way.

Company Rule

I have argued that according to *The Wealth of Nations*, the barbarian invasions that precipitated European feudalism led ultimately to the rise of a global economy that did not increase and diversify production as its advocates claim but suppressed it in the interests of exclusive groups. The scholarship on *The Wealth of Nations* has tended to overlook not only these analyses but also the crucial place of colonial India within the text. These two omissions are not coincidental: much more than the American colonies, British India typifies global economic degeneration. In fact, in *The Wealth of Nations*, as in the period's imagination more broadly, East India Company rule is *the* exemplary instance of modern antiproduction. Once we return the principle of free trade to this context, its critical function will become clear.

With the East Indies in particular as with the European colonies in general, Smith counterposed global trade's theoretical potential to its historical tragedy. He observed that the East Indies held even greater promise than the Americas did: "The discovery of a passage to the East Indies, by the Cape of Good Hope . . . opened, perhaps, a still more extensive range to foreign commerce than even that of America" (448). Elsewhere, he intensified the distinction: "The East Indies offers a market both for the manufactures of Europe and for the gold and silver . . . of America, greater and more extensive than both Europe and America put together" (632).[41] But he alluded to the East Indies' potential only to emphasize, characteristically, that it had been squandered: "Europe, however, has hitherto derived much less advantage from its commerce with the East Indies, than from that with America" (448). The reason for the failure, according to Smith, is that after the decline of the Portuguese Empire, European trade with the East Indies always occurred under the auspices of exclusive corporations: "The Portuguese monopolized the East India trade to themselves for about a century. . . . When the Dutch . . . began to encroach upon them, they vested their whole East India commerce in an exclusive company. The English, French, Swedes, and Danes have all followed their example, so that no great nation in Europe has ever yet had the benefit of a free commerce to the East Indies. No other reason need be assigned why it has never been so advantageous as the trade to America, which, between almost every nation of Europe and its own colonies, is free" (449).

When the English East India Company wrested Bengal from the Mughal Empire in 1765, an exclusive group of merchants become sovereign there. But sovereignty is precisely the role for which the classical segregation of economics from politics disqualified merchants: "No two characters," Smith observed, "seem more inconsistent than those of trader and sovereign" (819). Updating classical doctrine for modern society, Smith emphasized that while merchants inherently aspire to establish monopolies and "exclude as much as possible all rivals from the particular market where they keep their shop" (638), the sovereign must not merely abstain from trade but also protect the freedom thereof. In diametric opposition, Company rule "tends to make government subservient to the interests of monopoly" (638). Merchant companies, "by a strange absurdity, regard the character of the sovereign as but an appendix to that of the merchant, ... by means of which they may ... buy cheaper in India ... to sell with a better profit in Europe" (637).

Because monopoly capital and sovereign power become one in the colony, the antiproductive trajectory of European history is dramatically accelerated there. Remarkably, the Company's ruling principle was to suppress surplus production in order to ensure that it could always buy cheap and sell dear: the Company "endeavour[s] ... to reduce [the surplus produce] to what is barely sufficient for supplying [its] own demand" (637–38). When Company servants privately appropriated privileges the Mughal Empire had extended only to the Company's official trade, the consequences were even more devastating: "They will employ the whole authority of government ... to harass and ruin those who interfere with them in any branch of commerce. ... [Their] monopoly [tends] to degrade the cultivation of the whole country, and to reduce the number of its inhabitants" (639). As we have seen in *The Nabob* and shall see again in Burke's and Sheridan's speeches in the Hastings impeachment, the metropolitan imagination associated colonial rule precisely with such precipitous declines in production and population.

In *The Wealth of Nations'* discussions of the East Indies, then, a sense of European political economy very different from the one we associate with the text comes unmistakably into relief. Smith represented Indian colonial history in terms of wanton destruction, wherein "the natural genius" (635) of both the Dutch and the English East India Company revealed itself. Smith noted, "In the spice islands the Dutch are said to burn all the spiceries which a fertile season produces beyond what they expect to dispose of in Europe"; even in the islands they do not inhabit, they pay natives to destroy clove and nutmeg trees (636). Antiproduction is the necessary complement, Smith explained, to monopoly trade: "The best way, [VOC officials] imagine, to secure their own monopoly, is to take care that no more shall grow than what they themselves carry to the market" (4.7c, 636). Referring to the VOC's antiproductive measures as a "savage policy," Smith argued that their ultimate effect, if not their actual aim, was to depopulate the Spice Islands until there were only enough natives to supply the Dutch and no more (636).[42]

Turning from the VOC in the Spice Islands to the English Company in Bengal, Smith observed: "It has not been uncommon [for the chief] of a [Company] factory, to order a peasant to plough up a rich field of poppies ... to give the chief an opportunity of selling [opium] at a better price"; Company servants "attempted to restrain the production of the particular articles of which they had . . . usurped the monopoly [to the quantity] which they could expect to sell with such a profit as they might think sufficient" (636). It was in the Company's interests to decrease production, precisely because Bengal was already productive: the Company had "extended, either their dominion, or their depredations, over a vast accession of some of the richest and most fertile countries in India; all was wasted and destroyed" (753). In contrast to our received wisdom, Smith argued that European capital suppressed East Indian market economies.[43] He concluded that though the English Company had "not yet had time to establish in Bengal so perfectly destructive a system" as the VOC had in the Spice Islands, if its policy continued for "a century or two," it would (636–37).

If we connect Smith's discussions of Indian colonial history and premodern European history, we will see that, however aberrant the former seems, it merely intensifies the antiproductive tendencies of the latter. Lane, Steensgaard, and Parker have each argued that what early modern Europe actually exported to the rest of the world under the guise of merchant capital was its own warrior nomad caste—the *fidalgos,* conquistadors, *vrijburghers,* and nabobs—who used Europe's sophisticated war machinery to capture diverse forms of production and trade.[44] Arrighi has argued in the same vein that the effect of East India Company rule was precisely to turn India from the "natural course" of development toward Europe's retrograde order.[45] According to Smith, when the East India companies exported European development to the colonies, the mutually exclusive logics of the sovereign and the merchant collapsed into each other. The sovereign relinquished his public character and pursued monopoly trade; the merchant disavowed the logic of capital, reinvesting profit not in production or trade but rather in the expansion and militarization of the state.

Famine
The East India Company's antiproductive tendencies reached a nadir in the 1770–71 Bengal famine. The Company's Court of Directors estimated that one-third of the native population had starved to death; in Calcutta, Warren Hastings claimed 10 million had died.[46] By any measure, mortality during this time far exceeded that during precolonial famines: contemporary reports described corpses "piled on the streets of the capital."[47] In line with such reports, Smith believed the famine had little to do with the drought that preceded it—much less with any failure in

Bengali agricultural production—and everything to do with Company rule. *The Wealth of Nations'* "Digression concerning the Corn Trade" explained: "Drought is . . . scarce ever so universal as necessarily to occasion a famine, if the government would allow a free trade. . . . Some improper regulations . . . imposed by the servants of the East India Company upon the rice trade, contributed . . . to turn that dearth into a famine" (527). The reports from Bengal claimed that rather than let markets redistribute grain to distressed regions, Company officials and their agents monopolized rice and wheat, closed off supply lines from areas of abundance, and created the famine. They reportedly sent grain en masse from those areas where it was cheap to drought-stricken regions, where it was dear. As a consequence, even areas that produced grain ended up possessing none. The Company's own directors concluded that "the [peasants] were compelled to sell their rice to . . . monopolizing Europeans [who] could be no other than persons of some rank in our service."[48]

Scholars have taken Smith's comments about famine to express the essential premises of free-market ideology. But they have not studied these comments in the context of the Bengal famine, even though it occurred during Smith's initial composition of *The Wealth of Nations*. Once we explore the history of this famine, we will see that Smith's aim was less to call free trade into being than to delineate the history and political economy that stood in its way.

Smith's analysis of the Bengal famine depends on his tripartite division of "every civilized society" into "those who live by rent," "those who live by wages," and "those who live by profit" (365). He argued that unlike the wealth of the first two orders (the landlord and the peasant), the wealth of the third (the merchant) is not directly proportional to economic growth but, remarkably, inversely proportional to it: "The rate of profit does not, like rent or wages, rise with prosperity, and fall with the declension of the society. On the contrary, it is naturally low in rich, and high in poor countries, and it is always highest in the countries which are going fastest to ruin" (266). The rate of profit increases not with production but rather with degeneration, because as an economy produces less capital, it pays labor less and hence devalues it (266). When an economy devalues labor, the merchant profits from it more: "The diminution of . . . the funds destined for the maintenance of industry . . . lowers the wages of labour [and] raises the profits of stock. [The merchants'] goods cost them less, and they get more for them" (110–11). Merchant capital is distinguished by the fact that it depends on the degeneration of production; its strategy, Smith insinuated, is to ruin the economy.

When he defined "the highest ordinary rate of profit"—the rate at which an economy goes fastest to ruin—his example was British Bengal: "The profits of the trade which the servants of the East India Company carry on in Bengal may not perhaps be very far from this state" (113–14). As a laboratory in which the merchant corporation became autonomous of any sovereign principle, Bengal was Smith's model of ruin: "The great fortunes so suddenly and so easily acquired in Bengal and other British settlements in the East Indies may satisfy us that, as the wages of labour are very low, so the profits of stock are very high in those ruined countries" (111). When Smith alluded to the Bengal famine in Book 1, he insinuated that the merchant corporation's modus operandi is to starve labor. "In a country where the funds destined for the maintenance of labour were sensibly decaying [many would starve]. Want, famine, and mortality would immediately prevail in that class. . . . This perhaps is nearly the present state of Bengal. [In a fertile country] where, notwithstanding, three or four hundred thousand people die of hunger in one year, we may be assured that the funds destined for the maintenance of the labouring poor are fast decaying" (90–91). More than any other single event within *The Wealth of Nations'* purview, the famine illustrated Smith's dictum that merchant capital profits from ruin. The literal starvation of laborers during famine was for him only an extension of the general conditions of scarcity and want that the merchant corporation imposed on labor, in order to ensure that it did not become mobile.[49] Perhaps it was not by chance that even after the enormity of the 1770–71 famine, food shortages and starvation continued to plague Bengal, including in 1777, 1779, 1783, 1786–88, and 1793.[50]

But the scholarship on Smith's treatment of famine has revolved around how it apologizes for free markets rather than how it criticizes merchant capital. This focus reflects the fact that the "Digression concerning the Corn Trade" became "a sacred text for colonial famine policy."[51] E. P. Thompson noted, "In the nineteenth century class after class of administrators were sent out to India, fully indoctrinated at Haileybury College in Smith's 'Digression,' . . . ready to respond to the vast exigencies of Indian famine by resolutely resisting any improper interventions in the free operation of the market."[52] Thompson concluded that "these pages . . . were among the most influential [in history]. Their arguments discredited . . . traditional protective interventions in time of dearth [and] could be used to justify profiteering and hoarding."[53] There is an irony in all such uses of the "Digression," since the passage from it I have quoted specifically criticizes profiteering and hoarding. But for Thompson the "Digression" nonetheless marked the historical watershed between premodern "moral economy," in which social obligations regulated exchange relationships, and modern political economy, in which the market alone governs such relationships. He called *The Wealth of Nations* "a grand central terminus" where all the arguments "concerned to demolish the old paternalist market regulation" converged.[54] His analysis articulates the now-conventional view: *The Wealth of Nations* does not oppose but rather validates the main trajectory of European and global history.

But even as Thompson presumed to define Smith's view of the grain trade, he neglected Smith's historical analyses of that trade. Regardless of Smith's long discussions of medieval and contemporary markets in Books 3 and 4, respectively, Thompson insisted that the "Digression" was "counter-empirical. It did not want to know how actual markets worked, any more than its disciples do today." Two decades earlier, Thompson had written that the "Digression" "impresses less as an essay in empirical enquiry than as a superb, self-validating essay in logic."[55]

If the "Digression" appears now to be a logical exercise unconcerned with actual markets, I would suggest that the responsibility lies with those who turn Smith's historical analyses into abstract principles, whether they attack him as free-market apologist or defend him as such. In the former camp, Thompson turned Smith's treatment of the grain trade into a single principle: There must be *no* political intervention in the market regardless of dearth or famine. This reduction enabled Thompson to argue that the colonial officials who used the "Digression" to justify noninterventionist policies were "not vulgarizing the views of Dr Smith but enforcing these strictly."[56] In the latter camp, Hont and Ignatieff took exception to Thompson's reading of the "Digression," arguing that it ignored the tradition of moral philosophy on which Smith's "Digression" supposedly builds: "Smith was simply transposing into the language of markets an ancient jurisprudential discourse ... about how to ensure that the private individuation of God's dominion would not deny the propertyless the means of satisfying their needs."[57] Having identified the "Digression" with this tradition, Hont and Ignatieff could then argue that "the adequate subsistence of the poor, like everything else in the Smithian system, depended on growth led by increasing productivity in manufacturing."[58]

In counterresponse, Thompson commented tersely that "examining Smith's text solely in the light of its conjectured intellectual lineage, Hont and Ignatieff and their ilk forget that it was produced and had consequences in a real social world."[59] The problem with Hont and Ignatieff is not, however, that they dissociate the meaning of the "Digression" from its subsequent misapplication. The problem with them—as with Thompson—is that in their need to make *The Wealth of Nations* an apology for the present, they overlook Smith's historical vision and so misconstrue the text itself. The principle that there must be no intervention in the market regardless of famine is, contrary to Thompson's argument, nowhere present in the "Digression": the text in fact *explicitly* supported such intervention within these circumstances.[60] Nor, *pace* Hont and Ignatieff, does the "Digression" presuppose that industrial growth provides the poor "adequate subsistence"; as we have already observed, *The Wealth of Nations* explicitly argues that when industry precedes agriculture, its growth leads to the immiseration of labor (405).

In contrast to the notion that Smith believed in markets (rather than moral economy) to solve the problem of poverty, he argued in Book 3 that markets were fettered for deep historical reasons and in Book 4 that global capital would ensure they remain that way. If we return what Hont and Ignatieff described as "the Smithian system" or what Thompson and Brenner described in equally abstract terms as "Smith's model" to its historical contexts, we will see that it homes in on the grain trade for reasons very different from the ones they suggest.

As Smith's analysis of European history illustrates, monopolies on grain were for him the source not only of famine but also of what necessarily precedes it, general poverty. By the time of the 1770–71 famine, monopolies on grain appear to have impoverished the Bengal countryside. Reports from Bengal claimed that these monopolies compelled Bengali peasants to sell their grain *before* it had actually been harvested.[61] Because the peasants sold it before dearth arose, they were underpriced and hence did not profit from their labor. They consequently became too poor to buy even the seed they needed for the next harvest and were forced to take it on loan. Having mortgaged their harvest to such loans, they could not look for other buyers—or, for that matter, more profitable forms of production and exchange—if there were any. "The misery of the primary producer was," according to Datta, "the [merchant's] most potent weapon."[62] The monopoly conditions imposed on Bengali peasants had effectively immobilized them.

Smith argued that usury had expropriated the peasants' surplus, if not their very subsistence itself: "In Bengal, money is frequently lent to farmers at forty, fifty, and sixty per cent[,] and the succeeding crop is mortgaged for the payment . . .

[S]uch enormous usury must . . . eat up the greater part of [agricultural] profits" (111). As this comment explains, Bengali farmers were subject to usury in the form of both the seed loans they needed to sow grain and the cash loans they needed to pay the colonial state's unremitting tax demands.[63] The Company insisted on tax collection even at the height of the famine, managing to collect *more* rent then than at any other time since 1768. Hastings himself noted that tax collection was "violently kept up to its former standard," "notwithstanding the loss of at least one-third of the Inhabitants of the Province."[64] The Company could never give farmers a break, because as its military expenditures pushed it ever further into debt, it needed rent to pay for its commercial as well as its martial ventures. With its sovereign and commercial functions always compromising each other in this way, the Company—in contrast to Mughal regimes—could not afford to give starving peasants institutional relief. In this regard, Company rule was of a piece with British sovereignty, which had mortgaged itself to the unfathomable costs of modern war, thereby rendering the sovereign-subject "moral economy" no longer feasible.

When Smith alluded to the famine, he was clear about the kind of economy he was criticizing. Let's return to the language of the "Digression": "Some improper regulations, some injudicious restraints imposed by the *servants* of the East India Company upon the rice trade, contributed, perhaps, to turn [the drought] into a famine" (my emphasis). Smith claimed that *private* individuals, not political intervention, had caused the famine; he criticized a corporate body's use of sovereign power, not the operations of a moral economy.[65] The Company had produced, Smith observed, "a very singular government in which every member of the administration wishes to get out of the country as soon as he can, and to whose interest, the day after he has left it and carried his whole fortune with him, it is perfectly indifferent though the whole country was swallowed up by an earthquake" (640).

In sum, Smith argued in Book 3 that the medieval grain trade reflected the "retrograde" course of European development, and when he turned to the modern grain trade in Book 4, he suggested that it disseminated that retrograde development across the globe. The Bengal famine was for Smith the projection into another time and space of Europe's congenital defect, the difficulty it has had since the barbarian invasions to think of production outside the sovereign's prerogative to it. The historical context of colonial India makes clear that the "Digression," like *The Wealth of Nations* in general, is a critical exploration of the medieval and modern co-optation of markets, not the ur-ideology of market society. But what did Smith consider an adequate response to that co-optation, if not free-market ideology?

Collusion and Critique

Smith's criticism of East India Company rule contains both poles of his philosophy: (1) labor deserves the capital it produces, and (2) the state must not mortgage the commonwealth to colonial war. Both poles were charged in the years immediately after his death, the two sources, Rothschild notes, of "Smith's dangerous reputation."[66] Perhaps it is for this reason that they have been overlooked ever since. The axis that runs between them is the alliance of monopoly capital and sovereign power. As a consequence of this alliance, the expropriation of labor, on one hand, and the militarization of the state, on the other, reinforce each other, creating a downward economic spiral, the antithesis of progress. Hence, in Smith's vision, Bengal's ruin merely anticipates England's own, as his analogy of British India to the Roman provinces suggests (111).

Though Smith used Bengal to illustrate his belief that "the government of an exclusive company of merchants is [the worst] for any country whatever" (570), European nations make the point almost as well. He noted that "in the greater part of the commercial states of Europe, particular companies of merchants have ... perswade[d] the legislature to entrust to them ... the duty of the sovereign, together with all the powers ... connected to it" (733). When economies develop "unnaturally" in Smith's sense, exclusive groups of capitalists gain the capacity, Arrighi has explained, "to impose their class interest at the expense of the national interest." This is the "European developmental path" as *The Wealth of Nations* delineates it: not market-based growth but rather the increasing concentration "of capital and power."[67] Though Book 3 is the oldest part of *The Wealth of Nations*, the problematic consequences of this path remained at the center of Smith's concerns.[68] Two of the final texts he wrote during his lifetime—*The Wealth of Nations* 4.8 and *The Theory of Moral Sentiments* 6.2.2—focus on the private interests that influence British politics, illustrating Coats's, Haakonssen's, and Winch's suggestions that in the end Smith's scholarly aim was to disclose capital's sway over the state.[69]

In both *The Wealth of Nations* and private correspondence, Smith counseled extreme vigilance in regard to that influence:

The proposal of any new law ... which comes from [the merchants and the manufacturers], ought always to be listened to ... with the most suspicious attention. It comes from an order of men . . . who have generally an interest to deceive and even to oppress the publick. (267)

The capricious ambition of kings and ministers has not, during the present and preceding century, been more fatal to the repose of Europe, than the impertinent jealousy of merchants and manufacturers. [They] ought [not] to be the rulers of mankind. (493)

[Trade regulations are] in every case a complete piece of dupery, by which the interest of the State and the nation is constantly sacrificed to that of the some particular class of traders. (15 December 1783)

The regulations of Commerce are commonly dictated by those who are most interested to deceive and impose upon the Public. (1 November 1785)[70]

These passages hint at *The Wealth of Nations'* overarching response to the European path. If European history leads to the collusion of sovereign power and commercial wealth, Smith pulled the brake on history by revealing such collusion as its end. His thought does not, in other words, apologize for any past, present, or future configuration of markets but rather analyzes the genealogy, structure, and consequences of the global system, which intrinsically militates against any equitable configuration. This analysis is both a theoretical and a practical response, because it aims to produce, in opposition to state-corporate hegemony, a "Public" that thinks for itself, as each of the previous quotations attests. Whereas Smith aligned merchant rule with Draco, he aligned his own vision with Solon, the legislator who rewrote Draconian Law. According to Smith, Solon aimed to establish not the ideal law but merely "the best which the interests, prejudices, and temper of the times would admit of."[71] Smith's proposals to reform the British Empire presumed not to create an ideal society but only to "prepare the way for a better" (543).

We leftist scholars now say that the history of capital looks different from the peripheries. We might feel heartened to realize that more than two centuries earlier the author we take to be capital's master apologist argued that it did not look all that appealing in the center either. For him, the periphery revealed only more nakedly the essence of this history. *The Wealth of Nations* suggests that the images of degeneration that represented British India during the Enlightenment recognize the "unnatural" logic that governs European history and the global economy alike. British India was important for Smith because it brought into relief problems that turn out to be deep—in fact inherent—in the European histories of capital, the state, and their common origins. Smith's historical vision does not presuppose that progress is immanent in European development; he aligned the principle of free trade not with that path but rather with its critique. If *The Wealth of Nations* calls on the circulation of capital to fix the problems of European history, it does so understanding that the value of free trade lies in its always-latent potential to oppose monopoly's devastating and ever-present actuality.

Bentham's Universal Law

Perhaps it is no coincidence that the Enlightenment figure other than Smith most identified with modern political economy also responded to the Bengal famine. In a discussion the scholarship on him rarely references, Jeremy Bentham—often described as Smith's disciple—invoked the "millions" who "were swept off" in the famine and then alluded to the East India Company's explanation of their catastrophic deaths: "The famine . . . was owing, let us hope, to no other cause than the inclemency of the seasons, or the insuperable difficulties attending a new system of government."[72] Bentham pretended here to take the Company at its word, but his discretion was sly; later in the same essay, he blamed Company rule for Bengal's ruin: "If that country has hitherto escaped absolute destruction; if the lust of power, and the thirst of riches, have hitherto been kept within any tolerable bounds; we must attribute it to the force of the moral, not that of the political sanction; to manners, and not to laws" (187).

Since Stokes's magisterial study *The English Utilitarians and India*, generations of scholars have taken for granted the relationship between utilitarianism and British India, a relationship that shapes our understanding of both terms. The received account tells us that after the appointment of William Bentinck as governor-general of India in 1833, utilitarianism became the foundation of colonial law, and colonial India in turn became utilitarianism's laboratory.[73] The nexus of utilitarianism and colonial rule, first tested in India, would subsequently be tried in other parts of the empire. When our account returns to the origins of this nexus, it always discovers Bentham's ghostly figure waiting there, dictating the action from beyond his grave: "Mill will be the living executive—I shall be the dead legislative of British India."[74] This pronouncement echoes across the scholarly generations, handed down in some form from Bowring through Stephen and Stokes to Said, Winch, and Mehta, among others.[75] Along the way, Bentham became the symbol of an Enlightenment reason so sure of its rectitude that it presumed to rule in the absence of popular representation.[76] Said, for example, observed that "the influence of Bentham . . . on British rule in the Orient (and India particularly) . . . stressed the rational importance of a strong executive branch with various legal and penal codes, a system of doctrines on such matters as frontiers and land rents, and everywhere an irreducible supervisory, imperial authority."[77] Or, even more baldly, the words of Thompson: Bentham and Mill were "eager to impose administrative occidental despotism upon the East."[78]

Bentham's response to the famine forces us to reconsider the relationship of utilitarianism and colonial rule, seeing it not from an early nineteenth-century perspective, when utilitarianism was already ascendant, but rather from its late eighteenth-century origins. Bentham's allusions to the famine occur in one of the nearly countless manuscripts he chose not to publish, "Essay on the Influence of Time and Place in Matters of Legislation." Composed in 1782, it was first published, in French, only in 1802; the English original was finally published in 1843.[79] Though it was unquestionably the first utilitarian text about India, the critical literature has neglected the essay and, by extension, the Indian context of Bentham's thought, even while claiming that he arrogated to himself the right to make law for India.[80] In context, the essay makes clear that his thought, no less than Smith's, was a reaction *against* global political economy. Just as we rethought the function of "free trade" in Smith's work, so we can "universal law" in Bentham's, seeing it not as an apology for the global order but rather as the principle of its permanent critique.

Composed during the intense climate of reform that characterized the early 1780s, when the American Revolution called British imperial principles into question, the "Essay" critiques East India Company rule and reflects Bentham's general project to imagine a universal law the truly global empires of his time could apply across their breadth, "a common standard, by which the several systems of law prevailing in every country may respectively be compared."[81] It is therefore an addendum to the *Principles of Morals and Legislation*, a "universal jurisprudence" that aimed to replace English common law with a single, rational system concerned to maximize collective welfare.

Bentham chose Bengal as his test case in the "Essay" because Parliament's 1781 Administration of Justice Regulation demanded the East India Company articulate a law for Bengal in line with English standards; the Company had just begun the process when Bentham composed his essay. This effort—to create a state for conquered populations that were manifestly not British—was, Cohn observed, "without precedent in British constitutional history."[82] The "Essay" reveals how deeply Bentham had already immersed himself in the endeavor, since it footnotes not only Scrafton's *Reflections on the Government of Indostan* and Verelst's *View of the English Government in Bengal* but also two recondite tomes even the most avid colonial experts would have been hard-pressed to read, the *East India Reports of the House of Commons* (1772) and the *House of Commons Reports on East India Affairs* (1781). The "Essay" refers to such arcane points of contemporary East India affairs as the bribing of Mahomed Reza Cawn (176), the death of Lord Pigot, and the subsequent execution of Nundakumar (187).[83]

But Bentham claimed to have chosen Bengal as the test case for a universal law also because it was, according to him, England's antithesis in all significant respects. He referred to differences in geography, natural resources, climate, demography, jurisprudence, manners, customs, and religion, concluding finally that in "every circumstance, on which a difference . . . can be grounded" Bengal and England are "as different as can be" (172). Bengal was therefore his greatest imaginable challenge: "To a lawgiver, who having been bred up with English notions, shall have learnt how to accommodate his laws to the circumstances of Bengal, no other part of the globe can present a difficulty" (172). Once Bentham created a law for Bengal, his jurisprudence would effectively accommodate the full range of human diversity.

Yet, during the course of the "Essay," Bentham's focus undergoes an odd shift. Whereas the first part of the text describes fundamental differences between England and Bengal, the alien world the second part describes ceases to be Bengal and becomes instead British society in Bengal. Its defining characteristics turn out to be political and economic corruption: "The passion of avarice has implanted among the inhabitants of the English race in Bengal, two evil propensities: a propensity to practise extortion, to the prejudice of the subjected Asiatics [e.g., the collection of rent during famine]; and a propensity to practice peculation, to the prejudice of the public revenue [e.g., private monopolies on grain]. Hence arises a sort of tacit convention and combination on the part of every man, to support, assist, and protect every other in the practice of like enormities" (178–79). The shift in focus implies that English law has failed in Bengal not because it is insensitive to cultural difference but rather because it is amenable to corporate corruption: Company servants have made English law the instrument of their private interests. Bentham observed that for "the poor Hindoo" who sought justice in the face of such corruption but received only the "wanton and ridiculous vexations" of English law, it must have appeared "a deliberate plan for forcing him to deliver himself up . . . into the hands of the European professional blood-suckers" (187).

Ultimately, then, Bentham's shift of focus from Bengal to British society in Bengal enabled him to present his law as "universal" in the sense not that it accommodated all human difference but that it responded to a problem that suddenly spanned the globe: the corruption intrinsic to British mercantile rule, which rendered English customary law inadequate. From his analysis of colonial Bengal, Bentham "la[id] down the following propositions: 1st, That the English law is a great part of it such a nature, as to be bad every where: 2d, But that it would not only be, but appear worse in Bengal than in England: 3d, That a system might be devised, which, while it would be better for Bengal, would also be better even for England" (185). Bentham's "conclusion" here is, of course, the a priori premise that motivated all his jurisprudence—that is, far from being universally applicable, English law is universally invalid: "Enquire in East, West, South. . . . Enquire in Hindostan, in the West Indies, in South Africa, in Canada, in New Holland, in Mauritius, in Saint Helena, in the Seven Islands, over which, on pretence of protection, our rulers have extended their own yet rotten sceptre."[84] The order of Bentham's propositions implies that his desire to articulate a universal law followed from a prior desire to critique English common law's own universal pretensions. In contrast to that law, Bentham intended his law to oppose, not abet, the political economy of the British Empire.

According to Bentham, the "intrinsic defects" (185) of English common law included the fact not only that it was "a mass of nonsense and gibberish" but equally that "no efficient means of punishing the high officers of government are provided there" (187). He noted that "the standing principle" of the common law is that "the king is every thing" (187); the problem for him—indeed not only with English common law but with law as such—was that it aimed to preserve sovereign power, however corrupt it may have been.[85] Mercantile rule made this defect overwhelmingly evident: "A conquering republic is more oppressive to the conquered country than a conquering monarch: a monarch . . . is interested in preventing the exactions of his officers: in a republic, on the other hand . . . there exist[s] a tacit collusion among those that [possess] authority" (176). Bentham claimed that the experience of Bengal, "too fatal not to be severely felt, and too manifest to be dissembled," revealed the defect (185). In other words, the famine drew attention to the ungoverned agents of modern sovereignty: exclusive groups who use their privileged access to political power and armed force to pursue their private interests with devastating consequences.

Though Thompson and Said associate Bentham with the colonial state, his jurisprudence was organized, ironically, against it. Colonial Bengal is an essential context for Bentham's thought, because it exhibited the political economy he was reacting against in its most naked form. Echoing Smith, Bentham claimed that East India Company rule was "by far the worst constituted species of government conceivable": "a fluctuating body of merchants . . . residing at the opposite end of the world."[86] His aim was to formulate a law that would not shelter mercantile sovereignty but instead criminalize its typical forms of corruption. For example, after apparently taking the Company at its word on the famine, Bentham continued: "Without legislative precautions, a similar effect might perhaps be produced by the abuse of delegated power in that distant member of the British Empire" (175).

The energy behind Bentham's work lies not in the discovery of the perfect law but rather in the ceaseless disentangling of law from sovereign power. His expressed desire to be the "dead legislative of British India" was in fact ironic, as Pitts has convincingly argued. The quotation continues: "Twenty years after I am dead, I shall be a despot, sitting in my chair with Dapple [his walking stick] in my hand, and wearing one of the coats I wear now."[87] Our received accounts of Bentham have misplaced his irony—that is, his desire to think *against* the "despotism" intrinsic to European political economy and jurisprudence. His texts were, after all, critiques of the present—not what we have turned them into, the discourse of colonial rule.

The "Essay" does, however, conclude with a panegyric to the perfect law: "The laws have reached the maximum of their perfection, . . . when nations, having laid aside their arms and disbanded their armies by mutual agreement, . . . shall only pay almost imperceptible taxes: when commerce shall be free, so that what may be done by many, shall not be restricted exclusively to a small number; and when oppressive taxes, prohibitions, and bounties, shall not prevent its natural development" (193–94). The crimes Bentham's law opposes—war, monopoly, and the taxes necessary to finance them both—involve the collapsing of trade and sovereignty into each other. While Bentham did indeed presuppose that atomism is the precondition of modern politics, he opposed the mercantile state's attempt to turn that atomism away from the common welfare, toward its own. Thus, he aligned his law with capital's potential *against* its history. Like Smith, he pushed the logic of capital to its limit, articulating a set of legal principles intended to ensure that no exclusive group could monopolize it.

By virtue of the reforms the Administration of Justice Regulation set in train, colonial India became the model of universal reason that the British Empire disseminated across the globe. From the perspective of liberal thought, the British state had solved the paradox of devising an English law appropriate to Bengal. But Bentham felt otherwise and continued to insist that Britain surrender its colonies.[88] With the 1793 Act of Permanent Settlement, the British state began to model imperial reason not initially on any version of utilitarianism but on a Whig theory of property instead. It was, in other words, not a law organized against the abuse of sovereign power but rather an alliance of sovereign power and aristocratic capitalism that governed the empire's new development regime. Even after the 1813 Charter Act, when the forces of liberal reform finally gained access to colonial India, Bentham continued to condemn British rule as a "local monarchy."[89]

When utilitarianism finally began to shape colonial policy in India, the year *after* Bentham died, it had little in common with his philosophy. In fact, while Company officials aligned themselves with liberal and utilitarian ideology, they did not actually adopt Smith and Bentham's reforms but adhered to the historical patterns Smith and Bentham had critiqued. What we now refer to as nineteenth-century "free-trade" imperialism occurred until 1857 under the auspices, paradoxically, of Company rule. Throughout this period, the Company hewed to its original economic premises: control over trade is a sovereign prerogative, and labor deserves only its subsistence—precisely the premises that in Smith's view characterized European history and merchant capital, respectively.[90] Hence, though the 1813 Charter Act repealed the Company's monopoly on East Indian trade, the Company did not liberate markets but instead employed its military power to enforce both its commercial monopolies and its new, crushing system of rent collection (the Raiyatwari Settlement). At the same time, Company officials used the effective immunity they enjoyed in the colonies to redirect both commercial profit and property taxes away from state coffers to private hands: colonial law remained an instrument of sovereign corruption and economic privatization, as Bentham had observed. The unification of commercial and sovereign functions gave the Company an unprecedented capacity not only to withhold surplus from labor but also to accumulate capital without even investing in native productive forces. As a consequence, the Indian economy stagnated throughout the nineteenth century.

When we return Smith and Bentham to this context, we rediscover what was explosive in their thought. The point is, of course, not to deny its severe limitations: *The Wealth of Nations* and the "Essay" concern imperial reform, not anti-imperial revolution. The point is rather to recognize where these texts' critical distance from global modernity is greater than our own. When Smith and Bentham described European and colonial history in terms of the collusion of sovereign power and monopoly capital rather than the development of free trade or universal law, they laid a charge every bit as incendiary now as it was then.

5

NATION AND ADDICTION
Burke's and Sheridan's Speeches
in the Hastings Impeachment

The Heads of villages [were] tied together by the feet, . . . thrown over a bar, and there
beaten with bamboo canes upon the soles of their feet until their nails started from
their toes. . . . Falling upon them, . . . with sticks and cudgels, their tormentors attacked
them with such blind fury that the blood ran out of their mouths, eyes and noses. . . .
   . . . But, my Lords, there was more. Virgins whose fathers kept them from the sight
of the sun, were dragged into the public Court. . . . There in the presence of day, . . .
while their shrieks were mingled with the cries and groans of an indignant people, those
virgins were violated by the basest and wickedest of mankind. It did not end there. The
wives . . . differed only in this; that they lost their honour in the bottom of the most
cruel dungeons. . . . But they were dragged out, naked and exposed to the public view,
and scourged before all the people. . . . But it did not end there. . . . They put the nipples
of the women into the sharp edges of split bamboos and tore them from their bodies.
Grown from ferocity to ferocity, from cruelty to cruelty, they applied burning torches
and cruel slow fires (My Lords, I am ashamed to go further); those infernal fiends, in
defiance of every thing divine and human, planted death in the source of life.
   —Edmund Burke's testimony before the House of Lords about the methods
           used to extract taxes from the peasants of Rangpur (18 February 1788)[1]

Edmund Burke's *Reflections on the Revolution in France* (1790) offered a seminal
resolution to the dilemma of modern civil society: How can a community composed of private individuals each pursuing his own interests remain coherent?
According to the *Reflections*, if civil society is to avoid degenerating to savagery,
its ethics must remain rooted in national traditions, even as its economy is reoriented toward the market. While Burke accepted that commerce is the driving
force behind civil progress, he argued that commercial development becomes
anarchic when not informed by the nation's organic morality. Founded on the
twin pillars of church and aristocracy, the *Reflections*' concept of the nation famously became the basis of modern conservative thought in works like Russell

Kirk's *The Conservative Mind* (1953).[2] In recent years, postcolonial scholars such as Mehta, Gibbons, and Deane have taken up Burke's idea of the nation again, recasting its conservatism as a defense of singular, residual histories against a universal colonial reason.[3]

The focus on Burke's alleged belief in the nation, which ironically unites conservative and postcolonial scholars, needs to deemphasize the various aspects of his thought and life that call the nation into question. For example, Burke's premise that the nation originates in violence is much more deeply embedded in his vision of European history than his putative faith in church or aristocracy.[4] Furthermore, he devoted much of his professional career before the *Reflections* to rooting aristocratic corruption out of the state. A reading of Burke that accounted for these facts would need to reconsider the function "nation" serves in his thought, if not to valorize supposedly organic traditions. Such a reading might explain Burke's withering remarks about the British nation in his most extensive writing: not his aesthetic inquiry nor his analysis of the French Revolution but rather his parliamentary speeches and reports about British India, which occupy three volumes of his collected works. In regard to them, Burke declared at the very end of his life: "Let my endeavours to save the nation from that shame and guilt be my monument; the only one that I ever will have. Let everything I have done, said or written, be forgotten but this."[5]

From 1781, when Burke was appointed to head the House of Commons Select Committee on East Indian Affairs, until 1795, when the House of Lords acquitted former governor-general of India Warren Hastings of the charges Burke had brought against him, investigating India was Burke's primary professional obligation. In the process of heading the Select Committee, Burke became utterly expert in the arcane details of Indian affairs. In a way that the French Revolution never could, colonial India manifested for Burke the global economy's irresistible pull on the nation. This economy had arisen long before the Revolution and, as Burke emphasized, had already eroded the nation's pillars, in particular its moral sense.[6] In Burke's Indian speeches, the imperial order replaces that sense: as the East India Company constructs a global economy founded on the physical coercion of colonial labor, the British nation-state grows addicted to the products of that economy, loses the capacity to judge its crimes, and becomes implicated in its violence. The real complexity of Burke's attitude toward the nation comes into view against the background of colonial India; his texts on the subject exceed the Burkean concept of the nation.

But ironically, the now substantial body of scholarship on Burke and India—for example, Suleri (1992), Mehta (1999), Pitts (2005), and Dirks (2006)—has not altered our understanding of what fundamental terms like "nation" or "moral sense" meant to Burke. It has instead taken such terms at face value, reading his professed sympathy for the colonized as either a critique of imperialism or, conversely, a call for liberal imperialism.[7] This chapter contends—*pace* those who presuppose that Burke stood for national traditions against an abstract modernity or for moral sympathy against colonial iniquity—that he in fact placed no faith in either the nation or the moral sense: rather than conceive them as political resources, he treated them with extreme suspicion. The subtlety of Burke's thought lies precisely in how it uses such idealized categories only to empty them out in the end.

Burke staged his speeches in the Hastings impeachment as a series of theatrical performances expressing sentimentalized outrage at the East India Company's crimes: he hoped such performances would compel a nation bereft of moral sense to mimic it. Burke understood the nation to be based no longer in any set of organic traditions but rather only in such acts of imitation: the "nation" existed for him only rhetorically. His understanding of the nation as a rhetorical construct forces us to reconsider received interpretations of his thought. The following discussion suggests that at its deepest level Burke's use of the term "nation" did not advocate the national histories either of the colonizer or of the colonized but instead registered a global system that had corrupted both histories alike. Burke's nuanced understanding of imperial political economy ironized the very idea of nation and in doing so—I argue—comprehended the advent of a truly global modernity.[8]

The initial three sections of this chapter demonstrate how Burke's Indian writings employ his idea of the nation. The first discusses Burke's argument, prefiguring his subsequent condemnation of the French Revolution, that East India Company rule separated the nation from its "ancient constitution." The second explores Burke's allegation that the Hastings administration had consequently precipitated national degeneration within India. The third studies Burke's claim that the Company's influence in Parliament—which he considered to be the British nation's emblematic institution—threatened to import national degeneration from India back to Britain itself.

The final three sections disclose how Burke's Indian writings dismantle his idea of the nation piece by piece. The fourth focuses on Burke's private comments that Parliament was already so complicit with the Company that it could not be trusted with the impeachment. Burke attempted, therefore, to bypass Parliament and appeal directly to the British people, the only "nation" remaining after Parliament's corruption. In order to excavate Burke's actual view of this nation, the fifth section analyzes the previously unstudied parliamentary report he wrote on the opium trade, which he believed implicated the British public and Parliament alike in colonial violence. According to Burke, the nation-state's dependence on the global drug trade had already dissevered it from its ancient constitution. The sixth part argues that Burke's rhetoric appealed, as a consequence, not to the British public's moral sense but to its mimetic capacities: he treated the British nation not as a civil society, but—he confessed privately—as a mob. His rhetorical strategies make clear that he himself did not believe his theory of the nation.

Nation-State and Merchant-Colony

In 1786, twenty-one years after the East India Company had established British rule in India, Edmund Burke moved in the House of Commons to impeach Warren Hastings (governor-general of India, 1773–85) for the crimes his administration had committed in India, which Burke alleged included the violation of property, the destruction of native institutions, and the dishonoring of native women (6:77). After the Commons voted for his motion, Burke began the impeachment itself before the Lords in 1788, joined in the prosecution by Whig leader Charles James Fox and Richard Brinsley Sheridan, manager of Drury Lane Theatre and the most important dramatist of the period. London's fashionable society bought tickets to the four-day speech with which Burke opened the impeachment as if attending the theater. The speech drew a rapt, standing-room-only audience that included such prominent literary figures as Horace Walpole, Edward Gibbon, and Frances Burney. Burke brought the impeachment to a close six years later with an even longer nine-day "Speech in Reply." Referred to as "the greatest public sensation of the seventeen-eighties," the impeachment brought more attention than any other early modern event to Britain's relationship with colonial India.[9]

The impeachment concluded two decades of controversy around the East India Company: the 1766–67, 1772–73, and 1784 parliamentary investigations had each set out to determine why the Company had been unable to turn conquest into profit and the extent to which its employees had embezzled its revenue. But the origins of the vexed relationship between civil society and merchant imperialism lie further back, at the end of the sixteenth and the beginning of the seventeenth centuries, when European states first chartered East India companies and granted them sovereign powers, including the right to build fortresses, raise armies, make war, and govern European and native populations alike. This largely unprecedented transfer of sovereignty to private citizens effectively made Europe's overseas colonies experiments in civil society.[10]

The scholarship on Burke typically reads his political thought as a response to the French Revolution.[11] But because of the history just mentioned, colonial India makes more sense as the matrix of Burke's thought than the Revolution does; in any case, his analysis of the former precedes his analysis of the latter. His discussions of colonial India focus on the fact that private citizens assumed sovereign powers there. In this regard, his analysis resembles both Smith's and Bentham's, no doubt deriving in part from his reading of *The Wealth of Nations*, whose argument, Burke noted, he agreed with in all essentials.[12] Like Smith, Burke insisted that Company employees were not qualified to wield sovereign power because they lacked a public character. Alluding to the profiteering on grain that had occurred under the Company's purview and had led, at a minimum, to hundreds of thousands dead during the 1770–71 famine, Smith exclaimed: "How unjustly, how capriciously, how cruelly [the merchant companies] have commonly exercised [their sovereign rights], is too well known from recent experience."[13] Smith argued that the Company's interests were not continuous with India's interests but "directly opposite" to them, since merchant corporations inherently want to limit production to what they can themselves transport and sell, while the commonwealth depends instead on increasing circulation, production, and remuneration.[14] Burke noted, in the same vein, that the interests of the merchants who composed the East India Company were "separated both from the Country that sent them out and from the Country in which they are" (6:286).

In his critique of the East India Company, Smith insisted that there was a fundamental distinction between the sovereign and the merchant: "The [merchant] profession . . . in no country in the world carries along with it that sort of authority which naturally over-awes the people, and without force commands their willing obedience. . . . A council [of merchants] can command obedience only by the military force with which [it is] accompanied, and [its] government is therefore necessarily military and despotical."[15] Echoing Smith, Burke noted that the conceptual distinction between sovereign and merchant was nearly as old as Western political philosophy itself. He said that when the Company seized political power in 1757, "it became that thing which was supposed by the Roman Law so unsuitable, the same power was a Trader, the same power was a Lord" (6:283). Where Smith noted that Company rule made "government subservient to the interest of monopoly," Burke declared that the Company's government in India was "a State in disguise of a Merchant, a great public office in disguise of a Countinghouse" (6:283).[16]

Burke departed from Smith and Bentham only in a single salient point: against the degenerative tendencies of merchant rule, he offered not the logic of capital taken beyond the limits of mercantilism but rather the nation's traditional institutions. The *Reflections* famously located civil society's origins in the nation's ancient constitution.[17] According to the *Reflections*, the Glorious Revolution "was made to preserve our *antient* indisputable laws and liberties, and that *antient* constitution of government which is our only security for law and liberty" (8:271). An ancient constitution must be the basis of civil society, in Burke's view, because it alone reflects the nation's particular concepts of rights. A nation-state modeled on an ancient constitution is as close as humanity can get in Burke's thought to its prefallen condition, when natural law was transparent. The *Reflections* declared that Providence "willed . . . the necessary means of [human nature's] perfection—He willed therefore the state—He willed its connection with the source and original archetype of all perfection" (8:148).[18]

Burke's speeches in the impeachment argued for the importance of aligning state and nation before the *Reflections*. He went to great lengths to insist that India possessed its own ancient constitution, that it was a nation, and that it possessed a moral sense: "[The people of India] have laws; [rights;] and immunities, . . . they feel for honour, not only as much as your Lordships can feel for it [but] with a more exquisite and poignant sense than any people upon earth" (7:264–65). Ironically, Burke's knowledge of the Indian "ancient constitution" came almost entirely from the Orientalist scholarship Hastings himself had commissioned in order to shield himself from metropolitan criticism like Burke's that his administration was insensitive to Indian traditions.[19] Regardless of the irony, Burke argued that British rule in Bengal must work a "revolution" in the literal sense the 1688 settlement supposedly had, a turning back to or reconstruction of the nation's ancient constitution as the basis of its state. Noting that Bengal had been subject to native misrule, he observed that "it would have been a great deal to say that [the East India Company] came from the bosom of a free country, [carrying] with it . . . the liberty and spirit of a British constitution" (6:315).

But it "happened otherwise," Burke commented early in his opening speech; "it is now for us to think how we are to repair it" (6:315). Throughout the period that he headed the Commons Select Committee, Burke insisted that India should be governed by the British nation-state, not by a private corporation. He condemned Company rule in India because, in contrast to all previous empires, it was bereft of a national character: "When the Tartars entered into China and into Hindoostan, when all the Goths and Vandals entered into Europe, when the Normans came into England, they came as a Nation. The Company in India does not exist as a Nation" (6:285). The logic of Burke's speeches turns, above all, on this premise: Company rule had dissevered sovereign power from national traditions. If the Company's private monopoly on India had displaced it from the narrative of civil progress, unifying nation-state and colony would reintegrate India into history.

Nation v. Hastings

The efficacy of Burke's speeches in the prosecution would ultimately depend on his ability to make Hastings the embodiment of the Company's private interests. If Burke succeeded in doing so, it would be incumbent on the nation to prosecute Hastings, since those interests threatened national traditions not only in Bengal but also in England itself. In the binary opposition Burke articulated between the nation-state and the merchant-colony, he drew, as we have seen, on eighteenth-century political economy and political theory. But he borrowed the central trope around which he fashioned the impeachment—Hastings as a "decomposed civil being"—from the sentimental fiction about the nabob that preceded the trial.[20] Agnes Maria Bennett's *Anna, or the Memoirs of a Welch Heiress, Interspersed with Anecdotes of a Nabob* (1785) was among the most prominent of these texts.[21] As Burke would subsequently do with Hastings, Bennett placed her nabob—who is fathered by an "Irish adventurer, equally destitute of property, character, or principle"—in an adversarial relationship to the nation.[22] It follows from the fact that an adventurer fathers the nabob that he in turn develops a tendency toward "vicious pleasures" and "cruelty," becoming "a character the most complicated and contemptible of the human species," who "in no one voluntary act of his life [forgot] to conduct himself so as . . . to further his own interest."[23]

Historically, those who had been disenfranchised within Britain and hence turned to predation in the colonies did in fact occupy the lower rungs of the Company hierarchy.[24] The late eighteenth-century satire of the nabob as someone who attempts to efface his class origins by ostentatious shows of colonial wealth expressed the general awareness that Company servants tended to come from the lower classes. They appeared, as a consequence, to be dissociated from the property that classical republicanism claimed made men masters, provided them the leisure necessary to enter public service, and gave them political virtue.[25] But they seemed, at the same time, to be dissociated from the urban manners that Whig ideology claimed merchants gained by means of their participation in exchange relationships and consumer activities. Hence, the individuals who created the British Empire in India were thought to be beyond the pale of the nation even before they arrived in Asia.

Bennett's nabob welcomes his posting to British India, a "country where rape and murders are tolerated acts" and so one "less unpropitious [than Europe] to the free indulgence of the passions."[26] Once he arrives in India, "he [gives] a loose to the excesses of his nature, . . . adding avarice to the black catalogue of his vices."[27] Precisely because the colony lacks a civil society, it allows the merchant to degenerate to his natural "love of dominion." Burke followed Bennett in claiming that colonial India was the antithesis of civil society and, as a consequence, reinforced the worst aspects of the merchant's nature. He insisted that Hastings was known "in no other character than that of being a Bullock Contractor for some years, being fraudulent in that transaction, and afterwards giving fraudulent Contracts to others" (7:286). The colonies had merely brought out the viciousness intrinsic to Hastings, "a man bred in obscure, vulgar, and ignoble occupations and trained in sordid, base, and mercenary habits" (7:383).

Burke's speeches describe Hastings's moral degeneracy and antinational character ad nauseam, on the premise that these qualities proved his administration corrupt.[28] Burke portrayed Hastings while he sat before the Lords, for example, as incapable of showing them the deference they deserved: "We shall not in the whole history of parliamentary trials find anything similar to the demeanour of the prisoner at your bar . . . a want of decorum; an habitual depravity of mind, that has no sentiments of propriety, nor feeling for the relations of life."[29] Hinting at Hastings's class origins, Burke considered his supposed irreverence before the Lords evidence of a fundamental incivility ("an habitual depravity of mind"), because to be civilized, Burke implies, means to respect national traditions, chief among them the aristocracy. Hastings's lack of deference implies that he is bereft of the affections—"decorum," "sentiments of propriety," "feeling for the relations of life"—that are the nation's basis. Burke generalized his description of Hastings to the Company's servants in general, claiming that "such minds placed in authority . . . treat all ranks and distinctions with more pride, insolence, and arrogance, than those who have been born under canopies of state and swaddled in purple."[30]

Burke intended Hastings's supposed insolence toward the British aristocracy to corroborate the allegation that under Hastings's guidance, the Company had destroyed the institutions of Indian civil society. The largest part of Burke's speeches described the Company's subversion of three such institutions: land, markets, and government (immovable property, movable property, and the institution that guarantees the security of property). In each case, Burke portrayed the same kind of revolution: the Company replaced an ancient constitution that inscribed the wisdom of the past with a novel system that reflected the logic of mercantilism alone. Where Burke had hoped colonial rule would make India's ancient rights once again constitutional, passed down from generation to generation as an inviolable inheritance, the Company had instead effaced these rights with its own despotism, provoking the degeneration of civil society to the state of war.

The passage that appears at the beginning of this chapter—containing the graphic description of the Company torturing peasants unable to pay its exorbitant tax demands—was the most spectacular moment of the trial.[31] In the words of one historian, it "overwhelm[ed] [Burke's] audience with the horror of what he was describing."[32] Burke's descriptions of the Company agents emphasize that they have abandoned their civil selves and returned to savagery. The Company agents manifest their moral degeneracy in the most stereotypical ways imaginable: by means of cruelty, torture, and rape, the antitheses of the sympathetic relations that were supposed to bind civil society together.

But each of these acts also assaults an institution that, in Burke's view, was essential to the nation. First, the Company agents attack the native aristocracy: they torture "the Heads of villages," tying them "together by the feet," throwing them "over a bar," and beating them "with bamboo canes upon the soles of their feet until their nails started from their toes." Second, the agents violate the honor of native women, thereby inverting the chivalric values Burke insisted must regulate commercial society.[33] The tendency of the passage is to render public space uncivil, to turn even broad daylight into a gothic setting: "Virgins whose fathers kept them from the sight of the sun, were dragged into the public Court. . . . There in the presence of day, . . . [they] were violated by the basest and wickedest of mankind"; "[wives] were dragged out, naked and exposed to the public view, and scourged before all the people." The passage implies that Company rule makes the private interests of a decomposed civil self the only basis of public life. In the starkest terms imaginable, the merchant colony reverses the history of civil progress, returning the nation to barbarism.

A final point about Burke's opposition between national civilization and merchant barbarism: the nation his speeches concern is, in the end, not India but Britain. Marshall has argued that for Burke, "the possession of an Indian empire set off a deadly struggle between 'the force of money' and the 'preservation of our manners—of our virtues.'"[34] In line with Marshall's argument, Burke claimed that if the British were to preserve their own national character, the impeachment would be essential: he called it "a great *censorial* prosecution—for preserving the integrity, the purity, the noble simplicity of manners which used to characterise this Nation" (7:61–62). We could note Burke's equivocation here about whether the national character to which he referred has survived into the present or is merely a thing of the past. But his description of the impeachment implies nonetheless that the Company's ethical degeneracy threatened Britain's moral sense.[35]

Corruption

Having spent some decades as "the terror of the inhabitants of the East," Bennett's nabob returns to England, bringing with him the "disorders he had contracted in India."[36] The narrative energy that the figure of the nabob provides the sentimental fiction about returned Company servants stems not from what he has done in India but what he threatens to do in Britain. Bennett's nabob attempts to rape the governess of the estate in which *Anna* takes place. Less spectacularly, he "purchase[s] a borough, and b[uys] off the petitioning opponent; he [takes] his seat in the senate, and ma[kes] a speech *there*," always working outside "English laws," which are "the dread and hatred of his soul."[37]

Like the sentimental novelists who focused on British India, Burke had a vivid sense of the crimes the nabobs committed in India, but his real concern was their effect on Britain. He claimed that merchant imperialism corrupted the nation-state by means, above all, of Parliament—the institution, ironically, in which he made the claim. When East India Company influence led to the defeat of Fox's 1783 India bills, which Burke is thought to have authored and which called for a parliamentary committee to supervise Company rule, he insinuated that colonial wealth had begun to corrupt Parliament.[38] He described the bills' defeat in apocalyptic terms, as if the Company's influence within Parliament augured the end of the nation as such: "Did [the nation] not already exhibit marks of [an] awful dereliction? Yes.—The country was devoted to destruction: th[e] House, the venerable palladium of its liberties, was annihilated: the Constitution had received a shock, which it would never recover" (5:468). When Pitt's 1784 India Act replaced Fox's more radical India bills, the Crown acquired the right to appoint the parliamentary committee that would oversee Company rule. Burke considered the India Act a "shock" to the constitution, since it effectively established a Crown-Company oligarchy.[39] These events signified to Burke the moment in which the "monied men" gained control of the British state, forcing it to reap what it had sowed when it gave them the license to pursue their ambitions without restraint across the empire.

If eighteenth-century authors such as Hume and Gibbon gleaned from classical history the lesson that the republic's acquisition of empire undermines its very foundation, Burke inferred that this process of degeneration begins, in particular, with the influence of colonial wealth on the senate.[40] Montesquieu's *The Spirit of the Laws* described such wealth as a contagion that inevitably inflicts metropolitan society as well.[41] Burke used the metaphor of disease to argue that East Indian wealth threatened to destroy the British Empire altogether: "The downfall of the greatest empire this world ever saw, has been, on all hands agreed upon to have originated in the mal-administration of its provinces. Rome never felt within herself the seeds of decline, till corruption from foreign misconduct impaired her vitals" (6:63). Rome's vital organ was its senate: corruption here is the most dangerous, "[a] Horrible and foul enormity, because it poisons in the very medicine" (6:63).

When Burke first called for a parliamentary commission to supervise Company rule, he declared to the Commons: "You will teach the people that live under you, that it is their interest to be your subjects; and that, instead of courting the French, the Dutch, the Danes, or any other state, under heaven, to protect them, they ought only be anxious to preserve their connection with you; because, from you only they had to expect public proceeding, public trial, public justice" (5:137–38). If, by means of publicity, Parliament ensures that the state expresses the nation's will, then parliamentary supervision of the colonial government would unify the nation and the empire for the first time.[42] Burke's argument was that parliamentary control alone would make the empire a projection of national principles.[43] But after the defeat of Fox's India bills, Burke claimed that Parliament had begun "to suppress disagreeable truths, to screen a notorious delinquency, and, by a shocking medley of sophistry, impudence, and vague declamation, impose on the People of England, and keep them in the dark" (5:474). According to Burke, imperial wealth introduced a disjunction between the state and the nation because it led Parliament to abandon its role as an instrument of publicity.

Burke described the nabobs' apparent seizure of Parliament as the first move by Britain's "men of mere profit" to confiscate landed property from its traditional owners.[44] The nabobs' acquisition of power was of the same order as the French Revolution, since it replaced property with a moneyed interest. Property relations constitute not merely "the present order of things" but also "the very being of society" (8:164), according to Burke, because they reflect the nation's historical development. To the extent that it transforms property relations, merchant imperialism disrupts the essential continuity between state and history, both for the colonized and the colonizers, creating a modernity in which an arbitrary will rules. In his final speech before the Lords, Burke insisted that "Jacobinism never can strike a more deadly blow . . . than your lordships, if you were to acquit [Hastings], would strike against your own dignity and the very being of the society in which we live" (8:164). At the close of the speech, he characterized the Hastings impeachment as "a sacred trust" (8:439) that could by itself stop national degeneration on a global scale. He declared: "Never before was a cause of such magnitude submitted to any human tribunal" (8:439).

"A great public proceeding"

But Burke did not in fact trust the tribunal to judge the trial. Although he treated the Lords with deference when he was before them, he acknowledged privately that parliamentary corruption was so far advanced it precluded the possibility of a fair trial: "We know that we bring before a bribed tribunal a prejudged cause."[45] Burke's private denigration of Parliament dictated the trial's public unfolding. He chose the unusual procedure of impeachment, which Parliament had not employed in more than seventy years, because it enabled him to turn colonial affairs into a public spectacle: the daily press printed his speeches in the impeachment for a national reading audience.[46] Burke hoped the impeachment would bring publicity to East India Company rule even after Parliament itself had become complicit with the Company. Believing that colonial wealth had hollowed out the nation's emblematic institution, Burke turned to the nation itself.

He intentionally made his speeches dramatic rather than legalistic, because he wanted to bypass the representatives and appeal to the represented; he sought the judgment less of the senate than of the civil subject.[47] This turned out to be a different kind of justice altogether.

Burke emphasized—again in private correspondence—that the impeachment's real court of appeal was public opinion, not the Lords: "If we proceed under the publick Eye, I have no more doubt than I entertain of my existence, that all the ability, influence and power that can accompany a decided partiality in that tribunal can[not] save our criminal from a condemnation followed by some ostensible measure of Justice."[48] When he appealed to the British "public eye" for some "measure of justice"—rather than to a House of Lords that he now associated with "influence"—Burke appeared to participate in what Habermas calls an Enlightenment tendency to oppose the public sphere to political domination.[49] But though Burke's language here might lead one to infer that he intended to appeal to a rational public sphere, his understanding of the public was more complex. He was confident that it would side with him, not because he believed in its commitment to the principles of civil society but because he intended to manipulate it.[50] The "public sphere" for Burke was not the space in which democratic association leads to the refinement of reason, but rather where people learn to *mimic* civility.

Burke claimed that in contrast to the corrupted Lords, the nation he represented possessed natural sympathy: "My Lords, the commons of Great Britain are a rustic people. A tone of rusticity is the proper accent of those whom we represent. We are not acquainted with the urbanity and politeness of extortion and oppression. We know nothing of the sentimental delicacies of bribery and corruption" (7:240). Burke's traditional nation had to be rustic because only in pristine isolation from the imperial economy could it preserve natural sympathy. But the people whom Burke addressed were of course completely urban, the various metropolitan communities that constituted the daily press's reading public. They were precisely those who according to Burke engaged in the "extortion" and "oppression" of colonial labor, however indirectly, and hence felt compelled to conceal these crimes behind euphemism and false sentiment. It follows, therefore, that the judgment for which Burke looked from this reading public would have to have its source in something other than natural sympathy.

In fact, Burke insinuated that the actual nation that constituted his reading public—in contrast to the rustic nation that was the starting point of his political theory and occupied such a prominent place on the surface of his rhetoric—was deeply implicated in the torture it was supposed to judge. This is Burke's account of the first method of torture used on the Rangpuri peasants: "[Company agents] crushed and maimed those poor, honest, laborious hands which never had been lifted to their own mouths but with the scanty supply of the product of their own labour. These are the hands [which have] furnished the investment for China from which your Lordships and all this auditory and all this Country have every day for these fifteen years made that luxurious meal with which we all commence the day" (6:419). Burke's reference to the English breakfast alludes not only to the Chinese tea for which the East India Company exchanged the commodities and capital they acquired in Bengal but also to imperial luxury items such as sugar, coffee, and chocolate. Burke turned the torturing of the peasants' hands into a synecdoche for the production of these reified luxuries from Europe's various imperial outposts. His account opposes a colonial peasantry that labors for its meals and hence whose taste remains simple to the metropolitan public, whose habit of luxury consumption has transformed its very physiology: exotic goods, the essential elements in the eighteenth-century's degenerative theories of history, were thought to increase individual rapacity and hence to corrupt the body politic.[51] If civil society is modeled on sympathy, an imperial economy—Burke insinuated—is founded on torture, the diametrically opposed form of human exchange.

Burke emphasized the English nation's insensitivity to the suffering of its Indian subjects: "I am informed [that] the people of England will reject me . . . for having taken up the cause of the injured and oppressed fellow subjects of the people of England in India; for attempting to procure an atonement to Indian nations, who have been scourged by their iniquitous servants . . . miserable public!" (6:62). He referred to anyone who could read the accounts of Indian suffering "without shuddering" as the "most savage or hardest heart" (5:471), the product of "a corrupt and degenerate age" (7:241). Such degeneracy originated, Burke explained, not only in luxury consumption but also in the wealth the nabobs had brought back to Britain: they had bribed "the English nation by . . . the countless [hundreds of thousands] of rupees, poured into it from India," "fortunes that . . . do not leave a single Parish in [this Kingdom] unoccupied by the party and faction of the Defendant, which he has made by the oppression of the people of India" (7:234).[52]

The East India Company's exploitation of Bengali labor returned to England in a different form, Burke argued, in the taxes the state levied to service the national debt:

As certainly as we had regarded the sufferings and grievances of the Indians without mercy, our punishment would come without mitigation. What are these men [pointing to the Treasury Bench]? Are they not the Ministers of vengeance to a guilty, a degenerated, and unthinking nation? Yes.—They are . . . commissioned by the Great Sovereign of the world, who hath destined them his scourge, in loading with such a series of oppressive taxes as have no example, a people whose unprincipled ambition ha[s] rendered them infamous in both extremities of the globe. (5:468–69)[53]

Having supported an insensate imperial economy, the nation now had no choice but to pay its military costs; having been unconcerned with the expropriation of Indian peasants, it would take their place in turn. Burke placed as little trust in the moral sense of the people as he did in the open deliberations of Parliament, regardless of what we have assumed about his idea of the nation. The judgment Burke looked for in the Hastings trial could not have its source in the nation's moral sense because it had been replaced by the political economy of merchant imperialism.

Addiction

Burke's descriptions of this economy articulate a concept of the nation much more historically acute than the one we typically attribute to him. For example, when Burke commented that the peasants whom the Company tortured produce the English public's breakfast, he alluded in an exceptionally nuanced way to economic relationships that were reconstructing the nation around colonial violence. As mentioned, Burke's comment directs his audience's attention to the habit-forming commodities that constitute the English breakfast—tea, coffee, and sugar. The success of European imperialism in the New World, Africa, and Asia alike ultimately depended on such commodities—not, as we might imagine, on subsistence goods (e.g., foodstuffs, wool, or even cotton) or on the three traditional classes of long-distance trade items (precious metals, luxury manufactures, and enslaved human beings).[54] Narcotics were uniquely valuable, because their addictive properties enabled them to generate mass markets across the globe and become sources of historically unprecedented profit.

Britain's much-vaunted commercial and industrial revolutions originated, we are often told, in the development of a complex exchange network that included Indian Ocean, European, and New World circuits.[55] But these revolutions were predicated, more precisely, on the addictions merchant imperialism spread throughout the network. Because of its predilections for coffee and tea, England ended up consuming more sugar than any other place in the world. When the British state imposed duties on sugar, it effectively profited from each of these addictions at once.[56] The New World slave colonies that produced mass-marketed drugs—tobacco and alcohol as well as sugar—became essential markets for British and East Indian manufactures. The British state and the East India Company tended to reinvest the unprecedented profits of these newly global addictions less in the expansion of trade than in the equally unprecedented costs of modern war, conquest, and rule. Only the radical redistribution of wealth the drug trade produced could provide the state and the corporation the capital they needed in this regard.

There was one drug—present but occulted in Burke's description—that was absolutely necessary for the English breakfast but that rarely came into the English public's view. Burke noted that the peasants' "poor, honest, laborious hands . . . furnished the investment for China." Here, "investment" is a polysemous term that refers to the various products of Indian labor (e.g., territorial revenue and cotton textiles) that the Company exchanged for Chinese tea, which was the most popular Asian commodity in Western markets. But in this context, investment refers in particular to what would eventually become the main exchange item for tea, opium from Bihar and Bengal. While the term "investment" is purposefully ambiguous, we can be certain that Burke had opium in mind, because he had prepared the Select Committee's *Ninth Report* (1783), which detailed the colonial origins of the opium trade and its transformation into a source of the China investment.[57] The *Ninth Report* repeatedly identifies the term "investment" with opium.[58]

The report even describes the itineraries opium followed from Bengal to Canton: (1) through "the Markets of . . . the Coast of Malacca . . . to be invested in Merchandize saleable in China, or in Dollars to be had"; and (2) "directly to the Port of Canton."[59] Both trade routes were central to European imperial expansion. Though the scholarship on mercantilism typically considers the possession of New World bullion to be the precondition of European trade with the East Indies, it was opium that enabled European merchants to reconstruct that trade in their favor. Bullion gave them access only to Chinese middlemen, not to Asian producers themselves; it did not enable them to disrupt the Chinese trading networks that dominated the South China Sea.[60] In contrast, opium gave them a commodity that Asian producers would eventually desire even more desperately than European consumers wanted Indian Ocean goods. Once their opium addictions made them depend on European traders, Southeast Asian consumers had little choice but to abandon gift economies for monetized ones, and Chinese peasants, diverse agrarian economies for one centered on tea. Opium compelled them, in other words, to enter modes of production that rendered them even more susceptible to the pressure of merchant imperialism.

The Company recognized opium's effects: in fact, it considered opium to be poison, as both its official records and the *Ninth Report* document.[61] Not only did it initially refuse to sanction its servants' long-standing involvement in the opium trade within India but, as a consequence of the Qing state's ban on opium importation, it prohibited its ships from carrying opium from Bengal to its Canton Factory. But opium's illicit character only made it more attractive to Company servants trading privately, as the *Ninth Report* recognizes: "[Objects] of Export and Import were left open to young Men without mercantile Experience, and wholly unprovided with mercantile Capitals; but abundantly furnished with large Trusts of the Public Money, and with all the Powers of an absolute Government. In this Situation, a religious abstinence from all illicit Gain was prescribed to Men at Nine thousand Miles Distance from the Seat of Supreme Authority."[62] Burke insinuated here, as throughout the *Ninth Report*, that the Company was set up not to generate corporate profit but rather to enable private expropriation. Company servants tended to make their first fortunes in the opium trade, which became the most lucrative in Bengal despite the fact that it was outside the Company's purview.[63]

As soon as Hastings became governor-general of India (1773), he brought Bengali and Bihari opium into the Company's portfolio, making it a Company monopoly and subsequently an essential part of the China investment.[64] Hastings's professed intent was to prevent the servants from enriching themselves at the Company's expense. But monopoly drug trade of its nature generates a profit so lucrative that it tempts the individuals involved to embezzle it. In this case, as the *Ninth Report* observes, the corruption began at the highest levels. In 1781, Hastings himself gave the contract to manage the opium monopoly to a personal friend, Stephen Sullivan, who also happened to be the son of the East India Company chairman. Sullivan subsequently sold the contract to another Company servant, as if it were a commodity he had bought, thereby earning

£40,000 labor-free. In the "Speech on Fox's India Bill," Burke alluded to Sullivan's contract in order to emphasize that the Company's raison d'être was to enable its servants to expropriate public revenue:

> The stock is of no value. . . . Of what value is that, whether it rise to ten, or fall to six, or to nothing, to him whose son, before he is in Bengal two months . . . sells the grant of a single contract for forty thousand pounds? . . . All the relations of the Company are not only changed, but inverted. The servants in India are not appointed by the Directors, but the Directors are chosen by them. The trade is carried on with their capitals. To them the revenues of the country are mortgaged. (5:436–37)

According to Burke, the Company's directors, no less than its servants, aim not to increase the value of Company shares but to embezzle public revenue. The *Ninth Report* argues that the collusion between directors and servants generated so much private wealth that it overpowered Parliament's capacity to criminalize it—and by extension undermined the British state's very autonomy: "If such Confederacies . . . are suffered to pass without due Animadversion; the Authority of Parliament must become as inefficacious as all other Authorities have proved, to restrain the Growth of Disorders either in India or in Europe."[65]

The *Ninth Report* insists that the point of Hastings's "contract system," far from restraining Company servants, was to make their coercion of native labor absolute: according to the system's terms, "the Contractor . . . received a certain Price for his Commodity; but he was not obliged to pay any certain Price to the Cultivator; who, having no other Market than his, must sell it to him at his own Terms. . . . He is a Contractor of a new Species, who employs no Capital whatsoever of his own, and has the Market of Compulsion at his entire Command."[66] Picking up on the *Ninth Report*'s rhetoric, the first volume of *Capital* would present the contract system as an exemplary instance of primitive accumulation: "[Hastings's] favourites received contracts under conditions whereby they, cleverer than the alchemists, made gold out of nothing. Great fortunes sprang up like mushrooms in a day; primitive accumulation proceeded without the advance of even a shilling."[67] According to the *Ninth Report*, the system gave contractors the "Power and Influence to subdue the Cultivators of the Land to their own Purposes" and hence "to engage on the lowest possible Terms"; its aim was "to prevent the Cultivator from obtaining the natural Fruits of his Labour."[68] The China investment depended on the contract system's coercive power: peasants who do not have direct access to the market will not normally farm opium, because its cultivation is difficult.[69] During the motion to impeach Hastings, Burke commented: "Here [in England] the manufacturer and husbandman will bless the just and punctual hand, that in India has . . . wrung from [the peasant of Bengal] the very opium in which he forgot his oppressions and his oppressor" (5:403). Burke thus implied that not only the English breakfast but even the simple participation of returned Company servants in the British economy implicated the nation in the coercion of colonial labor.

The fortunes Company servants made from the opium trade served as the seed capital of the expansive financial infrastructure—including merchant houses, banks, and insurance companies—that arose from colonial wealth.[70] Those financial institutions helped the servants control colonial fiscal relations and commercialize native society at every level, including land, labor, and the state itself. Out of the opium and tea trades, small groups of super-rich capitalists sprang up across the British Empire, from London, Bombay, and Calcutta to Hong Kong and Canton. They aligned themselves ideologically with the other groups that represented imperial interests, in particular the sugar trade, and using their wealth to gain access to the seats of power in London, they created an imperial lobby that made the state serve the empire, even though it was clearly not profitable to the nation in general.

When Burke alluded to the Company's "investment," he knew exactly what he was talking about. In regard to the returned servants, he observed: "They enter into your senate; they ease your estates by loans; they raise their value by demand; they cherish and protect your relations which lie heavy on your patronage; and there is scarcely an house in the kingdom that does not feel some concern and interest that makes all reform appear officious and disgusting; and, on the whole, a most discouraging attempt. . . . All these things shew the difficulty of the work we have on hand: but they shew its necessity too" (5:403). Burke's reference to the torture that produced England's luxurious breakfast alludes to a colonial system that privatized economies from the New World to the Far East. Like the *Ninth Report* in general, it took precise aim at this congeries of private imperial interests while it was still in its formative stages.[71] Trocki notes, "Tobacco, sugar, and tea were the first [capitalist] objects [that conveyed] the complex idea that one could become different by consuming differently."[72] The addictions merchant imperialism encouraged worked against the will of the "nation," or rather redefined it, separating the state once and for all from the nation's ancient constitution.

Nation/Imitation

Burke's allusion to the English breakfast insinuated, in short, that the global economy had compromised the nation's moral sense. Because he could no longer appeal to that sense, he looked elsewhere for a judgment in the impeachment. Just before describing the torture of the Rangpuri peasants, Burke told the Lords, "You have had enough, you have had perhaps more than enough, of oppressions upon property and oppressions upon liberty, but here the skin was not touched" (6:418). If his recitation of the East India Company's crimes against civil society had not moved his audience, Burke implied that the graphic description of physical suffering to follow would. The *Philosophical Enquiry into the Sublime and the Beautiful* (1757) argued that such images of suffering intrinsically provoke an affective reaction.[73] Three decades later, Burke put the theories he had outlined there into practice. Just before the opening speeches, he privately confessed his willingness to be, in his words, "mobbish" in his attacks on Hastings, dwelling on episodes that, like the torture at Rangpur, would "if anything, work upon the popular Sense."[74] Burke insinuated that because the British public was bereft of a moral sense, he would have to describe the Company's crimes in lurid detail, in order to elicit a response from it. He saw the British nation not as a civil society but as a mob, and appealed to it as such: not to its moral sense but rather, in the absence thereof, to its affective reflexes.

Sheridan's speeches in the impeachment also did not hesitate to "touch the skin," working on the popular sense, if anything, only more mobbishly than Burke's did. Consider, for example, his account of how peasants responded to the Company's alleged devastation of their province in order to finance its army: "The natives, . . . on the banks of the polluted Ganges, panting for death, . . . tore more widely open the lips of their gaping wounds, to accelerate their dissolution, and while their blood was issuing, presented their ghastly eyes to Heaven, breathing their last and fervent prayer that . . . their blood . . . might . . . rouse the eternal Providence to avenge the wrongs of their country."[75] This passage would be collected, remarkably, in countless nineteenth- and early twentieth-century handbooks of rhetoric, oratory, and elocution. Observers considered another speech Sheridan gave during the impeachment (7 February 1787) to be "the most eloquent . . . ever delivered in Parliament."[76] Burke called it "the most astonishing effort of eloquence, argument, and wit, united, of which there was any record or tradition." Fox exclaimed that "all that he had ever heard—all that he had ever read when compared with it, dwindled into nothing, and vanished like vapour before the sun." And even Pitt declared that "it surpassed all eloquence of ancient or modern times."[77] Years later, Byron called it the "very best Oration . . . ever conceived or heard in this country."[78]

Yet this speech and the four, almost equally celebrated, that followed in June 1788 offer little to match these claims. What the speeches contain instead is Sheridan's sentimental excess, designed like Burke's to provoke corresponding emotions in their audience: "However degenerate an example [some] British subjects had exhibited in India, the people of England . . . felt as men should feel on such an occasion."[79] These speeches operated in accordance with the *Enquiry*'s dicta about "sympathy": it is (1) "a sort of substitution, by which we are put into the place of another man"; (2) "an instinct that works us . . . without our concurrence"; and, accordingly, (3) the very "principle" of artistic communion (1:220–22). That is to say, the speeches acted sympathy out, turned it into an aesthetic spectacle, and thereby *automatically* transmitted it to the audience. Burke and Sheridan intended their speeches to make a British public bereft of moral sense mimic it.[80] Their "eloquence," to the extent that it existed at all, lay wholly in their capacity to effect this "substitution."

Contemporary observers were fully aware that the orator's sentimental performance was supposed to produce a reflexive response in the auditor's sentimental consciousness and, furthermore, that this reflex was the very point of the occasion. The daily press described Sheridan's 1787 speech as "that torrent of eloquence which must excite in every breast sentiments of indignation against the atrocity which demanded it to flow."[81] A future governor-general of India wrote in private correspondence the following day: "I have not slept *one wink*. . . . The *bone* rose repeatedly in my throat, and the tears in my eyes—not of grief, but merely of strongly excited sensibility."[82] An account of Sheridan's 1788 speeches observed that "when Mr. Sheridan had concluded the admiration of his Auditors was too great for *silent* approbation. It unanimously burst forth in a tumult of applause, which the recollection of the scene as instantly suppressed."[83]

The *Enquiry* implies that the line between "sympathy" and "imitation" is a vanishing one. It explains that "as sympathy makes us take a concern in whatever men feel, so th[e] affection [of imitation] prompts us to copy whatever they do" (1:224). According to the *Enquiry*, sympathy and imitation are both "affections" in the literal sense, mental states brought about by one's mimetic relationship to another. By virtue of their mimetic structure, sympathy and imitation are the two bonds that hold society together according to the *Enquiry* (1:220, 224).

It follows, then, that if a political economy founded on coercion dulled the nation's sympathy, the act of imitation would be the only affection left to unify the nation. It follows, furthermore, that imitation would take on a life of its own. It would no longer refer back to an original moral sense or even to the nation's organic history. Rather than be based on natural sympathy, the act of imitation would, on the contrary, become its basis, spreading *simulacra* of sympathy across society. Burke suggested as much during the impeachment. He claimed that Parliament's failure to check the Company would turn colonial corruption into the basis of the national character: "If you once teach the people of England by the successes of [Company servants] . . . qualities directly the contrary to those by which they have hitherto been distinguished; if you make them a nation of concealers, a nation of dissemblers, a nation of Liars, . . . My Lords, . . . the character of England will be gone and lost" (7:63).

Mehta has described Burke's "writings on India [as] the most sophisticated and moving elaboration on the idea of sympathy" that we will find anywhere in his work.[84] I would suggest instead that Burke performed sympathy for this "nation of dissemblers," this semblance of a moral nation, attempting thereby to make it dissimulate its actual insensitivity toward colonial violence. For example, he collapsed melodramatically into the arms of Sheridan and his other colleagues immediately after describing the mutilation of the Bengali peasants.[85] Four months later, Sheridan's final speech in the opening of the impeachment precipitated a fainting spell not only in Sheridan himself, who fell now into Burke's waiting arms, but also in members of his audience, including, not coincidentally, the finest actress of the day, Sarah Siddons.[86] Burke would imitate this sentimental part again at the end of *five* of the closing sessions, insisting on each occasion that the physical strain of describing the Company's destruction of Indian society prevented him from continuing: "Your Lordships will spare my weakness. I have not spared myself. I cannot command and you cannot give greater bodily strength than a man has" (7:280–81).[87] Burke and Sheridan made their speeches dramatic performances, rather than merely legal arguments, because they believed their last resort was a nation that had lost the capacity to make moral judgments. The exaggerated theatricality of their appeal to the nation's moral sense insinuated that its basis lay wholly in imitation—or, we could say, in mob behavior.[88]

For the experience of "excited sensibility" that Burke and Sheridan's performances inspired, the British public spent as much as fifty guineas on a single admission ticket, waited for hours in the streets leading to Parliament before the speeches began, and nearly crushed each other to death in the frenzy to get the best seats.[89] Once they entered, they themselves became a part of the drama, its actors almost as much as they were its spectators. The galleries held not only members of London's high society but also European ambassadors dressed in full orders treating the impeachment as an occasion of state; the Duke of Newcastle's box contained the British queen and princesses. Hence, Burke's and Sheridan's speeches gave the audience the opportunity to display its "natural sympathy" publicly: the excitement around the impeachment waned after Burke's speeches, not to return until Sheridan's.

But a collective performance must to some extent also be a moment of collective self-consciousness. To be conscious that sentiment is a performance is willy-nilly to question its essential character, to consider the possibility that nothing exists behind the performance, nothing but imitation all the way down. Where one account of the audience's sentimental response claimed that "it flowed spontaneously from the fountain of our feelings.—It was involuntary in our natures," the future governor-general who so admired Sheridan's rhetoric also observed that his "art . . . drew attention entirely away from the *purpose* to the *performance*."[90] Intending to give the nation a model of how it should act, Burke and Sheridan turned themselves into an easily recognizable literary stereotype, the male protagonist of sentimental drama and fiction, unable to control his emotions in the face of women's suffering.[91] Having watched Sheridan faint, Gibbon commended the performance the next day: "I called this morning, he is perfectly well. A good actor!"[92] Sheridan had little compunction admitting the same: years later, when the Prince of Wales introduced him to Hastings, he disavowed the performance once and for all, "begging [Hastings] to believe that any part he had ever taken against him was purely political and that no one had greater respect for him than himself."[93] The public display of sentiment that was the peculiar characteristic of late eighteenth-century literary culture externalized virtue, but in doing so always implied that the nation's moral sense was literally nothing more than a show.[94] Those who participated in the spectacle of the impeachment appear to have gleaned the point.[95]

The concept of an inherently moral nation enabled Burke to imagine a reform of empire that would legitimize the imperial project, one in which the empire would become an ethical extension of an always ancient and always progressive nation-state.[96] Burke ended his opening speeches before the Lords by addressing not them but the nation in general, whom he called on to form a moral community with Britain's Indian subjects: "The sun in his beneficent progress round the world does not behold a more glorious sight than that of men, separated from a remote people by the material . . . barriers of nature, united by the bond of a social and moral community, all the Commons of England resenting as their own, the indignities and cruelties that are offered to all the people of India" (6:457–58). This stirring vision of a reformed, national empire looked forward to nineteenth-century apologies for empire, which claimed that, when Parliament eliminated the East India Company's monopoly in 1813, empire began to transcend the merchant's private interest and join the nation-state's progressive history—indeed, as the necessary agent of its propagation.

But the impeachment gave the lie to this apology: its rhetorical performances refuted the *Reflections'* theoretical declarations, revealing Burke's distrust of his own concept of the nation. His speeches displayed not confidence in the possibility that the British nation could reform its empire but rather his awareness that the British Empire had rendered the very idea of nation-as-moral-community absurd. We have inferred from the *Reflections* that Burke stood for the nation's untimely traditions against reason's universalizing principles. But Burke's speeches in the impeachment attest instead to his understanding that, long before the Revolution, empire had already vitiated the nation's moral sense. The style in which he addressed the nation presupposed that the imperial economy had emptied it of its ethical content, substituting in its place a mere simulacrum thereof. The nation's moral sense was for Burke only rhetorical: a trope, a performance, an act of mimesis.

When he employed terms such as "nation" or "tradition," Burke was therefore not indexing specific alternatives to Enlightenment reason, neither England's privileged history nor Ireland's or India's endangered histories. He used such terms instead to bring into being a moral audience that would otherwise not exist—and whose existence could in any case be only a dissimulation. The term "nation" registers the discrepancy between what Burke ideally wanted from Britain and what he actually saw there, between, for example, its moral claims, on one hand, and its economic practices, on the other. Having returned Burke's thought to the colonial history that as much as any context informed it, we can acknowledge, finally, that his invocation of the nation-as-moral-community comprehended a global economy—and, along with it, the contradictions that made any such nation impossible.

PART III

Progress (1790–1815)

6
ORIENTALISM AND THE PERMANENT FIX OF WAR
Voltaire contra Sir William Jones

Scholars of eighteenth-century British Orientalism often take issue with Edward Said's sweeping generalization that the discipline of Orientalism made the East available for rule.[1] Looking at a period to which Said only alluded but that nonetheless constitutes the first coincidence of Oriental studies and colonial rule, these scholars emphasize East India Company Orientalists' extraordinary respect for the cultures they studied. Their premises—that India and Europe were part of a common civilization whose roots stretched beyond antiquity; that Hindu theology was generally superior to Christian practice; and that colonial law must be founded on native jurisprudence—appear not to fit Said's model, in which an Orientalist "will to power over the Orient" silences the East.[2] Company Orientalism confounds our received ideas about "the imperial project," suggesting that eighteenth-century British India contained possibilities different from those of the centuries that followed, whose particular history has determined our theories of empire. Said's argument and the voluminous work it has spawned seem, in short, not to apply to the eighteenth century.

This chapter reexamines such claims by restoring Company Orientalism to its original context: the construction of a rule of property founded on native traditions. We will find, contrary to the claim that eighteenth-century Orientalism was more conciliatory than Said acknowledged, that it was in fact even more instrumental to colonial rule than he explained. The argument of this chapter is that the original purpose of Company Orientalism—the most troubling and perhaps precisely for that reason still the most overlooked—was to construct a radically different form of property ownership that could underwrite the cost of modern war. The Orientalist appeal to "native tradition" obscured this economy's absolute novelty.

To study Orientalism's earliest entanglement with colonial rule, we need to return to Warren Hastings's 1772 "Plan for the Administration of Justice," which would become the 1781 Administration of Justice Regulation.[3] Parliament had broached the question of what form Company sovereignty in Bengal should

take during its 1772 sessions because the Company had already failed so badly
in its primary sovereign obligation—the collection of property revenue—that
it was on the verge of bankruptcy, having allowed perhaps a third of Bengal's
native population to die of starvation during the previous year's famine.[4] Hastings intended his plan—which insisted that only a state modeled on Indian
tradition could protect native rights—to preempt parliamentary intervention.
His attempt to legitimize the rule of property by making it refer to native law
forced Company servants to master the prestige languages—Sanskrit and Persian in particular—in which the law was written.[5] Hence, the rule of property
engendered colonial Orientalism.

The most influential colonial Orientalist was Sir William Jones (1746–94), ar-
guably the most commanding scholar Orientalism has yet produced, the master
of more languages and the supposed origin of more practices and even disciplines
in the comparative study of culture than there is space here to name.[6] While heading Bengal Presidency's Supreme Court during the last decade of his brief life,
Jones also managed to compile from native-language originals the monumental
codifications—*Al Sirajiyyah; or The Mohamedan Law of Inheritance* (1792), *Institutes of Hindu Law* (1794), and *A Digest of Hindu Law* (1797)—that provided
the historic 1793 Act of Permanent Settlement its legal architecture.[7] Responding
to Parliament's determination that Hastings's policy of short-term leases had
failed to make colonial property profitable, the Permanent Settlement entitled
a native property-owning class to rent fixed in perpetuity. Its stated aim was to
encourage agricultural commerce by protecting the rights of native aristocrats,
thereby turning them into improving landlords. The theory of property behind
the Permanent Settlement, which spread from Bengal across the British Empire,
would subsequently form the ideological basis of the empire's progressive claims.[8]
While the Permanent Settlement achieved global significance—becoming the
subject of Ranajit Guha's *A Rule of Property for Bengal* (1963), an urtext for *Subaltern Studies*—its local authority lay in Jones's Islamic and Hindu legal codes.

In stark contrast to eighteenth-century British Orientalism itself, however,
the scholars who study it have been unconcerned with colonial property: they
have made arguments about Orientalism's political implications without attending to the specific realm of its political efficacy. They tend to invoke Jones—the
embodiment of the deep respect for Indian traditions supposedly characteristic
of eighteenth-century Orientalism—as a counterexample to Said's argument,
but without reference to the motives and consequences of his colonial juris-

prudence.[9] Ironically, Said also avoided the question of Orientalism's material relationship to colonial history but did so in contrast by considering the two terms identical. For Said, they form what he ingeniously described as "a *preposterous* transition": colonialism should have produced Orientalist knowledge but instead was produced by it.[10] Orientalist discourse was not only prior to colonial praxis but, according to Said, precisely *what* was put into practice. Hence, the history of colonial property does not and *cannot* exist in his narrative either.[11] If the motive behind Orientalism was an ultimately mysterious "will to power" or "will to govern," according to Said, in the specific case of Jones's Orientalist scholarship, it resurfaces in the form of an equally mysterious "impulse to codify."[12] To the extent that he provided immaterial explanations of Orientalism, Said shared its "textual attitude."[13] He drew attention to the reductive quality of his own textualism when he observed, "Once we begin to think of Orientalism as a kind of Western . . . will to govern over the Orient, we will encounter few surprises."[14]

In fact, Orientalism in its original colonial context still contains an extraordinary capacity to surprise. Indeed, it forces us out of the aporia "postcolonial theory" confronts between the equally forbidden paths of "textualism" or "culturalism," on one hand, and "economism," on the other.[15] To make sense of eighteenth-century British Orientalism, we will need to leave behind not only textual attitudes of all stripes but also the hoary materialism that sees "the logic of capital" behind all things. Here, remarkably, such materialism fails to explain even the establishment of modern property relations.

When Company Orientalists gave Indian property law a textual basis—in a form that would become seminal for the development of Indian history and historiography—they helped the Company simplify India's otherwise profoundly complicated and fluid system of property ownership.[16] Their authority legitimized the Company's attempts to fix and centralize the collection of rent, which culminated in the Permanent Settlement. Though it established modern property relations in Bengal, the Permanent Settlement famously *failed* to improve colonial property: the Bengali countryside became *less* productive after the Permanent Settlement. In itself, then, the logic of capital does not explain the utility of the Permanent Settlement or, for that matter, of Company Orientalism. We must look elsewhere for this explanation.

Though it has rarely been acknowledged, the Permanent Settlement succeeded according to a different logic entirely. By fixing Bengali rent in perpetuity, the Permanent Settlement gave the Company—if not what it should have wanted in the long term, a more productive economy—what it absolutely demanded in the short term, an apparently *fixed* source of capital that could serve as collateral in global financial networks. The Permanent Settlement enabled the Company to use debt to finance its conquest economy, whose cost had bankrupted it. Hence, when it made Indian history textual, eighteenth-century Orientalism did not reflect either the abstract imperatives of an Enlightenment "will to govern" or the material ones of capital accumulation. This Orientalism instead articulated the political economy of modern war.

In relying on debt financing to pay for its war-making capacity, the Company merely adopted the military-fiscal logic of European states, whose domestic production was insufficient for the unprecedented costs of modern warfare.[17] Perhaps we could say, then, that when the Permanent Settlement fixed Bengal within a system of property relations that was less productive but more capable of underwriting war than precolonial property had been, it brought to the colony not a failed version of European modernity but its undisclosed essence. Regardless, only this military-fiscal logic—states redirecting profit toward the cost of war rather than productive reinvestment—explains how colonial rule could afford to ruin native economies and, by extension, how ruined colonial and postcolonial economies are not aberrations within but in fact constitutive of modernity. When we replace Orientalism within this logic—which is with us now more powerfully than ever—we will observe the aims of Enlightenment critique and of Said's lifework come suddenly into a startling convergence.

This chapter contains four sections that study the history of Orientalism. The first explores Orientalism's little-studied precolonial genealogy, in which it formed an essential, if bizarre, chapter in the Enlightenment critique of governmental reason: Orientalism promised to recover ancient esoteric thought as an antidote to modern political degeneration. The second observes that when Jones's Orientalist publications became a Europe-wide phenomenon in the 1790s, they appeared to have realized Orientalism's original promise: they claimed to unify an ancient mythic system with modern political economy. The third studies Company Orientalists' actual proposals in regard to colonial property. These proposals betray Orientalist ideology: they were aligned neither with ancient traditions nor with capitalist production but rather with the Company's military fiscalism. Here, the actual function of Orientalism becomes clear: it helped fix a rule of property that could turn rent toward war and buried that rule so deeply in India's supposed ancient traditions that its modern logic became invisible. The final section asserts that the Permanent Settlement was the cutting edge of this logic, not an addendum to capitalist modernity: Jones's Orientalism enshrouded the fiscal imperatives of modern war in a mystified past for which European intellectuals had long pined. Two other sections provide literary excursuses: the first analyzes Voltaire's satire of Orientalist ideology; the second, Elizabeth Hamilton's apology for it.

Precolonial and Early Colonial Orientalism

Orientalism came to serve colonial rule with Hastings's plan, but its own history was older. In its precolonial form, far from being an instrument of historical progress, Orientalism was instead a critique of European history. Its roots lay in a debate under way since the seventeenth century between the Christian Church and its deist critics that aimed to settle, once and for all, the original form of natural reason. The official Christian line was that the original religion and civilization were Judaic: all religious practices outside the Judeo-Christian tradition were therefore merely corrupt versions of it, Hinduism a particularly strange variant. The church could claim as a consequence that its global proselytism merely brought lapsed Jews back into the fold. The deists argued, in diametric opposition, that it was not religions outside the Judeo-Christian tradition that were corrupt, but rather the reverse. Judaism was only as old as the Hebraic priestly caste, which arrogated all religious authority to itself, turned the original "natural religion" into a set of mysterious rites it alone controlled, and hence colluded with the rise of despotism. Enlightenment deism disavowed European history in the most radical way possible, since it considered this history's very origin and essence corrupt.

But to prove the Judeo-Christian tradition a corruption of an earlier religion, the deists needed evidence of that religion.[18] After the East India Company conquered Bengal in the middle of the eighteenth century, Hindu scriptures that supposedly predated the Old Testament became the deists' primary form of evidence. Like most of the Company Orientalists who followed in their immediate wake, the first two Company servants to enter the field of Orientalism, J. Z. Holwell and Alexander Dow, were deists.[19] Reviewed by major British periodicals and translated into multiple languages, Holwell's and Dow's studies attracted Europe-wide readerships far greater than previous Orientalist works had, because they supposedly contained scriptures that resolved the long-standing argument between Christianity and deism. Moses Mendelssohn, for one, commented with strange confidence that Holwell's Orientalist texts displayed a capacity "mit den Augen eines eingeborenen Braminen zu sehen."[20] Mendelssohn's epithet has the virtue at least of capturing Holwell's and Dow's essential ambition precisely: to convince a European readership that they had recovered natural reason before its historical corruption, that they had reproduced it textually, and hence that they saw with the eyes of a natural-born Brahmin.

Holwell and Dow each claimed, accordingly, to be the first European to reach civilization's "fountainhead." Holwell wrote: "it is . . . to be regretted, that in place of drinking at the fountain head, [previous authors] have swallowed the muddy streams which flowed from [corrupt commentaries]."[21] Dow commented similarly: "They took their accounts from any common Brahmin, with whom they chanced to meet, and never had the curiosity or industry to go to the fountain head."[22] Referring in general to the object of a quest that possesses the power to rejuvenate, "fountainhead" refers here, in particular, to Hindu scriptures supposedly so ancient that they contain natural reason; it implies that Europeans must study these scriptures if they are to reverse the process of decay that has shaped their history. The fountainhead alone stems from the time before despotism.

Holwell and Dow published their Orientalist studies during the late 1760s, when the Company's fiscal crisis forced it to debate the colonial rule of property; in fact, they were centrally involved in these debates. Reluctant before Hastings's plan to formulate its own policy of property management, the Company had instead grafted itself onto the Mughal economy. Typical of tributary systems, the ground rent peasants paid in this economy trickled up through many layers of sovereignty, from the peasantry through the landlord's agents to regional sovereigns and ultimately to the Mughal emperor. From the perspective of British property, where enclosure had greatly simplified property ownership, the multiple expropriations to which Indian peasants were subject appeared to be corrupt.[23] Hence Company officials blamed its fiscal crisis on "Asiatic despotism."

Holwell argued in Parliament that the Company must dispossess Bengali landlords—who he claimed took a disproportionate share of the agricultural surplus, thereby impoverishing both the peasants and the Company—and auction their property to the highest bidder.[24] But his position on colonial property was far from being merely theoretical. He had been Calcutta's chief magistrate in 1759, when the Company first faced the dilemma of how to collect property taxes from a territory larger than England itself; its options included gathering the rent itself or auctioning it to speculative capitalists. Under Holwell's influence, the Company chose the latter. Not coincidentally, Holwell became one of these speculative capitalists and subsequently the governor of Bengal (1760). He argued in *India Tracts* (1764) that if the Company aligned its rule of property with his proposals, "the East India Company would become, in a short time, the richest body of subjects in the world."[25]

Dow's position was strictly opposed to Holwell's. While also considering Bengal's problem to be Asiatic despotism, Dow insisted that the Company's own "ruinous policy of farming out the lands annually" exemplified such despotism.[26] He claimed, in regard to Bengal's decreasing population and production, that "we may date the commencement of decline from the day on which Bengal fell under the dominion of foreigners; who were more anxious to improve the present moment to their own emolument, than, by providing against waste, to secure permanent advantage to the British nation."[27] In response to the Company's method of auctioning its rent to the highest bidder, thereby rendering property radically unstable, Dow proposed that the Company fix the rent of "all the lands in Bengal and Behar, in perpetuity," thereby prefiguring the Permanent Settlement.[28]

Holwell's and Dow's analyses of the colonial property not only occurred alongside but also inflected the function of their Orientalism. They both presupposed that colonial rule gains legitimacy to the extent that it *appears* to preserve native traditions. Dow offered *The History of Hindostan*—his translation of a Persian-language narrative about the rise and decline of Indian empires, to which he appended his Orientalist essay—as an object lesson in the fate of despots: "The history now given to the public, presents us with a striking picture of the deplorable condition of a people subjected to arbitrary sway; and of the instability of empire itself, when it is founded neither upon laws, nor upon the opinions and attachments of mankind."[29] Holwell's *Interesting Historical Events*—his own narrative of Indian empires, which also contains an Orientalist essay—likewise called on the Company to replace Asiatic despotism with a sovereign form organically linked to its subject population: "The [Hindus] now labouring under *Mahometan* tyranny, [are] fated I hope, soon to feel the blessings of a mild *British* government."[30]

On one hand, Holwell's and Dow's recognition that the Company's sovereign legitimacy would depend on Orientalism was prescient. But on the other, it reflected Orientalism's past, which supposed that ancient esoteric traditions contained an antidote to modern political degeneration. From this perspective, the British had little choice but to turn to Orientalism, if they hoped to avoid despotism. Hence, when the Company's metropolitan critics argued that Company servants were unfit for sovereign power, Hastings showcased their Orientalism as proof of their public character: "The service has at no period more abounded with men of cultivated talents [and liberal knowledge;] which reflect the greater lustre on their possessors, by having been the fruit of long and laboured application, at a season of life, and with a licence of conduct, more apt to produce dissipation than excite the desire of improvement."[31] Hastings forwarded installments of the first Orientalist work his plan spawned—N. B. Halhed's *A Code of Gentoo Laws* (1776)—to London even before it was complete and sponsored a London edition afterward for the same reason.[32]

In fact, Hastings sponsored dual Calcutta and London publications not only of the *Code* but also of Charles Wilkins's translation of the *Bhagavad Gita*, a text that was exemplary of Hindu esoteric knowledge but irrelevant to the Company's administrative needs. In doing so, Hastings advertised the new relationship of sovereign power and native mysteries under colonial rule: the Company would be responsible for bringing those mysteries into the open. In his foreword to the *Bhagvat-Geeta* (1785), Hastings argued that Company Orientalism would leave a political and literary legacy much more valuable than the capital it extracted from its colonies: "Every instance which brings [the natives'] real character home . . . will impress us with a more generous sense of feeling for their natural rights. . . . But such instances can only be obtained in their writings: and these will survive when the British dominion in India shall have long ceased to exist, and when the sources which it once yielded of wealth and power are lost to remembrance."[33] Orientalism's critical attitude toward European history was, ironically, what enabled it to serve the Company so well, since it proved the Company to be antidespotic. When contemporary scholars praise eighteenth-century colonialism by foregrounding its Orientalist achievements, they merely recycle the Company's own arguments, as these quotations from Hastings illustrate.

In fact, though, the Orientalist critique of European history did not at all imply a genuine openness to Indian history. Orientalism's textual biases—that Indian "civilization" could be found only in ancient scriptures, that contemporary Indian culture was corrupt, and hence that Indian scripture had priority over Indian social practice—coincided only too neatly with the exigencies of colonial rule. These biases enabled Orientalism, when it arrived in the colony, to transform itself from Europe's tireless critic to empire's faultless servant. Company officials turned the scholarly discipline that deists had devised as a form of critique within Europe into a form of propaganda in the colony. The Company claimed that it had made ancient scriptures the basis of the state and property: it appeared to have brought myth and history paradoxically together, inaugurating a new age that would be identified with the work of Sir William Jones.

Voltaire and Orientalist Critique

But the Enlightenment—or at least its most famous philosopher and infamous deist—was alert to Orientalism's ideological tendencies even before the Company put it to work. Voltaire actually preceded Holwell and Dow in arguing that the evidence of an immemorial Indian civilization refuted the priority of the Judeo-Christian tradition. In works from *Essai sur les mœurs* (1756) to *Fragments historiques sur l'Inde* (1773) and *Lettres sur l'origine des sciences et sur celle des peuples de l'Asie* (1777), among many others, he insisted that "everything has come down to us from the banks of the Ganges."[34] He read both Holwell's and Dow's works immediately after their publication; claimed that Holwell's scriptures were the oldest textual expression of divine worship still extant and, even more bizarrely, that Dow's were antiquity's most beautiful monument; and concluded, "it is from the work of Holwell and Dow above all that we must learn."[35] But when Voltaire subsequently turned Holwell's and Dow's works into fiction in his novella *Les Lettres d'Amabed* (1769), he was anything but their earnest pupil. *Les Lettres d'Amabed* takes Orientalism's critique of European history to its limit, at which point it turns back on Orientalism itself: here the corruption Orientalism uncovers in European history constitutes history as such, Indian as well as European. Against the received wisdom that Voltaire advocated natural religion, this novella makes clear that the only form of reason in any sense "natural" for him is one that attempts to discern the corruption that exists everywhere and at all times.

Les Lettres d'Amabed puts the philosophical debate between the church and deism into play, in a style typical of Voltaire's *contes philosophiques*. At the same time, it returns to the origins of European colonial rule in India: the early sixteenth-century Portuguese conquests of Calicut and Goa, where the Roman Catholic Church established the eastern Inquisition. Its main characters represent the two sides in both these conflicts: on one hand, two Italian missionaries, Fa tutto and Fa molto, who practice a particularly corrupt form of Catholicism;

on the other, the newlywed Brahmins Amabed and Adaté and their own priest and guru, Shastasid, who practice a particularly pure form of Hinduism. The narrative opens on the question of civilization's origins, and Shastasid's first letter puts the question to rest. Writing from Madurai (known even in antiquity as "the Athens of the East") to Amabed in the ancient holy city of Benares, Shastasid explains that Christianity is merely "a feeble image of [Hindu] revelation."[36]

Though almost never given serious attention now, *Les Lettres d'Amabed* could scarcely be more historically provocative. Anticipating Frank, Perlin, and Pomeranz by more than two centuries, it argues that Asian, not European, economies have dominated world history, "reorienting" history precisely in Frank's sense of the term.[37] Amabed and Shastasid note that while China and India took the lead in agriculture and urbanization, creating the first civilizations (3–4), Europe remains comparatively unproductive: "These people of the Occident inhabit a poor country, which produces for them but very little silk, no cotton at all, no sugar, no spices" (5); "they lack for pepper, for cinnamon, for cloves, for tea, for coffee, . . . for incense, for aromatics, and for all that can render life agreeable" (8).

With equal prescience, *Les Lettres d'Amabed* argues that Asia's economic precedence refutes the Judeo-Christian practice of "universal history," Voltaire's bête noire. He traced this practice—premised on the idea of a single, profound meaning shining through all of history's stages—from the Pentateuch through the medieval chronicles to Bossuet's *Discours sur l'histoire universelle* (1679).[38] It continued in a different form in Hegel, Marx, and Leopold von Ranke, among many others. Amabed insists on the Eurocentrism of all such narratives: "It is a universal history of the whole world, in which not a word is said of [India's] ancient empire; nothing of the immense countries beyond the Ganges, nothing of China, nothing of the vast Tartary. . . . I can compare [European historians] only to the villagers who talk volubly of their own thatched cottages, and who do not know where . . . the capital [is]; or, rather, to those who think that the world ends at the limits of their own horizon" (7).

Les Lettres d'Amabed goes to the roots of this practice. With an anti-Semitism typical of Voltaire, Shastasid argues that the people whose historiography came to dominate European self-understanding had no history themselves, existing instead in a state of slavery: "At the time of Alexander there was in a corner of Phoenicia a little people of brokers and usurers, who had long been held in captivity [*qui avait été longtemps esclave*] in Babylon: they forged for themselves a history during captivity" (10).[39] Unwilling to acknowledge their own past, the

Jews instead created a history, Shastasid implies, out of the pagan myths that surrounded them. Voltaire's footnote explains that "the ancient Orphic verses called Bacchus . . . *Mosa*" and "fables concerning Bacchus were widely diffused in Arabia and Greece long before those nations were informed as to whether the Jews had a history or not" (63). *Les Lettres d'Amabed* insists that to understand the Judeo-Christian tradition, we must see it not as an origin but rather as a corruption: theologically as well as economically, it came after, co-opting practices that had served radically different values.

As mentioned, the Roman Catholic Church argued instead that the conversion of the heathens merely returned them to their original religion. The Portuguese conquistadors brought colonial rule to India in the name of the church, adding spiritual weight to their military adventurism by restoring the natives' true faith. Indeed, it was a papal bull (1455) that gave Portugal its imperial charter—its monopoly on the discovery, conquest, and commerce of Africa and Asia—in the first place. Gama assumed that lapsed Christians populated India, and when he finally arrived there, alighting on the shores of Calicut, he is said to have declared, "We come to seek Christians and spices."[40]

Les Lettres d'Amabed responds to this history by turning the idea of conversion inside out. Rather than disseminating the church's universal history, here conversion betrays it, revealing that European religions like European economies are not origins but rather corruptions.[41] Voltaire argued elsewhere that the Catholic Church took the baptism rites that accompany conversion from ancient Egyptian and Indian religion, removed these rites from their sacred context, and inserted them instead into a process whose end was secular, that is, promotion within the church hierarchy—a point *Les Lettres d'Amabed* also makes (39).[42] In this tale, baptism does not return Hindus to their uncorrupted origin but instead resituates Christianity in its own exceptionally corrupt history. Amabed and Adaté visit Goa, carrying letters of introduction from Fa tutto to Afonso de Albuquerque, the conquistador who first took Goa and ruled it. Once they arrive there, Tutto, reappearing as an officer of the Inquisition, asks them if they have been baptized. When they answer affirmatively, the Inquisition imprisons them on the charge of apostasy. Adaté explains: "This nation has a baptism, as we have. I am ignorant as to how our sacred rites have ever been conveyed to them. . . . They are so ignorant that they do not know that they received baptism from us a very few centuries ago. These barbarians have imagined that we had been of their sect, and that we had renounced their worship" (16–17). Whereas

Portuguese officials were appalled by the methods Jesuits used to convert Goans, Adaté discerns the history of corruption concealed within the ritual of baptism: "When the Father Fa tutto said . . . '*Io la convertero*' . . . he meant that he would make me return to *the religion of the brigands*" (17).[43]

Shastasid concludes simply that the Christians' "true divinity is gold; they go in search of this god to the other extremity of the world" (6). The novella implies that precisely because Europe lacks it own history and, by extension, the ability to trade with India on an equal footing, it has little choice but to rely on war: "They have to come from such a distance, through so many perils, to ravish our commodities . . . with arms in their hands. It is said that they have committed frightful cruelties at Calicut to obtain pepper" (8). Voltaire says nothing more concerning these "frightful cruelties," but the very terms of this allusion to the pepper trade make clear he knew exactly what he was talking about.

Even after its conquest of African and American territories had enabled it to acquire slaves and gold, respectively, the Portuguese Crown realized it would need control of the spice trade to gain hegemony among European states.[44] It recognized moreover that the Islamic sultanates surrounding the Indian Ocean derived much of their wealth from the spice trade, so seizing this trade would undermine their power and effectively launch another Crusade. In their attempt to wrest the Malabar pepper trade from Arab merchants, the conquistadors committed a list of atrocities so long its recitation becomes comically grotesque. Cabral, who captained the second Portuguese expedition to Calicut, and João da Nova, who captained the third, destroyed Arab ships and slaughtered the sailors aboard, burning many alive. They supposedly dismembered and defaced native sailors, *then* killed them, then piled their corpses on top of each other, before sending their ships back to shore. The Portuguese attacked not only merchant ships but also pilgrims to Mecca, whom they slaughtered as well. Cabral bombarded Calicut for days, as would Gama during the fourth expedition. In fact, by then, the Portuguese objective was simply to lay siege to Calicut.

Albuquerque finally acquired a monopoly on the pepper and spice trade at Calicut in 1513, after attacks in which tens of thousands of natives were said to have lost their lives. As a consequence of this monopoly, Portugal replaced Venice at the center of the European world economy. Voltaire would comment in *Essai sur les mœurs*: "After 1500 there was no pepper to be had at Calicut but by spilling blood."[45] But as the restraint of his own allusions suggests, Voltaire's point was less to incite moral outrage than to inculcate a historical vision capable of standing up to the claims of sovereignty. He wanted us to see, *prior* to every form of sovereign power, the processes of co-optation it conceals when it presents itself as originary.

Enacting reports about widespread Portuguese crimes against natives, including sexual abuse, the clergymen rape Adaté and her servant, Déra, while they are imprisoned in Goa (18–19, 23, 37).[46] A Portuguese captain saves her, and Amabad and Adaté sail for Rome to receive justice from the pope, but on the ship Déra is raped again (37). They arrive in Rome only to find the pope, Leon X, a syphilitic libertine whose interest in them is purely erotic: "He asked us how we made love in Benares, at what age the girls were usually married, if the great Brahma had a seraglio. . . . Finally, he dismissed us in recommending us to embrace Christianity, in embracing us, and in giving us little slaps on the buttocks in signs of good feeling" (59). *Les Lettres d'Amabed* managed somehow to disgust even Diderot, or so he protested: "This last work is without taste, without finesse, without invention, a tedious repetition of all the old smutty jokes that the author has recited against Moses and Jesus Christ, prophets and apostles, the Church, popes, cardinals, priests, and monks. . . . I don't like religion, but I don't hate it enough to find this good. The idea, true or false, that the Mosaic theology originated in India leads to these letters, and this idea is not Voltaire's, who makes it popular with this small work, and there are better." It was, Diderot concluded, "a lot of garbage" (*force ordures*).[47]

Perhaps Diderot had missed Voltaire's point. Here, it was ultimately *not* to satirize the church or *écraser l'infâme* but rather to present its practices as exemplary of history as such. *Les Lettres d'Amabed* opposes the Brahmins' natural religion to the Catholics' political corruption but does not advocate the former. When the Brahmins are drawn into the latter, historical process, the conversion and rebirth they experience as "Europeans" mocks the very idea of spiritual rebirth, since it offers them not the consciousness that precedes political corruption but instead one that is much more attuned to it and hence capable of negotiating the absolutely corrupt time into which European colonialism has hurtled them.[48] Voltaire's point is that we learn ultimately from the material history of corruption, not the textual expression of "natural religion." So *Les Lettres d'Amabed* presents the church less as the object of satire than as the very source, however perverse, of Enlightenment, which lay for Voltaire not in ethical ideals but in the knowledge of the political and economic interests concealed behind them. The church turns out to be a particularly appropriate guide to that knowledge: a monsignor explains to Amabed that "'the viceregents [*les vices-Dieu*] will so abuse the good-will of men that in the end they will make them intelligent'" (58).[49] About him, Amabed writes: "This monsignor seems to me very shrewd; I am improving myself greatly with him, and I already feel myself to be quite different [*tout autre*]" (52).[50]

Regardless of Voltaire's professed admiration for Holwell and Dow, his Brahmin characters are caricatures of their Orientalist texts: Amabed, Adaté, and Shastasid figure Orientalism's purely textual understanding of civilization's origins. No less than Judeo-Christian universal history, Orientalism imagined a time before corruption that could serve as the template for a world-historical future free of despotism. But in Voltaire's own creation story—in contradistinction to the Christian, deist, and Orientalist ones—corruption is originary; here, it is corruption all the way down, so to speak. For Voltaire, corruption occurs whenever a ruling power expropriates a cultural practice from its own world, turns it toward other ends, and obscures its different history. To him, form has no content outside this process of conversion, apart from the meanings different types of power successively impose on it. "Corruption" is ultimately just Voltaire's term for what we now call "genealogy": he thinks history always in terms of genealogies, *not* in terms of degeneration (or development) from a prehistoric and prepolitical origin. Voltaire's critical method inspires a conversion in Amabed—not from Hinduism to Christianity but rather from a view of history in terms of origin and decay to one in terms of genealogy without origin or end—that makes him "quite different" from what he had been, suddenly more sophisticated about the nature of sovereign power.

This philosophical tale's wit lies in the fact that rather than simply choose the deist line over the Christian one, as we might expect Voltaire to do, it opposes both. *Les Lettres d'Amabed* keeps its focus on the always-material processes that lie behind any metaphysical system and betray it, natural reason no less than the Judeo-Christian tradition. Company Orientalists continued the practice of conversion in their own way: they justified colonial rule by claiming that it returned Hindus to their original religion. But where Orientalism enthroned the Brahminic scriptures, Voltaire used them *only* as a critical principle against the self-proclaimed originality of the Judeo-Christian tradition: in his view, Indian religions, no less than European ones, are intrinsically corrupt. Enlightenment critical method dictated for Voltaire that we imagine the state never in terms of the moment before corruption—as Holwell, Dow, and Hastings's 1772 plan insisted—but always in terms of an endless process of corruption itself. Voltaire's aim was to prevent his own method from spawning a new metaphysical principle—to forestall, in brief, the dialectic of Enlightenment. In this regard, he foresaw the colonial future: British intellectuals, William Jones primus inter pares, reimagined ancient Eastern civilization as the prototype of a state beyond political degeneration *and*, paradoxically, the foundation for East India Company rule. In diametric opposition, by pushing Orientalism to its limit, Voltaire's incendiary polemic negated its own ideological tendencies—an achievement Diderot above all would have admired if he had discerned it there.

Jones and Mythic Law

Soon after arriving in Bengal, Jones echoed the claim of having reached the Hindu fountainhead that both Holwell and Dow had made two decades before. Introducing himself in the "Hymn to Surya" (1786) as one of the first Europeans to have learned Sanskrit, he described it as the "celestial tongue" that "draws orient knowledge from its fountains pure."[51] Agreeing with Holwell and Dow that ancient Hinduism contained manifestations of natural reason, he claimed in his seminal essay "On the Gods of Greece, Italy, and India" (1788) that "we may infer a general union or affinity between the most distinguished inhabitants of the primitive world, at the time when they deviated . . . from the rational adoration of the only true God."[52] He suggested moreover that this original civilization had global influence: "We shall, perhaps, agree . . . that Egyptians, Indians, Greeks and Italians, proceeded originally from one central place, and that the same people carried their religion and sciences into China and Japan: may we not add, even to Mexico and Peru?" Reversing centuries of Islamic tyranny and millennia of Brahmin priestcraft, Jones's recovery of the pure source of "orient knowledge" claimed to make once again public in both India and Europe the spiritually integrated reason natural to "prehistoric" humanity.

The Romantic generation accepted Jones's claims without hesitation. Offering a different world-historical origin, Jones's Orientalism famously assisted their ambition to create a radically new aesthetic. His 1789 translation of Kalidasa's Sanskrit play *Sakuntala* heralded what Raymond Schwab's *The Oriental Renaissance* refers to as the "*Sakuntala* Era."[53] For Herder, it was further proof that India was humanity's fatherland. He recommended it to Goethe, who in turn passed his love of it down to Schiller. Contemporary scholars have hailed Jones's "A Hymn to Náráyana" as seminal for the subsequent history of Romanticism.[54]

But this poem was, ironically, no less central to the colonial rule of property. Jones reused the creation myth with which the poem begins to preface *Institutes of Hindu Law; or, The Ordinances of Menu.*[55] In importing his own creation myth into the *Manava-Dharmasastra* (or *The Laws of Manu*), he aimed to give his translation of what is generally considered to be the oldest text of Hindu law the *appearance* of antiquity and hence greater authority. Jones's preface to *The Mahomedan Law of Succession to the Property of Intestates* (1782) had already argued that his legal scholarship returned to the "fountain head."[56] But his preface to *Institutes of Hindu Law* made the argument much more elaborate. Here Jones not only accepted the general belief that Manu was "the oldest [and] the holiest of legislators" in India but also suggested that his laws were "one of the oldest compositions existing" anywhere in the world.[57] Jones speculated, furthermore, that Manu ("Menu or Menus in the nominative and Menos in an oblique case") was linked to Minos of Crete: "Though perhaps he was never in *Crete*, yet some of his institutions may well have been adopted in that Island, whence Lycurgus, a century or two afterwards, may have imported them to *Sparta*."[58] In that case, Jones's publication of *The Laws of Manu* reestablished not only the original Hindu law but one origin of non-Hebraic law as such: "If Minos, the son of Jupiter, . . . was really the same person as Menu, the son of Brahma, we have the good fortune to restore, by means of *Indian* literature, the most celebrated system of heathen jurisprudence, and this work might have been entitled *The Laws of* Minos." The Romantic generation was only too ready to adopt Jones's speculative prehistory: Goethe, Herder, Fichte, Schelling, Novalis, the Schlegels, Blake, Coleridge, Shelley, and Emerson, among many others, were fascinated by *The Laws*' unification of mythic and practical functions.

If the point of the creation myth was to authorize Jones's translation of the law, the point of the translation was, as mentioned, to provide the 1793 Permanent Settlement with its legal architecture. Jones considered the legal codes on which he labored tirelessly during the final years of his life to be his most valuable contributions to history, not his many other Orientalist works nor the Indo-Aryan thesis, for which he is much more famous: he aspired to be "the Justinian . . . of the East."[59] Jones wanted Orientalism, in other words, to serve the demands of colonial property, as Holwell and Dow had foreseen it must. Jones's Orientalism gave the East India Company's revolutionary rule of property the appearance of an ancient origin, folding it into the "*Sakuntala* Era," at least as far as his European reading public was concerned. *The Laws of Manu* simultaneously authorized the

Permanent Settlement and drew attention away from its material context and consequences. Its logic seemed to be dictated by immemorial traditions.

In fact, though, the Orientalist discovery of the fountainhead replaced the fluid processes of Indian history with the rigid structures of colonial political economy. According to the Orientalists, the essence of India was necessarily religious, and religion comprised only certain original texts, which themselves had no history—except for their *subsequent* corruption by priestcraft and despotism. This history was in any event reversible, since the Orientalists could recover the scriptures in their original form and restore their proper signification. But while the Company presumed to rescue Hinduism from Brahminic corruption and hence to undermine priestly power, they actually colluded with Brahminism's deeply partisan narrative of Indian history, because they relied on Brahmin informants.[60] Contrary to the premises of the Orientalists and their informants, the Vedas and Sastras were not created at some originary moment but instead transmitted orally across generations. Although it is true that they were written and rewritten as they were transmitted, the writing was only an aid to memory. It did not stabilize their form but instead incorporated into it the historical traces of their infinitely layered composition.

For example, in order to maintain their priestly function, the Brahmins often compromised with other sects, introducing the gods of independent religions into their own pantheon. Ancient Indian religion needs to be seen, therefore, as the religions—with an absolutely necessary emphasis on plurality—of autonomous sects or social segments that did not consider themselves part of a single theology.[61] The history of the Vedas and the Sastras includes, furthermore, the Brahmins' gradual rise to hegemony, a consequence in part of their royal appointment as landowners during the first millennium AD. From this position, they built institutions of religious learning that presented their beliefs as divine revelations obtaining from the origins of time. The Brahmin priestly caste designed its scriptures to be the embodiment of the reason that precedes history, but precisely in this design these scriptures contain a complex genealogy, a history of endless corruption.

The attributes that made scripture essential to Brahminic hegemony—its capacity to dehistoricize and delocalize what were in fact particular practices—also enabled it to fulfill the Orientalist effort to locate the supposed origins of Indo-European civilization. More to the point, the Orientalists' interest in Sanskrit texts reflected their appreciation of the hegemonic functions these texts had served and the new ones toward which the Company could turn them.[62] But the crucial difference between Brahminic and Company authority was that in the former case the transmission of texts remained perforce largely oral and hence open to endless contextual variability. In contrast, the Company brought the printing press to India. Print effectively codified the *Manava-Dharmasastra* and turned it from the customary law of a single caste into the universal law of all Hindus. Whether in the case of the Sastras or Shari'a, the Company's legal codifications made the interpretation of law *more* orthodox than it had previously been. It was only after "Hindu civilization"—which, if it existed at all, comprised radically heterogeneous and conflicting forces—became identical with a set of supposedly timeless scriptures that colonial rule could fix it both temporally and spatially, making it appear static rather than susceptible to development through historical time.

The Orientalist quest for the origins of civilization disseminated Brahmin ideology—which in the precolonial period had only a local or regional function—from the centralized structures that colonialism introduced to India: not only printing presses but also educational institutions and, not least of all, the judicial system.[63] In the process, colonial rule made Brahminism's claim to be the origin of Hinduism a self-fulfilling prophecy. The Indian nationalism that emerged during the nineteenth century in opposition to colonial rule derived, ironically, from the Orientalist construction of Hinduism and its central tenets of a sacred book and the theological sovereignty of one sect over all. Insisting on its own antiquity and hence authority, this new Hinduism dictated which practices belonged to the essence of India and which were mere corruptions to be excluded or marginalized. It transformed into far-reaching ideology what the Orientalists first recovered as supposedly authentic theology. Regardless of subsequent scholarship that has delineated the constantly changing legal culture of precolonial India, the mistaken priority Jones gave the *Manava-Dharmasastra* has still not been reversed. The separate postcolonial civil codes that apply to Hindus and Muslims attest to the enduring significance of the Orientalists' supposed reconstruction of Hindu and Muslim legal traditions. "Indian history" is the effect of the deist attempt to refute the Judeo-Christian claim on world history and, ultimately, of the East India Company and the British state's radically centralizing tendencies. When it claimed to uncover the pure waters of the fountainhead, the early Orientalist construction of ancient Indian civilization concealed the profane history that actually gave it rise.

Precolonial and Early Colonial Sovereignty

Colonial Orientalism emerged within a peculiar sovereign form, which the scholarship on Orientalism has overlooked. Early modern innovations in war making—known now as the "military revolution"—had increased the cost of war far in excess of what royal treasuries afforded, forcing European sovereigns to revolutionize their fiscal systems as well: they began to depend on piracy, monopoly trade, colonial rule, and ultimately debt financing.[64] Despite its quasi-sovereign status, the East India Company had purposefully avoided this military-fiscal logic, attempting instead to reap the profits of trade—however monopolistic—without incurring the cost of war and conquest. But its victory at the Battle of Plassey (1757) finally and irrevocably pulled the Company into military fiscalism: from this point forward, its military expenditures always exceeded its revenue, and it attempted in response ceaselessly to expand the territory from which it drew its rent and on which it imposed its monopolies. Trapped in this vicious cycle of war debt and war as an economic strategy to escape debt, the Company became a sovereign form categorically different from those that had occupied Indian soil. It had demands on its revenue absolutely unknown to prior forms of Indian sovereignty: for example, its obligation as a joint-stock company to pay investors a regular dividend and as a monopoly trader to buy all of Bengal's export commodities. And since the British state depended on the Company's finance capital, Bengali property was hostage not only to the Company's own military-fiscal exigencies but also to the British state's, to wars it had fought and would fight continents away.

These pressures led the Company to extract wealth from Bengali property in a historically unprecedented way: Hastings himself concluded that where the English Crown extracted one-fifth of British agricultural profit in rent, the Company extracted nine-tenths of Bengali surplus value.[65] It introduced a number of drastic innovations in order to do so, bringing in speculative capitalists to collect rent; monetizing rent; ascribing the ownership of property not to communities but rather to private individuals, whom it thus made responsible for the rent; and incorporating previously rent-free lands.[66] Regardless of what Company Orientalism claimed, the Company could *not* in fact afford actually to base its rule of property on native traditions. It was the Company—not the precolonial system—that extracted more than the Bengali economy could bear.

Holwell and Dow experienced these transformations directly: like the official Orientalists who followed in their wake, they knew what the Company's fiscal needs entailed. Hence, while their Orientalist publications called for the reconstruction of native traditions as the basis of colonial rule, their own concepts of property demanded a wholly new political economy. Holwell designed his plan of auctioning Bengali rent to speculative capitalists "to appeal to cash-hungry British MPs."[67] He testified before Parliament that "if [Bengali rent] now amounts to Three Millions Sterling, the real produce is three or four times as much" and that to obtain the latter sum, the Company must lease Bengali land "to the best Bidders": "there would be few Persons to account with, and much therefore saved in the Collections."[68] Though Hastings opposed Holwell's plan precisely because it failed to respect preexisting traditions of property, it eventually became the orthodox approach, and Hastings himself instituted it when he became governor in 1772.

Although Dow criticized Holwell's policy, his alternative proposal that the Company protect native property rights by permanently fixing rent demanded, nonetheless, the "military conquest of the whole subcontinent" and the reform of all its sovereign institutions accordingly.[69] Dow's intention in fixing rent was not to return to ancient traditions but to create a native class of comprador property owners whom the Company could use to pacify its subjects: "To give them property would only bind them with stronger ties to our interest; and make them more our subjects; or, if the British nation prefers the name—more our slaves."[70] Once Holwell's plan of auctioning rent had run its course, Dow's proposal for fixing rent would take over. But in either case, these plans, though opposed to each other, both fundamentally reconstructed Indian property by formulating a rule in which all intermediate owners (or sovereigns) across the subcontinent's radically heterotopic geography would be eliminated.

Holwell's and Dow's concept of sovereignty set the pattern for Company policy: as its economic and hence territorial ambitions became infinite, the Company followed the European state-form in reconceptualizing sovereignty as absolute power, the absence of any other sovereign or extractive entity. This stark reconceptualization characterizes the transformation of the Company from Clive's victory at Plassey in 1757 (when it ceased to be a primarily seaborne power and, rapidly militarizing itself, began to expand its territorial possessions) to Hastings's plan in 1772 (when it effectively declared its autonomy from the Mughal Empire).[71] At that time, in response to the Company's fiscal crisis, Hastings not only dispossessed the Bengal property-owning class and auctioned off their rent but also rejected the idea of power sharing, arresting native governors and stopping the Company's stipulated payment to the Mughal emperor. Soon thereafter, Hastings would proclaim, albeit prematurely, that "every intermediate power is removed, and the sovereignty of the country wholly and absolutely vested in the Company."[72]

In short, then, Company Orientalists were concerned from the very origins of colonial rule not to preserve Indian civilization but rather to replace it with European absolutism. They recognized that the Company would as a consequence need Orientalism to mystify this utterly modern sovereign form. Behind the facade of ancient traditions was a process characteristic of colonial history generally: the colonial state aimed to centralize authority by reifying formerly fluid legal practices. In the process, it created a sovereign power that was "singular," existing "not alongside other legal and political authorities but above them."[73]

Though Company officials referred to the precolonial expropriation of peasant labor as "fraud" and "corruption," sovereign ruthlessness—while no doubt actual—had been of necessity circumscribed: the many levels of precolonial sovereignty each administered relatively few subalterns and possessed a correspondingly limited capacity to concentrate wealth and power.[74] Gift economies obtained at every level, enforcing a delicate balance of extraction and reciprocation in the exercise of sovereignty. In contrast, the Company could not afford to return any part of the peasants' surplus to them, because the cost of modern war had always already laid claim to it. The Company itself created the economic crises it typically blamed on the precolonial structure of sovereignty, precisely by undoing the circumscribed nature of that sovereignty. The rule of property claimed to be the ultimate response to these crises, even though they were in fact manifestations of the historical rupture colonialism itself had induced.

Hamilton and Orientalist Ideology

The Permanent Settlement entitled Bengal's property-owning class (or *zamindars*) to rent fixed in perpetuity on the premise that it would enable them to stop rack-renting their own tenants and to improve their property. Improvement would lead in turn to a market in land, which alongside the Company's effort to protect commerce would liberate the circulation of native capital. In the process, the zamindars would become a capitalist class, bringing native traditions in line with modern political economy. The principle of aristocratic capitalism that lay behind the Permanent Settlement eventually spread, as mentioned, from Bengal across the British Empire.[75] The empire's claim to transform native elites into

gentleman farmers enabled it finally to separate itself from the stigma of mercantile degeneration and attach itself instead to the idea of progress.[76] British
print culture *first* began to describe colonial India in terms of the British state's
progressive ideals, rather than the Company's degenerative political economy,
only at this time (the 1790s).[77] During these years, it transformed the Enlightenment critique of empire into a *post*-Enlightenment ideology thereof: namely,
that the British Empire defended traditional property rights against the anarchic tendencies of revolutionary France.[78] Company Orientalism lay at the very
essence of this ideology.

   Not coincidentally, the most important novel of the 1790s about British
India, one of the first to represent it in terms of progress, focuses on Company
Orientalism. In fact, an Orientalist sets Elizabeth Hamilton's *Translations of the
Letters of a Hindoo Rajah* (1796) on its way. The eponymous Rajah describes
his initial encounter with Captain Percy: "He spoke to me in the Persian language; of which, as well as the Arabic, and the different dialects of Hindostan,
he was *perfect master.* . . . He had set out many months before, from Calcutta,
with an intention of travelling through the northern parts of Hindostan, in
order to trace the antiquities of the most ancient of nations."[79] Percy represents
the Company servants Jones gathered together in the Royal Asiatick Society of
Bengal (est. 1784), which pioneered the scholarly discipline of Indology, and in
particular to one of the society's founding members, Hamilton's own brother
Charles, who until his untimely death from tuberculosis in 1792 was a prominent Orientalist. Hastings commissioned him to translate *Al-Hidayah*, a Persian
code of Islamic law that the Company would use to codify its Muslim subjects'
traditional rights.[80] The novel quotes extensively from Company Orientalism,
including Halhed's *A Code of Gentoo Laws*, Wilkins's *Bhagvat-Geeta*, and Jones's
Sacontala. Hamilton dedicated the novel to Hastings ("the honoured patron, and
friend, of a beloved, and much lamented brother"), lauding him for his support
of Orientalism. Hence, while *Les Lettres d'Amabed* fictionalizes the Orientalism
that preceded Hastings's plan, *The Letters of a Hindoo Rajah* fictionalizes the
Orientalism that followed it. But where the former text undermines Orientalist ideology, the latter—designed as anti-Jacobin propaganda—reinforces it. In
fact, the novel reiterates Hastings's rhetoric precisely: the Rajah observes that
"to the knowledge of Persian, many [Company servants] add a considerable
degree of information in the Shanscrit language. The time of vacation from
immediate service, wasted by the Mussulman Commanders in voluptuous in-

dolence, is spent by these more enlightened men, in studies which add to their stock of knowledge. . . . It is by these strangers that the annals of Hindostan . . . shall be restored" (1:190).

After Percy dies from the injuries he has suffered in war, the Rajah reverses Percy's journey, in order to reach the source of his knowledge. As it follows the Rajah, the novel's itinerary provides a map of British imperial ideology. Like Amabed's, the Rajah's travels take him away from the holy city of Benares, but he travels not to the Portuguese colony in Goa and to Rome but rather to the East India Company fort in Calcutta and to London—and, at the novel's close, to the English countryside, where he experiences the rule of property firsthand. The narrative corresponds, therefore, to the Orientalist model of colonial rule: it joins Indian myth to English political economy.

The novel picks up on the Orientalist leitmotif that Jones employed yet again in his tenth-anniversary address to the Royal Asiatick Society: "In history, as in law, we must not follow streams, when we may investigate fountains"; the Rajah refers to "the beloved of Brahma" as "the pure fountain of all human wisdom" (1:93).[81] But Hamilton emphasizes that the Rajah has access to such wisdom only because Company Orientalists have reconstructed it. In order to "read those divine mysteries, over which the wisdom of our holy Bramins has thrown a veil" (1:168), the Rajah recites Jones's "Hymn to Náráyana," which, Hamilton's footnote explains, "is so expressive of the sentiments of the Rajah, that the translator has taken the liberty of inserting it" (169). Recall that Jones used this poem, which would powerfully influence Romantic art, to preface *Institutes of Hindu Law*. Only two years after Jones's death, Hamilton already credits him with turning ancient esotericism into an inspiration for modern aesthetics. More to the point of this chapter, the novel defends British rule by arguing that it alone possesses the scholarly competence to align ancient mysteries with global modernity.

When the Rajah reaches the English countryside, he meets the gentleman farmer Darnley, whose commitment to "Agricultural improvement" (2:311) recalls the Permanent Settlement's aristocratic capitalism.[82] No less than the Permanent Settlement, the novel presents the moral economy of aristocratic capitalism as the solution to degenerative tendencies of British mercantilism, which is the novel's main satirical object.[83] Aristocratic capitalism brings the novel, in other words, to a happy ending. The Rajah's introduction to Darnley is prefaced by an anecdote told by one of Darnley's tenants, Gilbert Grub, about an inheritance of 150 guineas that one of Grub's relatives bequeathed to Darnley, since it was Darnley alone who had supported him throughout his life. But Darnley conceives himself to be a trustee appointed for the fair distribution of the inheritance to all of Grub's kinspeople: "'God forbid . . . I should take a far-thing, that my conscience told me was the property of another!'" (2:307). This tableau near the novel's conclusion offers the aristocratic capitalist's commitment to traditional property rights as an emblem of the British counterrevolution's global ideology.

A Spatio-temporal Fix for Bengal

But regardless of its own claims, the Permanent Settlement did not align ancient Indian traditions with modern political economy. Instead, it accelerated the history of colonial enfeudalization.[84] Rather than improve their property, the zamindars chose to use their state-protected status to intensify the rack-renting of their tenants, whose rights the colonial government chose not to protect in deference to the moral economy aristocrats (like Darnley) formed with their tenants. The peasants' surplus underwrote the zamindars' urbane lives as absentee landlords in Calcutta, comfortably removed from the source of their income. Bengal gradually reverted to preindustrial modes of production, ultimately becoming a noncompetitive sphere from which the British Empire could extract primary goods and devalued labor. These facts now constitute a history we know too well, recounted from *A Rule of Property for Bengal* to the volumes of *The New Cambridge History of India* and beyond.[85] What our histories do not explain is the logic behind the Permanent Settlement's construction of an unproductive colonial economy. From the perspective of a *capitalist* modernity, such an economy appears to be aberrant. Guha eloquently encapsulates this perspective: "Capitalism which had built up its hegemony in Europe by using the sharp end of Reason found it convenient to subjugate the peoples of the East by wielding the blunt head."[86]

In fact, the explanation of the Permanent Settlement lies not in capitalism as it is conventionally understood but rather, as Robert Travers's recent studies make clear, in military fiscalism. Despite its stated aim to ensure that the zamindars would keep enough rent to reinvest it in improvement, the Permanent Settlement did *not* lower the Company's revenue demands but kept them at the high levels of the preceding decades, in proportion to its military costs.[87] The Company's most pressing need was to show potential creditors that it had a *fixed* source of revenue that could serve as collateral in the global financial networks emerging all around it. The Company needed to impose a "spatio-temporal fix"—to use David Harvey's term—on Bengal or, in other words, to extract a fixed quantity of rent over a given period of time.[88]

Hence, the Permanent Settlement not only fixed the Company's revenue demand in principle but also insisted on the collection of this fixed demand in practice. Where the Mughal Empire accepted discrepancies between the rate at which it assessed its lands and the amount the zamindars could pay in any given season, the Permanent Settlement insisted its demand be paid in full, even if they were forced to sell their lands to do so.[89] As a consequence, the *majority* of the zamindars did in fact sell their lands. In the process, the Permanent Settlement established the tripartite structure (landlord-tenant-labor)—famously at the origins of capitalist wage labor—that already characterized British property relations, thereby pulling Bengal into modernity. When the principles behind the Permanent Settlement were disseminated across the British Empire, modernity would drag many more colonies along. But with rent mortgaged to war in the colonies, capitalism's original tripartite structure led not to productive dynamism but instead to economic sclerosis. One could argue that this colonial difference—the sacrifice of production to the exigencies of war—is in fact modernity's essence.[90] Regardless, it was no coincidence that the main period of the British Empire's territorial expansion (1795–1805) occurred immediately after the establishment of the Permanent Settlement, even as Bengali agriculture was being ruined. Using debt to finance war, the British state and the East India Company bankrupted colonial property.

Jones's legal codes argue that the Company's rule of property merely restored its subjects' ancient traditions: he claimed that "the old Hindus . . . were absolute proprietors of their land" and, furthermore, that "[man's] right of property . . . distinguishes [him] from other animals and from things inanimate" in Islamic thought.[91] But the Permanent Settlement was in reality an absolutely novel arrangement by means of which colonial officials, throwing up their hands at the fluidity and diversity of local property relations, imposed a fixed and universal principle in their place.[92] The supposedly ancient aristocracy that the Permanent Settlement entitled had been, far from nobility, the Mughal Empire's tax collectors. When it fixed their property rights, the Permanent Settlement effectively turned these erstwhile taxmen into a comprador class that depended on the Company to protect its expropriation of peasant labor. At the same time, the Permanent Settlement stripped them of the sovereignty they had exercised over their property and markets. In doing so, it simplified the Bengali economy, rerouting revenue streams toward the Company. The Permanent Settlement was, in short, the Company's most thorough attempt to replace the heterotopia that characterized native property with a British model of absolute sovereignty.

Jones's codes claim that the Company aimed ultimately to join "the old jurisprudence of [India]" with "the improvement of a commercial age."[93] He insisted that fixed rent demands would make colonial rule a "blessing" to the natives as well as "a durable benefit" to the British.[94] From this avowedly capitalist perspective, the value of the codes lay in the fact that, whatever their "defects," they are "revered, as the word of the Most High, by nations . . . whose well directed industry would add largely to the wealth of *Britain*."[95] Hence, the codes presumed to lay the groundwork for subsequent economic development. However convincing, Jones's argument here is as false as his claim that ancient traditions justify the colonial rule of property. The Permanent Settlement played its role in global financial networks without providing a durable source of revenue, much less serving Europe's "commercial interests." As short-term collateral, colonial property was more valuable when it was fixed than when it was productive. The historical significance of Jones's legal codes lay in their capacity to authorize this fixed structure, wherein colonial property realized its value. Jones unwittingly acknowledged that value: he noted that the "resources of *Bengal*" will "continually increase" only "when [landowners] shall have well grounded confidence, that the proportion of [the land tax] will never be raised, *except for a time on some great emergency, which may endanger all they possess*."[96] Colonial property never ceased to be mortgaged to modern war, because it was not an exception but the rule. The Orientalists' scholarly-textual tendency to reify Indian history matched the Company's military-fiscal need to "fix" the Indian economy perfectly. When colonial Orientalism and the colonial rule of property are placed, as they in fact occurred, side by side, their underlying logic suddenly reappears: it involves neither a will to know nor the rise of a capitalist modernity but rather the reorientation of property toward war, the historical rupture Orientalism facilitated and still now obscures.

A few months before his death, Said wrote the foreword to the twenty-fifth-anniversary edition of *Orientalism*, in the immediate aftermath of the U.S. occupation of Iraq; he drew attention to the essay's historical context by concluding it, simply, with a date ("May 2003"). Within the foreword proper, both at its outset and its end, Said made clear that he considered *Orientalism* in particular and the intellectual vocation in general to be instruments of Enlightenment.[97] His references to Enlightenment evoke Kant's definition of *Aufklärung*: "the public use of reason," a type of thought that steps outside state and professional rationality and subjects them to criticism.[98] This "attitude" of the Enlightenment—an open-ended critique meant to lead not to a new sovereign form but rather, in Kant's terms, to "an exit from one's self-incurred immaturity," or in Said's, to "liberation"—describes precisely the intellectual and political stance Said assumed throughout his public life.[99] An irony of postcolonial studies over the past two decades—when it has increasingly critiqued what it refers to as Enlightenment reason in the name of a nonstatist politics—is that in doing so, it extends this Enlightenment project.[100] Those who disavow this tendency within postcolonial studies place the responsibility for it squarely on Said's shoulders.[101] But unlike them, he realized that exile from the state-form was the telos of the Enlightenment's own critical method. In Said's exilic demand for a ceaselessly critical orientation toward one's own time and place—an untimeliness or what he would call in his final work "lateness"—the Enlightenment returns in its most intransigent form.[102] Though this fact is rarely acknowledged, the Enlightenment itself bequeathed the critique of governmental reason to postcolonial studies.

Hired by the nascent colonial state, Orientalism started its own professional career in the late eighteenth century. But what state interests did this professional reason serve? Until we consider this question, we cannot begin to work through the specific relationship of Orientalism to imperialism "analytically and historically," as Said insisted we must.[103] Until we answer it, we cannot know the substance of the modernity from which our critical method must free itself. Said's own temperament and training, if not his critical ideals, colluded in avoiding the question: *Orientalism* turned colonial history into a textual process in spite of itself. If "Orientalism overrode the Orient," the study of Orientalism has equally overridden the material specificities of colonial history.[104] However schematically, this chapter has attempted to account for that history. It reveals the essence of the modern state-form to be neither the stereotypically capitalist imperative to turn the colony into a space of always increasing production *nor* the stereotypically imperialist imperative to let it remain a source of tribute, a feudal aberration trapped within a modern trajectory.[105] The history in which Orientalism and colonial rule came together fits neither of these narratives. It foregrounds instead the antiproductive exigencies of war, which depended above all on the European state's capacity to fix the colonial economy spatially and temporally. This endeavor depended, in turn, on the textual protocols of Orientalism for its legitimacy. This now obscure history troubles both that era's sovereign claim to have aligned ancient property rights with modern political economy and our own scholarly premise that either the Enlightenment will to govern or the logic of capital lies at the heart of modernity. Attention to this colonial history, since it interrupts all such narratives, is part of a simultaneously Enlightenment and postcolonial project, every bit as pertinent to our own hyperarmed and indebted present as it is to the colonial past.

7
HISTORY, ANACHRONISM, VIOLENCE
Morgan's Missionary *and Scott's* Guy Mannering

Studies of the historical novel conventionally read it as the literary form of progress. They tend to do so according to either a Hegelian-Marxist concept of progress, like Lukács in his seminal work *The Historical Novel*, or a liberal concept of progress, like much recent scholarship. In the former case, the historical novel discloses the otherwise invisible relationship between the reified appearance of things, on one hand, and concrete forms of labor, on the other.[1] In the latter case, the historical novel performs aesthetically what capitalism achieves materially, turning traditional value systems toward a modern principle of universal value.[2] In either case, the historical novel works for progress, subsuming otherwise geographically and temporally divergent realms into the univocal course of world history.

The rise of the historical novel concludes the literary history this book has studied. With this genre, the Enlightenment vision of colonial rule as a *degenerative* military-monopoly system begins to turn instead into a post-Enlightenment vision of colonial rule as the *progressive* transformation of tradition into modernity. It is no coincidence that two of the historical novel's earliest instances—Lady Morgan's *The Missionary* (1811) and Sir Walter Scott's *Guy Mannering* (1815)—focus on colonial India: in the early nineteenth century, the opposition between tradition and modernity appeared to be playing itself out there more momentously than any other place in the British Empire. *The Missionary* uses this opposition, accordingly, to explain native mutinies within the colonial army; *Guy Mannering* does so to explain native insurgency against colonial rules of property. By the early nineteenth century, then, colonial violence had ceased to be a sign of colonial rule's degeneracy and instead become a correlate of historical progress.

Though both novels use the idea of progress to understand the roots of colonial violence, the actual institutions of progress did not yet exist in British India. The previous chapter noted that the idea of progress began to shape the dominant representation of British India only during the 1790s. This chapter considers an even stranger paradox: the material history of progress began to shape colonial India later still, only after the 1813 Charter Act. As the historical novel concludes this book's literary history, so the Charter Act marks the decline of the corresponding period in political economy, the mercantile era. This act eliminated both the East India Company's monopoly on Indian trade and its prohibition of missionaries, thereby throwing British India open to the agents of both liberalism and evangelism. Only after the Charter Act can we can properly identify colonial rule in India with progress in any sense.

Early British India demands therefore that we think outside the analytic frame of progress, in which modern history is always a conflict between traditional modes of production and the forces of capitalist reorganization. We tacitly adopt this frame whenever we presuppose an idea of progress, whether we advocate a Hegelian-Marxist version of it as Lukács did or we critique a liberal version of it as recent scholarship has. In either case, we enclose historical conflict within a dialectic whose direction is already decided: history has unfolded in a certain way, whether we like it or not; fulfilling our intellectual responsibilities depends on understanding this history alone.[3] If we instead think outside the analytic frame of progress, we may be able to understand literature outside it as well—indeed, how literature calls it into question.

In its reading of the historical novel's relationship to "progress," this chapter differs from the prevailing scholarship. Its counterintuitive premise is that if we want to think outside progress, the early historical novel will be an exemplary guide. Precisely to the extent that it represents historical conflict as the progressive transformation of "obsolete" forms of life, the historical novel contains traces of those lives and their different values. Dramatizing the work of progress, the historical novel helps us undo that work and reimagine life outside progress's historical continuum. It interrupts the work of progress whenever it represents the histories that we consider merely antecedent to our own in terms of values that cannot be assimilated to ours.[4] In other words, the historical novel exits progress, when we read it not as progress's dutiful henchman—unfailingly "faithful," as Lukács would have it, to history—but rather as literature: a mode of representation that questions history's limits.[5]

This chapter preserves the Enlightenment's vision of colonial rule within the different dispensation we inhabit—in which the collusive relationship of militarized states and monopoly corporations has become only more powerful and hence in which that vision has acquired even greater urgency. When the historical novel interrupts progress, it makes the Enlightenment's critical vision available in a form that is pertinent to us now. It hints at alternative histories, rich with forms of production, meaning, and value that the idea of progress and our own analytical methods alike have abandoned. Such histories can now only haunt our very different kind of knowing, but their spectral presence still has the power to disturb the complacency of that knowledge.

The Missionary

Not only had the Company always prohibited evangelism but the first Company official to vet the idea of evangelism publicly did so only in 1805, when Company chaplain Claudius Buchanan called for "*civilizing* the natives" in his *Memoir of the Expediency of an Ecclesiastical Establishment for British India.*[6] Even then, though, Buchanan imagined evangelism to be the Company's antidote, not its instrument: Christianity would ameliorate the Company's extraction of India's resources. Buchanan asked rhetorically: "From [India] we export annually an immense wealth to enrich our own country. What do we give in return?" (40). But Buchanan realized that the Company could not afford to civilize its subjects: "It is easy to govern the Hindoos in their ignorance, but shall we make them as wise as ourselves! The superstitions of the people are no doubt abhorrent from reason; they are idolatrous in their worship, and bloody in their sacrifices; but their manual skill is exquisite in the labours of the loom; they are a gentle and obsequious people in civil transaction" (41).[7] Buchanan understood that the Company legitimized its rule by appearing to be an organic extension of native tradition; it had no interest in appearing, and even less in being, a progressive force.

But he understood as well that the Company's political economy was becoming obsolete: "Every character of our situation seems to mark the present aera, as that intended by Providence, for our taking in to consideration the moral and religious state of our subjects in the East" (2). With the Napoleonic blockade of European markets, British industrial capital desperately needed other outlets. Increasingly powerful, it was about to end the Company's two-century-old monopoly on trade with India. It would subsequently attempt to cultivate Indian taste, moving it away from its own textile production—its "exquisite" "labours of the loom" that had dominated world markets for centuries—toward the consumption of British textiles, whose export would spur the British Industrial Revolution. We will return to this history later: for now we need only observe that Buchanan's *Memoir* did not shift the Company's attitude but instead sparked a public debate in which the Company defended its position.[8]

This debate was interrupted by reports of a native uprising. Two hours after midnight on 10 July 1806, in the East India Company fort at Vellore (Madras Presidency), 1,800 sepoys carried out a mutiny that they had been plotting for months.[9] Having secured the fort's armaments, they entered the officers' quarter and opened fire on the men sleeping there. Once finished, the sepoys had gained control of the fort, having killed perhaps 130 and wounded approximately 90 of the 370 British colonists stationed there. Retribution came as quickly and violently as the uprising: arriving from Arcot the next morning, British dragoons retook the fort immediately, killing hundreds of sepoys in the process.

Contemporaneous accounts generally identify an order issued by Army Commander in Chief Sir John Cradock as the immediate cause of the mutiny.[10] Intending to introduce the troops to proper military discipline, the order replaced the sepoys' turban with a British-designed topi and forbade them to display any marks of their caste or religion. From the moment the order was instituted in March 1806, the troops rejected the topi, choosing to parade with their heads covered only by handkerchiefs, while deriding their English officers as "dogs." Cradock arrested, court-martialed, and whipped the sepoys in response. But after the uprising Governor William Bentinck paradoxically pardoned 600 mutineers (albeit also sentencing 37 natives to death, including 6 "blown from the mouth of a cannon"), and rescinded the turban order.[11] From the first days after the mutiny, one strand of its scant historiography claimed that the sepoys became violent because the turban order violated their religious sensibilities. Bentinck took this claim for granted in private correspondence with Cradock immediately after the mutiny: "I am not surprised by the general apprehension of the sepoys that their religious customs are no longer to be respected. Under these circumstances the clause [about the turban] becomes a bad one and . . . wisdom appear[s] to require that it should be immediately abandoned."[12]

After reports about Vellore reached London, the debate Buchanan had started about the Company's ban on evangelism revolved around the violence at Vellore, involving more than twenty-five authors in a pamphlet war and, eventually, both the *Quarterly* and *Edinburgh* reviews.[13] The Company's directors used the mutiny to advance their case against evangelism even more vehemently, presenting the mutiny as evidence of the violence evangelism would inevitably incite. They argued that the origins of the mutiny lay in "opposition to the innovations in the customs and religious institutions of the sepoys, fanned to heat by general rumours of their forced conversion to Christianity" and censored Buchanan for the *Memoir*'s attack on Indian religion.[14]

The Vellore Mutiny became a footnote to *The Missionary*, whose author, Lady (Sydney Owenson) Morgan, was already famous across Europe not only for *The Wild Irish Girl* but also for her political radicalism during the Napoleonic Wars.[15] *The Missionary* follows the early seventeenth-century voyage of the Portuguese monk Hilarion from Lisbon to Goa as the new Apostolic Nuncio of India. He subsequently leaves Goa to proselytize in the autonomous province of Kashmir but instead falls in love with the novel's Indian heroine, Luxima. The greater part of the novel describes their romance. Near its close, Inquisition officers from Goa imprison Hilarion for his indiscretions with Luxima. Having just escaped imprisonment herself, she discovers him as he is about to burn at the stake. Delirious from her detention, she imagines that he is her husband and the Inquisition fire is his Hindu funeral pyre, and she begins to commit sati. Hilarion breaks free from the officers' grasp to save her, but they attack him, and the dagger they mean for him finds Luxima instead. This stabbing provides the "impulse" for an Indian uprising that European forces quickly defeat.[16]

To gloss this fictional uprising, Morgan turned back to the historical one at Vellore. Like the contemporaneous accounts of the mutiny, *The Missionary*'s footnote describes it as a conflict between tradition and modernity: "An insurrection of a fatal consequence took place in *Vellore* so late as 1806, and a mutiny at Nundydrag and Benglore occurred about the same period: both were supposed to have originated in the religious bigotry of the natives, suddenly kindled by the supposed threatened violation of their faith from the Christian settlers" (248–49). Brief though it is, the footnote deftly encapsulates the basic terms the novel uses to dramatize the uprising and, by extension, the colonial encounter. According to it, the factors that produce colonial violence are European colonial rule's apparent "violation" of native religious traditions, on one hand, and the "religious bigotry" or irrationality of those traditions, on the other. Echoing both Bentinck and the Company directors, the footnote reduces colonial conflict to a confrontation between two stages on the continuum of historical progress.

But the irony of the Company's position that the sepoys rose up in response to the prospect of "forced conversion to Christianity" was that there was only one missionary in the whole of Madras Presidency.[17] And the irony of the footnote's implication that the Company threatened the sepoys' faith was that it refused to lend even this single missionary any support.

PROGRESS

The anachronism at the center of *The Missionary* is the representation of colonial rule in terms of progress before progress had entered British India. This
anachronism will remain invisible to us as long as we understand colonialism as
a conflict between "modernity" and "tradition." The emergence of these categories in the early nineteenth century effectively disabled the eighteenth-century
critique of empire: the alignment of modernity and tradition with colonial rule
and native society, respectively, rendered the former historically necessary and
the latter obsolete. The discussion of *The Missionary* that follows aims not to
provide a comprehensive reading of the novel but rather to consider the operation of such categories within it, where they evacuate native resistance of its
politics. This discussion argues that when "modernity" and "tradition" become
terms of historical analyses, they play into empire's hands.

Although the scholarship on *The Missionary* has not discussed its footnote
to the Vellore Mutiny, it is less the case that Morgan used the mutiny to gloss one
moment in her novel than that she used her whole novel to gloss the mutiny,
upon the analysis of which the future of progress in India seemed to depend. The
novel was published during the debates that preceded Parliament's historic 1813
renewal of the Company's charter. Hence with *The Missionary*, the nascent genre
of the historical novel became involved in the interpretation of colonial violence
in India. It was well suited for the task. Born in colonial spaces, first with Maria
Edgeworth and Morgan in Ireland and later with Scott in Scotland, the historical novel aimed to replace the colonial history of violence with an aesthetics of
reconciliation.[18] It performed this substitution by using romantic relationships to
allegorize colonial conflict. *The Missionary*'s Luxima, the High "Priestess" (38) of a
Brahmin sect, adapts a role Morgan developed for *The Wild Irish Girl*'s Glorvina,
a Celtic "princess," the female embodiment of national traditions. The romantic
allegory implies the possibility of "union" between not only synchronically divided geographies within empire (colony and metropole) but also diachronically
divided temporalities in the progress of society (tradition and modernity). The
romantic relationship implies that colonial conflict occurs not between fundamentally different orders that have been unified violently but rather between two
moments on a single continuum that could be joined organically.

But *The Missionary* is set in the early seventeenth century, when Goa's imperial situation was uniquely complex: while Goa was a Portuguese colony, Portugal
had become part of the Spanish Empire. The retrospective placement enables the

novel to distinguish empire outside Europe from empire within—in other words, to differentiate British India from colonial Ireland and the Napoleonic Empire. The novel opens by looking forward to the Portuguese revolution against the Spanish Empire (1640): "The spring of national liberty . . . produced one of the most singular and perfect revolutions which the history of nations has recorded" (1). The Portuguese revolution—and perhaps by implication colonial insurgency within Europe, such as the unsuccessful Jacobite (1745) and United Irishmen (1798) rebellions against Britain, as well as the continental nationalisms against Napoleonic France—differ essentially from the Indian uprising at Vellore. Though Morgan was known internationally for her commitment to the revolutionary value of European nationalism, *The Missionary* implies that any revolt founded on Indian traditions would be intrinsically premature: they remain trapped in mythic consciousness and hence do not engender but rather block progress.

If colonial rule is, for Morgan, the precondition of Indian social progress, exposure to mythic consciousness is, conversely, the precondition of European spiritual fulfillment, enabling the colonist to become psychically integrated and rule traditional society more effectively. Having recovered the "nature" that lies dormant within himself by means of his relationship with Luxima, Hilarion calls for a colonial rule that is correspondingly sensitive to Hindu consciousness. To the Jesuits who deliver him to the Inquisition, Hilarion explains: "It is by a previous cultivation of [the Hindus'] moral powers [that] we may hope to influence their religious belief; it is by teaching them to love us that we can lead them to listen to us; it is by inspiring them with respect for our virtues, that we can give them confidence in our doctrine" (226).

Even though the novel purports to criticize colonial rule and to point the way toward its reform, the novel's criticism ironically prefigures—practically verbatim—the Company's very own administrative minutes:

When we have gained their attachment by mild and liberal treatment, they will gradually adopt from us new customs and improvements, which under a severe and suspicious government they would have rejected. [Thomas Munro]

It is not enough to give new laws, or even good courts; you must take the people along with you, and give them a share in your feelings, which can be done by sharing theirs. [Mountstuart Elphinstone]

The most important of the lessons we can derive from past experience is to be slow and cautious in every procedure which has a tendency to collision with the habits and prejudices of our native subjects. . . . We should adopt all we can of [native institutions] into our system. . . . All that Government can do is, . . . by adapting its principles to the various feelings, habits, and character of its inhabitants, to give time for the slow and silent operation of the desired improvement. [Sir John Malcolm][19]

In his seminal study of nineteenth-century imperial ideology, *The English Utilitarians and India*, Stokes referred to the generation of colonial administrators who emerged early in the century—most prominently, Madras governor Munro and his disciples, Bombay governor Elphinstone and Elphinstone's successor, Malcolm—as "romantic."[20] According to the historical narrative of both Stokes and Bearce, a romantic ideology motivated these administrators to oppose the Permanent Settlement with the supposedly Indian custom of personal government, which created a "sympathetic" bond between ruler and ruled. Such a narrative takes these officials at their word; as the previous passages illustrate, their own writings advanced this vision of early nineteenth-century Company policy, presenting it as an attempt to be sensitive to Indian traditions and forestall immature rebellion. *The Missionary*'s critique of colonial rule adopts the very terms colonial rule used to defend itself.

But the novel does not merely mirror colonial ideology; it tellingly supports progress much more wholeheartedly than the Company itself did—notwithstanding the fact that Morgan was internationally famous for her resistance to the British Empire. Like Buchanan, Hilarion believes that because Hinduism is essentially irrational, it must be "perfectly eradicated" (181) and "universally subverted" (184).[21] In contrast, Company bureaucrats gave little support to missionary activity even after Parliament legalized it in 1813.[22] For example, both Munro and Elphinstone opposed missionaries, with Munro actively punishing administrators who used their positions to spread Christianity. The Company was always only too willing to enact greater sympathy for native traditions, not because it wanted to provide progress an opening gambit but because it had created those "traditions."[23] Anachronisms of this kind are the ruse of colonial history: as long as we overlook them, we remain trapped within the ideology of progress.

VIOLENCE

As we have already observed, native violence was the precondition of colonial rule's "sympathy" for native traditions: for example, Bentinck rescinded the turban order not when the sepoys first rejected it but only after they had killed or maimed more than half the British officers at Vellore. Colonial rule is innately aware of the native capacity for violence; this awareness is present both in the administrative minutes just quoted and in Hilarion's comments to the Jesuits. But colonial discourse does not merely insist on the native's inherently violent nature; as recent postcolonial historiography attests, it also empties native violence of its political content.[24] Hence, while *The Missionary* opposes Buchanan's evangelism, it nonetheless reiterates his attitude toward native violence: "[Hindoos] are described by competent judges as being of a spirit vindictive and merciless; exhibiting itself at times in a rage and infatuation, which is without example among other people" (37). As Morgan placed "religious bigotry" at the source of native violence, so Buchanan placed "infatuation" there. In either case, native violence is prepolitical; native consciousness is intrinsically incapable of politics.

Buchanan took his examples of native violence from an article published in *Asiatick Researches* by former governor-general of India Lord Teignmouth, one of the few evangelical members of the Royal Asiatick Society. Like *The Missionary's* uprising, Teignmouth's examples all involve natives who become self-destructive when they attempt to act politically. Here is one example: "In 1791, *Soodishter Mier*, . . . the farmer of land paying revenue . . . in the province of *Benares*, was summoned to appear before . . . the duty collector of the district where he resided. He positively refused to obey the summons, [and] several people were deputed to enforce the process. . . . On their approaching his house he cut off the head of his deceased son's widow, and threw it out."[25] In each of Teignmouth's anecdotes, a native man refuses the rule of property in a form that appears to make no sense. The anecdote's representation of the fundamental difference between the colonial and precolonial orders prevents us from taking the latter seriously. By presenting native political consciousness as absolutely unreasonable, Teignmouth's anecdotes make the rule of property identical with political reason as such.

On the opposite side of the debate from Buchanan, East India Company proprietor Thomas Twining argued against evangelism on the premise that, because religious traditions constitute native consciousness, violating them would incite a mass uprising: "The people of India are not a political, but a religious people. . . . *They* venerate their Shastah and Koran, with as much enthusiasm as *we* our Magna Carta . . . if ever the fatal day shall arrive, when religious innovation shall set her foot in that country, indignation shall spread from one end

198 History, Anachronism, Violence

of Hindostan to the other; and the arms of fifty millions of people will drive us from that portion of the globe, with as much ease as the sand of the desert is scattered by the wind."[26] Even as Twining imagines a subcontinent-wide revolution, he describes a spontaneous act that would not make but erase history. Even in the act of revolution, Indians remain "not a political, but a religious people." The representation of native violence as fundamentally irrational served both sides in the metropolitan debate on colonial policy: the argument for evangelism on the grounds that it would civilize the natives and the argument against it on the grounds that it would provoke them.

But this representation of native violence also served a more profound logic. Such reports informed what would become the most influential exposition of world-historical progress, Hegel's *Lectures on the Philosophy of World History*, which references "English reports" of Hindu ascetic self-mutilation, sati, mass suicide, and infanticide. Hegel's frequently cited dictum that "the generic principle of the Hindoo Nature" is "the character of Spirit in a state of Dream" is the logical extension of these reports, echoing Buchanan's and Morgan's references to "infatuation" and "enthusiasm," respectively.[27] Like theirs, Hegel's idea of the Hindu dream-state implies that Indian attempts at political action are historically empty. He explains that "what we call historical truth . . . —intelligent, thoughtful comprehension of events, and fidelity in representing them,— nothing of this sort can be looked for among the Hindoos" (170).[28] The native's dream-state prevents him from grasping the dialectical relationship between material reality and human consciousness and hence from understanding either historically: "In a dream, the individual ceases to be conscious of self as such, in contradistinction from objective existences" (147). The incapacity to think historically entails the inadequacy of native politics and rationality: History "is an essential instrument in developing and determining [a rational political condition]. Because the Hindoos have no History in the form of annals, . . . they have no History in the form of transactions, . . . no growth expanding into a veritable political condition" (170).

Hindu "spirit" realizes itself therefore by means of religious ritual rather than of historical knowledge: it loses itself in a prehistorical experience of the "Absolute" that obliterates the opposition between subject and object. Echoing colonial reports, Hegel argues that Hindus are self-destructive, their violence against themselves merely the other side of their passivity and inaction: "However pusillanimous and effeminate the Hindoos may be in other respects, it is

evident how little they hesitate to sacrifice themselves to the Highest,—to An-
nihilation" (156). Indian consciousness is, therefore, "extravagant"—literally,
a wandering outside history's progressive trajectory. Hindu spirit "can only
come to a . . . consciousness of itself, by extravagating in a boundlessly wild
imagination" (174).

A half century after the Vellore Mutiny, before and during the 1857 Great
Mutiny it prefigured, Marx picked up on Hegel's idea: "This undignified, stag-
natory, and vegetative life, . . . this passive sort of existence evoked on the other
part . . . wild, aimless, unbounded forces of destruction, and rendered murder
itself a religious rite in Hindustan."[29] Here Marx stands on his head side by side
with Hegel, able like him to think of native violence only in idealist terms. In
order to locate the historical dialectic in a single space and time, originating
necessarily in Europe and spreading outward irreversibly from there, Hegel and
Marx needed to disregard extra-European forms of insurgency. The explanation
of native violence in terms of irrational religious tradition was as necessary for
Hegel and Marx as for the Company and its liberal critics: neither the philosophy of history nor modern political economy could afford to acknowledge the
precolonial order's historical legitimacy.

They all agreed, in other words, on the historical necessity that colonial rule
eliminate native productive relations.[30] None of them noticed the exceptionally
perverse anachronism implicit in their assumption that European modernity—
armed to the teeth and irredeemably in debt—would liberate forces of production supposedly enchained in other parts of the world. Once the European-led
dialectic annulled non-European modes of production—whether materially
under the pressure of monopoly corporations or conceptually under the pressure of liberal, Hegelian, or Marxist concepts of history—those emptied forms
could be situated onto a single historical continuum. But in themselves, such
forms remain stubbornly outside European models of progress, suggesting other
historical dialectics, guided by forms of reason Hegel and Marx were in no position to comprehend or value.

Morgan republished *The Missionary* in 1859, its explanation of native violence meant now to spell out the necessity of the Great Mutiny's failure.[31] But
by then the metropolitan debate was over: most European observers were on
the side of historical progress. Marx observes somewhere that world history occurs twice. He forgot to add: the first time as anachronistic fiction, the second,
as scientific materialism.[32]

MUTINY

Is it even possible now, so belatedly, to raise the question again of what happened at Vellore? The argument that the violence responded to a religious offense soon won the day, yet even after the mutiny, both the Hindu priests and the imams at Vellore insisted that the turban order contained no such offense.[33] What did such colonial violence signify before the analytic frame of progress redescribed it as the "wild" and "aimless" expression of a "vegetative life"?

We know at least that the planned mutiny ranged far beyond Vellore, as *The Missionary*'s footnote begins to comprehend ("An insurrection of a fatal consequence took place in *Vellore* . . . and a mutiny at Nundydrag and Benglore occurred about the same period"). In fact, "Vellore Fever" spread across Madras Presidency, up and down both the Coromandel and Malabar coasts. In July 1806, approximately ten thousand sepoys at Hyderabad refused to wear the topi and began to deride their British officers as well.[34] By the last week of that month, the sepoys at Wallajahabad also threatened to massacre the British officers there. In October, a British officer reported the mutiny at Nandidurg: "[A] rising amongst our men was to take place this night for the purpose of massacring all the Europeans. We have taken post in Captain Bayner's house, and without [immediate assistance] the most serious consequences to us, will most probably ensue."[35] One month after the Nandidurg sepoys were supposed to assassinate their officers, the sepoys at Pallamcottah planned the same. Infiltrating the garrison at Quilon, insurgents from Madras Presidency planned a mutiny there as well. In fact, Company investigations found plans to mutiny in every South Indian cantonment. In August, Bentinck wrote privately to Munro that "the conspiracy has extended beyond all belief and has reached the most remote parts of our army."[36] In October he wrote to Minto, "For many nights together after the mutiny at Vellore, I and every individual went to bed in the uncertainty of rising alive."[37]

We also know something about the sepoys who plotted these mutinies. They came primarily from rural areas and, in the case of Vellore, from the class of peasant-warriors who ruled agrarian villages or from South India's generations-old mercenary communities.[38] They joined the Company army because its conquest of South India left them few other sources of military employment. The Company had more or less completely brought all the southern princely states (Mysore, Arcot, Tanjore, and Travancore) to an end in the years immediately before the mutiny. This mass extinction of native sovereignty included not only powerful states such as these but also the "little kingdoms"—ruled by "poligars" or *palaiyakkarars*—that composed the southern and western parts of Madras Presidency. Many of the Vellore sepoys had served under a palaiyakkarar: the Company recruited Vellore's 23rd Regiment from the Tirunelvelli district, which the palaiyakkarar Kattaboma Naik had ruled until the Company executed him in 1801, whereas the 18th Regiment's 2nd Battalion, stationed at Bangalore, consisted of men who had served Tipu Sultan. But the Company employed only a small percentage of the soldiers who were demobilized when their sovereigns were dispossessed; the rest, still armed, were left jobless. When the Company took the Ceded Districts (formerly part of Mysore) from the Nizam of Hyderabad in exchange for military protection, the British commanding officer noted that the area "swarm[ed] with armed men who have no employment."[39]

If the sepoys had little choice but to turn to the Company, it depended on them even more. Unable to commandeer troops from the British state (which had its own wars to fight) or pay their salaries when the state could part with them, the Company had begun to turn to natives during the 1740s.[40] While the sepoys enabled the Company to expand its territorial possessions, these conquests only made the Company ever more dependent on the sepoys, since the cost of the wars the Company fought to expand the territory from which it collected revenue always exceeded that revenue, put it more deeply into debt, and drove it back to war. Caught in this vicious cycle, the Company employed ever increasing numbers of sepoys: by the time of the mutiny, the Madras army contained about fifteen hundred Europeans and thirty to forty thousand natives.

The sepoys entered the Company's service expecting the kind of mutual obligation that had defined their relations with native sovereigns.[41] But the Company had little practice in such relations. Perhaps more to the point, it often withheld the sepoys' wages to satisfy the more urgent financial demands of its creditors, its shareholders, and the indebted British state. Even when the sepoys received a salary, it tended to be roughly one-sixth of what European soldiers earned. The Company recognized the sepoys' grievances, Cradock suggesting that they were at the root of the mutiny and Bentinck himself acknowledging that "the sepoys have now fought with us for near a century . . . under every hardship and in arrears for many months."[42] The real reason Bentinck did not punish the vast majority of the Vellore sepoys was that Madras Presidency's future hung precariously on what little good faith he could inspire in them. But even he realized, as he noted in private correspondence, that "no dependence can be placed upon any of our native troops."[43] Company sovereignty left the sepoys no alternative but to serve it and at the same time disavowed any obligation to them. In place of the princely states' elaborate structure of patronage, the Company built only "jails and courthouses," as one native contemporary observed.[44]

But the princes were not forgotten. The most prominent among them were the sons of Tipu Sultan, the Company's most formidable opponent during the late eighteenth century. Apparently mindless of what they represented to the sepoys—a form of sovereignty premised on mutual obligation—the Company showed exceptionally poor judgment by transferring Tipu's sons and all their retainers to Vellore.[45] In doing so, the Company unwittingly reconstituted within the walls of its own garrison precisely the sovereign form it thought it had destroyed when it defeated and assassinated Tipu in 1799. Roughly three thousand of Kattaboma's former dependents who had taken part in the resistance he led in 1799–1800—which culminated in his public hanging—followed Tipu's family, relocating from the tip of India to the countryside around the fort. The Vellore sepoys rose up explicitly in the name of this other sovereign form, which the specters of Tipu and Kattaboma represented. For example, they allied themselves with the followers of the palaiyakkarars, recognized as their king the dethroned Nizam of Hyderabad and as their leader Tipu's son (who claimed incidentally that he would double their salaries), flew Tipu's flag when they gained control of the fort, and aimed to restore Tipu's line in Mysore. Ironically, the Company's failure to make its revenue match its military expenditures precipitated both the material destruction of precolonial sovereignty and its symbolic reactivation.

Long before Cradock issued the turban order, Muslim holy men (fakirs) performing "the Hindustani Drama"—a puppet show in which Muslims, aided by the French, drove the British from the battlefield—were reported at each of the garrisons.[46] The fakirs brought a proclamation from Medina calling on Muslims to dethrone the Company and reestablish Islamic rule. A court of inquiry revealed the fakirs to be conspirators in disguise and the conspiracy, which involved Maratha and French support, to have spread from Mysore to the other garrisons by means of both the fakirs and secret agents. Indeed, the other garrisons knew of the plans for the Vellore Mutiny before it occurred.

We can infer at the very least that the history of the mutiny was much more complicated than the analytic frame of progress can appreciate. Religion played a part, but its function was far from anything we could call "traditional." Religion—whatever that term ultimately signifies in a context such as this—appears here to have facilitated, not forestalled, native political agency.[47] More to the point, it is not clear how one could disentangle religion from politics in the mutiny—much less argue that the former compromised the latter. Regardless, the religious offense the turban order posed to Islamic and Hindu principles, if it posed any, was not the mutiny's cause, whose preconditions were much too materially rich to bear such abstraction.

Yet the turban order was in almost every instance—not only at Vellore but also Hyderabad, Bangalore, Nandidurg, and beyond—the signal conspirators chose to initiate a mutiny.[48] Even when the soldiers themselves had no objections to wearing the topi, the surrounding townspeople jeered them for doing so—in some cases refusing to let townswomen marry any sepoy whose dress conformed to European style—until the sepoys too rejected the topi. Why? What history did the turban contain justifying the violence enacted in its name? We turn now to *Guy Mannering*, because it is haunted by this history.

Guy Mannering

Accounts of the historical novel tend to begin with Scott, even though both Morgan's and Maria Edgeworth's narratives preceded his own. Jameson has commented that in Lukács's study, the historical novel "springs fully grown from Sir Walter Scott's imagination"; Lukács himself observed that "the new historical art begin[s] with Scott."[49] According to Lukács, Scott first put the new concept of "history as the concrete precondition of the present" into narrative form.[50] In Lukács's account, as in many recent studies, it is Scott's "immeasurable influence" that popularizes this kind of narration in the Western literary tradition.[51] Lukács championed Scott for precisely the same reason that Jameson has championed Lukács: Scott's historical novels, like Lukács's dialectical criticism, enable literature "to open a totalizing and mapping access to society as a whole."[52] In other words, literature discloses the relationship between base and superstructure, thereby providing knowledge of the social "totality"—the precondition, we have already observed in regard to Hegel, of reason, politics, and progress as such. To the extent that literature fails to do this, it must be subjected, Jameson insists, to ideological critique.

Like Morgan's first novel, *The Wild Irish Girl* (1806), Scott's first, *Waverley* (1814), focused on the coming of progress to one of Britain's domestic colonies. And like Morgan's second novel, *The Missionary*, Scott's second, *Guy Mannering*, projects its precursor's focus on progress to colonial India. As if to give aesthetic form to *The Missionary*'s call for the reconciliation of mythic consciousness and colonial rule, *Guy Mannering* is a historical novel governed, paradoxically, not by progress but by a curse; rather than materialist, the novel is haunted. The haunting implies that until the agents of progress acknowledge the traditional forces they have dispossessed, those forces will interrupt progress. Hence, the plot joins the course of progress only at the very end, when its protagonists— British military officers returned from colonial India—release it from the curse and superintend its development. These officers are qualified to do so because they embody a colonial rule that has brought progress to India and consequently models the reconciliation of tradition and modernity.

According to Lukács, Scott's novels gave "a perfect artistic expression of . . . the historical defense of progress."[53] An irony of Lukács's endorsement of Scott within *The Historical Novel*'s Hegelian model of literary history is that Hegel himself referred to Scott as a *seichter Kopf*, a shallow mind.[54] Hegel was much more attuned than Lukács to Scott's narrative extravagances, the fantastic vagaries to which Scott subjected his plots before he resolved them progressively. The historical novel necessarily possesses narrative tendencies that wander away from progress before they are brought into line with it. These tendencies cannot be understood in terms of progress and hence confound totalizing knowledge, however dialectical it claims to be. The following analysis of *Guy Mannering* concentrates on what haunts it, on the premise that the literary—as the interruption of any perspective that stakes the claim of "knowledge" and "universality"—must lie ultimately not in what hews to the dialectic but rather in what unfolds extravagantly.

PREHISTORY

Not only is the turban a motif in *Guy Mannering* but it represents a hard-won sensitivity toward non-European traditions. In its initial occurrence, it adorns the gypsy soothsayer, Meg Merrilies. When we first encounter her, she is "equipt in a habit which mingled the national dress of the Scottish common people with something of an eastern costume," which we learn later is a turban.[55] Merrilies is the matriarch of a "colony" of gypsy characters "who had for a great many years enjoyed their chief settlement upon the estate of Ellangowan" (34), the rural setting on the southwest coast of Scotland where much of the novel takes place. The turban insinuates a resemblance between the novel's gypsy characters and the British Empire's Indian subjects that, far from incidental, goes to the heart of the supposedly conflictual relationship between tradition and modernity.

When the laird of Ellangowan, Godfrey Bertram, is appointed justice of the peace for the surrounding area, he embarks on the "improvement" of his property. In a fashion typical of eighteenth-century Scotland, he "ruthlessly" prosecutes the "poachers, black-fishers, orchard-breakers, and pigeon-shooters" (33) who had operated on his estate.[56] Bertram's final act in the enclosure of Ellangowan is the dispossession of the gypsies. Occurring around 1765—the year that the East India Company became sovereign over Bengal—Bertram's dispossession of the gypsies determines the shape of the novel: as they pass Bertram on the road out of Ellangowan, Merrilies pronounces the curse that haunts the plot.

The simultaneity of Bertram's dispossession of the gypsies and the Company's conquest of Bengal might be coincidental, but the parallel between Bertram's gypsy tenants and the Company's Indian subjects is not. Though Europeans had traditionally assumed that gypsies originated in Egypt, studies from the late eighteenth century—reinforced by Company Orientalism—proposed India as their origin; by the time of the novel's publication, the latter view was generally accepted. The "Indian theory" of gypsy origins had two pillars, first articulated by Heinrich Grellman's *Dissertation on the Gipsies* (trans. 1787): Romani and Hindustani were part of the same language family; and gypsies emerged from India's outcastes. Scott himself advocated this theory in a sequence of contributions to *Blackwood's Magazine* and in the notes to the Magnum Opus edition of *Quentin Durward*.[57] Rearticulating the idea that gypsies had emerged from India's outcastes, Scott refers to Bertram's gypsy tenants as "the Parias of Derncleugh" (38), the part of Ellangowan where they reside.

While Scott adorned his lead gypsy character in stereotypically Indian clothes, he clearly intended the expulsion of the gypsies to gesture beyond colonial India to dispossessed people across the globe. For example, he refers to the conflict between Bertram and the gypsies as "the Scottish Maroon war" (40), alluding to the First and Second Maroon Wars in Jamaica (1730–39 and 1795–96, respectively), in which the descendants of African slaves engaged in guerrilla warfare against British forces, inspiring revolt and plans to revolt across the West Indies.[58] And he prefaced the novel's eighth chapter with a John Leyden poem, "Scenes of Infancy": "So the red Indian, by Ontario's side, / Nursed hardy on the brindled panther's hide, / As fades his swarthy race, with anguish sees / The white man's cottage rise beneath the trees" (40). The novel's theme of dispossession is particularly appropriate for this period—of the Revolutionary and Napoleonic Wars—when the British Empire underwent unprecedented expansion, not only in India but also in the Caribbean, South Africa, Ceylon, and Java, as well as various offensives in Egypt and the Arabian peninsula.

Scott wrote *Guy Mannering*, furthermore, at the moment when the Scottish clearances reached their own "awful climax."[59] Just before beginning the novel, he sailed around Scotland for the first time in his life, seeing the consequences of the clearances firsthand. The act of dispossession that begins the novel, therefore, telescopes different spaces along the British Empire's global rule of property: the story of Ellangowan's improvement is at the same time a narrative of colonial property as such.[60]

Scott described the gypsies of Derncleugh in terms of the consciousness that precedes the rule of property, identifying them in the process with various non-European peoples:

The wildness of [the gypsies'] character, and the indomitable pride with which they despised all regular labour, commanded a certain awe, . . . not diminished by the consideration, that these strollers were a vindictive race . . . restrained by no checks . . . from taking desperate vengeance upon those who had offended them. These tribes were, in short, the *Parias* of Scotland, living like wild Indians among European settlers. (36–37)

Like Teignmouth, Scott described a consciousness that exists outside the rule of property and as a consequence responds to any perceived offense violently.[61] He attributed this consciousness not only to gypsies, Native Americans, and Indian outcastes in the present but also to Celtic peoples in the past. Hence, Bertram's own line begins, ironically, with nomads bereft of property: "His genealogical-tree . . . bore heathen fruit of . . . darker ages. [T]hey had been formerly the stormy chiefs of a desart, but extensive domain, and the heads of a numerous tribe. . . . They had made war, raised rebellions, been defeated, beheaded, and hanged, as became a family of importance, for many centuries" (7–8).[62]

As it represents the epochal transformation produced by the rule of property, the novel foregrounds its concern for those worlds—whether ancient Scottish, precolonial Indian, Native American, or gypsy—that exist under the threat of extinction. But like *The Missionary*'s, *Guy Mannering*'s sensitivity to such worlds always presupposes their obsolescence: they exist in the present only as relics of the past. Such a presupposition is implicit in the post-Enlightenment understanding of colonial rule as a diachronic conflict between tradition and modernity. This understanding enables us to humanize progress by making it "sensitive" to tradition but never to oppose it, since it is by definition historically inevitable.

THE CURSE

Merrilies's curse on Godfrey Bertram refers to his newborn son, Henry, and his unborn daughter:

This day . . . Ye have riven the thack off seven cottar houses—look that your ain roof-tree stand the faster. . . . There's thirty hearts there, that wad hae wanted bread ere ye had wanted sunkets, and spent their life-blood ere ye had scratched your finger. . . . Our bairns are hinging at our weary backs—look that your braw cradle at hame be the fairer spread up—not that I am wishing ill to little Harry, or to the babe that's yet to be born— God forbid—and make them kind to the poor, and better folk than their father. (44)

Merrilies's prophecy makes clear that Bertram's dispossession of the gypsies violates the code of mutual obligation between lord and subject, and she accordingly curses him with the decay of Ellangowan and the loss of his son. But she also foresees a more sensitive generation of Bertrams—"kind to the poor, and better folk than their father"—that will supervise Ellangowan's renovation.

Merrilies's curse sets into motion a highly complicated plot that not only contains the eighteenth century's primary tropes about empire but also cancels their prior meaning and elevates them into a post-Enlightenment vision. In the summary that follows, however, we need keep in mind only the plot's mythic pattern, which the critical literature on *Guy Mannering* has not recognized, and the plot's conclusion, in which British military officers from colonial India superintend the reconciliation of historical stages and so release the plot from mythic time. The novel practices formally what it preaches historically: it allows the mythic character whose dispossession begins the narrative to shape time, until she has been appeased.

In the days after Bertram dispossesses the gypsies, tea-smuggling pirates shoot Bertram's agent in the enclosure of Ellangowan, which targeted not only the gypsies but also thieves and smugglers. Bertram's agent dies while holding Bertram's son, Henry. Waiting in the wings watchfully over the Bertram family as always, Merrilies takes Henry for safekeeping, thereby enacting the stereotypical role of the gypsy who kidnaps the child, but rewriting it so that it leads not to the loss of identity but rather to the preservation of the lineage. Heartbroken about the loss of her son, Bertram's wife dies immediately after giving birth to a daughter. The pirates take Henry from Merrilies and send him to Holland, from where he is eventually shipped to India as a clerk in the Dutch East India Company (VOC). One of Bertram's employees, the lawyer Gilbert Glossin, has conspired with the pirates in the agent's murder and Henry's abduction in order to ensure that the estate would have no legal heir. After Henry's abduction, Glossin undermines Bertram's finances and becomes his creditor.

Having fallen willy-nilly into the world of the VOC, Henry resists the temptations of degenerate merchant capital by enlisting in the British colonial army. Henry's choice of vocation reiterates Guy Mannering's: he is an English aristocrat also of a decaying line who, like Henry, chooses the colonial army over colonial trade. After a decorated career dating back to the conquest of Bengal, Mannering becomes Henry's commanding officer. Their vocation ensures that a martial character disdaining commerce characterizes imperialists in this novel. They symbolize British India's turn-of-the-century transformation from the Company's degenerative tendencies to the liberal state's progressive policies.[63] This transformation involved the rise of a trained colonial civil service—begun in India and subsequently transferred to southern Africa, Ceylon, Malaya, and Java—whose education was modeled on a military curriculum. The civil service's claim to the civic virtue traditionally ascribed to the aristocrat enabled the empire to distance itself from the charges of corruption previously directed at Company rule.

Henry's abduction precipitates transitions across dialectically related historical stages, from the decaying aristocracy, to emerging merchant capital, to the progressive British Empire. These transitions convey an absolutely essential historical ideology—or, we could say, teleology. The Second British Empire resolved the conflict between aristocratic honor and merchant interest (which we have observed in every chapter of this book) by re-creating the figure of the aristocrat in the colony. It appeared in this way to subordinate the operation of the global economy to the ethos of mutual obligation. Henry's rejection of a mercantile in favor of an aristocratic vocation finally undoes Merrilies's curse, which imagined future generations of the Bertram aristocracy more sensitive to the dispossessed.

A second moment repeats Henry's original abduction and reverses it. At a fort on the colonial frontier, Mannering challenges Henry to a duel, on the premise that Henry has cuckolded him. Mannering's wife, shocked by the impression that he has killed Henry, pines away for some months before dying, leaving him their teenage daughter, Julia. Mannering retires from the army and settles in the vicinity of Ellangowan, for which he immediately felt a profound kinship when he first visited it on a tour of Scotland years before. Henry, though, had not died: wounded in the duel, he was kidnapped by native bandits. After months as their hostage, he escapes, voyaging to Scotland in pursuit of Mannering's daughter, Julia, the actual object of his desire.

The second moment in the mythic cycle transports Henry from the imperial periphery, through the hands of the natives the British army was pacifying there, back to a domestic periphery desperately in need of the rule of property. The two moments form a pattern composed of a shooting; an abduction by bandits who exist outside the rule of property; the death of a mother bereaved both times by Henry's apparent death; the partial orphaning of a daughter; and the radical transformation of Henry's identity. The repetitions suggest mythic time, organized by a force more powerful than modern reason. Henry's epic success in mastering mythic time qualifies him to guide progress: his experience of native culture provides him the Orientalist knowledge that informed the colonial rule of property and the rise of modern historical consciousness alike.

The narrative revisits Ellangowan only in late 1782—near the end of the American Revolution and the East India Company's Second Maharatha War (1780–82), at the origin of the Second Empire. Ellangowan's mortgaged condition resembles the British state's: its wars in America had placed it close to bankruptcy as well. Henry and Mannering intervene at this point, embodying a colonial rule based on respect for traditional society rather than ruthless expropriation. Led by Merrilies, Henry captures the Dutch pirate who had shot his father's agent seventeen years earlier and who provides evidence that the financier Glossin abducted Henry in order to acquire Ellangowan. Glossin's imprisonment near the novel's end enables Henry to repossess Ellangowan "amid the shouts of the tenantry and the neighborhood" and "Mannering to superintend certain improvements which he had recommended to Bertram."[64]

The implication of Anglo-Indian officers releasing time from its mythic pattern is that colonial India points the way toward progress. In *Guy Mannering*, colonial India becomes a model for history and, by extension, for the historical novel as well. But though the novel often alludes to the history of colonial India, it never represents it in detail.[65] The omission is essential: only absent its own history—only once the content of that history has been annulled, abstracted, and elevated—could colonial India become a model for world history. The next section returns to this absented history, which *Guy Mannering* simultaneously indicates and occludes. Taking the historical novel's own allusions as its guide, it revisits the histories "world history" could not contain.

COLONIAL PROPERTY

The novel's trajectory implies that colonial India helps Henry become "kind to the poor, and better folk than [his] father" when he finally returns to Scotland. It begs the question, therefore, of how the colonial state treated Indian "folk" during this time. The East India Company's relationship with its tenants was the question that most preoccupied it from its acquisition of colonial sovereignty (1765) to the Act of Permanent Settlement (1793). But the Permanent Settlement—which vested property rights in zamindars who had been the Mughal Empire's tax collectors—hardly made this question disappear. Rather than become the improving landlords the Company envisioned, the zamindars became rentiers, refusing to reinvest the wealth they extracted from their tenants back into the land. Hence, the Permanent Settlement did not encourage a capitalist agricultural economy but instead enfeudalized the Bengali countryside. Its failure only intensified parliamentary debates about the colonial rule of property, which reached their high point just before Parliament's 1813 renewal of the Company's charter.

In response to its failure, the East India Company began to vest property rights no longer in the zamindar but in the *raiyat* (peasant). The Raiyatwari (peasant-wise) Settlement paid close attention to the world of the raiyat, at least in theory surveying and assessing each peasant farm individually.[66] Where the Permanent Settlement conceived of property rights in universal terms, the Raiyatwari Settlement appeared to study them instead in their village contexts. It presented itself—and has been subsequently read—as an attempt, therefore, to rescue native tradition. The 1812 *Report* of the parliamentary Select Committee explains that "the active and intelligent investigations of the Company's servants [has] added to the stock of information . . . respecting local institutions, and the Hindoo system of Financial economy, as contra-distinguished from the altered and perverted form, which it assumed under the Mahommeddan governments."[67] The *Report* describes the new rule of property as "a system [to] conciliate the feelings of the native inhabitants . . . by a respect for their institutions" and claims that it is rooted in "the ancient laws and local usages of the country."[68]

It is no coincidence that the Company officials I quoted in the context of *The Missionary* (Munro, Elphinstone, and Malcolm)—whom Stokes and Bearce cite as examples of colonial rule's new sensitivity to Indian tradition—were responsible for establishing the Raiyatwari Settlement in Madras and Bombay presidencies. It was the Raiyatwari Settlement that made colonial rule appear "kind to the poor" and "better folk" than it had previously been. The replacement of

Godfrey Bertram's ruthlessness toward his estates' marginal inhabitants with Henry Bertram's sensitivity toward them recapitulates the replacement of the Permanent Settlement with the Raiyatwari system precisely. The system's emergence occurred just before the composition of *Guy Mannering*, and Scott knew Malcolm, among many other Company servants, personally.[69]

The Company's "sensitivity" to traditional property relations was a reaction to the violence incited by its own rules of property, which no less than Godfrey Bertram's had disregarded the customary rights both of peasants and of nomads.[70] The Permanent Settlement had dispossessed the former, since it recognized the landlord's rights alone. Hungry for land, dispossessed peasants migrated to *adivasi* (tribal) areas and disrupted the order of tribal society as well. In the case of nomads, the Company engaged, conversely, in forced settlement, in order to expand the territory from which it drew rent and to simplify the property relations that obtained there. Like the British state in regard to Highlanders and Irish pastoralists, the Company considered societies outside the rule of property depraved—and proved its point by provoking their violent resistance.

The Raiyatwari system's sensitivity to local diversity followed these cruder attempts to eradicate precisely that diversity and was in fact only a more advanced stage in the process. Its motive was not to preserve native traditions but instead to eliminate native sovereignty. By claiming that traditional property rights resided in peasants alone, the Company justified its rejection of native claims to sovereign power—and hence to territorial revenue.[71] Referring to Munro's plan to impose the Raiyatwari system over a large swath of Madras Presidency, Stein has commented: "He was proposing nothing less than the completion, by administrative means, of the military conquest of the Baramahal territory. . . . It was the perceived task of civil administration . . . to divest ancient local lordships of any capacity to resist or overturn Company rule."[72] The *Report* claims accordingly that the Raiyatwari Settlement protects the peasant from "the poligars, and other chiefs," who supposedly showed no respect for the peasant's property rights.[73] The Company's supposed commitment to the raiyat gave it a ready-made argument for its own territorial expansion: the *Report* observes that "one circumstance appears . . . to make the situation of . . . the natives under [British rule] superior to what it was under their Mahomeddan rulers[:] the *unity* of its authority, . . . which keeps every other power, in subordination to its own."[74]

The Company executed Kattaboma Naik precisely because he resisted its revenue demands. At first glance, the violence of its response—in which it killed several thousand of his followers and hanged both Kattaboma and his brother—seems illogical, because Kattaboma was a petty ruler, possessing neither much wealth nor the capacity to undermine the Company's authority. But the Company went to such lengths—unprecedented in the history of Indian sovereignty—because it wanted to make Kattaboma an example of what would happen to native sovereigns who dared defy the Company. Kattaboma's execution announced the entrance of the Company's absolutist form of sovereignty into Madras Presidency's farthest reaches: it would protect "the sanctity of regular payments of revenue" by any means necessary.[75]

The Company could not afford to share revenue with other sovereigns, because its economy was based on territorial expansion, not agricultural improvement, regardless of its claims.[76] Scott understood this economy exactly, as a conversation between Mannering and a guest at Margaret Bertram's funeral demonstrates:

> "I am afraid . . . we have not done with your old friend Tippoo Saib yet— . . . he'll give the Company more plague; and I am told, but you'll know for certain that East India Stock is not rising."
>
> "I trust it will, sir, soon."
>
> "Mrs. Margaret . . . has some India bonds. . . . It would be desirable now for the trustees and legatees to have the Colonel's advice about the time and mode of converting them into money." (215)

Henry will eventually use his relative's legacy, including her East India shares, to pay off Ellangowan's creditors and take back the estate. This conversation implies that native resistance is a problem because it threatens the value of that stock. But this was a peculiar kind of value. The very prospect of the Company's military victories over Indian princes such as Tipu—and hence of its accession to increased territorial revenue—made Company shares appreciate.[77] The capital that the British public invested in the Company by buying its shares enabled it to pursue new conquests, make its shares appreciate further, and satisfy the demands of its investors by generating a form of profit unrelated to increased productivity or indeed to economic production in any sense. The colonial economy came to rely therefore not on the improvement of property but rather on the conquest of territory. War as an economic strategy makes sense until it leads to bankruptcy, the Company's recurrent condition during this period and the precondition of its renewed concern with agricultural improvement. The very effort to defeat Tipu made the Company's debt soar to unprecedented heights by the time the

Company achieved it in 1799. In short, this conversation contains—in however occulted a form—the Enlightenment's critique of colonial rule: that its aim is not improvement and progress but rather global privatization in the interests of war.

TRADITION

Although the kinship of colonial law and the peasant's ancestral traditions under the Raiyatwari Settlement made it appear "kind to the poor," it actually enforced a series of momentous transformations.[78] It enclosed "waste lands" that had been shared in common and sold them. It compelled the raiat to produce not for himself and his family but rather for export to volatile South Asian and global markets. It made the raiat's property rights less secure, notwithstanding its own claims, because it renegotiated those rights annually. And it required the raiat to pay his taxes in cash, as a consequence of which he often became indebted to moneylenders and subsequently lost his land. Intentionally or not, the Raiyatwari Settlement turned Madras Presidency into a source of indentured labor for other parts of the British Empire.

The Settlement inherited its principles, furthermore, not from Indian traditions but, ironically, from the "yeoman economic individualism" of *Scottish* agrarianism.[79] Those who put the Raiyatwari Settlement in place in India—Alexander Reade as well as Munro, Elphinstone, and Malcolm—were in fact all Scottish. But the Scottish roots of Indian colonial property lie deeper still. From the Second Empire's origins in 1783, the Company turned to property management as a remedy to its failing war economy and undertook detailed statistical studies of Indian political economy and geography modeled on Arthur Young's surveys of Scotland. Grounded in Scottish Enlightenment stage theory, the surveys produced anthropologies of Indian peoples that appeared to display the colonial state's deep appreciation of its tenants' cultures but that simultaneously always rendered those cultures "traditional," historically prior and hence more primitive. The practices that made British India a prototype for the imperial state and the renovation of Scottish property in *Guy Mannering* came, paradoxically, from Scotland in the first place. Scott's ingenuity was to recognize that because Scottish agrarianism informed the colonial rule of property across the Second Empire, he could use late eighteenth-century Scotland to encapsulate many different colonial terrains.

The model of Young's surveys would spread from India and Ceylon through the Cape of Good Hope to Canada.[80] The Raiyatwari system would influence subsequent rules of property as well, and the forms of dispossession it engendered would become equally widespread, ranging from Southeast Asia to Canada and beyond. Along the way, colonial "improvement" rent the fabric of native economies so completely that it rendered them unproductive: the Raiyatwari Settlement itself was largely responsible for creating a "static" and apparently "timeless village India," the trope with which Indian tradition remains identified today. It was, ironically, the early nineteenth-century colonial rule of property that traditionalized India, literally forming the ground on which historical progress would subsequently take place.

The colonial rule of property failed to make native agriculture more productive, because, as noted previously, it redirected agricultural profit toward war.[81] The East India Company paid for its conquests with India's own wealth, using local revenue, for example, to finance the colonial army. In the novel as well, "improvement" depends on wealth that precedes it. Merrilies gives Henry "the treasure of the tribe" to help him recover Ellangowan; the only part he returns to the gypsies is what he uses to pay for her funeral (341). Mannering plans to build a "Bungalow" (354) for himself at Ellangowan: the very term he uses to name his country house insinuates its East Indian provenance.[82] He responds to the criticism that his ambitious plans for Ellangowan's improvement "will take the estate of Ellangowan on its back, and fly away with it": "Why then, we must ballast it with a few bags of sicca rupees" (354). This allusion is particularly rich, since it was the Company's demand that the princely states subsidize the Company army in *sicca* (silver) rupees that incited peasant insurgency in the first place and eventually forced the princes to cede territory in lieu of payment.

Like Hegel's *Lectures on the Philosophy of World History, Guy Mannering* presupposes therefore that "prehistorical" forms of life must be sacrificed to progress. But because progress ultimately takes a sympathetic form in the novel, those lives consent to their own sacrifice. Merrilies guides Henry to the Dutch pirate-smuggler who killed his father's agent seventeen years before. In the moment before Henry captures the Dutch smuggler, the smuggler fatally wounds Merrilies—her death therefore repeating Luxima's. As she lies dying, Merrilies embraces her fate: "I swore . . . to mysell, that if I lived to see the day o' [Henry's] return, I would set him in his father's seat if every step was on a dead man. I have keepit that oath. I will be ae step mysell" (337). She was a "victim," Henry realizes, of "her fidelity to his family" (340).

The vulnerability of nomads and pastoralists to the Company's relentless expansion gave them little choice but to participate in their own erasure. The Company used these groups as guides to the alien terrains over which it fought.[83] Its "respect" for natives was the corollary of its dependence on them. In the absence of such dependence—for example, with Australian aboriginals—British respect for indigenous culture was in short supply. When Henry first returns to Ellangowan, Merrilies suddenly appears before them, and Julia commands him to "give that dreadful woman something, and bid her go away." He responds simply, "I cannot. . . . I must not offend her" (325). Though he has no concern to protect her form of life, he will need her during his conquest of Ellangowan.

Rather than let the gypsies return to Ellangowan, Henry fulfills Merrilies's dying wish by building a cottage for himself where they had lived; there is, in other words, no place for gypsies in Henry's new rule of property. In art as in life: at the same that he wrote *Guy Mannering*, Scott used the phenomenal profits of his first novel to construct his own version of Ellangowan, Abbotsford, of which he eventually became the mock "laird."[84] His attitude toward the gypsies who occupied the property rehearsed Godfrey Bertram's exactly. Considering them "thorough desperadoes" and "the worst class of vagabonds," he made sure that the justice of the peace cleared the land completely before he began construction.[85] Here too progress needed to sacrifice what preceded it.

THE TURBAN

The Indian "costume" with which Scott first adorns Merrilies reappears after Mannering returns to Ellangowan: he spends his leisure drawing the turbans of the Company's defeated adversaries. His daughter, Julia, describes him, for example, "resuming the folds of a [Maharatha]'s turban in tranquility" (181). Mannering sketches another turban during a learned disquisition on tribals: "He had . . . got into a long description of the peculiar notions and manners of a certain tribe of Indians, who live far up the country, and was illustrating them by making drawings on Miss Bertram's work-patterns, three of which he utterly damaged, by introducing among the intricacies of the pattern his specimens of Oriental costume," which include "India turbans and cummerbands" (180). Whether worn by Merrilies or the Maharatha, the turban symbolizes a premodern culture that the rule of property must both respect and civilize. Mannering's portrait of the Maharatha repeats Scott's portrayal of the gypsy; in both cases, the labor of mimesis conveys sensitivity to native traditions. The novel presents itself, in other words, as the antithesis of 1806 military dress code in Madras Presidency.

It is worth noting that when Mannering's sketch overwrites Julia's work pattern, Indian clothes symbolically destroy English ones. But the priority *Guy Mannering* accords the turban rewrites a more complicated history. East India Company textiles such as the turban, the shawl, and the cummerbund became such fashionable commodities in Britain that they spurred a domestic manufacturing industry in imitation at the turn of the nineteenth century.[86] In order to outcompete India's centuries-old weaving industry, British capitalists mechanized textile production by devising principles that would form the basis of the Industrial Revolution. Indian cotton production could not respond to British mechanization in kind, because it involved hereditary occupations through which highly specialized and region-specific knowledge was passed down. The act of mimesis at the heart of the Industrial Revolution, in contrast to Mannering's, aimed not to preserve Indian tradition but rather to render it obsolete.

In fact, Parliament banned Indian textiles from British markets at the turn of the nineteenth century and forced the Indian colonies to import English textiles duty-free at the same time.[87] The year before Scott published *Guy Mannering*, English cottons flooded Indian markets, leading ultimately to the destruction of a textile economy that had dominated Indian Ocean trade for centuries, to the ruin of the countryside that supplied this economy, and to the creation of yet another generation of landless laborers. This moment marks a global shift: while India suddenly needed to import textiles for the first time in its history, Britain began to mass-produce cotton cloth, thereby stimulating the Industrial Revolution. The British economy's reliance on cotton would militate against the abolition of slavery in America and redirect subsistence agriculture across the empire to cotton export production instead.

Guy Mannering has no illusions about why the forces of progress imitate the culture of the dispossessed. The novel parodies the act of imitation, thereby detaching it from its original object and reflecting on the act itself. Julia's sketch of Hyder Ali (Tipu Sultan's father, who resisted colonial rule throughout the 1770s) mocks Mannering's portraits: she exclaims, "I succeeded in making a superb Hyder-Ally last night" (160). Julia's flippant attitude toward the object of her mimesis, in contradistinction to her father's earnestness, emphasizes not only that the representation of the defeated is the victors' prerogative but also that it becomes merely a style for them.[88] Where Mannering's mimesis implies that the

British Empire has absorbed—and so elevated—Indian tradition, Julia's insinuates that the continuity of colonial rule with native history occurs only after the
latter has been emptied of its content and turned into an abstraction.

Parodic versions of native tradition abounded in Scott's life: for example, it
was Scott himself who invented clan-specific tartan kilts, for a pageant celebrating the king's visit to Edinburgh. Though such kilts soon became the very symbol
of Scottish tradition, they have been described as a "bizarre travesty of Scottish
history" that had existed in no form therein.[89] Scott developed the equally bizarre
habit of dressing his servants in mock feudal garb, explaining that when his servant John Waynes finishes his work, "he solemnly exchanges his working jacket for
an old green one of mine, and takes the air of one of Robin Hood's followers."[90]
Here as in early nineteenth-century colonial India, an economy in which value
has become abstract imitates an older one in which it is supposed to have been
organic. The act of mimesis is meant to create continuity with the past but ironically emphasizes a more profound discontinuity: the past becomes reproducible
only after it has been turned into a shell of itself, bereft of its content. "Tradition"
is a modern anachronism, an extension of modern abstraction, "the creation of
the modern world" in Wallerstein's words, and "its ideological scaffolding."[91]

But clothes did in fact contain the trace of a radically different history throughout the colonial period. In diametric contrast to the Company, precolonial princes
generally recognized a sovereign obligation to return part of the revenue they
extracted from their subjects by purchasing the products of their labor, textiles
in particular.[92] These purchases were not market exchanges; the sovereign was
expected to be concerned with neither the commodity's appropriate price nor
his own material needs. The purchase exchanged much more than abstract value:
products of human labor were thought to contain a portion of the laborer's very
being—and subsequently, of the one who gifted them. When the prince purchased
a commodity from his subjects or gifted it to others, he ensured that his sovereignty and their subjecthood interpenetrated each other—not just economically
but also ontologically. His legitimacy rested on the extent to which his purchases
and gifts returned to his subjects the taxes he extracted from them and hence on
the extent to which he joined his being with theirs. With legitimacy conceived
in this way, the sovereign could separate himself from the local economy only
with great difficulty.

In regard to the ontological exchange between sovereign and subject, cloth
was thought to work a less instantaneously powerful, but more portable and

durable, transformation than food.[93] One's being was contained in one's clothes in direct proportion to the tightness of the weave—silk preserving one's being most securely, for example. Hence, while precolonial India exported more cloth than any other region of the world, the vast majority of its cloth was instead gifted in one direction or the other, up to the sovereign or back down to the laborer. Along the way, cloth became the medium of sovereignty itself; Bayly has observed that "Indian society spoke partly in the idiom of cloth."[94] *Guy Mannering* recalls this archaic tongue: the gypsies "were said anciently to have repaid" the Lords of Ellangowan for the protection they received from them by "sp[inning] mittens for the lady, and knitt[ing] boot-hose for the Laird" (37). Turbans were particularly expressive, since they were thought to contain male virility and, in Islam, a holy man's *barkat*, or charisma. We should note, in the context of the Vellore Mutiny, that there was no greater offense than to tear the turban off a man's head.

It was no coincidence that the East India Company placed its primary settlements—Bombay, Calcutta, and Madras—in India's textile-production centers.[95] The Company aimed to redirect that production toward exiguous costs native princes had never known. The Raiyatwari Settlement must be understood in this context: by falsely advertising the Company's continuity with native tradition, the settlement obscured the Company's overriding concern to turn its subjects' labor into the abstract capital of the European military-fiscal economy. The Company was intrinsically opposed to preexisting sovereign-subject relations. It wanted to make the legitimacy of the sovereign directly proportional not to its ontological intimacy with its subjects but to its capacity to suppress their resistance. The previously quoted observation that the Company built nothing but "jails and courthouses" acquires its full historical significance in this light—the Company had subordinated political economy to policing and production to war.

In the process, it undermined its own legitimacy. When the Company replaced the turban with the topi in Madras Presidency, it signaled the transformation of one type of sovereignty, in which cloth was the medium of reciprocity, into another, in which it became the medium of expropriation instead. When the sepoys used the Company's ban on turbans as the cue to mutiny, they implicitly rejected this concept of sovereignty. They aimed to replace the Company with the Islamic princes it had dethroned—and perhaps with the largely Islamic order of sovereignty whose eventual demise the East India companies' entrance into the Indian Ocean trading world had foretold two centuries earlier. The sepoys' revolt defended the turban against a sovereign form that claimed to preserve native traditions but that had in fact turned them into abstractions. It seems that, far from acting irrationally, the sepoys knew exactly what they were doing.[96]

For its part, cotton cloth carried the spirit of the mutiny across the history of India. The colonial state's refusal to purchase native textiles helped provoke the 1857 Great Mutiny: emphasizing that cotton imports harmed native life, rebels recruited aggrieved weavers to the cause.[97] A half century later, the Swadeshi campaign famously called for the boycott of imported textiles and encouraged native production instead. Later still, through his Khadi campaign and his own iconic wearing of *khaddar* (homespun cotton), Gandhi reactivated cotton cloth's precolonial associations. He claimed that in the act of weaving their own clothes, Indians would literally create a revolution in the very being of their nation— hence, the image of the spinning wheel enshrined at the center of the Indian flag. To repeat Moor Zogoiby's inference from his grandfather's habit of wearing homespun cotton in *The Moor's Last Sigh*, Indian colonial resistance always understood a simple but historically profound imperative: "To change your masters, change your clothes."[98] Anticolonial industrialists such as the Birlas and the Tatas drew a different lesson from the popular resonance of Gandhi's anti-industrial message: imitating the production of homespun cotton, their Bombay factories turned it into a source, ironically, of industrial profit.

.   .   .

When we imagine "tradition" to come from a distant past, we make history anachronistic. If we presuppose that the historical novel concerns the transition from "tradition" to "modernity," we imprison it likewise within this anachronism. We could, however, read the historical novel as the representation not of this false transition but rather of the modern invention of tradition itself. Whenever *Guy Mannering* reflects on the imitation of the past, it calls both historical and critical commonplaces into question. No less than eighteenth-century texts, though in more occulted ways, *Guy Mannering* aligns European modernity not with progress but rather with a degenerative military-monopoly system. And like those earlier texts as well, its historical vision is haunted by the Indian Ocean's radically different forms of sovereignty and production. Their spectral presence within the text always disturbs its progressive unfolding.

The aim of this chapter, as of this book in general, has been to read literature in a way that is sensitive to the global conditions it now inhabits. The mercantile era (whose afterlife we still inhabit, though our period goes by a different name) began by declaring the state the only sovereign entity—and merchant companies a telling exception to this Europe-wide rule. In other words, at the roots of modern sovereignty lies an alliance between hegemonic states and exclusive corporations. As each of the preceding chapters has demonstrated, the modus operandi of this alliance has been to search for economies that are more productive and less militarized than itself and to impose monopoly conditions on them. To obscure this constitutive act of violence, sovereign institutions must claim that their practices are continuous with their subjects' histories. They must replace those histories with an absolutely anachronistic discourse of "tradition" that naturalizes their own methods of expropriation.

The literature of the long eighteenth century does not merely mimic sovereign discourses but also necessarily intervenes therein. From Restoration drama and the rise of the novel to the origins of colonial Orientalism and the historical novel, all the works I have discussed interrupt these discourses by touching on the histories they needed to obscure. Each of these works—by Dryden, Defoe, Sterne, Foote, Smith, Bentham, Burke, Voltaire, and even Scott—allude in exceptionally precise ways to European violence in the Indian Ocean and to the native economies that existed there before. The histories indexed by such allusions do not constitute the history we know; they are rather what our history needed to exile. But they nonetheless persist in literature as the trace of other worlds and other ways of seeing. Their presence there turns literature into a different mode of historical perception—one that, if we were open to it, would call all our claims to knowledge into question, the scholar's no less than the sovereign's. The trace of these histories activates the critical energy of the Enlightenment in particular and of literature in general, which recalls what we have forgotten, thinks beyond what we know, and hence stops progress in its tracks.

Reference Matter

NOTES

INTRODUCTION

1. See Suleri, *Rhetoric of English India*, 4–7, 24–74; Teltscher, *India Inscribed*, 2, 6–7, 109–56, 192–228; Raman, *Framing "India,"* 3, 5, 13, 155–236.

2. See Muthu, *Enlightenment against Empire*, 1–12, 259–83; Pitts, *Turn to Empire*, 3–6, 25–121, and "Enlightenment against Empire," in Israel, *Enlightenment Contested*, 590–602.

3. Foucault, "What Is Critique?" 382–98, 392.

4. Fanon, *Wretched of the Earth*, 311–12. See Said, *Freud and the Non-European*, 21.

5. Guha, *A Rule of Property*, xiv. This comment is from the second edition (1982).

6. Said, *Orientalism*, 3, 42, 121.

7. Chatterjee, *Politics of the Governed*, 6. See also Guha, *History at the Limit of World-History*, 27; Chatterjee, *Nationalist Thought*, 39.

8. Chakrabarty, *Provincializing Europe*, 4, 20, and *Habitations of Modernity*, 278.

9. Chakrabarty, *Provincializing Europe*, 148.

10. Berman, *Enlightenment or Empire*, 8; Sarkar, "Orientalism Revisited," 242.

11. Chakrabarty, *Provincializing Europe*, 5; Aravamudan, *Tropicopolitans*, 328; Mufti, *Enlightenment in the Colony*, 5, 26. In the same vein, see Eagleton, "Nationalism," 30.

12. Chakrabarty, *Provincializing Europe*, 5; Prakash, "Writing Post-Orientalist Histories," 183 (my emphasis).

13. See, for example, Sahlins, *Culture in Practice*, 501–3.

14. Adorno and Horkheimer, *Dialectic of Enlightenment* (1999), 6; Hardt and Negri, *Empire*, 80; Chakrabarty, *Provincializing Europe*, 93; Nandy, "Politics of Secularism," 90; Laclau, *Emancipation(s)*, vii; Spivak, *Critique of Postcolonial Reason*, 429–30; Nussbaum, *The Global Eighteenth Century*, 2. See Schmidt, "Introduction: What Is Enlightenment?" 20–21. Cf. Adorno, *Critical Models*, 159.

15. Guha, *Dominance without Hegemony*, 14–16, 63; Guha's discussion draws on Marx, *Grundrisse*, 408, 410, 540.

16. Chakrabarty, *Provincializing Europe*, 70.

17. Eagleton, *The Function of Criticism*, 9, 10, 12.

18. Ibid., 12, 16, 27.

19. Ibid., 26.

20. Chakrabarty, *Provincializing Europe*, 29–30.

21. Ibid., 71.

22. Wallerstein, "The Bourgeois(ie)," 148. The quotation that follows is on the same page.

23. Deleuze and Guattari, *Anti-Oedipus*, 230. The quotation that follows is on 233.

24. Ibid., 233.

25. Parker, *Military Revolution*, xix, 89, 136, 174–75; Subrahmanyam, *Portuguese Empire*, 161.

26. Said, *Orientalism*, 5, 2–3, 7–8. The quotation is on 3.

27. Spivak, *Critique*, 141–42 (on "ab-using" the Enlightenment); Chakrabarty, *Provincializing Europe*, 4–5 (on the Enlightenment's "indispensability").

28. Subrahmanyam, "Introduction," 10.

29. Wallerstein, *Unthinking Social Science*, 202–17; Braudel, *Afterthoughts*, 64, and *Perspective of the World*, 486; Arrighi, *Long Twentieth Century*, 10–12.

30. Braudel, *Wheels of Commerce*, 230.

31. See Washbrook, "Progress and Problems," 60, 63–64, 66, 68, 72, "Economic Depression," 239, and "South India," 498–99. See also Bose, *A Hundred Horizons*, 13. Washbrook, "Economic Depression," 63, cites Perlin, "Proto-industrialisation and Pre-colonial South Asia," 30–95, and Chaudhuri, "Markets and Traders."

32. Braudel, *Wheels of Commerce*, 230.

33. In regard to that identification, see, for example, Wallerstein, "Eurocentrism and Its Avatars," 93–107; Wolf, *Europe*, 5–8; Young, *Colonial Desire*, 44; Porter, *Creation of the Modern World*, 425.

34. Diderot, *Political Writings*, 177–78; Raynal, *Histoire* 5:2–3. On Diderot, commerce, and colonization in the *Histoire*, see Pagden, "The Effacement of Difference," 130; Anthony, *Diderot's Politics*, 215–16. On Diderot's critique of East India companies and monopoly commerce, see Muthu, *Enlightenment against Empire*, 98–103. On Diderot's idea of the decay of civilizations, see Wokler, "Diderot, Denis," 67.

35. Ferguson, *Essay on the History of Civil Society*, 201.

36. Stephen, *English Literature and Society*, 21–23; Rothschild, *Economic Sentiments*, 16–17.

37. Pocock, *Barbarism and Religion*, 4:240. See Raynal, *Philosophical and Political History*, 1:107–8.

38. Pocock, *Barbarism and Religion*, 4:233, 239, 245.

39. Frank, *ReOrient*, 85.

40. Ibid., 91; Parthasarathi, *Transition to a Colonial Economy*, 5.

41. Davenant, *Political and Commercial Works*, 1:94. See the discussion in Arrighi, *Long Twentieth Century*, 35.

42. Hegel, *Reason in History*, 74, and *Die Vernunft in der Geshichte*, 143–44.

43. Hegel, *Reason in History*, 89.

44. Deleuze and Guattari, *Anti-Oedipus*, 194.

45. Mehta, *Liberalism and Empire*, 153; Dirks, *Scandal of Empire*, 282.

46. On the Hegelian transformation of Kantian critique into the driving force of history, see Hardt and Negri, *Empire*, 81–83. On the danger of reading Hegel back into Kant, see Muthu, *Enlightenment against Empire*, 164.

47. Israel, *Enlightenment Contested*, 591. See also Travers, *Ideology and Empire*, 250; Pagden, *Lords of All the World*, 6, 10, 196; Pocock, *Barbarism and Religion*, 4:232–33, 238, 245.

48. Bayly, *Birth of the Modern World*, 300. See also Pitts, *Turn to Empire*, 1.

49. For the political and economic differences between the largely unarmed trade that occurred in the Indian Ocean before European colonialism and the monopoly commerce that accompanied the colonial era, see Washbrook, "South India," 510, 512; Pearson, "India and the Indian Ocean," 79–82; Abu-Lughod, *Before European Hegemony*, 275; Chaudhuri, *Trade and Civilisation*, 14; Bayly and Fawaz, "Introduction," 18; Bose, "Space and Time," 377–78; Bose and Jalal, *Modern South Asia*, 27.

50. Kant, *Toward Perpetual Peace*, 14, and *Was ist Aufklärung?* 16. On this telos as the "boundless development of . . . diverse ways of life," see Wood, "Kant's Philosophy of History," 254. On "Idea for a Universal History" and difference, see Pagden, *Lords of All the World*, 190.

51. Kant, *Toward Perpetual Peace*, 12.

52. Ibid., 12; Kant, *Was ist Aufklärung?* 14.

53. Kant, *Toward Perpetual Peace*, 14, and *Was ist Aufklärung?* 16.

54. Kant, *On History*, 23. The more recent translation is "because of war, . . . the ever-growing burden of debt" (Kant, *Toward Perpetual Peace*, 14). In regard to military fiscalism, see Brewer, *Sinews of Power*, 21–130; Bayly, "First Age of Global Imperialism," 28–47.

55. See Virilio, *Pure War*, 11–12; Arrighi, *Long Twentieth Century*, 92, 99.

56. Kant, *On History*, 13.

57. Ibid., 12; Kant, *Was ist Aufklärung?* 4. The more recent translation is "this absurd course of human activity" (Kant, *Toward Perpetual Peace*, 4).

58. On the absence of historical reason in "Idea for a Universal History," see Deleuze, *Kant's Critical Philosophy*, 75.

59. On Enlightenment antipathy toward the state, see Muthu, *Enlightenment against Empire*, 280–82.

60. Condorcet, *Sketch*, 105, and *Esquisse*, 196.

61. Condorcet, *Sketch*, 194.

62. Ibid., 176.

63. Ibid., 199; Condorcet, *Esquisse*, 379.

64. Condorcet, *Sketch*, 176. On the analogous call for revolution in *Histoire des deux Indes*, see Pocock, *Barbarism and Religion*, 4:245.

65. Condorcet, *Sketch*, 194.

66. Defoe, *General History of the Pyrates*, 53. On the capture of the Mughal fleet, see Scammell, "European Exiles," 653, 656, 661.

67. Ackroyd, "Foreword," ix–x.

68. Defoe, *The King of Pirates*, 71.

69. Ibid., 73.

70. Ibid., 70 (my emphasis).

71. See Wallerstein, *Historical Capitalism with Capitalist Civilization*, 58–59.

72. On these trades, see Bayly, *Rulers, Townsmen, and Bazaars*, 151, 154, 238.

73. Spivak, *Critique*, 239.

74. Guha, *Dominance without Hegemony*, 67; Chatterjee, *Politics of the Governed*, 7; Bhabha, *Location of Culture*, 62; Aravamudan, *Tropicopolitans*, 307.

75. Adorno and Horkheimer, *Dialectic of Enlightenment* (1997), 26–27, 118–19; Horkheimer, *Eclipse of Reason*, 32, 96, 129, and "Reason against Itself," 360.

76. Adorno and Horkheimer, *Dialectic of Enlightenment* (1997), 24; Horkheimer and Adorno, *Dialektik der Aufklärung*, 40.

77. Adorno and Horkheimer, *Dialectic of Enlightenment* (1997), 24, 25, 26–27.

78. The concluding sentence of Adorno and Horkheimer, *Dialectic of Enlightenment* (1997), 208; Horkheimer and Adorno, *Dialektik der Aufklärung*, 234. See also the concluding sentences to Horkheimer, "Reason against Itself," 366–67, and *Eclipse of Reason*, 187.

79. Young, *White Mythologies*, 39, 40.

80. Foucault, "What Is Enlightenment?" 45, see also 38. See Scott, *Conscripts of Modernity*, 180.

81. Foucault, "What Is Critique?" 388, 393.

82. Foucault, "What Is Enlightenment?" 42.

83. Chakrabarty, *Provincializing Europe*, 108–9.

84. This form of thinking is for the Frankfurt School a feature of all thought, as old as mythology itself: see Adorno and Horkheimer, *Dialectic of Enlightenment* (1997), 11; Benjamin, *Selected Writings*, vol. 2, pt. 2, 578.

85. Adorno, *History and Freedom*, 89.

86. Horkheimer and Adorno, *Dialectic of Enlightenment*, 103.

87. Adorno, *Aesthetic Theory*, 178.

88. Ibid., 5.

89. Spivak, *Death of a Discipline*, 71.

90. Derrida, *Mémoires: For Paul de Man*, 73, and *Mémoires: Pour Paul de Man*, 83.

91. Ibid.

92. Defoe, *The King of Pirates*, 60.

93. Ibid.

94. Ibid., 60–61 (my emphasis).

95. On the impossibility of seeing pre-industrial forms of labor in our terms, see Baudrillard, *Mirror of Production*, 100–101. On the absence of printed native responses to colonialism in the eighteenth century, see Joseph, *Reading the East India Company*, 19. On exchange as part of a total way of life before the rise of market society, see Mauss, *The Gift*, 3–6; Polanyi, *The Great Transformation*, 48–52; Giddens, *Contemporary Critique*, 80–81.

96. On this version of the subaltern, see Chakrabarty, "Globalisation," 142, and *Provincializing Europe*, 110. On "the memory of the anonymous," see Benjamin, *Selected Writings*, 3:406.

CHAPTER 1

1. See Aravamudan, *Tropicopolitans*, 29–33. For studies that consider *Oroonoko* exemplary of modernity, see Gallagher, *Nobody's Story*; Ferguson, "*Oroonoko*"; Ferguson, "Juggling"; Brown, "Romance of Empire"; McKeon, *Origins of the English Novel*, 111–13; Spengeman, "Earliest American Novel"; Davis, *Factual Fictions*, 106–10.

2. For a discussion of the debate on the transition from feudalism to capitalism, see Subrahmanyam, "Introduction," 2–6. See also Pirenne, *Economic and Social History*; Hilton, *Transition*; Brenner, "Agrarian Class Structure"; "Origins of Capitalist Development"; "Dobb on the Transition"; and "Bourgeois Revolution"; Aston and Philpin, *The Brenner Debate*; Chatterjee, "Modes of Power."

3. Aravamudan, *Tropicopolitans*, 29.

4. Both works involve, finally, a non-European heroine whose chastity the merchants would or do violate and who in response wants to end her life. The names of the heroines resemble each other—Ysabinda in the earlier work, Imoinda in the latter—and, however trivial, the similarity suggests *Amboyna*'s influence on Behn's composition of *Oroonoko*.

5. Curtin, *Cross-Cultural Trade*, 137; Pearson, "India and the Indian Ocean," 82–83; Chaudhuri, "Reflections," 439; Bayly and Fawaz, "Introduction," 18; Turner, *Spice*, 37.

6. Dryden, *Works*, 10. All subsequent references will be cited in the text by act, scene, and line or page. Besides the studies cited in subsequent notes, the scholarship on *Amboyna* includes Schille, "'With Honour Quit the Fort'"; Hoxby, *Mammon's Music*, 80–90; Fludernik, "Noble Savages"; Markley, "Violence and Profits."

7. Wolf, *Europe*, 109, 125; Rosecrance, *Rise of the Trading State*, 72. See Turner, *Spice*, 61, for a list of goods that Romans traded for spices, "above all bullion."

8. Prakash, "Restrictive Trading Regimes," 329; Clay, *Economic Expansion*, 127. The quotation comes from Clay, 128.

9. Arrighi, *Long Twentieth Century*, 40–41; Wolf, *Europe*, 109; Ormrod, *Rise of Commercial Empires*, 6.

10. See Curtin, *Cross-Cultural Trade*, 149; Meilink-Roelofsz, *Asian Trade*, 5.

11. McKeon, *Origins of the English Novel*, 166. See the discussion in Griffin, "Social World of Authorship," 43.

12. Wood, *Pristine Culture*, 3–6; Wallerstein, "Bourgeois(ie) as Concept," 146.

13. Hill, *Some Intellectual Consequences*, 31.

14. Arrighi, *Long Twentieth Century*, 39–45.

15. See Rosecrance, *Rise of the Trading State*, 67, 79.

16. Wallerstein, *Modern World-System II*, 39, 60–61. See also Israel, *Dutch Primacy*, 410–13.

17. Curtin, *Cross-Cultural Trade*, 151.

18. Foucault, *Security, Territory, Population*, 298.

19. Wallerstein, *Modern World-System I*, 210; Arrighi, *Long Twentieth Century*, 44.

20. Beaud, *History of Capitalism*, 26, cites the quotation from Marx.

21. Hallward, "Scipio and Victory," 110. On the classical segregation of politics and economics and the modern collapsing of the two, see Arendt, *The Human Condition*, 12–73.

22. Pincus, *Protestantism and Patriotism*, 262, cites this pamphlet (by John Darell). For Dryden's reading of it, see Markley, *The Far East*, 149.

23. Spanish colonists operated out of the Spice Island Ternate as well as Manila and helped defend the *Estado da Índia* against the VOC: Knaap, "Crisis and Failure," 152; Markley, "Riches, Power," 502.

24. Subrahmanyam, *Portuguese Empire*, 136.

25. See Prabhakaran, *Historical Origin*, 45, 58; Parker, *Military Revolution*, 106, 132; Schnurmann, "Wherever profit leads us," 481; Andrews, *Trade, Plunder and Settlement*, 265; Furber, *Rival Empires of Trade*, 34.

26. Curtin, *Cross-Cultural Trade*, 153.

27. Clay, *Economic Expansion*, 135–36.

28. Wolf, *Europe*, 125.

29. Subrahmanyam, *Portuguese Empire*, 108–10, 112. See also Wolf, *Europe*, 113.

30. Subrahmanyam, *Portuguese Empire*, 108, 112, 142–43; Steensgaard, *Asian Trade Revolution*, 95. See also Curtin, *Cross-Cultural Trade*, 141–42; Andrews, *Trade, Plunder and Settlement*, 258–59, 261; Pearson, "India and the Indian Ocean," 83–85; Furber, *Rival Empires of Trade*, 259.

31. Cited by Steensgaard, *Asian Trade Revolution*, 83.

32. Ibid., 85–86.

33. Harris, *Sick Economies*, 15–17 (Harris cites Quétel, *History of Syphilis*, 16).

34. Winn, *John Dryden*, 239. *A True Relation of the Unjust* was first published imme-

diately after the massacre but republished the year before Dryden wrote *Amboyna* with
the addition of much of the Spice Islands' history that had occurred during that time.

35. Das Gupta, "Maritime Trade of Indonesia," 243, 252–54, 257. See also Musgrave,
"Economics of Uncertainty," 343, 346; Subrahmanyam, *Portuguese Empire*, 160–61, 163,
214; Curtin, *Cross-Cultural Trade*, 151; Arrighi, *Long Twentieth Century*, 139; Wolf, *Europe*,
237; Glamann, *Dutch-Asiatic Trade*, 7–8; Parker, *Military Revolution*, 106; Andrews, *Trade,
Plunder and Settlement*, 259–60.

36. Steensgaard, *Asian Trade Revolution*, 56.

37. Curtin, *Cross-Cultural Trade*, 154. See also Furber, *Rival Empires of Trade*, 44, 52;
Prakash, "Restrictive Trading Regimes," 324; Glamann, *Dutch-Asiatic Trade*, 92; Davies,
Primer, 55–56; Das Gupta, "Maritime Trade of Indonesia," 243, 264, 268; Steensgaard,
Asian Trade Revolution, 133; Prakash, "Restrictive Trading Regimes," 321; Prabhakaran,
Historical Origin, 63; Wolf, *Europe*, 239.

38. Davies, *Primer*, 56. See also Prakash, "Restrictive Trading Regimes," 325; Furber,
Rival Empires of Trade, 45, 48, 52; Davies, *Primer*, 54–57; Das Gupta, "Maritime Trade of
Indonesia," 265; Steensgaard, *Asian Trade Revolution*, 134; Wolf, *Europe*, 238; Anonymous, *A
True Relation*, 7, 44; Canfield, *Heroes & States*, 112; Dearing, "Commentary" to *Amboyna*, 282.

39. Anonymous, *A True Relation*, 4, 63, 83.

40. Musgrave, "Economics of Uncertainty," 347. See also Subrahmanyam, *Portuguese
Empire*, 212–13; Steensgaard, *Asian Trade Revolution*, 407; Prakash, "Restrictive Trading
Regimes," 329–30; Das Gupta, "Maritime Trade of Indonesia," 269, 330; Curtin, *Cross-
Cultural Trade*, 154.

41. Musgrave, "Economics of Uncertainty," 347–48; Steensgaard, *Asian Trade Revolution*, 146, 153, 410; Das Gupta, "Maritime Trade of Indonesia," 268; Anonymous, *A True
Relation*, unnumbered page in preface. See also Steensgaard, *Asian Trade Revolution*, 9,
171; Arrighi, *Long Twentieth Century*, 139.

42. Andrews, *Trade, Plunder and Settlement*, 268; Furber, *Rival Empires of Trade*, 44;
Bassett, "The 'Amboyna Massacre' of 1623," 1–19, 4; Steensgaard, *Asian Trade Revolution*, 116.

43. Israel, *Conflicts of Empires*, 308–9, 314. See also Ormrod, *Rise of Commercial
Empires*, 32–33; Parker, *Military Revolution*, 132; Kaul, *Poems of Nation*, 54, 65, 289; Clay,
Economic Expansion, 176, 188–90; Hill, *Some Intellectual Consequences*, 35, 37; Wilson,
Profit and Power, 99; Bassett, "Trade of the English East India Company," 145–57, 43;
Curtin, *Cross-Cultural Trade*, 155–56; Chaudhuri and Israel, "English and Dutch East
India Companies," 408–9.

44. Chaudhuri and Israel, "English and Dutch East India Companies," 408.

45. Foucault, *Security, Territory, Population*, 286, 289–94.

46. Ibid., 294.

47. Pincus, *Protestantism and Patriotism*, 449.

48. Schnurmann, "Wherever profit leads us," 477; Raman, *Framing "India,"* 224; Stone,
Crisis of the Aristocracy, 10, 334–38, 364–70, 384; Kaul, *Poems of Nation*, 295; Clay, *Economic
Expansion*, 193. See also Wallerstein, *Historical Capitalism*, 62–63, 105–6.

49. For the ascription of aristocratic and royalist values to Dryden and Restoration
theater more broadly, see Zwicker, "John Dryden," 192–93, 201–2; Kewes, "Dryden's Theatre," 131–32; Dharwadker, "Restoration Drama and Social Class," 140–41, 143, 146; Orr,
Empire on the English State, 140–41.

50. McKeon, *Origins of the English Novel*, 169.

51. On Dryden's use of contradiction, see Sherman, "Dryden and the Theatrical Imagination," 17; Love, "Restoration and Early Eighteenth-Century Drama," 113.

52. Wilson, *Profit and Power*, 25. See also Turner, "From Revolution to Restoration," 791; Hill, *Some Intellectual Consequences*, 16; Israel, *Conflicts of Empires*, xix; Sim and Walker, *Discourse of Sovereignty*, 5.

53. See Staves, *Players' Scepters*, 3; Hughes, "Restoration and Settlement," 130, 132. See also Munns, "Theatrical Culture I," 94.

54. Dryden, *Selected Poems*, 39. See the discussion in McKeon, *Politics and Poetry*, 101.

55. Hughes, "Restoration and Settlement," 128; Kaul, *Poems of Nation*, 67, 69; Dryden, *Selected Poems*, 9.

56. Kaul, *Poems of Nation*, 65–66, 69, 292. See also Turner, "From Revolution to Restoration," 792; Sim and Walker, *Discourse of Sovereignty*, 115–16; Staves, *Players' Scepters*, 46; Canny, "Origins of Empire," 21–22.

57. Dryden, *Selected Poems*, 19. See the discussion in Brown, "Dryden and the Imperial Imagination," 62.

58. On the desanctification and nominalization of the word in Restoration drama, see Staves, *Players' Scepters*, xiv.

59. Behn, *Oroonoko*, 102–6, 129–31, 133–34, 139. On the character of Oronooko in regard to the novel, empiricism, and skepticism, see McKeon, *Origins of the English Novel*, 113; Davis, *Factual Fictions*, 109.

60. See Owen, *Restoration Theatre and Crisis*, 200.

61. Anonymous, *A True Relation*, 21.

62. Birdwood, *Register of Letters*, 33, 136. Raman, *Framing "India,"* 218, first led me to these letters in the Oriental & India Office Collections.

63. Bassett, "The 'Amboyna Massacre' of 1623," 2.

64. Birdwood, *Register of Letters*, 39.

65. Barnard, "Dryden and Patronage," 215; Winn, *John Dryden*, 232, 240–42; Raman, *Framing "India,"* 208.

66. Griffin, *Literary Patronage in England*, 72–73, 82; Barnard, "Dryden and Patronage," 202.

67. Spurr, "England 1649–1750," 8; Winn, *John Dryden*, 232; Griffin, *Literary Patronage in England*, 75; Clay, *Economic Expansion*, 275.

68. Kewes, "Dryden's Theatre," 141; Winn, *John Dryden*, 241; Hughes, "Restoration and Settlement," 133; Owen, "Restoration Drama and Politics," 130.

69. Kewes, "Dryden's Theatre," 131–32; Griffin, *Literary Patronage in England*, 72, 86; Zwicker, "Dryden and the Problem of Literary Modernity," 283. See also Kewes, *Authorship and Appropriation*, 2–3.

70. Kewes, "Dryden's Theatre," 131.

71. See Zwicker, "Dryden and the Poetic Career," 154; Brown, "Dryden and the Imperial Imagination," 73.

72. See Kaul, *Poems of Nation*, 74–75.

73. Roman ruins had recently been uncovered within London's city limits: see Kaul, *Poems of Nation*, 293.

74. Winn, *John Dryden*, 240.

75. Plutarch, *Plutarch's Lives*, 1:460.

76. Hallward and Charlesworth, "The Fall of Carthage," 485–88. See also Wilson, *Profit and Power*, 5; Prabhakaran, *Historical Origin*, 14–15, 55, 69; Wallerstein, *Modern World System II*, 46.

77. See Weber, *General Economic History*, 203.

78. See Hallward and Charlesworth, "The Fall of Carthage," 475–84.

79. Ormrod, *Rise of Commercial Empires*, 34.

80. Plutarch, *Plutarch's Lives*, 1:458.

81. See the discussions in Markley, *The Far East*, 156–57; and in Hoxby, *Mammon's Music*, 136–37.

82. See Kewes, "Dryden's Theatre," 133; Kaul, *Poems of Nation*, 293.

83. See Anderson, *Passages*, 19, 24, 26.

84. See Markley, *The Far East*, 158, on *Annus Mirabilis*; Kaul, *Poems of Nation*, 57, on "The Character of Holland."

85. Marvell, *Complete Poems*, 115.

86. East India Company to Sir John Webster, Home Miscellanies H42, f. 56. Pincus, *Protestantism and Patriotism*, 267, first drew my attention to this letter.

87. See Wallerstein, "Bourgeois(ie) as Concept," 150: "The argument that capitalism is a unique kind of historical system in that it alone has kept the economic realm autonomous from the political seems to me a gigantic misstatement of reality, albeit a highly provocative one."

CHAPTER 2

1. Lukács, *Theory of the Novel*, 56. For a parallel explanation of this epistemological transformation, see Jameson, *Postmodernism*, 410–11.

2. The reading of *Mansfield Park* in Said, *Culture and Imperialism*, 84–97, operates on this model.

3. Armstrong, *Desire and Domestic Fiction*, 75, 73. On the eighteenth-century country house, see also Williams, *The Country and the City*, 105.

4. See Thompson, *Models of Value*, 25.

5. Lukács, *Theory of the Novel*, 80; Jameson, *The Political Unconscious*, 79.

6. Thompson, *Models of Value*, 89.

7. See Hunter, *The Reluctant Pilgrim*.

8. Armstrong, *Desire and Domestic Fiction*, 15.

9. McKeon, *Origins of the English Novel*, 336, 332.

10. Watt did not consider *Robinson Crusoe* prototypical, because it lacks a bourgeois family: see Watt, *Rise of the Novel*, 60–92; Greene, "*Captain Singleton*."

11. Kroll, "Defoe and Early Narrative," 33. For discussions of *Captain Singleton*, besides the other works cited in these notes, see Novak, *Economics*; Richetti, *Popular Fiction*, *Defoe's Narratives*, and *Life of Daniel Defoe*; Baer, "'Complicated Plot of Piracy'"; Trotter, *Circulation*; Brown, *Ends of Empire*; Turley, "Piracy, Identity, and Desire"; Wheeler, *The Complexion of Race*; Lamb, *Preserving the Self*.

12. Rosecrance, *Rise of the Trading State*, 80–81. See also Carruthers, *City of Capital*, 78–79, 146–50; Evans, "Evolution," 344–45; Chaudhuri and Israel, "English and Dutch East India Companies," 437.

13. See Carruthers, *City of Capital*, 149, 151; Chaudhuri and Israel, "English and Dutch East India Companies," 408, 436–37; Chaudhuri, *Trading World*, 7.

14. Starr, *Defoe & Spiritual Autobiography*, 40. Aravamudan, *Tropicopolitans*, 76, sees "the trope of conversion" and hence the return to "bourgeois domesticity" operating across Defoe's novels.

15. Aravamudan, *Tropicopolitans*, 79, argues instead that *Captain Singleton* "rationalizes the rise of venture capitalism."

16. Defoe, *Life, Adventures, and Pyracies*, 1. Cited hereafter in the text.

17. On the interrelationship of aristocratic ideology, rank, parentage, and romance, see McKeon, *Origins of the English Novel*, 131–33.

18. See Novak, *Defoe and the Nature of Man*, 5, 20–21.

19. In a section entitled "The Myth of Singleness," Brown notes that "Defoe's novels are based on a notion of radical egocentricity" (*Institutions of the English Novel*, 54).

20. For other allusions to the prospect of hanging, see Defoe, *Life, Adventures, and Pyracies*, 139, 144, 177, 182, 258, 269.

21. Turley, *Rum, Sodomy, and the Lash*, 45. See also Linebaugh, *The London Hanged*, 19; Rediker, *Between the Devil and the Deep Blue Sea*, 283; Senior, *A Nation of Pirates*, 121–22.

22. For a list of such publications, see Turley, *Rum, Sodomy, and the Lash*, 46.

23. Faller, *Crime and Defoe*, 5.

24. In regard to the former claim, see Greene, "*Hostis Humani Generis*;" Heller-Roazen, *The Enemy of All*.

25. De Schweinitz, *Rise and Fall of British India*, 43.

26. Keynes, *A Treatise on Money*, 2:156–57. See also De Schweinitz, *Rise and Fall of British India*, 43; Thomson, *Sir Francis Drake*, 156.

27. Barber, *British Economic Thought*, 5.

28. Senior, *A Nation of Pirates*, 10, 18, 36, 77–79; Weber, *General Economic History*, 202. See also Turley, *Rum, Sodomy, and the Lash*, 25, 37.

29. See Senior, *A Nation of Pirates*, 46, 49, 50–58, 110, 122, 127.

30. Ibid., 127.

31. Defoe, *A True Account*, 21.

32. The 18 October 1707 issue of Defoe's *Review* 4:425–26.

33. Ibid., 428. A similar argument is made in Defoe, *A True Account*, 20–21. See Novak, *Daniel Defoe*, 569.

34. Works written by or attributed to Defoe that also represent the global economy in terms of piracy include *The King of Pirates*; *A New Voyage round the World, by a Course Never Sailed Before*; *A General History of Pyrates* (2 vols.); *The Life and Adventures of Capt. John Avery*; and *Colonel Jack*. Rediker, *Between the Devil and the Deep Blue Sea*, 255, claims that "Defoe was the first historian of [these early eighteenth-century] pirates."

35. Turley, *Rum, Sodomy, and the Lash*, 29, 32, 62; Kincaid, *British Social Life in India*, 26; Stern, "British Asia and British Atlantic," 708. See also Chaudhuri and Israel, "English and Dutch East India Companies," 436; Das Gupta, *Indian Merchants*, 94.

36. Defoe, *Robinson Crusoe*, 230.

37. Prabhakaran, *Historical Origin*, 63.

38. For this concept of "immanent" meaning, see Lukács, *Theory of the Novel*, 56, 80.

39. See Lawson, *East India Company*, 20, 24, 44.

40. Maloni, *European Merchant Capital*, vii, 5, 12, 15–16, 18, 30, 32. See also Subrahmanyam, "A Note on the Rise of Surat," 23–33, 31, 32.

41. Guha, *India in the Seventeenth Century*, 196. The original title of Careri's travels was *Giro del Mondo* (Napoli, 1699–1700).

42. Refai, "Sir George Oxinden," 575, 577; Chaudhuri, *Trading World of Asia*, 19. See also Watson, "Fortifications," 73, 78–79; Bhaumik, "Bengal Wars," 126; Chaudhuri and Israel, "English and Dutch East India Companies," 434; Barber, *British Economic Thought*, 44; Habib, Review of *Indian Merchants*, 829.

43. Maloni, *European Merchant Capital*, 43. See also Sen, *Empire of Free Trade*, 3, 13.

44. Pincus, "Whigs, Political Economy," 69–72. See also Stern, "British Asia and British Atlantic," 701.

45. Barber, *British Economic Thought*, 44–45. See also Pincus, "Whigs, Political Economy," 72–73, 80.

46. Chaudhuri, *Trading World of Asia*, 20.

47. Barber, *British Economic Thought*, 45.

48. Defoe, *Anatomy of Exchange-Alley*, 15, 53–54; Beresford and Rubinstein, *The Richest of the Rich*.

49. Watson, "Fortifications," 73.

50. Defoe, *Anatomy of Exchange-Alley*, 62–63.

51. Ibid., 13. See Dale, *The First Crash*, 22–25. In regard to Defoe's criticism and "detestation" of the East India Company, see Novak, *Daniel Defoe*, 185, 365–66.

52. These traders could also be interlopers, common before the merger of the two Companies, who enabled Company servants to repatriate the profits of their private trade: see Carruthers, *City of Capital*, 148. Such interlopers were involved in piracy: see Barendse, *The Arabian Seas*, 476. See also Watson, *Foundation for Empire*, 16, 36, 57–61, 69, 73–79; Marshall, *East Indian Fortunes*, 3; Maloni, *European Merchant Capital*, 39; Watson, "Fortifications," 81, 86.

53. Maloni, *European Merchant Capital*, 34.

54. Ibid., 34–35. See also Stern, "British Asia and British Atlantic," 708; Thomson, *Mercenaries, Pirates, and Sovereigns*, 40; Barendse, *The Arabian Seas*, 476–77.

55. Maloni, *European Merchant Capital*, 35. For an example of the Company attempting to mollify native merchants in the face of English piracy, see Surat Factory Records, g/36/6, 15–18 (8, 17, and 18 November 1700).

56. Kincaid, *British Social Life*, 26; Maloni, *European Merchant Capital*, 34. See also Barendse, *The Arabian Seas*, 476–77; Das Gupta, *Indian Merchants*, 98.

57. Watson, *Foundation for Empire*, 102, observes that Company servants trading privately "were essentially secretive about their activities."

58. Chaudhuri and Israel, "English and Dutch East India Companies," 409. See also Clay, *Economic Expansion* 2:161–62, 165.

59. Defoe, *The Trade to India*, 42.

60. Barber, *British Economic Thought*, 56–57.

61. Watson, *Foundation for Empire*, 75; Maloni, *European Merchant Capital*, 38.

62. Defoe, *A Brief State*, 13. In the same vein, see Defoe, *The Just Complaint*, 12, 31.

63. Novak, *Daniel Defoe*, 282; Defoe, *The Trade to India*, 42–43.

64. Defoe, *The Just Complaint*, 13; Novak, *Daniel Defoe*, 553–54; Chaudhuri, *Trading*

World of Asia, 11; Linebaugh, *The London Hanged*, 19–20; Douglas, "Cotton Textiles in England," 39. See also Davenant, *Essay on the East-India-Trade*, 21; Anonymous, *An Hue-and-Cry after East-India-Goods*, 4, 7–8.

65. Defoe, *The Trade to India*, 27, 30, 35.

66. Ibid., 27, 33, 34 (my emphasis).

67. Ibid., 25.

68. Defoe, *A Brief*, 47.

69. Defoe, *Anatomy of Exchange-Alley*, 46.

70. For a different account of the relationship of imperialism and civil society in Defoe, see Neill, "Crusoe's Farther Adventures."

71. Defoe, *Robinson Crusoe*, 54, 55, 58, 279.

72. The *OED* notes: "OE. had *gecyndnys* in sense 'generation, nation': but the existing word is of later formation."

73. Lukács, *Theory of the Novel*, 61.

74. Armstrong, *Desire and Domestic Fiction*, 73.

75. Ibid., 75.

76. Lukács, *Theory of the Novel*, 60, 62.

77. Thompson, *Models of Value*, 89.

78. Hume, *Essays*, 482.

79. In regard to the novel's "historicity," see McKeon, *Origins of the English Novel*, 39–47.

80. For approaches to literature that focus on such discrepancies, in contrast to Lukács's focus on totality, see Adorno, *Aesthetic Theory*, 7; de Man, *Aesthetic Ideology*, 179; Spivak, "'Breast-Giver,'" 88. In regard to the novel and totality, see McKeon, *Theory of the Novel*, 180.

CHAPTER 3

1. Kant, *Grounding for the Metaphysics of Morals*, 36.

2. See, for example, Watts, *Cultural Work of Empire*, 158; Nicholson, *Writing and the Rise of Finance*, 3; Skinner, *Sensibility and Economics*, 1–4.

3. I owe the distinctions that follow largely to Jonathan Lamb.

4. See, for example, Markley, "Sentimentality as Performance," 211; Mullan, *Sentiment and Sociability*, 126. See the discussion in Skinner, *Sensibility and Economics*, 3–4.

5. Bowen, *Revenue and Reform*, 12–13, 16.

6. Ibid., 24.

7. See Curtis, *Letters of Laurence Sterne*, 302–3, 405, 410; Wright and Sclater, *Sterne's Eliza*, 35–36, 168; New and Day, *Florida Edition*, xxi; Cash, *Laurence Sterne*, 269. On Sterne as the century's most influential sentimentalist, see Mullan, "Sentimental Novels," 239.

8. See Wright and Sclater, *Sterne's Eliza*, 2, 7–8, 18–20, 42, 45–46, 50, 54, 74; Cash, *Laurence Sterne*, 271–72.

9. Sterne's editor, Wilbur Cross, named the manuscript, first discovered in 1878, *Journal to Eliza*, but its first page is actually headed "Continuation of the Bramine's Journal" (New and Day, *Florida Edition*, xxvi, xl). Sterne's and Draper's pet names for each other, "bramin" and "bramine," alluded to Sterne's profession and Draper's Indian origins (Curtis, *Letters*, 299).

10. Keymer, "Sentimental Fiction," 573; Curtis, *Letters*, 316. All other quotations from

Sterne's letters to Draper or to *The Bramine's Journal* are from Curtis and will be cited hereafter in the text.

11. See Bowen, *Revenue and Reform*, 1, 19–20, 22–23, 51, 56–58, 62; Smith, *British Imperialism*, 6–7.

12. The quotation, cited by Bowen, *Revenue and Reform*, 56, is from the *Monthly Review* 36 (1767): 148.

13. Bowen, *Revenue and Reform*, 64. See also Travers, "'The Real Value of the Lands,'" 517–58, 525, 537.

14. Bowen, *Revenue and Reform*, 99.

15. Medalle, *Letters*, 2:69.

16. New and Day, *Florida Edition*, 390, observe, helpfully, that "tuberculosis often attacks . . . the genitals."

17. See Keymer, "Sentimental Fiction," 572.

18. Smith, *British Imperialism*, 6.

19. Parker, *Military Revolution*, xix, 89, 136, 175.

20. Carruthers, *City of Capital*, 14, 116.

21. See ibid., 5, 6, 18, 80.

22. Nicholson, *Writing and the Rise of Finance*, 4–5.

23. Rothschild, *Economic Sentiments*, 38–41. See also Morgan, "Mercantilism and the British Empire," 181.

24. Cited by Nicholson, *Writing and the Rise of Finance*, 16, from *Defoe's Review*, number 142.

25. Pocock, *The Machiavellian Moment*, 426.

26. See, for example, Parker, *Military Revolution*, xix.

27. See Festa, *Sentimental Figures*, 109.

28. Keymer, "Sentimental Fiction," 594; New and Day, *Florida Edition*, lii.

29. Laurence Sterne, *Life and Opinions*, 454. See Keymer, "Sentimental Fiction," 594.

30. Nicholson, *Writing and the Rise of Finance*, 8, quotes Stephen, *English Literature and Society*, 51.

31. Curtis, *Letters*, 314, 413.

32. On Sterne, death, and the style of *The Bramine's Journal*, see Lamb, "Sterne's System of Imitation."

33. Medalle, *Letters*, 2:27.

34. Lamb, *Sterne's Fiction*, 4, refers to Sterne's "figurative language" as "irreducibly equivocal."

35. See Wright and Sclater, *Sterne's Eliza*, 74, 88–89, 136; Curtis, *Letters*, 461–62.

36. Curtis, *Letters*, 463.

37. Wright and Sclater, *Sterne's Eliza*, 137.

38. See Bowen, *Revenue and Reform*, 23, 28, 76, 103, 126, 131; Travers, "Ideology and British Expansion," 7–27, 16.

39. Bowen, *Revenue and Reform*, 85; Edwardes, *The Nabobs at Home*, 45.

40. The quotation is from Holzman, *The Nabobs in England*, 96.

41. Trefman, *Sam. Foote*, 1.

42. Boswell, *Life of Johnson*, 5:37. See Freeman, "Best Foote Forward," 574.

43. Chatten, *Samuel Foote*, 14.

44. Trefman, *Sam. Foote*, 11.

45. Taylor, *Plays by Samuel Foote*, 11–12, 34; Trefman, *Sam. Foote*, 4, 7, 9–10. See also Chatten, *Samuel Foote*, 15, 20–21.

46. On the hostility the nabob's estate buying produced during this period, see Raven, *Judging New Wealth*, 222.

47. Quoted in Bowen, *Revenue and Reform*, 22 (my emphasis), from Pownall, *The Right, Interest, and Duty*, 4.

48. See Rothschild, *Economic Sentiments*, 39; Bowen, *Revenue and Reform*, 22–23, 118.

49. Taylor, *Plays by Samuel Foote*, 85. All other quotations from *The Nabob* will be to this edition, cited hereafter in the text.

50. Bowen, *Revenue and Reform*, 5–9, 134. See also Bayly, *Origins of Nationality*, 255.

51. Bowen, *Revenue and Reform*, 6, 12. See also Smith, *British Imperialism*, 18.

52. Holzman, *The Nabobs in England*, 50.

53. Buchan, "The East India Company," 52–61, 56–57; Bowen, *Revenue and Reform*, 31–32, 38–41. See also Cain and Hopkins, *British Imperialism*, 86.

54. Osborn, "India and the East India Company," 204, 212–13. See also Bowen, *Revenue and Reform*, 125–26.

55. Bowen, *Revenue and Reform*, 103, 128–29.

56. Edwardes, *The Nabobs at Home*, 55–57. See also Holzman, *The Nabobs in England*, 8–13; Bowen, *Revenue and Reform*, 28, 95.

57. Pocock, *Virtue, Commerce, and History*, 144–46.

58. Ibid., 146. In this regard, see two poems from the period: Touchstone, *Tea and Sugar*; and Clarke, *The Nabob*. For a discussion, see Juneja, "The Native and the Nabob," 190–91.

59. Gibbon, *Letters*, 2:78 (cited in Trefman, *Sam. Foote*, 189).

60. See Taylor, *Plays of Samuel Foote*, 14–15.

61. Backscheider and Howard, *Plays of Samuel Foote*, 1:vii, xii, xx, xviii.

62. Taylor, *Plays of Samuel Foote*, 1, 36. See also Backscheider and Howard, *Plays of Samuel Foote*, 1:xviii–xix, xv.

63. Quoted in Backscheider and Howard, *Plays of Samuel Foote*, 1:xvii.

64. Ibid., 1:x–xi (from Foote, *Letter from Mr. Foote*).

65. See Pagden, "The Effacement of Difference," 130.

66. Bowen, *Revenue and Reform*, 134–35.

67. Gibbon, *Letters*, 1:366 (quoted in Bowen, *Revenue and Reform*, 171). Gibbon's comment came after a hearing in 1773, but Bowen makes clear that the tenor of the hearings was similar.

68. Charles Dibdin, quoted in Backscheider and Howard, *Plays of Samuel Foote*, 1:xii.

69. See Bowen, *Revenue and Reform*, 119–20, 125, 128.

70. See Cain and Hopkins, *British Imperialism*, 92–95. See also Brewer, *Sinews of Power*, 173–78; Bowen, *Revenue and Reform*, 188.

71. See Bowen, *Revenue and Reform*, 126–27; Rothschild, *Economic Sentiments*, 39.

72. For a different reading emphasizing the distinctions between Thomas and Mite, see O'Quinn, *Staging Governance*, 43–73, esp. 62 and 72.

73. Smith, *British Imperialism*, 11. See also Bowen, *Revenue and Reform*, 122, 125.

74. Bowen, *Revenue and Reform*, 25–26, 153, 163–64, 188. See also Derry, *Politics*, 15.

75. See Bowen, *Revenue and Reform*, 108, 112–14, 121. He refers, for example, to Harry Verelst.

76. Smith, *British Imperialism*, 16. See also Black, *British Foreign Policy*, 34–36; Arrighi, *Long Twentieth Century*, 160; Morgan, "Mercantilism and the British Empire," 176; Bayly, *Rulers, Townsmen and Bazaars*, 235; Chung, "Britain-China-Trade Triangle," 416; Osborn, "India and the East India Company," 214–15, 219.

77. Compare with Scott, *History of Sir George Ellison*, 76: "Of all Mr. Ellison's charities, none gave him such exquisite delight as the release of prisoners confined for debt." See also arch-sentimentalist Mackenzie, *The Lounger*, 173–76 (issue dated 3 December 1785), where the good nabob Truman uses his colonial wealth to repay family debts and to restore the ancient family seat. See Mullan, "Sentimental Novels," 244; Juneja, "The Native and the Nabob," 184, 187–88; Sencourt, *India in English Literature*, 206–9.

78. Anonymous, *The Disinterested Nabob*, 2:91. Cited hereafter in the text by volume and page number. None of the previously mentioned secondary works about the nabob comment upon this novel.

79. See Raven, *Judging New Wealth*, 197; Smith, *British Imperialism*, 23.

80. Staves, "Construction of the Public," 178–79.

81. See Smith, *British Imperialism*, 24; Madden and Fieldhouse, *Imperial Reconstruction*, 178–79.

82. Black, *British Foreign Policy*, 35; Mui and Mui, "William Pitt," 464, and "The Commutation Act," 252. See also Bowen, *Revenue and Reform*, 25.

83. Richards, "The Opium Industry," 48; Travers, "'The Real Value of the Lands,'" 553. See also Barui, *Salt Industry of Bengal*, 2, 5, 14, 49, 52–53, 85–86, 109; Bowen, *Revenue and Reform*, 71–72; Marshall, *East Indian Fortunes*, 16, 114.

84. *Fort William*, 5:282, 283.

85. Barui, *The Salt Industry of Bengal*, 112–13.

86. Bolts, *Considerations on Indian Affairs*, 188–89 (cited by Barui, *Salt Industry of Bengal*, 18).

87. Forest, *Selections from the Letters*, 1:196, 197.

88. Barui, *Salt Industry of Bengal*, 12, 25–27, 109.

89. Ibid., 38, 51–57, 87, 94; Bayly, *Rulers, Townsmen and Bazaars*, 57–58, 151–52, 261–62.

90. Barui, *Salt Industry of Bengal*, 61.

91. See Viswanathan, "The Naming of Yale College," for one such history.

92. On the disappearance of the nabob as a negative figure from public discourse, see Juneja, "The Native and the Nabob," 191; Holzman, *The Nabobs in England*, 98; Osborn, "India and the East India Company," 215.

CHAPTER 4

1. McNally, *Political Economy*, 152; Rothschild, *Economic Sentiments*, 69. Both authors are concerned to refute the claim.

2. Frank, "Roots of Development," 121; Arrighi, *Adam Smith in Beijing*, 42; Copley, "Reading the *Wealth of Nations*," 17.

3. Copley, "Reading the *Wealth of Nations*," 4; Coats, "Adam Smith and the Mercantile System," 219–20.

4. Pocock, "Adam Smith and History"; Fleischacker, *On Adam Smith's "Wealth of Nations."* Subsequent notes cite the works of the other scholars .

5. See Muthu, "Adam Smith's Critique," 193–202; Travers, "British India," 146–53.

6. Copley and Sutherland, *Adam Smith's "Wealth of Nations,"* xii.

7. Arrighi, *Adam Smith in Beijing,* 43, 50, refutes the belief that Smith advocated self-regulating markets, the invisible hand, and the technical division of labor.

8. Smith, *Wealth of Nations,* 626. Cited hereafter in the text. Smith lifted the claim from Diderot in the *Histoire des deux Indes*: see Raynal, *Philosophical and Political History,* 1:1. See also Marx and Engels, *The Communist Manifesto,* 80.

9. Brenner, "Origins of Capitalist Development," 37.

10. Ibid., 33.

11. Smith, *Lectures on Jurisprudence,* 341. See Rothschild, *Economic Sentiments,* 55, 62, 69; Rosenberg, "Adam Smith on Profits," 378–79. Smith's mentor Hume also insisted on the importance of labor receiving surplus and hence mobility: see, for example, Hume, *Political Essays,* 103. Marx, *Capital,* 1:736, misunderstands Smith in this regard.

12. See Sowell, "Adam Smith," 13.

13. In regard to *The Wealth of Nations'* concept of the struggle for liberty, see Sutherland, "Introduction," xiii.

14. I disagree here with the widespread claim that *The Wealth of Nations* defends "commercial society": see, for example, Pitts, *Turn to Empire,* 34; Heilbroner, "The Paradox of Progress," 526.

15. Coats, "Adam Smith and the Mercantile System," 219.

16. Rosenberg, "Adam Smith on Profits," 383. In a similar vein, see Brenner, "Origins of Capitalist Development," 33; Parker, "Look, No Hidden Hands," 128–29; Hollander, "Historical Dimension," 72.

17. Coats, "Adam Smith and the Mercantile System," 219, 221.

18. Smith, *Correspondence,* 286–87 (my emphasis), letter of 1 November 1785.

19. For Smith's use of the term "natural" without metaphysical connotations, see Coats, "Adam Smith and the Mercantile System," 223; Pitts, *Turn to Empire,* 266. Hollander, "Historical Dimension," 72, notes that "a general notion of the temporal priority of agriculture over commerce during the course of 'normal' development [was] characteristic of the Scottish historical literature."

20. See McNally, *Political Economy,* 242.

21. Arrighi, *Adam Smith in Beijing,* 34.

22. Cf. Anderson, *Passages,* 33, 35, 38, 55–56, 60, 66, 96, 109–15, 267.

23. Smith makes the same point in *Lectures on Jurisprudence,* 185.

24. Smith's criticism of large landholdings and primogeniture militates against attempts like McNally's to identify him with classical republicanism: see Winch, *Adam Smith's Politics,* 141; McNally, *Political Economy,* 191, 202.

25. See Skinner, "Adam Smith," 157.

26. In the same vein, see *The Wealth of Nations,* 397, and *Lectures on Jurisprudence,* 48, 300, 302.

27. In regard to the medieval fear of grain monopolies, see Rashid, "Policy of Laissez-Faire," 493.

28. On the rise of corporations and "the corporation spirit," see *The Wealth of Nations,* 140–44.

29. Arrighi, *Adam Smith in Beijing,* 25–26, 57, 69; Frank, *ReOrient,* 13.

30. Smith's account of Europe's unnatural history in Book 3 refutes both the claim

in Marx, *The Poverty of Philosophy*, 121, that for the political economists "there has been history, but there is no longer any" and the elaboration of this claim in McNally, *Political Economy*, 261, 265.

31. See Rothschild, "Global Commerce," 9.

32. Hont and Ignatieff, "Needs and Justice," 44. Hont and Ignatieff's reading of Smith originated immediately after Smith's death: see Trevor-Roper, "Idea of the Decline and Fall," esp. 417 and 424.

33. The identification of "the tyrant" and "the monopolist" is at least as old as Aristotle: see Aristotle, *Politics*, 27.

34. See Hoxby, *Mammon's Music*, 27–30; Haller and Davies, *The Leveller Tracts*, 151–53.

35. See, for example, Pitts, *Turn to Empire*, 32; Winch, "Adam Smith's 'Enduring Particular Result,'" 259–60.

36. Coats, "Adam Smith and the Mercantile System," 225.

37. Ibid., 234; Rosenberg, "Adam Smith on Profits," 381–82.

38. Arrighi, *Long Twentieth Century*, 20. See also Muthu, "Adam Smith's Critique," 195–96.

39. Braudel, *La Dynamique du capitalisme*, 56; Arrighi, *Long Twentieth Century*, 20.

40. See the fanciful gloss of Friedman, "Adam Smith's Relevance for 1976," 8: "We are in a similar state today—except that we must broaden the 'tribes' of 'monopolists' to include . . . trade unions, school teachers, welfare recipients."

41. *Wealth of Nations*, 222–23, discusses at length the value of the East Indies trade to Europe.

42. On famine and mass starvation as consequences of Dutch policy, see Davies, *Primer*, 54–57.

43. Ironically, it was not Smith but Marx who insisted that Company rule was progressive: see Marx, *First Indian War of Independence*, 18–19.

44. Parker, *Military Revolution*, 112, citing Lane, *Venice and History*; and Steensgaard, "Violence and the Rise of Capitalism."

45. Arrighi, *Adam Smith in Beijing*, 35.

46. See Travers, "Ideology and British Expansion," 18; Banerjee, "Grain Traders and the East India Company," 181; Datta, *Society, Economy, and the Market*, 286–87, and "Merchants and Peasants," 149–50, 159.

47. Datta, *Society, Economy, and the Market*, 244, 260; Banerjee, "Grain Traders and the East India Company," 180.

48. Hunter, *Annals of Rural Bengal*, 421.

49. See Wallerstein, *Historical Capitalism with Capitalist Civilization*, 39; Harvey, *The Limits to Capital*, xxiv.

50. Datta, "Merchants and Peasants," 143.

51. Ahuja, "State Formation and 'Famine Policy,'" 152.

52. Thompson, *Customs in Common*, 276.

53. Ibid., 282.

54. Ibid., 201.

55. Ibid., 283, 203. Thompson's first essay in the debate, "The Moral Economy of the English Crowd in the Eighteenth Century," published in *Past and Present* 50 (1971), was reprinted in *Customs in Common*, 185–258. His response to Hont and Ignatieff's criticism, "The Moral Economy Reviewed," was published in *Customs in Common*, 259–351.

56. Thompson, *Customs in Common*, 278–79.

57. Hont and Ignatieff, "Needs and Justice," 2.

58. Ibid., 21.

59. Quoted in Copley, "Introduction," 8, from the 1993 Penguin edition (Harmondsworth) of *Customs in Common*, 273.

60. *Wealth of Nations*, 539: "To hinder ... the farmer from sending his goods at all times to the best market is evidently to sacrifice the ordinary laws[,] *an act of legislative authority* which ought to be exercised only ... *in cases of the most urgent necessity*" (my emphasis). Throughout the "Digression," Smith describes free trade as the "palliative" of dearth and the "preventative" of famine (527 and 532), but never claims that it is the only response to a famine that *already* exists.

61. See Datta, "Merchants and Peasants," 142, 151–52, 155, 158, 162.

62. Ibid., 154.

63. Ibid., 155, 161. See also Datta, *Society, Economy, and the Market*, 256–57, 287–89; Gough, Wood, and Barrientos, *Insecurity and Welfare Regimes*, 264–65.

64. Forrest, *Selections from the State Papers*, 2:265, 264.

65. Thompson, *Customs in Common*, 281, incorrectly took this quotation as a critique of "well-intentioned interventions."

66. Rothschild, *Economic Sentiments*, 55, 62, 68–69.

67. Arrighi, *Adam Smith in Beijing*, 92–93.

68. In regard to the first claim, see Hollander, "Historical Dimension," 79–80; Skinner, "Adam Smith," 154; in regard to the second, see Muthu, "Adam Smith's Critique," 199.

69. Coats, "Adam Smith and the Mercantile System," 219–20, 228; Haakonssen, "Adam Smith," 820; Winch, *Adam Smith's Politics*, 144; Ross, *Life of Adam Smith*, 352.

70. Smith, *Correspondence*, 262, 286.

71. In the same vein, see Smith, *Theory of Moral Sentiments*, 274–75.

72. Bentham, *Works* (1962), 174–75. Cited hereafter in the text.

73. See Metcalf, *Ideologies of the Raj*, 29; Cain and Hopkins, *British Imperialism*, 324–25.

74. Bentham, *Works* (1843), 10:450.

75. Stephen, *English Utilitarians*, 300; Stokes, *English Utilitarians and India*, 68; Winch, "Bentham on Colonies and Empire," 153–54; Mehta, *Liberalism and Empire*, 6. See the excellent discussion in Pitts, "Jeremy Bentham," esp. 69, 73, 85, and 88, from which I take these citations; Winch, *Classical Political Economy*, 159–60; Zastoupil, *John Stuart Mill and India*, 13, 18.

76. See, for example, Prakash, "Who's Afraid of Postcoloniality?" 192.

77. Said, *Orientalism*, 214–15.

78. Thompson, *Customs in Common*, 174.

79. Bentham, *Traités de législation civile et pénale*; Bentham, *Works* (1843), vol. 10.

80. Exceptions are Majeed, *Ungoverned Imaginings*; Pitts, "Jeremy Bentham."

81. Bentham, *Limits of Jurisprudence Defined*, 330. The quotation in the following sentence in the text is from Bentham, *Introduction to Principles*, 294. See Majeed, *Ungoverned Imaginings*, 130.

82. Cohn, "Law and the Colonial State," 131.

83. Bentham's private correspondence described his project to study Nathaniel Brassey Halhed's *A Code of Gentoo Laws* (1776). See Bentham, *Correspondence*, 2:62–63; Franklin, "Introduction," in *A Code of Gentoo Laws*, viii.

84. Bentham, *Colonies, Commerce, and Constitutional Law*, 153, quoted in Pitts, "Jeremy Bentham," 65.

85. Steintrager, *Bentham*, 50.

86. Quoted by Mack, *Jeremy Bentham*, 396.

87. Pitts, "Jeremy Bentham," 83.

88. Ibid., 57, 62, 64–65; Schultz and Varouxakis, "Introduction," 12–13. See "Emancipate Your Colonies! Addressed to the National Convention of France, 1793," in Bentham, *Rights, Representation, and Reform*, 291.

89. "Plan of Parliamentary Reform, in the Form of a Catechism," in Bentham, *Works* (1843), 3:463. See Majeed, *Ungoverned Imaginings*, 25.

90. Washbrook, "South India," 506–9, 514–16, and "Progress and Problems," 89. See also Cain and Hopkins, *British Imperialism*, 324; Stokes, *English Utilitarians and India*, 61, 77–78.

CHAPTER 5

1. Burke, *Writings and Speeches*, 6:419–20. Cited hereafter in the text by volume and page.

2. Kirk, *The Conservative Mind*. On Burke's influence on "Victorian conservatism," see Clark, "Introduction," 110–11.

3. Mehta, *Liberalism and Empire*, 21–22, 41–42, 123, 134, 142–43; Gibbons, *Edmund Burke and Ireland*, 16, 166–67; Deane, *Foreign Affections*, 87.

4. Eagleton, "Capitalism and Form," 120–21.

5. Private correspondence dated 28 July 1796 in Burke, *Works*, 8:492. The letter continues, "I blame myself exceedingly for not having employed the last year in this work . . . to rescue this dull and thoughtless people from the punishments which their neglect and stupidity will bring upon them for their systematic iniquity and oppression."

6. See Eagleton, *Ideology of the Aesthetic*, 31–69, for Burke's ambivalent relationship to the moral sense tradition.

7. Mehta, *Liberalism and Empire*, 21–22, and Pitts, *Turn to Empire*, 60, are in the former camp; Suleri, *Rhetoric of English India*, 45–48, and Dirks, *Scandal of Empire*, 313–14, the latter.

8. Gibbons, *Edmund Burke and Ireland*, 83, quotes O'Brien, *Edmund Burke as an Irishman*, 155: "He was master of an irony so grave as sometimes to be taken by more than the simple for sober earnest."

9. Musselwhite, "Trial of Warren Hastings," 78.

10. See Thomson, *Mercenaries, Pirates, and Sovereigns*, 32, 35; Lloyd, *The British Empire*, 13–14; and Pearson, "Merchants and States," 87–92.

11. See, for example, Ferguson, "Burke," 611–12, 618–19.

12. Macpherson, *Burke*, 21–22.

13. Smith, *Wealth of Nations*, 754.

14. Ibid., 637–38. See Whelan, *Edmund Burke and India*, 39–40.

15. Smith, *Wealth of Nations*, 638.

16. Ibid.

17. Pocock, *Politics, Language, and Time*, 208–11.

18. See the discussions in Williams, *Culture and Society*, 10; Whitney, *Primitivism*, 193–205.

19. See Makdisi, *Romantic Imperialism*, 100, 112.

20. I take the phrase "decomposed civil being" from Pagden, "Effacement of Difference," 134.

21. On Bennett's popularity, see Lovell, *Consuming Fiction*, 53.

22. Bennett, *Anna*, 1:70.

23. Ibid., 73–74.

24. Trumpener, *Bardic Nationalism*, 171.

25. See Pocock, *Virtue, Commerce, and History*, 195–96, and "Introduction," xx–xxi.

26. Bennett, *Anna*, 1:146, 91.

27. Ibid., 91.

28. For the argument that Burke's rhetoric was instead an attempt to scapegoat Hastings, see Suleri, *Rhetoric of English India*, 49–74; Teltscher, *India Inscribed*, 166.

29. Burke, *Speeches*, 1:461.

30. Burke, *Works*, 8:106.

31. Teltscher, *India Inscribed*, 167.

32. P. J. Marshall's headnote in Burke, *Writings and Speeches*, 6:418.

33. For the resemblance between this passage and the *Reflections'* signature account of the attack on Marie Antoinette, see Kramnick, *The Rage of Edmund Burke*, 136–38, 152–53; Rawson, *Satire and Sentiment*, 160–61.

34. P. J. Marshall's headnote in Burke, *Writings and Speeches*, 6:34, from Burke's speech of 7 May 1789.

35. This topos recurs in Phebe Gibbes, *Hartly House, Calcutta*: see Anonymous, *Hartly House*, esp. 278–79.

36. Bennett, *Anna*, 1:91, 96.

37. Ibid., 98–99, 111.

38. For the circumstances of the bills' defeat, see Samet, "A Prosecutor and a Gentleman," 402; Marshall, *Impeachment of Warren Hastings* , 20–26, 34–35.

39. On Burke's opposition to Crown influence in Parliament, see Macpherson, *Burke*, 22–23.

40. Pocock, *Virtue, Commerce, and History*, 146.

41. Montesquieu, *Spirit of the Laws*, 369–73. See Dobie, "Exotic Economies." See also Montesquieu's explanation of the relationship between territorial acquisition and the corruption of republics, 120.

42. For the development of the principle of publicity in opposition to state secrets, see Habermas, *Structural Transformation*, 52–54.

43. On Burke's belief in the impossibility of extending parliamentary representation to the Indian colonies themselves, see Whelan, *Edmund Burke and India*, 23–32.

44. Pocock, *Virtue, Commerce, and History*, 197, notes that Burke considered the Jacobin seizure of church lands to be "the central, the absolute and the unforgivable crime of the Revolutionaries."

45. Burke, *Correspondence*, 5:241 (10 December 1785).

46. See Dickinson, *Liberty and Property*, 49–50.

47. Marshall, *Impeachment of Warren Hastings*, 70–71.

48. Burke, *Correspondence*, 5:357 (1 November 1787). Musselwhite, "Trial of Warren Hastings," 92, notes that Burke believed the most important forum in the impeachment to be not the Lords but the press and public opinion. Habermas, *Structural Transformation*,

96, notes that while the Physiocrats believed the public should scrutinize public matters, their British contemporaries believed it could compel lawmakers.

49. Habermas, *Structural Transformation*, 11, 14.

50. Sentimental rhetoric was thought to be capable of shaping "the collective sentiments of society" or "public opinion"—itself a new idea—in the interests of philanthropic causes: see Ellis, *The Politics of Sensibility*, 15–16.

51. Sekora, *Luxury*, 66–67.

52. The first quotation is from Burke, *Works*, 8:388.

53. For the similar critique in Smith and Bentham, see Knorr, *British Colonial Theories*, 175–95, 251–68.

54. Trocki, *Opium*, 22, 28.

55. See, for example, Hobsbawm, *Industry and Empire*, 36.

56. See Mintz, *Sweetness and Power*, 159; Trocki, *Opium*, 28–29.

57. P. J. Marshall's headnote in Burke, *Writings and Speeches*, 5:195.

58. *Ninth Report from the Select Committee* (1783) in Burke, *Writings and Speeches*, 5:194–333, 247, 271, 279.

59. Burke, *Writings and Speeches*, 5:281.

60. See Trocki, *Opium*, 8–9, 31, 53.

61. Ibid., 32; Burke, *Writings and Speeches*, 5:270.

62. Burke, *Writings and Speeches*, 5:247–48.

63. Trocki, *Opium*, 6, 9.

64. Ibid., 9, 46–47.

65. Burke, *Writings and Speeches*, 5:286.

66. Ibid., 276.

67. Marx, *Capital*, 1:917.

68. Burke, *Writings and Speeches*, 5:270, 273.

69. Trocki, *Opium*, 21.

70. See ibid., 9–10, 29–39; Mintz, *Sweetness and Power*, 157–62.

71. In a private correspondence to Henry Dundas, head of the Board of Control (25 March 1787), Burke wrote: "A body of men, united in a close connexion of common guilt . . . and possessed of a measure of wealth and influence which perhaps you yourself have not calculated at any thing like its magnitude, is . . . actually formed in this country. This faction is at present ranged under Hastings as an Indian leader. . . . If [it] should now obtain a triumph it will be very quickly too strong for your ministry" (quoted in Marshall, *Impeachment of Warren Hastings*, 23).

72. Trocki, *Opium*, 53.

73. See Gibbons, *Edmund Burke and Ireland*, 2; Deane, *Foreign Affections*, 88–89.

74. Burke, *Correspondence*, 6:197–98, 5:372.

75. Sheridan, *The Celebrated Speech*, 33.

76. Sheridan, *Speech of R. B. Sheridan, Esq. on Wednesday*, iii.

77. Quoted in Sheridan, *Speeches*, 1:272.

78. Byron, *Letters and Journals*, 3:239, quoted in Suleri, *Rhetoric of English India*, 53, and in Kelly, *Richard Brinsley Sheridan*, 151.

79. Sheridan, *Speech of R. B. Sheridan, Esq. on Wednesday*, 6.

80. For a discussion of the relationship between theater, public spectacle, sympathy, and its mechanical operation in the *Enquiry*, see Lamb, *Preserving the Self*, 259–61. For an example of sympathy as the effect of mimicry, see Sterne, *A Sentimental Journey*, 201. For discussions of sentiment and mimicry, see Ellis, *Politics of Sensibility*, 72–76; Lamb, *Preserving the Self*, 264–67.

81. Sheridan, *Speech of R. B. Sheridan, Esq. on Wednesday*, iii.

82. Minto, *Life and Letters*, 124. See Kelly, *Richard Brinsley Sheridan*, 144.

83. Sheridan, *Speech of R. B. Sheridan, Esq. on Summing Up*, 28.

84. Mehta, *Liberalism and Empire*, 170.

85. Sheridan's wife fainted just before: see Hastings, *Trial of Warren Hastings*, 8. See Mullan, *Sentiment and Sociability*, 109–10, for a discussion of sympathy and bodily collapse: "The body's collapse is the sign of virtue *in extremis*."

86. Kelly, *Richard Brinsley Sheridan*, 148.

87. On the sentimental topos of "virtue in distress," see Brissenden, *Virtue in Distress*, 91: "It was the frailty of virtue . . . which brought the tears of sensibility brimming to the eye of the tender hearted reader."

88. Lamb, *Preserving the Self*, 256–57, explores the idea that sympathy is a mechanical reaction and suggests that it was thought to resemble "mob instinct." For the classic argument that sympathy arises not from a separate "moral sense" but rather from an involuntary imitation, see Hume, *Treatise of Human Nature*, 575–76. In a similar vein, see Smith, *Theory of Moral Sentiments*, 191. See Bell, *Sentimentalism, Ethics*, 39–49; Mullan, *Sentiment and Sociability*, 46–47.

89. See Kelly, *Richard Brinsley Sheridan*, 146–47.

90. The first quotation is from *The Celebrated Speech*, 51; the second, from Minto, *Life and Letters*, 209, cited in Morwood, *Life and Works*, 121.

91. For an analysis of the sentimental male protagonist, see Van Sant, *Eighteenth-Century Sensibility*, 98–115; Todd, *Sensibility*, 40–41. From 1740 to 1780, drama was largely sentimental, exemplified in particular by Sheridan's plays. In his most famous play, *The School for Scandal* (1777), the man of sentiment is named "Joseph Surface." As sentimental hero, Burke bears a direct relationship to Harley, the protagonist of the exemplary sentimental novel *The Man of Feeling* (1771). One of its central sentimental tableaus is Harley's sympathy for a suffering old man who had been a soldier in India, had helped an Indian imprisoned by his officers escape, and hence had been court-martialed and tortured. See Mackenzie, *The Man of Feeling*, 85–102; Richetti, *English Novel in History*, 261.

92. Gibbon, *Letters*, 1:109.

93. Quoted in Morwood, *Life and Works*, 117.

94. For a subtle account of how sympathy always risks appearing to be merely a show, see Van Sant, *Eighteenth-Century Sensibility*, 121–24. Motooka, *Age of Reasons*, 20–21, observes "a curious phenomenon in the reception history of sentimental fiction: the frequency with which readers feel compelled to debate whether a given sentimental work is really sentimental, or . . . in fact a parody of the sentimental."

95. As Gibbons, *Edmund Burke and Ireland*, 104, notes, Paine claimed that "Burke had reduced ethics to mere aesthetic effects": see Paine, *Rights of Man*, 51.

96. See Deane, *Foreign Affections*, 8–9; Dirks, *Scandal of Empire*, xii.

CHAPTER 6

1. See, for example, Macfie, *Orientalism*, 57–58; Clarke, *Oriental Enlightenment*, 26; MacKenzie, *Orientalism*, 26; Smith, "Orientalism and Hinduism," 46, 60.

2. Said, *Orientalism*, 94.

3. Majeed, *Ungoverned Imaginings*, 17, 26; Franklin, "Introduction," in *Institutes of Hindu Law*, v.

4. Cohn, "Law and the Colonial State," 133.

5. Cohn, "Command of Language," 282.

6. His languages included Greek, Latin, Hebrew, French, Italian, Spanish, Portuguese, Arabic, Persian, Sanskrit, and Chinese. His works set precedents for comparative literature; grammars of Arabic, Hindi, and Bengali; the modern translation of Arabic literature into European languages; the Indo-European thesis; modern linguistics (Aarsleff, *Study of Language in England*, 134); and Romanticism (Abrams, *The Mirror and the Lamp*, 87–98). See Franklin, "Introduction," in *Sir William Jones*, xix, xxiii, xxvi, and headnotes, 104–5, 337, 348, 355; Rocher, "Foreword," 3–7.

7. Rocher, "Foreword," 10; Mukherjee, *Sir William Jones*, 3–4, 132; Majeed, *Ungoverned Imaginings*, 29. H. T. Colebrooke completed *The Digest* after Jones's death, but Jones spent the final six years of his life working on it (Franklin, "Introduction," in *Institutes of Hindu Law*, xi).

8. Bayly, *Imperial Meridian*, 155–57.

9. See, for example, Cannon, *Life and Mind of Oriental Jones*, xv, and "Oriental Jones," 48; Franklin, "Introduction," in *Sir William Jones*, xxiii–xiv, and headnote, 355; Macfie, *Orientalism*, 58; Irwin, *For Lust of Knowing*, 293; Prakash, "Writing Post-Orientalist Histories," 386; Makdisi, *Romantic Imperialism*, 116.

10. Said, *Orientalism*, 96.

11. While Said acknowledged Jones as Orientalism's "undisputed founder" (ibid., 78), he dates colonial Orientalism's onset to Napoleon's 1798 Egyptian invasion (Said, *Orientalism*, xvii).

12. Said, *Orientalism*, 94, 78.

13. Ibid., 92–93.

14. Ibid., 94.

15. See Sarkar, *Writing Social History*, 84; Dirks, "From Little King to Landlord," 175, for criticisms of the former; and Guha, "Preface," and "Aspects of the Historiography of Colonial India," vii, 1; Prakash, "Postcolonial Criticism," 13, for criticisms of the latter.

16. Cohn, "Law and the Colonial State," 146–47, 150.

17. See Cain and Hopkins, *British Imperialism*, 73–74.

18. Byrne, *Natural Religion*, 86–87. See also Marshall, *British Discovery*, 3.

19. Rocher, "British Orientalism," 219. See also Marshall, *British Discovery*, 5. Guha, *Rule of Property*, 25: "We owe the beginnings of Indological studies to this body of literature."

20. Quoted in Franklin, "Introduction," in *Interesting Historical Events*, xii.

21. Holwell, *Interesting Historical Events*, 2:63.

22. Dow, *History of Hindostan*, 1:lxxiii.

23. Travers, "Ideology and British Expansion," 15–16.

24. Ibid., 15; Travers, "'The Real Value of the Lands,'" 525. See also Franklin, "Introduction," in *Interesting Historical Events*, xiii; Mukhopadhyay, *Agrarian Policy*, 26–27.

25. Quoted in Travers, "Ideology and British Expansion," 15.

26. Ibid., 16; Dow, *History of Hindostan*, 3:xcv.

27. Dow, *History of Hindostan*, 3:lxxvii.

28. Ibid., 3:cxix.

29. Ibid., 1:xi.

30. Holwell, *Interesting Historical Events*, 1:5.

31. Hastings, "Letter to Nathaniel Smith," 189.

32. Rocher, "British Orientalism," 224; Franklin, "Introduction," in *A Code of Gentoo Laws*, vii; Brockington, "Warren Hastings and Orientalism," 94.

33. Hastings, "Letter to Nathaniel Smith," 189. The metropolitan press of the 1790s used this passage almost verbatim to defend colonial rule: see Trautmann, *Aryans and British India*, 24–25.

34. Voltaire, *Lettres sur l'origine des sciences*, 4 (my translation).

35. *Fragments historiques sur quelques revolutions dans l'Inde*, in Voltaire, *Œuvres complètes*, 22:248 (my translation). On Voltaire's knowledge of works on India, see Jovicevich, *Les Lettres d'Amabed*, xxxv–xlii. See also Rocher, *Ezourvedam*, 3–4.

36. Voltaire, *Complete Tales*, 2:5. Cited hereafter in the text.

37. Frank, *ReOrient*; Pomeranz, *The Great Divergence*; Perlin, *Invisible City*.

38. See Pocock, *Barbarism and Religion*, 2:104–6. On Voltaire, India, and historiography, see Viswanathan, *Outside the Fold*, 192–93.

39. Jovicevich, *Les Lettres d'Amabed*, 9.

40. Turner, *Spice*, 15; Prabhakaran, *Historical Origin*, 24–25, 31.

41. On conversion in *Les Letters d'Amabed*, see Howells, "Processing Voltaire's *Amabed*," 153–62.

42. Voltaire, *Philosophical Dictionary*, 60.

43. Prabhakaran, *Historical Origin*, 48–49.

44. Ibid., 25, 35, 37, 40–41, 45. See also Pearson, "India and the Indian Ocean," 74, 83; Das Gupta, "Maritime Trade of Indonesia," 251; Abu-Lughod, *Before European Hegemony*, 276.

45. Voltaire, *Essai sur les mœurs*, 2:310 (my translation).

46. Prabhakaran, *Historical Origin*, 47.

47. Quoted in Jovicevich, *Les Lettres d'Amabed*, xxxiii (from a private correspondence, date and recipient unknown, in Denis Diderot, *Œuvres complètes*, 6:367). My thanks to Claudio Pikielny for translating the final term.

48. Howells, "Processing Voltaire's *Amabed*," 154–56, 160.

49. Jovicevich, *Les Lettres d'Amabed*, 52.

50. Ibid., 47.

51. Jones, *Sir William Jones*, 152. See Majeed, *Ungoverned Imaginings*, 37–38.

52. Jones, *Works*, 1:320. Jones disagreed with Holwell that Hinduism necessarily predated Judaism: see Dodson, *Orientalism, Empire*, 28.

53. See Schwab, *Oriental Renaissance*, 57–64; Franklin, "General Introduction," in *Interesting Historical Events*, x; Rocher, "Foreword," 8.

54. Franklin, headnote to "A Hymn to Náráyana," in *Sir William Jones*, 104–5. "A

Hymn to Náráyana" is the opening text of McGann, *New Oxford Book of Romantic Period Verse.*

55. Schwab, *Oriental Renaissance,* 195. See also Majeed, *Ungoverned Imaginings,* 21–24; Rocher, "Weaving Knowledge, 54; Franklin, "Introduction," in *Institutes of Hindu Law,* x.

56. Jones, *Works,* 8:163.

57. Jones, *Institutes of Hindu Law,* iv, v.

58. Ibid., viii, ix.

59. Jones, *Sir William Jones,* xxvii, and *Letters,* 2:699, discusses being the "Justinian of India." For Jones's importance to subsequent Indian legal history, see Majeed, *Ungoverned Imaginings,* 16; Ibbetson, "Sir William Jones as a Comparative Lawyer," 17–42.

60. Cohn, "Command of Language," 293–94; Dodson, *Orientalism, Empire,* 49–50. See also Viswanathan, "Colonialism and the Construction of Hinduism," 26–27, 37; Veer, "Sati and Sanskrit," 255.

61. Thapar, "Imagined Religious Communities?" 222.

62. Veer, "Sati and Sanskrit," 257–59. See also Cohn, "Notes," 7, and "Command of Language," 328; Thapar, "Imagined Religious Communities?" 218; Bayly, "British and Indigenous Peoples, 35; Majeed, *Ungoverned Imaginings,* 26–27.

63. See Thapar, "Communalism," 1–21, and "Imagined Religious Communities?" 218, 228–29; Hutchinson and Smith, *Nationalism,* 7–8; Chakravarti, "Whatever Happened to the Vedic *Dasi?*" 27–87; Majeed, *Ungoverned Imaginings,* 36; Ludden, "Orientalist Empiricism," 271; Rocher, "British Orientalism," 229; Niranjana, *Siting Translation,* 18; Kopf, *British Orientalism,* 180–87; Cohn, "Command of Language," 317–19.

64. Parker, *Military Revolution,* 174. See also Cain and Hopkins, *British Imperialism,* 91–94; Bayly, *Origins of Nationality,* 259.

65. Travers, "'The Real Value of the Lands,'" 524, 539.

66. Mukhopadhyay, *Agrarian Policy,* 13.

67. See Travers, "'The Real Value of the Lands,'" 525–27.

68. Evidence of Zephaniah Holwell, 30 March 1767, Additional Manuscript 18469, fols. 13 and 14. Travers, "'The Real Value of the Lands'" drew my attention to this manuscript.

69. Franklin, "Introduction," in *History of Hindostan,* ix, xi.

70. Dow, *History of Hindostan,* iii, cxx.

71. See Travers, "Ideology and British Expansion," 15, 17–18, and "'The Real Value of the Lands,'" 529.

72. Letter of March 1773 to the chairman of the directors, in Gleig, *Memoirs,* 1:293 (quoted in Travers, "Ideology and British Expansion," 17).

73. See Benton, *Law and Colonial Cultures,* 128–29, 131. The quotation refers to the colonial state in 1924.

74. Bose, "Space and Time," 377.

75. See Gray, "Peculiarities of Irish Land Tenure," 142.

76. Travers, "'The Real Value of the Lands,'" 550; Cain and Hopkins, *British Imperialism,* 14–15, 34–35, 45.

77. See "'Cornwallis Triumphant': War in India and the British Public in the Late Eighteenth Century," in Marshall, *Trade and Conquest,* 69–71.

78. See Colley, *Britons,* 150; Metcalf, *Ideologies of the Raj,* 35.

79. Hamilton, *Hindoo Rajah,* 1:10–11. Cited hereafter in the text by volume and page.

Rajan, "Feminizing the Feminine," 153, notes that *Hindoo Rajah* went through five editions from 1796 to 1811.

80. See Kelly, *Women, Writing and Revolution*, 128–43.

81. Jones, *Works*, 3:210–11. On Jones's repeated use of the term "fountain" in this context, see Majeed, *Ungoverned Imaginings*, 37.

82. Hamilton refers to the Rajah's correspondent in this epistolary novel as a zamindar ("Zimeendar of Cumlore").

83. See Bayly, *Imperial Meridian*, 155–57. For a different interpretation claiming that "Hamilton is [blind to the] infectious aspects of the Orient," see Leask, *British Romantic Writers*, 101.

84. Guha, *Rule of Property*, 200; Dirks, "From Little King to Landlord," 199; Bayly, *Indian Society*, 2.

85. See, for example, Metcalf, *Ideologies of the Raj*, 20–21.

86. Guha, *Rule of Property*, xiv.

87. Travers, "'The Real Value of the Lands,'" 548.

88. See Wallerstein, "Bourgeois(ie) as Concept," 146–47; and Harvey, *The New Imperialism*, 43–44, 115–24, for the argument that the monopoly imposition of "spatio-temporal control" or a "spatio-temporal fix" is fundamental to capitalism and imperialism, respectively.

89. See Bayly, *Origins of Nationality*, 250, 258; Travers, "'The Real Value of the Lands,'" 549, 555–56. See also Guha, *Rule of Property*, 130; Thompson, "Changing Perceptions of Land Tenures," 121; Butler, "Orientalism," 401.

90. Wallerstein, "Bourgeois(ie) as Concept," 139: "The number of national bourgeoisies that are said to have 'betrayed' their historic roles turns out not to be small but very large—indeed, the vast majority."

91. *Al Sirajiyyah; or, The Mohammedan Law of Inheritance*, in Jones, *Works*, 8:208, 207.

92. See Travers, "'The Real Value of the Lands,'" 521, 549; Mukhopadhyay, *Agrarian Policy*, 10, 12.

93. Jones, *Institutes of Hindu Law*, iv.

94. Jones, *Works*, 8:209.

95. Jones, *Institutes of Hindu Law*, xvi, iv.

96. Jones, *Works*, 8:209, 209–10 (my emphasis).

97. See Said, *Orientalism* (2003), xvi: "The ongoing and literally unending process of emancipation and enlightenment that, in my opinion, frames and gives direction to the intellectual vocation"; "the human, and humanistic, desire for enlightenment and emancipation is not easily deferred, despite the incredible strength of the opposition to it. . . . I would like to believe that *Orientalism* has had a place in the long and often interrupted road to human freedom."

98. Kant, "An Answer to the Question," 59–60.

99. Foucault, "What Is Enlightenment?" 42; Kant, "What Is Enlightenment?" 58; Said, *Culture and Imperialism*, 214, 268, 273, 276.

100. See Chakrabarty, *Habitations of Modernity*, 34–36, and *Provincializing Europe*, 107; Guha, *History at the Limit of World-History*, 5, 14–23, 34–47; Prakash, "Who's Afraid of Postcoloniality?"

101. Sarkar, *Writing Social History*, 84.

102. Said, *On Late Style.*

103. Said, *Orientalism*, 123.

104. Ibid., 96. For an insistence on the importance of "socioeconomic" analyses, see Said, *Orientalism*, xxiii.

105. Spivak, *Critique of Postcolonial Reason*, 89, 220, 222, sees the colony—and the East India Company colony in particular—as "successful imperialism" because it was a "tribute-paying economic formation."

CHAPTER 7

1. Lukács, *The Historical Novel*, 19–63.

2. See Trumpener's excellent study *Bardic Nationalism*, 128–57. In addition to the studies cited in subsequent notes, see also Maxwell, "The Historical Novel"; Orel, *The Historical Novel from Scott to Sabatini*; Simmons, *Reversing the Conquest*; Manzoni, *On the Historical Novel*; Shaw, *Forms of Historical Fiction*; Lascelles, *The Story-Teller Retrieves the Past*; Fleischman, *The English Historical Novel.*

3. See Guha, "The Prose of Counter-Insurgency," 62, for the argument that sequential analysis—the basic structure of historiography—is a form of counterinsurgency.

4. I refer here to what Chakrabarty, *Provincializing Europe*, 63, 250, calls "History 2s—pasts 'encountered by capital as antecedents but not as belonging to its own life-process.'" He is paraphrasing Marx, *Theories of Surplus Value*, 3:468.

5. Lukács, *The Historical Novel*, 59. See Guha, *History at the Limit of World-History*, 5–6.

6. Buchanan, *Memoir*, 29. Cited hereafter in the text.

7. On the incompatibility of the civilizing mission's ethical ideals and colonial rule's political exigencies, see Arendt, *Origins of Totalitarianism*, 123–57.

8. Embree, *Charles Grant*, 141–42, 189–90; Philips, *The East India Company*, 159–60.

9. See Bandyopadhyay, *Tulsi Leaves*, 5; Gupta, *Lord William Bentinck*, 182–83, 186; Philips, *The East India Company*, 160. For a detailed account of the mutiny, see Brereton, "Mutiny at Vellore." In addition to the other studies cited on the mutiny, see also Gupta, "The Vellore Mutiny"; Joshi, "The Martyrs of Vellore Mutiny," 29–32; Moodley, "Vellore 1806"; Mill, *History of British India*, 7:115–45; Anonymous, *Letter from an Officer at Madras.*

10. See Gupta, *Lord William Bentinck*, 175–76, 187–88; Bandyopadhyay, *Tulsi Leaves*, 5–6.

11. Bandyopadhyay, *Tulsi Leaves*, 6.

12. A letter from Bentinck to Cradock dated 14 July 1806, quoted in Gupta, *Lord William Bentinck*, 187.

13. Philips, *The East India Company*, 169. See also Fisch, "Pamphlet War"; Embree, *Charles Grant*, 240; Gupta, *Lord William Bentinck*, 210.

14. Quoted in Philips, *The East India Company*, 160 (March 1807).

15. On the reception history of *The Missionary*, see Lew, "Sidney Owenson," 40.

16. Morgan, *The Missionary*, 248. Cited hereafter in the text.

17. See Gupta, *Lord William Bentinck*, 214.

18. Trumpener, *Bardic Nationalism*, 128–32, 137–46, 167. See Joseph, *Reading the East India Company*, 171, for a discussion of the East India Company's own reliance on "sexual allegory" involving "a figure of . . . native insurrection (the Hindu man), a figure of potential violation (the Hindu woman), . . . and a figure of benevolent protection (the Company)."

19. The first two quotations come from Bearce, *British Attitudes toward India*; the last, from Stokes, *English Utilitarians and India*, 23.

20. Stokes, *English Utilitarians and India*, 10.

21. On Hilarion's conversion of Luxima to Christianity, see Viswanathan, *Outside the Fold*, 27–31.

22. See Washbrook, "South India," 484; Bearce, *British Attitudes toward India*, 142–43.

23. See Mani, "Contentious Traditions," 113, 116; Chakravarti, "Whatever Happened to the Vedic *Dasi*? 31.

24. See, for example, Guha, "Prose of Counter-Insurgency," 45; Chakrabarty, *Habitations of Modernity*, 15.

25. *Asiatic Researches*, 4:335.

26. Marshall, *Problems of Empire*, 189–90.

27. Hegel, *Lectures*, 147, 156–57, 159. Cited hereafter in the text.

28. On Hegel's idea of the Hindu dream-state, see Niranjana, *Siting Translation*, 25–26; Inden, "Orientalist Constructions of India," 425–28.

29. Marx, *First Indian War of Independence*, 18, from the 25 June 1853 issue of the *New York Tribune*.

30. Hegel, *Lectures*, 149; Marx, *First Indian War of Independence*, 18, 19.

31. Morgan, *Luxima*.

32. The first two sentences of *The Eighteenth Brumaire of Louis Bonaparte*: Marx and Engels, *Selected Works*, 1:225; Hegel, *Lectures*, 325. Marx took the idea from Engels: Mazlish, "The Tragic Farce of Marx, Hegel, and Engels," 335–37.

33. Gupta, *Lord William Bentinck*, 176–77.

34. Ibid., 189–90; Chinnian, *First Struggle for Freedom*, 26, 30, 53, 68–72, and *The Vellore Mutiny*, 3.

35. Quoted in Chinnian, *First Struggle for Freedom*, 30.

36. Quoted in Gupta, *Lord William Bentinck*, 192.

37. Ibid., 192.

38. Ibid., 178–79, 211, 216; Frykenberg, "Conflicting Norms," 52. See also Chinnian, *First Struggle for Freedom*, 42.

39. Quoted in Gupta, *Lord William*, 181.

40. Ibid., 170; Gupta, "The Vellore Mutiny," 91. See also Bayly, *Origins of Nationality*, 259, and "The British and Indigenous Peoples," 28; Frykenberg, "Conflicting Norms," 53. In regard to the increasing use of sepoys, see also Ahuja, "Origins of Colonial Labour Policy," 164; Bayly, *Imperial Meridian*, 128.

41. Frykenberg, "Conflicting Norms," 52. See also Chinnian, *The Vellore Mutiny*, 4; Gupta, *Lord William Bentinck*, 173, 188.

42. Quoted in Gupta, *Lord William Bentinck*, 173.

43. Quoted in ibid., 192.

44. Quoted in Bayly, *Origins of Nationality*, 197.

45. See Gupta, *Lord William Bentinck*, 177–80, 184, 190; Chinnian, *The Vellore Mutiny*, 1–3, 25.

46. See Chinnian, *First Struggle for Freedom*, 32, 42, 45–48, 50, 74.

47. Veer, *Religious Nationalism*, 49, notes that late eighteenth-century Hindu and

Muslim devotionalists resisted British authority not on religious grounds but in the name of basic civil principles. In the same vein, see Chandra, *The Sannyasi Rebellion*, iii.

48. See Chinnian, *First Struggle for Freedom*, 18, 22, 24, 42; Gupta, *Lord William Bentinck*, 189; Bandyopadhyay, *Tulsi Leaves*, 7.

49. Jameson, "Introduction," 2; Lukács, *The Historical Novel*, 89.

50. Lukács, *The Historical Novel*, 21.

51. Ibid., 63. See also Lee, *History Lessons*, 16; Humphrey, *The Historical Novel*; Alexander and Hewitt, *Scott and His Influence*; "The Waverly-Model and the Rise of Historical Romance," chapter 2 of Dekker, *The American Historical Romance*.

52. Jameson, "Introduction," 7. See also Jameson, *Marxism and Form*, xi, 6, 8, 171, 205.

53. Lukács, *The Historical Novel*, 63.

54. Hegel, *Werke in zwanzig Bänden*, 11:566 (quoted in Humphrey, *The Historical Novel*, vii).

55. Scott, *Guy Mannering* (1999), 23. Cited hereafter in the text. In addition to the other studies listed on *Guy Mannering*, see Lincoln, *Walter Scott and Modernity*, 89–120; Trumpener, "The Time of the Gypsies," 849; Jordan, "Management of Scott's Novels," 2:146–52; McMaster, *Scott and Society*, 158–61.

56. See Brown, *Walter Scott*, 37.

57. Garside, "Picturesque Figure and Landscape," 162–63.

58. See Duffy, "War, Revolution," 135–36.

59. Sutherland, *Life of Walter Scott*, 182, 190.

60. See Trumpener, *Bardic Nationalism*, 190; Garside, "Picturesque Figure and Landscape," 163–64; "Waverley and the Cultural Politics of Dispossession," chapter 4 of Makdisi, *Romantic Imperialism*.

61. *Guy Mannering*'s description of gypsies repeats British colonial discourse across the empire in both demeaning nomadic and pastoral societies for their lack of property and romanticizing them as "redolent of an age of heroism and innocence" (Bayly, *Imperial Meridian*, 154).

62. On the idea that "the Indian present could be seen as the British past," see Cohn, "Representing Authority in Victorian India," 167.

63. See Bayly, *Origins of Nationality*, 261, *Imperial Meridian*, 120, 161, and "The British and Indigenous Peoples," 32.

64. Scott, *Guy Mannering* (1830), 4:226. The Magnum Opus edition amends the original quotation, restored in the Edinburgh edition, 353: "superintend certain operations."

65. Sutherland, *Life of Sir Walter Scott*, 182, observes that "the most intriguing hole in [*Guy Mannering*'s] patchwork is Colonel Mannering's twenty-odd years in India."

66. Bayly, *Imperial Meridian*, 157; Kapil, "Ryotwari System," 45.

67. *Fifth Report*, 166.

68. Ibid., 3, 4.

69. Scott grew up in a section of Edinburgh, George Square, famously full of nabobs. Relations who served in colonial India included his eldest brother Robert, uncle William Russell, cousin James Russell, brother-in-law Charles Carpenter, and David Halliburton. Friends who did so included John Leyden and Adam Ferguson's son James. Scott also knew Lord Minto, the Governor-General of India (1807–14), and Robert Dundas—who

nearly became governor-general of India and took Scott with him—was an old school friend. See Claire Lamont's annotations in Scott, *Chronicles of Canongate*, 360; Millgate, "Introduction," xvii; Sutherland, *Life of Walter Scott*, 154.

70. See Bayly, *Imperial Meridian*, 101, 154, 158–59, and *Origins of Nationality*, 50, 251, 258, 288; Singh, *Birsa Munda*, xx–xxi; Bose, "Space and Time," 377–78.

71. Stein, *Thomas Munro*, 60.

72. Ibid., 59. See also Ludden, "India's Development Regime," 256.

73. *Fifth Report*, 166.

74. Ibid.

75. Bayly, *Origins of Nationality*, 264–65, 268.

76. See Bose, "Space and Time," 377; Bayly, "The British and Indigenous Peoples," 23.

77. See Bayly, *Origins of Nationality*, 251, 259–60, 263–64, 297, and *Imperial Meridian*, 120; Washbrook, "Progress and Problems," 73, 74; Arrighi, *Long Twentieth Century*, 160.

78. See Bayly, *Imperial Meridian*, 158–59; Wolf, *Europe*, 250–51, 269.

79. See Bayly, *Imperial Meridian*, 125, 156–57, 159; Kapil, "Ryotwari System," 45; Metcalf, *Ideologies of the Raj*, 25. Just as the aristocratic capitalist Darnley concludes *Translations of the Letters of a Hindoo Rajah* in the wake of the Permanent Settlement, the Scottish "yeoman" farmer Dinmont (331) helps bring *Guy Mannering* to its conclusion in the wake of the Raiyatwari Settlement.

80. See Bayly, *Imperial Meridian*, 125–26, 157–59; Washbrook, "India," 3:399, "South India," 505–6, 516, "Economic Depression," 239, and "Progress and Problems," 81.

81. See Washbrook, "South India," 507–8; Bayly, *Origins of Nationality*, 251, and "The British and Indigenous Peoples," 23, 25.

82. The term "bungalow" originated in the late seventeenth century from the Hindi *bangla*, "belonging to Bengal" (*OED*).

83. See Bayly, "The British and Indigenous Peoples," 29, 32.

84. Sutherland, *Life of Sir Walter Scott*, 155.

85. Garside, "Picturesque Figure and Landscape," 169.

86. See Claire Lamont's "Introduction" and annotations to *The Surgeon's Daughter*, where the turban reappears, in Scott, *Chronicles of Canongate*, xxv–xxvi, 402; Chaudhuri, "Structure of Indian Textile Industry," 178–82.

87. See Wolf, *Europe*, 248, 251, 278, 280, 287; Chaudhuri, "Structure of Indian Textile Industry," 178; Chaudhuri and Israel, "English and Dutch East India Companies," 408.

88. On the pervasive visual images of Tipu Sultan in British print culture, see Bayly, *Origins of Nationality*, 253–54. On Tipu and the Maharathas as "fossilized embodiments of a past which the British . . . had created in the late eighteenth and early nineteenth centuries," see Cohn, "Representing Authority," 192.

89. Trevor-Roper, "The Invention of Tradition," 19, 29–30.

90. From a letter dated "Abbotsford, 21st March 1813," in Lockhart, *Memoirs*, 1:446 (also quoted in Garside, "Picturesque Figure and Landscape," 170).

91. Wallerstein, *Historical Capitalism*, 75.

92. See Bayly, *Rulers, Townsmen and Bazaars*, 58–59, and *Origins of Nationality*, 190, 202.

93. See Bayly, *Origins of Nationality*, 174–75, 180–81, 189, 197.

94. Ibid., 190.

95. Chaudhuri, "Structure of Indian Textile Industry," 136; Bose, "Space and Time," 371. See also Washbrook, "South India," 503; Bayly, *Origins of Nationality*, 202–3.

96. The Vellore Mutiny occurred at the same time as a famine in Madras Presidency: Gough, Wood, and Barrientos, *Insecurity and Welfare Regimes*, 265.

97. Bayly, *Origins of Nationality*, 197–98, 200–202.

98. Rushdie, *The Moor's Last Sigh*, 54.

BIBLIOGRAPHY

Aarsleff, Hans. *The Study of Language in England, 1780–1860.* Princeton, N.J.: Princeton University Press, 1967.

Abrams, M. H. *The Mirror and the Lamp: Romantic Theory and the Critical Tradition.* New York: Oxford University Press, 1953.

Abu-Lughod, Janet. *Before European Hegemony: The World System A.D. 1250–1350.* Oxford: Oxford University Press, 1989.

Ackroyd, Peter. "Foreword." In *The King of Pirates,* by Daniel Defoe. London: Hesperus, 2002.

Additional Manuscript 18469. Department of Manuscripts. British Library. London.

Adorno, Theodor. *Aesthetic Theory.* Minneapolis: University of Minnesota Press, 1997.

———. *Critical Models: Interventions and Catchwords.* New York: Columbia University Press, 1998.

———. *History and Freedom: Lectures 1964–1965.* Cambridge, U.K.: Polity, 2006.

Adorno, Theodor, and Max Horkheimer. *Dialectic of Enlightenment.* London: Verso, 1997.

———. *Dialectic of Enlightenment.* New York: Continuum, 1999.

Ahuja, Ravi. "The Origins of Colonial Labour Policy in Late Eighteenth-Century Madras." *International Review of Social History* 44.2 (1999): 159–95.

———. "State Formation and 'Famine Policy' in Early Colonial South India." In *Land, Politics and Trade in South Asia,* edited by Sanjay Subrahmanyam, 147–85. Oxford: Oxford University Press, 2004.

Alexander, J. H., and David Hewitt, eds. *Scott and His Influence: The Papers of the Aberdeen Scott Conference, 1982.* Aberdeen: Association for Scottish Literary Studies, 1983.

Anderson, Perry. *Passages from Antiquity to Feudalism.* London: Verso, 1996.

Andrews, Kenneth. *Trade, Plunder and Settlement: Maritime Enterprise and the Genesis of the British Empire, 1480–1630.* Cambridge: Cambridge University Press, 1984.

Anonymous. *The Disinterested Nabob.* 3 vols. London: S. Hazard, 1788.

———. *Hartly House, Calcutta.* London: Pluto Press, 1989.

———. *An Hue-and-Cry after East-India-Goods.* London: John Harris, 1701.

———. *A Letter from an Officer at Madras . . . Exhibiting . . . the Late Unfortunate Insurrection in the Indian Army.* London: J. Murray, 1810.

———. *A True Relation of the Unjust, Cruell, and Barbarous Proceedings against the English at Amboyna.* London: William Hope, 1672.

Aravamudan, Srinivas. *Tropicopolitans: Colonialism and Agency, 1688–1804.* Durham, N.C.: Duke University Press, 1999.

Arendt, Hannah. *The Human Condition.* Chicago: University of Chicago Press, 1998.

———. *The Origins of Totalitarianism.* New York: Harcourt Brace, 1979.

Aristotle. *The Politics and the Constitution of Athens.* Cambridge: Cambridge University Press, 1996.

Armstrong, Nancy. *Desire and Domestic Fiction: A Political History of the Novel*. New York: Oxford University Press, 1987.

Arrighi, Giovanni. *Adam Smith in Beijing: Lineages of the Twenty-first Century*. London: Verso, 2007.

———. *The Long Twentieth Century: Money, Power, and the Origins of Our Times*. London: Verso, 1994.

Asiatic Researches. 22 vols. New Delhi: Cosmo Publications, 1979.

Aston, T. H., and C. H. E. Philpin, eds. *The Brenner Debate: Agrarian Class Structure and Economic Development in Pre-industrial Europe*. Cambridge: Cambridge University Press, 1985.

Backscheider, Paula, and Douglas Howard, eds. *The Plays of Samuel Foote*. 3 vols. New York: Garland, 1983.

Baer, Joel. "'The Complicated Plot of Piracy': Aspects of English Criminal Law and the Image of the Pirate in Defoe." *The Eighteenth Century: Theory and Interpretation* 23 (1982): 3–26.

Bandyopadhyay, Premansu Kumar. *Tulsi Leaves and the Ganges Water: The Slogan of the First Sepoy Mutiny at Barrackpore 1824*. Kolkata: K. P. Bagchi, 2003.

Banerjee, Kum Kum. "Grain Traders and the East India Company: Patna and Its Hinterland in the Late Eighteenth and Early Nineteenth Centuries." In *Merchants, Markets and the State in Early Modern India*, by Sanjay Subrahmanyam, 163–89. Oxford: Oxford University Press, 1990.

Barber, William. *British Economic Thought and India 1600–1858: A Study in the History of Development Economics*. Oxford: Clarendon Press, 1975.

Barendse, R. J. *The Arabian Seas: The Indian Ocean World of the Seventeenth Century*. Armonk, N.Y.: M. E. Sharpe, 2002.

Barnard, John. "Dryden and Patronage." In *The Cambridge Companion to John Dryden*, edited by Steven Zwicker, 199–220. Cambridge: Cambridge University Press, 2004.

Barui, Balai. *The Salt Industry of Bengal, 1757–1800: A Study in the Interaction of British Monopoly Control and Indigenous Culture*. Calcutta: K. P. Bagchi, 1985.

Bassett, D. K. "The 'Amboyna Massacre' of 1623." *Journal of Southeast Asian History* 1.2 (September 1960): 1–19.

———. "The Trade of the English East India Company in the Far East, 1623–84." *Journal of the Royal Asiatic Society of Great Britain and Ireland* (1960): 32–47, 145–57.

Baudrillard, Jean. *The Mirror of Production*. St. Louis, Mo.: Telos Press, 1975.

Bayly, C. A. *The Birth of the Modern World, 1780–1914: Global Connections and Comparisons*. Malden, Mass.: Blackwell, 2004.

———. "The British and Indigenous Peoples, 1760–1860: Power, Perception and Identity." In *Empire and Others: British Encounters with Indigenous Peoples, 1600–1850*, edited by Martin Daunton and Rick Halpern, 19–41. London: UCL Press, 1999.

———. "The First Age of Global Imperialism c. 1760–1830." *Journal of Imperial and Commonwealth History* 26.2 (May 1998): 28–47.

———. *Imperial Meridian: The British Empire and the World, 1780–1830*. New York: Longman, 1989.

———. *Indian Society and the Making of the British Empire*. New York: Cambridge University Press, 1988.

———. *Origins of Nationality in South Asia: Patriotism and Ethical Government in the Making of Modern India.* Oxford: Oxford University Press, 1998.

———. *Rulers, Townsmen, and Bazaars: North Indian Society in the Age of British Expansion, 1770–1870.* Cambridge: Cambridge University Press, 1983.

Bayly, C. A., and Leila Fawaz. "Introduction: The Connected World of Empires." In *Modernity and Culture: From the Mediterranean to the Indian Ocean*, edited by Leila Fawaz and C. A. Bayly, 1–27. New York: Columbia University Press.

Bearce, George. *British Attitudes toward India 1784–1858.* Oxford: Oxford University Press, 1961.

Beaud, Michel. *A History of Capitalism 1500–2000.* New York: Monthly Review Press, 2001.

Behn, Aphra. *"Oroonoko," "The Rover" and Other Works.* London: Penguin, 1992.

Bell, Michael. *Sentimentalism, Ethics and the Culture of Feeling.* New York: Palgrave, 2000.

Benjamin, Walter. *Selected Writings.* 4 vols. Cambridge, Mass.: Harvard University Press, 1996–2003.

Bennett, Agnes Maria. *Anna; or Memoirs of a Welch Heiress.* 4 vols. London: William Lane, 1785.

Bentham, Jeremy. *Colonies, Commerce, and Constitutional Law: Rid Yourselves of Ultramaria and Other Writings on Spain and Spanish America.* New York: Oxford University Press, 1995.

———. *The Correspondence of Jeremy Bentham.* 12 vols. London: Athlone, 1963.

———. *An Introduction to Principles of Morals and Legislation.* Oxford: Clarendon Press, 1996.

———. *The Limits of Jurisprudence Defined: Being Part Two of an Introduction to the Principles of Morals and Legislation.* New York: Columbia University Press, 1945.

———. *Rights, Representation, and Reform: Nonsense upon Stilts and Other Writings on the French Revolution.* Oxford: Clarendon Press, 2002.

———. *Traités de législation civile et pénale.* 3 vols. Paris: Bossange, Masson et Besson, 1802.

———. *The Works of Jeremy Bentham.* 11 vols. London: Simpkins Marshall, 1843.

———. *The Works of Jeremy Bentham.* Vol. 1. New York: Russell & Russell, 1962.

Benton, Lauren. *Law and Colonial Cultures: Legal Regimes in World History, 1400–1900.* Cambridge: Cambridge University Press, 2002.

Beresford, Philip, and William Rubinstein. *The Richest of the Rich: The Wealthiest 200 People in Britain since 1066.* Petersfield, U.K.: Harriman House Publishing, 2007.

Berman, Russell. *Enlightenment or Empire: Colonial Discourse in German Culture.* Lincoln: University of Nebraska Press, 1998.

Bhabha, Homi. *The Location of Culture.* London: Routledge, 2004.

Bhaumik, Pradip. "Bengal Wars." In *Historical Dictionary of the British Empire*, edited by James Olson and Robert Shadle, 126–28. Westport, Conn.: Greenwood Press, 1996.

Birdwood, Sir George, ed. *The Register of Letters &c. of the Governor and Company of Merchants of London Trading into the East Indies 1600–1619.* London: Bernard Quaritch, 1965.

Black, Jeremy. *British Foreign Policy in an Age of Revolutions, 1783–1793.* New York: Cambridge University Press, 1994.

Bolts, William. *Considerations on Indian Affairs.* London: J. Almon, 1772.

Bose, Sugata. *A Hundred Horizons: The Indian Ocean in the Age of Global Empire.* Cambridge, Mass.: Harvard University Press, 2006.

———. "Space and Time on the Indian Ocean Rim: Theory and History." In *Modernity and Culture: From the Mediterranean to the Indian Ocean*, edited by Leila Fawaz and C. A. Bayly, 365–88. New York: Columbia University Press.

Bose, Sugata, and Ayesha Jalal. *Modern South Asia: History, Culture, Political Economy*. New York: Routledge, 2004.

Boswell, James. *Life of Johnson*. 6 vols. Oxford: Oxford University Press, 1964.

Bowen, H. V. *Revenue and Reform: The Indian Problem in British Politics*. Cambridge: Cambridge University Press, 1991.

Braudel, Fernand. *Afterthoughts on Material Civilization and Capitalism*. Baltimore: Johns Hopkins University Press, 1977.

———. *La Dynamique du capitalisme*. Paris: Arthaud, 1985.

———. *The Perspective of the World*. Berkeley: University of California Press, 1992.

———. *The Wheels of Commerce*. Berkeley: University of California Press, 1982.

Brenner, Robert. "Agrarian Class Structure and Economic Development in Pre-industrial Europe." *Past & Present* 70 (February 1976): 30–75.

———. "Bourgeois Revolution and Transition to Capitalism." In *The First Modern Society: Essays in English History in Honour of Lawrence Stone*, edited by A. L. Beier, David Cannadine, and James Rosenheim, 271–304. Cambridge: Cambridge University Press, 1989.

———. "Dobb on the Transition from Feudalism to Capitalism." *Cambridge Journal of Economics* 2.2 (1978): 121–40.

———. "The Origins of Capitalist Development: A Critique of Neo-Smithian Marxism." *New Left Review* 104 (July–August 1977): 25–92.

Brereton, J. M. "Mutiny at Vellore." *Blackwood's Magazine* 320 (1976): 335–52.

Brewer, John. *The Sinews of Power: War, Money, and the English State, 1688–1783*. London: Routledge, 1989.

Brissenden, R. F. *Virtue in Distress: Studies in the Novel of Sentiment from Richardson to Sade*. New York: Barnes & Noble, 1974.

Brockington, J. L. "Warren Hastings and Orientalism." In *The Impeachment of Warren Hastings*, edited by Geoffrey Carnall and Colin Nicholson, 91–108. Edinburgh: Edinburgh University Press, 1989.

Brown, David. *Walter Scott and the Historical Imagination*. London: Routledge & Kegan Paul, 1979.

Brown, Homer. *Institutions of the English Novel: From Defoe to Scott*. Philadelphia: University of Pennsylvania Press, 1997.

Brown, Laura. "Dryden and the Imperial Imagination." In *The Cambridge Companion to John Dryden*, edited by Steven Zwicker, 59–74. Cambridge: Cambridge University Press, 2004.

———. *Ends of Empire: Women and Identity in Early Eighteenth-Century Literature*. Ithaca, N.Y.: Cornell University Press, 1993.

———. "The Romance of Empire: *Oroonoko* and the Trade in Slaves." In *The New Eighteenth Century: Theory, Politics, and English Literature*, edited by Felicity Nussbaum and Laura Brown, 41–61. New York: Methuen, 1987.

Buchan, P. Bruce. "The East India Company 1749–1800: The Evolution of a Territorial Strategy and the Changing Role of the Directors." *Business and Economic History* 23.1 (Fall 1994): 52–61.

Buchanan, Claudius. *Memoir of the Expediency of an Ecclesiastical Establishment for Brit-ish India*. Cambridge, Mass.: Hilliard & Metcalf, 1811.

Burke, Edmund. *The Correspondence of Edmund Burke*. 10 vols. Chicago: University of Chicago Press, 1958–78.

———. *The Speeches of the Right Honourable Edmund Burke on the Impeachment of War-ren Hastings*. Vol. 1. London: George Bell & Sons, 1891.

———. *The Works of the Right Honourable Edmund Burke*. Vol. 8. London: George Bell & Sons, 1890.

———. *The Writings and Speeches of Edmund Burke*. 9 vols. Oxford: Clarendon Press, 1981–2000.

Butler, Marilyn. "Orientalism." In *The Romantic Period*, edited by David Pirie, 395–447. New York: Penguin, 1994.

Byrne, Peter. *Natural Religion and the Nature of Religion: The Legacy of Deism*. New York: Routledge, 1989.

Byron, George Gordon. *Letters and Journals*. Cambridge, Mass.: Belknap Press, 1974.

Cain, P. J., and A. G. Hopkins. *British Imperialism: Innovation and Expansion 1688–1914*. New York: Longman, 1993.

———. *British Imperialism, 1688–2000*. London: Longman, 2002.

Canfield, J. Douglas. *Heroes & States: On the Ideology of Restoration Tragedy*. Lexington: University Press of Kentucky, 2000.

Cannon, Garland. *The Life and Mind of Oriental Jones: Sir William Jones, the Father of Modern Linguistics*. Cambridge: Cambridge University Press, 1990.

———. "Oriental Jones: Scholarship, Literature, Multiculturalism, and Humankind." In *Objects of Enquiry: The Life, Contributions, and Influences of Sir William Jones (1746–1794)*, edited by Garland Cannon and Kevin Brine, 25–50. New York: New York University Press, 1995.

Canny, Nicholas. "The Origins of Empire: An Introduction." In *The Origins of Empire: British Overseas Enterprise to the Close of the Seventeenth Century*, edited by Nicho-las Canny, 1–33. Vol. 1 of *The Oxford History of the British Empire*. Oxford: Oxford University Press, 1998.

Carruthers, Bruce. *City of Capital: Politics and Markets in the English Financial Revolu-tion*. Princeton, N.J.: Princeton University Press, 1996.

Cash, Arthur. *Laurence Sterne, the Later Years*. New York: Methuen, 1986.

Chakrabarty, Dipesh. "Globalisation, Democratisation and the Evacuation of History?" In *At Home in Diaspora: South Asian Scholars and the West*, by Jackie Assayag and Véronique Bénéï, 127–47. New Delhi: Permanent Black, 2003.

———. *Habitations of Modernity: Essays in the Wake of Subaltern Studies*. Chicago: Uni-versity of Chicago Press, 2002.

———. *Provincializing Europe: Postcolonial Thought and Historical Difference*. Princeton, N.J.: Princeton University Press, 2000.

Chakravarti, Uma. "Whatever Happened to the Vedic *Dasi*? Orientalism, Nationalism and a Script for the Past." In *Recasting Women: Essays in Indian Colonial History*, edited by Kumkum Sangari and Sudesh Vaid, 27–87. New Brunswick, N.J.: Rutgers University Press, 1990.

Chandra, A. N. *The Sannyasi Rebellion*. Calcutta: Ratna Prakashan, 1977.

Chatten, Elizabeth. *Samuel Foote*. Boston: Twayne Publishers, 1980.

Chatterjee, Partha. "More on Modes of Power and the Peasantry." In *Subaltern Studies II*, edited by Ranajit Guha, 311–49. Delhi: Oxford University Press, 1983.

———. *Nationalist Thought and the Colonial World: A Derivative Discourse*. Minneapolis: University of Minnesota Press, 1993.

———. *The Politics of the Governed: Reflections on Popular Politics in Most of the World*. New York: Columbia University Press, 2004.

Chaudhuri, K. N. "Markets and Traders in India during the Seventeenth and Eighteenth Centuries." In *Economy and Society: Essays in Indian Economic and Social History*, edited by K. N. Chaudhuri and Clive Dewey, 143–62. Delhi: Oxford University Press, 1979.

———. "Reflections on the Organizing Principle of Premodern Trade." In *The Political Economy of Merchant Empires*, edited by James Tracy, 421–42. New York: Cambridge University Press, 1991.

———. "The Structure of Indian Textile Industry in the Seventeenth and Eighteenth Centuries." *Indian Economic and Social History Review* 11.2–3 (June–September 1974): 127–82.

———. *Trade and Civilisation in the Indian Ocean: An Economic History from the Rise of Islam to 1750*. Cambridge: Cambridge University Press, 1985.

———. *The Trading World of Asia and the English East India Company, 1660–1760*. Cambridge: Cambridge University Press, 1978.

Chaudhuri, K. N., and Jonathan Israel. "The English and Dutch East India Companies and the Glorious Revolution of 1688–9." In *The Anglo-Dutch Moment: Essays on the Glorious Revolution and Its World Impact*, edited by Jonathan Israel, 407–38. New York: Cambridge University Press, 1991.

Chinnian, Perumal. *The First Struggle for Freedom in South India in 1806: Sporadic Events after the Vellore Mutiny*. Erode, India: Siva Publications, 1983.

———. *The Vellore Mutiny, 1806: The First Uprising against the British*. Madras: P. Chinnian, 1982.

Chung, Tan. "The Britain-China-Trade Triangle (1771–1840)." *Indian Economic and Social History Review* 11.4 (December 1974): 411–31.

Clark, J. C. D. "Introduction." In *Reflections on the Revolution in France: A Critical Edition*, by Edmund Burke. Stanford: Stanford University Press, 2002.

Clarke, J. J. *Oriental Enlightenment: The Encounter between Asian and Western Thought*. London: Routledge, 1997.

Clarke, Richard. *The Nabob: or, Asiatic Plunderers*. London: J. Townsend, 1773.

Clay, C. G. A. *Economic Expansion and Social Change: England 1500–1700*. Vol. 2. London: Cambridge University Press, 1984.

Coats, A. W. "Adam Smith and the Mercantile System." In *Essays on Adam Smith*, edited by Andrew Skinner and Thomas Wilson, 218–36. Oxford: Clarendon Press, 1975.

Cohn, Bernard. "The Command of Language and the Language of Command." In *Subaltern Studies IV*, edited by Ranajit Guha, 276–329. New Delhi: Oxford University Press, 1985.

———. "Law and the Colonial State in India." In *History and Power in the Study of Law: New Directions in Legal Anthropology*, edited by June Starr and Jane Collier, 131–52. Ithaca, N.Y.: Cornell University Press, 1989.

———. "Notes on the History of the Study of Indian Society and Culture." In *Structure and Change in Indian Society*, edited by Milton Singer and Bernard Cohn, 3–28. Chicago: Aldine, 1968.

———. "Representing Authority in Victorian India." In *The Invention of Tradition*, edited by Eric Hobsbawm and Terence Ranger, 165–209. Cambridge: Cambridge University Press, 1983.

Colley, Linda. *Britons: Forging the Nation 1707–1837*. New Haven, Conn.: Yale University Press, 1992.

Condorcet, Jean-Antoine-Nicolas de Caritat. *Esquisse d'un tableau historique des progrès de l'esprit humain*. Paris: Agasse, 1795.

———. *Sketch for a Historical Picture of the Progress of the Human Mind*. New York: Noonday Press, 1955.

Copley, Stephen. "Introduction: Reading the *Wealth of Nations*." In *Adam Smith's "Wealth of Nations": New Interdisciplinary Essays*, edited by Stephen Copley and Kathryn Sutherland, 1–22. Manchester, U.K.: Manchester University Press, 1995.

Copley, Stephen, and Kathryn Sutherland, eds. *Adam Smith's "Wealth of Nations": New Interdisciplinary Essays*. Manchester, U.K.: Manchester University Press, 1995.

Curtin, Philip. *Cross-Cultural Trade in World History*. New York: Cambridge University Press, 1984.

Curtis, Lewis, ed. *Letters of Laurence Sterne*. Oxford: Clarendon Press, 1965.

Dale, Richard. *The First Crash: Lessons from the South Sea Bubble*. Princeton, N.J.: Princeton University Press, 2004.

Das Gupta, Arun. "The Maritime Trade of Indonesia: 1500–1800." In *India and the Indian Ocean, 1500–1800*, edited by Ashin Das Gupta and M. N. Pearson, 240–75. Calcutta: Oxford University Press, 1987.

Das Gupta, Ashin. *Indian Merchants and the Decline of Surat c. 1700–1750*. Wiesbaden: Franz Steiner, 1979.

Datta, Rajat. "Merchants and Peasants: A Study of the Structure of Local Trade in Grain in Late Eighteenth-Century Bengal." In *Merchants, Markets and the State in Early Modern India*, by Sanjay Subrahmanyam, 139–62. Oxford: Oxford University Press, 1990.

———. *Society, Economy, and the Market: Commercialization in Rural Bengal c. 1760–1800*. New Delhi: Manohar, 2000.

Davenant, Charles. *An Essay on the East-India-Trade*. London, 1696.

———. *The Political and Commercial Works*. 5 vols. London: R. Horsfield, 1771.

Davies, D. W. *A Primer of Dutch Seventeenth Century Overseas Trade*. The Hague: Martinus Nijhoff, 1961.

Davis, Lennard. *Factual Fictions: The Origins of the English Novel*. New York: Columbia University Press, 1983.

Deane, Seamus. *Foreign Affections: Essays on Edmund Burke*. Notre Dame, Ind.: University of Notre Dame Press, 2005.

Dearing, Vinton. "Commentary" to *Amboyna*. In *The Works of John Dryden*, vol. 12, edited by Vinton Dearing, 251–442. Berkeley: University of California Press, 1994.

Defoe, Daniel. *The Anatomy of Exchange-Alley*. London: E. Smith, 1719.

———. *A Brief State of the Question*. London: W. Boreham, 1719.

———. *Defoe's Review*. 22 vols. New York: AMS Press, 1965.

———. *A General History of the Pyrates*. Mineola, N.Y.: Dover Publications, 1999.

———. *The Just Complaint of the Poor Weavers*. London: W. Boreham, 1719.

———. *The King of Pirates*. London: Hesperus, 2002.

———. *The Life, Adventures, and Pyracies, of the Famous Captain Singleton*. Oxford: Oxford University Press, 1990.

———. *Robinson Crusoe*. New York: Penguin, 1985.

———. *The Trade to India Critically and Calmly Consider'd*. London: W. Boreham, 1720.

———. *A True Account of the Design and Advantages of the South-Sea Trade*. London: J. Morphew, 1711.

Dekker, George. *The American Historical Romance*. Cambridge: Cambridge University Press, 1987.

Deleuze, Gilles. *Kant's Critical Philosophy: The Doctrine of the Faculties*. Minneapolis: University of Minnesota Press, 1984.

Deleuze, Gilles, and Felix Guattari. *Anti-Oedipus: Capitalism and Schizophrenia*. Minneapolis: University of Minnesota Press, 1983.

De Man, Paul. *Aesthetic Ideology*. Minneapolis: University of Minnesota Press, 1996.

Derrida, Jacques. *Mémoires: For Paul de Man*. New York: Columbia University Press, 1986.

———. *Mémoires: Pour Paul de Man*. Paris: Galilée, 1988.

Derry, John. *Politics in the Age of Fox, Pitt and Liverpool*. New York: Palgrave, 2001.

De Schweinitz, Karl. *The Rise and Fall of British India: Imperialism and Inequality*. London: Methuen, 1983.

Dharwadker, Aparna. "Restoration Drama and Social Class." In *A Companion to Restoration Drama*, edited by Susan Owen, 140–60. Oxford: Blackwell, 2001.

Dickinson, H. T. *Liberty and Property: Political Ideology in Eighteenth-Century Britain*. New York: Holmes & Meier, 1987.

Diderot, Denis. *Political Writings*. New York: Cambridge University Press, 1992.

Dirks, Nicholas. "From Little King to Landlord: Colonial Discourse and Colonial Rule." In *Colonialism and Culture*, edited by Nicholas Dirks, 175–208. Ann Arbor: University of Michigan Press, 1992.

———. *The Scandal of Empire: India and the Creation of Imperial Britain*. Cambridge, Mass.: Harvard University Press, 2006.

Dobie, Madeleine. "Exotic Economies and Colonial History in the *Esprit des lois*." *Studies on Voltaire and the Eighteenth Century* 362 (1998): 145–67.

Dodson, Michael. *Orientalism, Empire, and National Culture: India, 1770–1880*. New York: Palgrave Macmillan, 2007.

Douglas, Audrey. "Cotton Textiles in England: The East India Company's Attempt to Exploit Developments in Fashion 1660–1721." *Journal of British Studies* 8.2 (May 1969): 28–43.

Dow, Alexander. *The History of Hindostan*. 3 vols. London, 1770–72.

Dryden, John. *Selected Poems*. London: Penguin, 2001.

———. *The Works of John Dryden*. Vol. 12. Berkeley: University of California Press, 1994.

Duffy, Michael. "War, Revolution and the Crisis of the British Empire." In *The French Revolution and British Popular Politics*, edited by Mark Philp, 118–45. Cambridge: Cambridge University Press, 1991.

Eagleton, Terry. "Capitalism and Form." *New Left Review* 14 (March–April 2002): 119–31.

———. *The Function of Criticism*. London: Verso, 2005.

———. *The Ideology of the Aesthetic*. Cambridge, Mass.: Harvard University Press, 1990.

———. "Nationalism: Irony and Commitment." In *Nationalism, Colonialism, and Litera-ture*, by Terry Eagleton, Fredric Jameson, and Edward Said. Minneapolis: University of Minnesota Press, 1990.

Edwardes, Michael. *The Nabobs at Home*. London: Constable, 1991.

Ellis, Markman. *The Politics of Sensibility: Race, Gender and Commerce in the Sentimental Novel*. New York: Cambridge University Press, 1996.

Embree, A. T. *Charles Grant and British Rule in India*. New York: Columbia University Press, 1962.

Evans, Frank. "The Evolution of the English Joint Stock Limited Trading Company." *Columbia Law Review* 8.5 (May 1908): 339–61.

Faller, Lincoln. *Crime and Defoe: A New Kind of Writing*. New York: Cambridge University Press, 1993.

Fanon, Frantz. *The Wretched of the Earth*. New York: Grove, 1963.

Ferguson, Adam. *An Essay on the History of Civil Society*. New York: Cambridge University Press, 1995.

Ferguson, Frances. "Burke and the Response to the Enlightenment." In *The Enlightenment World*, edited by Martin Fitzpatrick, Peter Jones, Christa Knellwolf, and Iain McCalman, 610–20. New York: Routledge, 2004.

Ferguson, Margaret. "Juggling the Categories of Race, Class and Gender: Aphra Behn's *Oroonoko*." *Women's Studies* 19 (1991): 159–81.

Ferguson, Moira. "*Oroonoko*: Birth of a Paradigm." *New Literary History* 23.2 (1992): 339–59.

Festa, Lynn. *Sentimental Figures of Empire in Eighteenth-Century Britain and France*. Baltimore: Johns Hopkins University Press, 2006.

Fifth Report from the Select Committee of the House of Commons on the Affairs of the East India Company. London, 1812.

Fisch, Jarg. "A Pamphlet War on Christian Missions in India 1807–1809." *Journal of Asian History* 19.1 (1985): 22–70.

Fleischacker, Samuel. *On Adam Smith's "Wealth of Nations."* Princeton, N.J.: Princeton University Press, 2004.

Fleischman, Avrom. *The English Historical Novel: Walter Scott to Virginia Woolf*. Baltimore: Johns Hopkins University Press, 1971.

Fludernik, Monica. "Noble Savages and Calibans: Dryden and Colonial Discourse." In *Dryden and the World of Neoclassicism*, edited by Wolfgang Gortschacher and Holger Klein, 273–88. Tübingen, Germany: Stauffenburg, 2001.

Foote, Samuel. *A Letter from Mr. Foote, to the Reverend Author of the Remarks, Critical and Christian, on the Minor*. London: T. Davies, 1760.

Forrest, G. W., ed. *Selections from the Letters, Despatches, and Other State Papers Preserved in the Foreign Department of the Government of India, 1772–1785*. 3 vols. Calcutta: Superintendent of Government Printing, 1890.

———, ed. *Selections from the State Papers of the Governors-General of India*. 4 vols. Oxford: Blackwell, 1910–26.

Fort William–India House Correspondence and Other Contemporary Papers Relating Thereto. 21 vols. New Delhi: National Archives of India, 1949–85.

Foucault, Michel. *Security, Territory, Population*. New York: Palgrave Macmillan, 2007.

———. "What Is Critique?" In *What Is Enlightenment?: Eighteenth-Century Answers and*

Twentieth-Century Questions, edited by James Schmidt, 382–98. Berkeley: University of California Press, 1996.

———. "What Is Enlightenment?" In *The Foucault Reader*, edited by Paul Rabinow, 32–50. New York: Pantheon, 1984.

Frank, Andre Gunder. "On the Roots of Development and Underdevelopment in the New World: Smith and Marx vs. the Weberians." *International Review of Sociology* 10.2–3 (1974): 109–55.

———. *ReOrient: Global Economy in the Asian Age*. Berkeley: University of California Press, 1998.

Franklin, Michael. "General Introduction." In *Interesting Historical Events*, by John Zephaniah Holwell. New York: Routledge, 2000.

———. "Introduction." In *A Code of Gentoo Laws, or, Ordinations of the Pundits*, by N. B. Halhed. New York: Routledge, 2000.

———. "Introduction." In *The History of Hindostan*, by Alexander Dow. New York: Routledge, 2000.

———. "Introduction." In *Institutes of Hindu Law, or The Ordinances of Menu*, by William Jones. New York: Routledge, 2000.

———. "Introduction." In *Interesting Historical Events*, by J. Z. Holwell. New York: Routledge, 2000.

———. "Introduction." In *Sir William Jones: Selected Poetical and Prose Works*, by William Jones. Cardiff: University of Wales Press, 1995.

Freeman, Terence. "Best Foote Forward." *Studies in English Literature, 1500–1900* 29.3 (Summer 1989): 563–78.

Friedman, Milton. "Adam Smith's Relevance for 1976." In *Adam Smith and the "Wealth of Nations": 1776–1976 Bicentennial Essays*, edited by Fred Glahe, 7–20. Boulder: Colorado Associated University Press, 1978.

Frykenberg, Robert. "Conflicting Norms and Political Integration in South India: The Case of the Vellore Mutiny." *Indo-British Review* 13.1 (1987): 51–63.

Furber, Holden. *Rival Empires of Trade in the Orient 1600–1800*. Minneapolis: University of Minnesota Press, 1976.

Gallagher, Catherine. *Nobody's Story: The Vanishing Acts of Women Writers in the Marketplace, 1670–1820*. Berkeley: University of California Press, 1994.

Garside, Peter. "Picturesque Figure and Landscape: Meg Merrilies and the Gypsies." In *The Politics of the Picturesque: Literature, Landscape and Aesthetics since 1770*, edited by Stephen Copley and Peter Garside, 145–74. New York: Cambridge University Press, 1994.

Gibbon, Edward. *The Letters of Edward Gibbon*. 3 vols. London: Cassell, 1956.

Gibbons, Luke. *Edmund Burke and Ireland: Aesthetics, Politics, and the Colonial Sublime*. Cambridge: Cambridge University Press, 2003.

Giddens, Anthony. *A Contemporary Critique of Historical Materialism*. Vol. 1. Berkeley: University of California Press, 1981.

Glamann, Kristoff. *Dutch-Asiatic Trade 1620–1740*. The Hague: Martinus Nijhoff, 1981.

Gleig, G. R., ed. *Memoirs of the Life of the Right Honourable Warren Hastings*. 3 vols. London: Richard Bentley, 1841.

Gough, Ian, Geoffrey Wood, and Armando Barrientos. *Insecurity and Welfare Regimes in*

Asia, Africa and Latin America: Social Policy in Development Contexts. Cambridge: Cambridge University Press, 2004.

Gray, Peter. "The Peculiarities of Irish Land Tenure, 1800–1914: From Agent of Impoverishment to Agent of Pacification." In *The Political Economy of British Historical Experience, 1688–1914,* edited by Donald Winch and Patrick O'Brien, 139–64. Oxford: Oxford University Press, 2002.

Greene, Jody. "*Captain Singleton*: An Epic of *Mitsein*?" *The Eighteenth Century: Theory and Interpretation* 52.3–4 (Fall–Winter 2011).

———. "*Hostis Humani Generis*." *Critical Inquiry* 34.4 (Summer 2008): 683–705.

Griffin, Dustin. *Literary Patronage in England, 1650–1800.* Cambridge: Cambridge University Press, 1996.

———. "The Social World of Authorship 1660–1714." In *The Cambridge History of English Literature, 1660–1770,* edited by John Richetti, 37–60. Cambridge: Cambridge University Press, 2005.

Guha, J. P., ed. *India in the Seventeenth Century: Being an Account of the Two Voyages to India by Ovington and Thevenot, to Which Is Added the Italian Travels of Careri.* New Delhi: Associated Publishing House, 1984.

Guha, Ranajit. *Dominance without Hegemony: History and Power in Colonial India.* Cambridge, Mass.: Harvard University Press, 1997.

———. *History at the Limit of World-History.* New York: Columbia University Press, 2002.

———. "On Some Aspects of the Historiography of Colonial India." In *Subaltern Studies I,* edited by Ranajit Guha, 1–8. New Delhi: Oxford University Press, 1982.

———. "Preface." In *Subaltern Studies I,* edited by Ranajit Guha, vii–viii. New Delhi: Oxford University Press, 1982.

———. "The Prose of Counter-Insurgency." In *Selected Subaltern Studies,* edited by Ranajit Guha and Gayatri Chakravorty Spivak, 45–84. New York: Oxford University Press, 1988.

———. *A Rule of Property for Bengal: An Essay on the Idea of Permanent Settlement.* Durham, N.C.: Duke University Press, 1996.

Gupta, Maya. *Lord William Bentinck in Madras and the Vellore Mutiny, 1803–7.* New Delhi: Capital Publishers, 1986.

———. "The Vellore Mutiny, July 1806." *Journal of Indian History* 49.1–3 (1971): 91–112.

Haakonssen, Knud. "Adam Smith (1723–1790)." In *Routledge Encyclopedia of Philosophy,* edited by Edward Craig, 8:815–22. New York: Routledge, 1998.

Habermas, Jürgen. *The Structural Transformation of the Public Sphere: An Inquiry into a Category of Bourgeois Society.* Cambridge, Mass.: MIT Press, 1989.

Habib, Irfan. Review of *Indian Merchants and the Decline of Surat, c. 1700–1750,* by Ashin Das Gupta. *American Historical Review* 89.3 (June 1984): 829.

Haller, William, and Godfrey Davies, eds. *The Leveller Tracts, 1647–1653.* New York: Columbia University Press, 1944.

Hallward, B. L. "Scipio and Victory." In *Rome and the Mediterranean,* edited by S. A. Cook, F. E. Adcock, and M. P. Charlesworth, 83–115. Vol. 8 of *The Cambridge Ancient History.* Cambridge: Cambridge University Press, 1930.

Hallward, B. L., and M. P. Charlesworth. "The Fall of Carthage." In *Rome and the Mediterranean,* edited by S. A. Cook, F. E. Adcock, and M. P. Charlesworth, 466–94. Vol. 8 of *The Cambridge Ancient History.* Cambridge: Cambridge University Press, 1930.

Hamilton, Eliza. *Translation of the Letters of a Hindoo Rajah.* 2 vols. London: G. & J. Robinson, 1801.

Hardt, Michael, and Antonio Negri. *Empire.* Cambridge, Mass.: Harvard University Press, 2000.

Harris, Jonathan Gil. *Sick Economies: Drama, Mercantilism, and Disease in Shakespeare's England.* Philadelphia: University of Pennsylvania Press, 2004.

Harvey, David. *The Limits to Capital.* London: Verso, 1999.

———. *The New Imperialism.* New York: Oxford University Press, 2003.

Hastings, Warren. "Letter to Nathaniel Smith, from *The Bhagvat-Geeta.*" In *The British Discovery of Hinduism in the Eighteenth Century,* edited by P. J. Marshall, 184–91. Cambridge: Cambridge University Press, 1970.

———. *The Trial of Warren Hastings, Esq. Late Governor General of Bengal.* London: S. Bladon, 1788.

Hegel, Georg Wilhelm Friedrich. *Lectures on the Philosophy of History.* Translated by John Sibree. London: G. Bell & Sons, 1902.

———. *Reason in History: A General Introduction to the Philosophy of History.* New York: Liberal Arts Press, 1953.

———. *Die Vernunft in der Geschichte.* Vol. 8 of *Sämtliche Werke.* Leipzig: Felix Meiner, 1920.

———. *Werke in Zwanzig Bänden.* Frankfurt am Main: Suhrkamp, 1970.

Heilbroner, Robert. "The Paradox of Progress: Decline and Decay in *The Wealth of Nations.*" In *Essays on Adam Smith,* edited by Andrew Skinner and Thomas Wilson, 524–39. Oxford: Clarendon Press, 1975.

Heller-Roazen, Daniel. *The Enemy of All: Piracy and the Law of Nations.* New York: Zone Books, 2009.

Hill, Christopher. *Some Intellectual Consequences of the English Revolution.* Madison: University of Wisconsin Press, 1980.

Hilton, Rodney, ed. *The Transition from Feudalism to Capitalism.* New York: Verso, 1992.

Hobsbawm, Eric. *Industry and Empire: The Making of Modern English Society, 1750 to the Present Day.* New York: Pantheon, 1986.

Hollander, Samuel. "The Historical Dimension of *The Wealth of Nations.*" In *Adam Smith and Modern Political Economy,* edited by Gerald O'Driscoll Jr., 71–84. Ames: Iowa State University Press, 1979.

Holwell, J. Z. *Interesting Historical Events.* 3 vols. London, 1765–71.

Holzman, James. *The Nabobs in England: A Study of the Returned Anglo-Indian, 1760–1785.* New York: Columbia University Press, 1926.

Home Miscellanies H42. India Office Records. British Library. London.

Hont, Istvan, and Michael Ignatieff. "Needs and Justice in the *Wealth of Nations:* An Introductory Essay." In *Wealth and Virtue: The Shaping of Political Economy in the Scottish Enlightenment,* edited by Istvan Hont and Michael Ignatieff, 1–44. Cambridge: Cambridge University Press, 1983.

Horkheimer, Max. *Eclipse of Reason.* New York: Continuum, 1985.

———. "Reason against Itself: Some Remarks on Enlightenment." In *What Is Enlightenment?: Eighteenth-Century Answers and Twentieth-Century Questions,* edited by James Schmidt, 359–67. Berkeley: University of California Press, 1996.

Horkheimer, Max, and Theodor Adorno. *Dialectic of Enlightenment: Philosophical Fragments*. Stanford: Stanford University Press, 2002.

———. *Dialektik der Aufklärung: Philosophische Fragmente*. Vol. 3 of *Gesammelte Schriften*, by Theodore Adorno. Frankfurt am Main: Suhrkamp, 1984.

Howells, Robin. "Processing Voltaire's *Amabed*." *British Journal for Eighteenth-Century Studies* 10.2 (Autumn 1987): 153–62.

Hoxby, Blair. *Mammon's Music: Literature and Economics in the Age of Milton*. New Haven, Conn.: Yale University Press, 2002.

Hughes, Derek. "Restoration and Settlement: 1660 and 1688." In *The Cambridge Companion to English Restoration Theatre*, edited by Deborah Payne Fisk, 127–41. New York: Cambridge University Press, 2000.

Hume, David. *Essays: Moral, Political, and Literary*. Indianapolis: Liberty Fund, 1987.

———. *Political Essays*. Cambridge: Cambridge University Press, 2003.

———. *A Treatise of Human Nature*. Oxford: Clarendon Press, 1978.

Humphrey, Richard. *The Historical Novel as Philosophy of History: Three German Contributions: Alexis, Fontane, Döblin*. London: Institute of Germanic Studies, University of London Press, 1986.

Hunter, J. Paul. *The Reluctant Pilgrim: Defoe's Emblematic Method and Quest for Form in Robinson Crusoe*. Baltimore: Johns Hopkins University Press, 1966.

Hunter, W. W. *Annals of Rural Bengal*. New York: Johnson Reprint, 1970.

Hutchinson, John, and Anthony Smith, eds. *Nationalism*. New York: Oxford University Press, 1994.

Ibbetson, David. "Sir William Jones as a Comparative Lawyer." In *Sir William Jones, 1746–1794: A Commemoration*, edited by Alexander Murray, 17–42. Oxford: Oxford University Press, 1998.

Inden, Ronald. "Orientalist Constructions of India." *Modern Asian Studies* 20.3 (1986): 401–46.

Irwin, Robert. *For Lust of Knowing: The Orientalists and Their Enemies*. London: Allen Lane, 2006.

Israel, Jonathan. *Conflicts of Empires: Spain, the Low Countries and the Struggle for World Supremacy 1585–1713*. London: Hambledon, 1997.

———. *Dutch Primacy in World Trade, 1585–1740*. Oxford: Oxford University Press, 1989.

———. *Enlightenment Contested: Philosophy, Modernity, and the Emancipation of Man, 1670–1752*. Oxford: Oxford University Press, 2006.

Jameson, Fredric. "Introduction." In *The Historical Novel*, by Georg Lukács. Lincoln: University of Nebraska Press, 1983.

———. *Marxism and Form: Twentieth-Century Dialectical Theories of Literature*. Princeton, N.J.: Princeton University Press, 1974.

———. *The Political Unconscious: Narrative as a Socially Symbolic Act*. Ithaca, N.Y.: Cornell University Press, 1981.

———. *Postmodernism, or, The Cultural Logic of Late Capitalism*. Durham, N.C.: Duke University Press, 1991.

Jones, Sir William. *Institutes of Hindu Law; or, The Ordinances of Menu*. London: J. Sewell, 1796.

———. *The Letters of Sir William Jones*. 2 vols. Oxford: Clarendon Press, 1970.

———. *Sir William Jones: Selected Poetical and Prose Works*. Cardiff: University of Wales Press, 1995.

———. *The Works of Sir William Jones*. 13 vols. London: John Stockdale, 1807.

Jordan, Elaine. "The Management of Scott's Novels." In *Europe and Its Others*, edited by Francis Barker, Peter Hulme, Margaret Iverson, and Diana Loxley, 2:146–61. Colchester, U.K.: University of Essex Press, 1985.

Joseph, Betty. *Reading the East India Company, 1720–1840: Colonial Currencies of Gender*. Chicago: University of Chicago Press, 2004.

Joshi, J. C. "The Martyrs of Vellore Mutiny." *Quarterly Review of Historical Studies* 28.4 (1989): 29–32.

Jovicevich, Alexandre. *Les Lettres d'Amabed, de Voltaire*. Paris: Éditions universitaires, 1961.

Juneja, Renu. "The Native and the Nabob: Representations of the Indian Experience in Eighteenth-Century English Literature." *Commonwealth Literature* 27.1 (1992): 183–98.

Kant, Immanuel. "An Answer to the Question: What Is Enlightenment?" In *What Is Enlightenment?: Eighteenth-Century Answers and Twentieth-Century Questions*, edited by James Schmidt, 58–64. Berkeley: University of California Press, 1996.

———. *Grounding for the Metaphysics of Morals*. Indianapolis: Hackett, 1993.

———. *On History*. New York: Macmillan, 1963.

———. *Toward Perpetual Peace and Other Writings on Politics, Peace, and History*. New Haven, Conn.: Yale University Press, 2006.

———. *Was ist Aufklärung?: Ausgewählte kleine Schriften*. Leipzig: Felix Meiner, 1999.

Kapil, Fathima. "Ryotwari System in Madras Presidency." *Quarterly Review of Historical Studies* 28.4 (1989): 45–52.

Kaul, Suvir. *Poems of Nation, Anthems of Empire: English Verse in the Long Eighteenth Century*. Charlottesville: University Press of Virginia, 2000.

Kelly, Gary. *Women, Writing and Revolution 1790–1827*. Oxford: Clarendon Press, 1993.

Kelly, Linda. *Richard Brinsley Sheridan: A Life*. London: Sinclair Stevenson, 1997.

Kewes, Paulina. *Authorship and Appropriation: Writing for the Stage in England, 1660–1710*. New York: Oxford University Press, 1998.

———. "Dryden's Theatre and the Passions of Politics." In *The Cambridge Companion to John Dryden*, edited by Steven Zwicker, 131–55. Cambridge: Cambridge University Press, 2004.

Keymer, Thomas. "Sentimental Fiction: Ethics, Social Critique and Philanthropy." In *The Cambridge History of English Literature, 1660–1770*, edited by John Richetti, 572–601. Cambridge: Cambridge University Press, 2005.

Keynes, John Maynard. *A Treatise on Money*. London: Macmillan, 1965.

Kincaid, Dennis. *British Social Life in India, 1608–1937*. London: Routledge & Kegan Paul, 1973.

Kirk, Russell. *The Conservative Mind, from Burke to Santayana*. Chicago: H. Regnery, 1953.

Knaap, Gerrit. "Crisis and Failure: War and Revolt in the Ambon Islands, 1636–7." In *Warfare and Empires*, by Douglas Peers, 151–76. Aldershot, U.K.: Ashgate, 1997.

Knorr, Klaus. *British Colonial Theories, 1570–1850*. Toronto: University of Toronto Press, 1944.

Kopf, David. *British Orientalism and the Bengal Renaissance: The Dynamics of Indian Modernization, 1773–1835*. Berkeley: University of California Press, 1969.

Kramnick, Isaac. *The Rage of Edmund Burke: Portrait of an Ambivalent Conservative.* New York: Basic Books, 1977.

Kroll, Richard. "Defoe and Early Narrative." In *The Columbia History of the British Novel,* edited by John Richetti, John Bender, Deirdre David, and Michael Seidel, 23–49. New York: Columbia University Press, 1994.

Laclau, Ernesto. *Emancipation(s).* London: Verso, 1996.

Lamb, Jonathan. *Preserving the Self in the South Seas.* Chicago: University of Chicago Press, 2001.

———. *Sterne's Fiction and the Double Principle.* Cambridge: Cambridge University Press, 1989.

———. "Sterne's System of Imitation." *Modern Language Review* 76.4 (October 1981): 794–810.

Lane, Frederic. *Venice and History: The Collected Papers of Frederic C. Lane.* Baltimore: Johns Hopkins University Press, 1966.

Lascelles, Mary. *The Story-Teller Retrieves the Past / Historical Fiction and Fictitious History in the Art of Scott, Stevenson, Kipling, and Some Others.* Oxford: Clarendon Press, 1980.

Lawson, Philip. *The East India Company: A History.* London: Longman, 1993.

Leask, Nigel. *British Romantic Writers and the East: Anxieties of Empire.* New York: Cambridge University Press, 1992.

Lee, Joan Skinner. *History Lessons: Refiguring the Nineteenth-Century Historical Novel in Spanish America.* Newark, Del.: Juan de la Cuesta, 2006.

Leur, J. C. van. *Indonesian Trade and Society: Essays in Asian Social and Economic History.* The Hague: W. Van Hoeve, 1955.

Lew, Joseph. "Sidney Owenson and the Fate of Empire." *Keats-Shelley Journal* 39 (1990): 39–65.

Lincoln, Andrew. *Walter Scott and Modernity.* Edinburgh: Edinburgh University Press, 2007.

Linebaugh, Peter. *The London Hanged: Crime and Civil Society in the Eighteenth Century.* London: Verso, 2003.

Lloyd, T. O. *The British Empire 1558–1983.* Oxford: Oxford University Press, 1984.

Lockhart, John. *Memoirs of the Life of Sir Walter Scott, Bart.* Vol. 1. Philadelphia: Carey, Lea, & Blanchard, 1837.

Long, Douglas. *Bentham and Liberty: Jeremy Bentham's Idea of Liberty in Relation to His Utilitarianism.* Toronto: University of Toronto Press, 1991.

Love, Harold. "Restoration and Early Eighteenth-Century Drama." In *The Cambridge History of English Literature, 1660–1770,* edited by John Richetti, 109–31. Cambridge: Cambridge University Press, 2005.

Lovell, Terry. *Consuming Fiction.* London: Verso, 1987.

Lukács, Georg. *The Historical Novel.* Lincoln: University of Nebraska Press, 1983.

———. *The Theory of the Novel.* Cambridge, Mass.: MIT Press, 1978.

Ludden, David. "India's Development Regime." In *Colonialism and Culture,* edited by Nicholas Dirks, 247–87. Ann Arbor: University of Michigan Press, 1992.

———. "Orientalist Empiricism: Transformations of Colonial Knowledge." In *Orientalism and the Postcolonial Predicament: Perspectives on South Asia,* edited by Carol Breckenridge and Peter van der Veer, 250–78. Philadelphia: University of Pennsylvania Press, 1993.

Macfie, A. L. *Orientalism.* New York: Longman, 2002.

Mack, Mary. *Jeremy Bentham: An Odyssey of Ideas.* London: Heinemann, 1962.

Mackenzie, Henry. *The Lounger.* Edinburgh: William Creech, 1786.

———. *The Man of Feeling.* New York: Oxford University Press, 1987.

MacKenzie, John. *Orientalism: History, Theory, and the Arts.* Manchester, U.K.: Manchester University Press, 1995.

MacLean, Gerald. *Time's Witness: Historical Representations in English Poetry, 1603–1660.* Madison: University of Wisconsin Press, 1990.

Macpherson, C. B. *Burke.* New York: Hill & Wang, 1980.

Madden, Frederick, and David Fieldhouse, eds. *Imperial Reconstruction, 1763–1840: The Evolution of Alternative Systems of Colonial Government.* New York: Greenwood Press, 1987.

Majeed, Javed. *Ungoverned Imaginings: James Mill's "The History of British India" and Orientalism.* Oxford: Clarendon Press, 1992.

Makdisi, Saree. *Romantic Imperialism: Universal Empire and the Culture of Modernity.* Cambridge: Cambridge University Press, 1998.

Maloni, Ruby. *European Merchant Capital and the Indian Economy: A Historical Reconstruction Based on Surat Factory Records 1630–88.* New Delhi: Manohar Publications, 1992.

Mani, Lata. "Contentious Traditions: The Debate on Sati in Colonial India." In *Recasting Women: Essays in Indian Colonial History,* edited by Kumkum Sangari and Sudesh Vaid, 88–126. New Brunswick, N.J.: Rutgers University Press, 1990.

Manuel, Frank. *The Eighteenth Century Confronts the Gods.* Cambridge, Mass.: Harvard University Press, 1959.

Manzoni, Alessandro. *On the Historical Novel.* Lincoln: University of Nebraska Press, 1984.

Markley, Robert. *The Far East and the English Imagination, 1600–1730.* Cambridge: Cambridge University Press, 2006.

———. "Riches, Power, Trade and Religion: The Far East and the English Imagination, 1600–1720." *Renaissance Studies* 17.3 (September 2003): 494–516.

———. "Sentimentality as Performance: Shaftesbury, Sterne and the Theatrics of Virtue." In *The New Eighteenth Century,* edited by Felicity Nussbaum and Laura Brown, 210–30. New York: Methuen, 1987.

———. "Violence and Profits on the Restoration Stage: Trade, Nationalism, and Insecurity in Dryden's *Amboyna.*" *Eighteenth Century Life* 22.1 (1998): 2–17.

Marshall, P. J., ed. *The British Discovery of Hinduism in the Eighteenth Century.* Cambridge: Cambridge University Press, 1970.

———. *East Indian Fortunes.* Oxford: Clarendon Press, 1976.

———. *The Impeachment of Warren Hastings.* New York: Oxford University Press, 1965.

———, ed. *Problems of Empire: Britain and India 1757–1813.* London: Allen & Unwin, 1968.

———. *Trade and Conquest: Studies on the Rise of British Dominance in India.* Brookfield, Vt.: Variorum, 1993.

Marvell, Andrew. *The Complete Poems.* New York: Penguin, 1985.

Marx, Karl. *Capital: A Critique of Political Economy.* 3 vols. New York: Penguin, 1976.

———. *The First Indian War of Independence, 1857–1859.* Moscow: Progress Publishers, 1975.

———. *Grundrisse.* Harmondsworth, U.K.: Penguin, 1973.

———. *The Poverty of Philosophy.* New York: International Publishers, 1963.

————. *Theories of Surplus Value*. Vol. 3. Moscow: Progress Publishers, 1978.

Marx, Karl, and Friedrich Engels. *The Communist Manifesto*. Harmondsworth, U.K.: Penguin, 1967.

————. *Selected Works in Two Volumes*. London: Lawrence & Wishart, 1950.

Mauss, Marcel. *The Gift: The Form and Reason for Exchange in Archaic Societies*. New York: Norton, 1990.

Maxwell, Richard. "The Historical Novel." In *The Cambridge Companion to Fiction in the Romantic Period*, edited by Richard Maxwell and Katie Trumpener, 65–87. Cambridge: Cambridge University Press, 2008.

Mazlish, Bruce. "The Tragic Farce of Marx, Hegel, and Engels: A Note." *History and Theory* 11.3 (1972): 335–37.

McGann, Jerome, ed. *New Oxford Book of Romantic Period Verse*. Oxford: Oxford University Press, 1993.

McKeon, Michael. *The Origins of the English Novel 1600–1740*. Baltimore: Johns Hopkins University Press, 1987.

————. *Politics and Poetry in Restoration England: The Case of Dryden's "Annus Mirabilis."* Cambridge, Mass.: Harvard University Press, 1975.

————, ed. *Theory of the Novel: A Historical Approach*. Baltimore: Johns Hopkins University Press, 2000.

McMaster, Graham. *Scott and Society*. Cambridge: Cambridge University Press, 1981.

McNally, David. *Political Economy and the Rise of Capitalism: A Reinterpretation*. Berkeley: University of California Press, 1988

Medalle, Mrs, ed. *Letters of the Late Rev. Laurence Sterne*. 2 vols. Vienna: R. Sammler, 1797.

Mehta, Uday. *Liberalism and Empire: A Study in Nineteenth-Century British Liberal Thought*. Chicago: University of Chicago Press, 1999.

Meilink-Roelofsz, M. A. P. *Asian Trade and European Influence in the Indonesian Archipelago between 1500 and about 1630*. The Hague: Martinus Nijhoff, 1962.

Metcalf, Thomas. *Ideologies of the Raj*. Cambridge: Cambridge University Press, 1994.

Mill, James. *History of British India*. 10 vols. London: J. Madden, 1858.

Millgate, Jane. "Introduction." In *Guy Mannering*, by Walter Scott. New York: Penguin, 2003.

Minto, Gilbert Elliot. *Life and Letters of Sir Gilbert Elliot, First Earl of Minto, from 1751 to 1806*. London: Longmans, Green, 1874.

Mintz, Sidney. *Sweetness and Power: The Place of Sugar in Modern History*. New York: Penguin, 1986.

Montesquieu, Baron de. *The Spirit of the Laws*. New York: Hafner, 1949.

Moodley, Devadas. "Vellore 1806: The Meanings of Mutiny." In *Rebellion, Repression, Reinvention: Mutiny in Comparative Perspective*, edited by Jane Hathaway and Geoffrey Parker, 87–101. Westport, Conn.: Praeger, 2001.

Morgan, Kenneth. "Mercantilism and the British Empire." In *The Political Economy of British Historical Experience, 1688–1914*, edited by Donald Winch and Patrick O'Brien, 165–92. Oxford: Oxford University Press, 2002.

Morgan, Lady (Sydney). *Luxima, the Prophetess: A Tale of India*. London: C. Westerton, 1859.

————. *The Missionary, an Indian Tale*. New York: Franklin, 1811.

Morwood, James. *The Life and Works of Richard Brinsley Sheridan*. Edinburgh: Scottish Academic Press, 1985.

Motooka, Wendy. *The Age of Reasons: Quixotism, Sentimentalism, and Political Economy in Eighteenth-Century Britain.* New York: Routledge, 1998.

Mufti, Aamir. *Enlightenment in the Colony: The Jewish Question and the Crisis of Postcolonial Culture.* Princeton, N.J.: Princeton University Press, 2007.

Mui, Hoh-Cheung, and Lorna Mui. "The Commutation Act and the Tea Trade in Britain 1784–1793." *Economic History Review* 16.2 (1963): 234–53.

———. "William Pitt and the Enforcement of the Commutation Act, 1784–1788." *English Historical Review* 76.300 (July 1961): 447–65.

Mukherjee, S. N. *Sir William Jones: A Study in Eighteenth-Century British Attitudes to India.* Cambridge: Cambridge University Press, 1968.

Mukhopadhyay, Subhas Chandra. *The Agrarian Policy of the British in Bengal: The Formative Period, 1698–1772.* Allahabad, India: Chugh Publications, 1987.

Mullan, John. "Sentimental Novels." In *The Cambridge Companion to the Eighteenth-Century Novel,* edited by John Richetti, 236–54. Cambridge: Cambridge University Press, 1996.

———. *Sentiment and Sociability: The Language of Feeling in the Eighteenth Century.* Oxford: Clarendon Press, 1988.

Munns, Jessica. "Theatrical Culture I: Politics and Theatre." In *The Cambridge Companion to English Literature 1650–1740,* edited by Steven Zwicker, 82–103. New York: Cambridge University Press, 1998.

Musgrave, Peter. "The Economics of Uncertainty: The Structural Revolution in the Spice Trade, 1480–1640." In *Spices in the Indian Ocean World,* edited by M. N. Pearson, 337–50. Aldershot, U.K.: Ashgate, 1996.

Musselwhite, David. "The Trial of Warren Hastings." In *Literature, Politics, and Theory: Papers from the Essex Conference, 1976–84,* edited by Francis Barker, Peter Hulme, Margaret Iversen, and Diana Loxley, 77–103. New York: Methuen, 1986.

Muthu, Sankar. "Adam Smith's Critique of International Trading Companies: Theorizing 'Globalization' in the Age of Enlightenment." *Political Theory* 36.2 (April 2008): 185–212.

———. *Enlightenment against Empire.* Princeton, N.J.: Princeton University Press, 2003.

Nandy, Ashis. "The Politics of Secularism and the Recovery of Religious Tolerance." In *Mirrors of Violence: Communities, Riots and Survivors in South Asia,* edited by Veena Das, 69–93. Delhi: Oxford University Press, 1990.

Neill, Anna. "Crusoe's Farther Adventures: Discovery, Trade, and the Law of Nations." *Eighteenth Century: Theory and Interpretation* 38.3 (1997): 213–30.

New, Melvyn, and W. G. Day, eds. *The Florida Edition of the Works of Laurence Sterne.* Vol. 6, *"A Sentimental Journey" and Continuation of the "Bramine's Journal."* Gainesville: University Press of Florida, 2002.

Nicholson, Colin. *Writing and the Rise of Finance.* Cambridge: Cambridge University Press, 1994.

Niranjana, Tejaswini. *Siting Translation: History, Post-structuralism, and the Colonial Context.* Berkeley: University of California Press, 1992.

Novak, Maximillian. *Daniel Defoe: Master of Fictions.* New York: Oxford University Press, 2001.

———. *Defoe and the Nature of Man.* London: Oxford University Press, 1963.

———. *Economics and the Fiction of Daniel Defoe.* Berkeley: University of California Press, 1962.

Nussbaum, Felicity, ed. *The Global Eighteenth Century*. Baltimore: Johns Hopkins University Press, 2003.

O'Brien, William. *Edmund Burke as an Irishman*. Dublin: M. H. Gill, 1926.

O'Quinn, Daniel. *Staging Governance: Theatrical Imperialism in London, 1770–1800*. Baltimore: Johns Hopkins University Press, 2005.

Orel, Harold. *The Historical Novel from Scott to Sabatini: Changing Attitudes toward a Literary Genre, 1814–1920*. London: St. Martin's, 1995.

Ormrod, David. *The Rise of Commercial Empires: England and the Netherlands in the Age of Mercantilism, 1650–1770*. Cambridge: Cambridge University Press, 2003.

Orr, Bridget. *Empire on the English State, 1660–1714*. Cambridge: Cambridge University Press, 2001.

Osborn, Jeremy. "India and the East India Company in the Public Sphere of Eighteenth-Century Britain." In *The Worlds of the East India Company*, edited by H. V. Bowen, Margarette Lincoln, and Nigel Rigby, 201–21. Woodbridge, U.K.: Boydell, 2002.

Owen, Susan. *Restoration Theatre and Crisis*. New York: Oxford University Press, 1996.

Pagden, Anthony. "The Effacement of Difference: Colonialism and the Origins of Nationalism in Diderot and Herder." In *After Colonialism: Imperial Histories and Postcolonial Displacements*, edited by Gyan Prakash, 129–46. Princeton, N.J.: Princeton University Press, 1995.

———. *Lords of All the World: Ideologies of Empire in Spain, Britain and France c. 1500–c. 1800*. New Haven, Conn.: Yale University Press, 1995.

Paine, Thomas. *Rights of Man*. New York: Penguin, 1984.

Parker, Geoffrey. *The Military Revolution: Military Innovation and the Rise of the West, 1500–1800*. Cambridge: Cambridge University Press, 1996.

Parker, Noel. "Look, No Hidden Hands: How Smith Understands Historical Progress and Societal Values." In *Adam Smith's "Wealth of Nations": New Interdisciplinary Essays*, edited by Stephen Copley and Kathryn Sutherland, 122–43. Manchester, U.K.: Manchester University Press, 1995.

Parthasarathi, Prasannan. *The Transition to a Colonial Economy: Weavers, Merchants, and Kings in South India*. Cambridge: Cambridge University Press, 2001.

Pearson, M. N. "India and the Indian Ocean in the Sixteenth Century." In *India and the Indian Ocean 1500–1800*, edited by Ashin Das Gupta and M. N. Pearson, 71–93. Calcutta: Oxford University Press, 1987.

———. "Merchants and States." In *The Political Economy of Merchant Empires*, edited by James Tracy, 41–116. New York: Cambridge University Press, 1991.

Perlin, Frank. *Invisible City: Monetary, Administrative and Popular Infrastructures in Asia and Europe*. Aldershot, U.K.: Ashgate, 1992.

———. "Proto-industrialisation and Pre-colonial South Asia." *Past & Present* 98.1 (1983): 30–95.

Philips, C. H. *The East India Company 1784–1834*. Manchester, U.K.: Manchester University Press, 1961.

Pincus, Steven. *Protestantism and Patriotism: Ideologies and the Making of English Foreign Policy, 1650–1668*. Cambridge: Cambridge University Press, 1996.

———. "Whigs, Political Economy, and the Revolution of 1688–89." In *"Cultures of Whiggism": New Essays on English Literature and Culture in the Long Eighteenth Century*, edited by David Womersley, Paddy Bullard, and Abigail Williams, 62–85. Newark: University Press of Delaware, 2005.

Pirenne, Henri. *Economic and Social History of Medieval Europe.* London: Routledge & Kegan Paul, 1972.

Pitts, Jennifer. "Jeremy Bentham: Legislator of the World?" In *Utilitarianism and Empire,* edited by Bart Schultz and Georgios Varouxakis, 57–91. New York: Rowman & Littlefield, 2005.

———. *A Turn to Empire: The Rise of Imperial Liberalism in Britain and France.* Princeton, N.J.: Princeton University Press, 2005.

Plutarch. *Plutarch's Lives.* Edited by Arthur Hugh Clough. Translated by John Dryden. 2 vols. New York: Modern Library, 2001.

Pocock, J. G. A. "Adam Smith and History." In *The Cambridge Companion to Adam Smith,* edited by Knud Haakonssen, 270–87. Cambridge: Cambridge University Press, 2006.

———. *Barbarism and Religion.* 4 vols. Cambridge: Cambridge University Press, 1999–2005.

———. "Introduction." In *Reflections on the Revolution in France,* by Edmund Burke. Indianapolis: Hackett, 1987.

———. *The Machiavellian Moment: Florentine Political Thought and the Atlantic Republican Tradition.* Princeton, N.J.: Princeton University Press, 1975.

———. *Politics, Language, and Time: Essays on Political Thought and History.* New York: Atheneum, 1971.

———. *Virtue, Commerce, and History: Essays on Political Thought and History, Chiefly in the Eighteenth Century.* Cambridge: Cambridge University Press, 1985.

Polanyi, Karl. *The Great Transformation: The Political and Economic Origins of Our Time.* Boston: Beacon, 2001.

Pomeranz, Kenneth. *The Great Divergence: China, Europe, and the Making of the Modern World Economy.* Princeton, N.J.: Princeton University Press, 2000.

Porter, Roy. *The Creation of the Modern World: The Untold Story of the British Enlightenment.* New York: Norton, 2000.

Pownall, Thomas. *The Right, Interest, and Duty of Government, As Concerned in the Affairs of the East Indies.* London: S. Bladon, 1773.

Prabhakaran, M. B. *The Historical Origin of India's Underdevelopment: A World-System Perspective.* New York: University Press of America, 1990.

Prakash, Gyan. "Postcolonial Criticism and Indian Historiography." *Social Text* 31/32 (1992): 8–19.

———. "Who's Afraid of Postcoloniality?" *Social Text* 49, 14.4 (Winter 1996): 187–203.

———. "Writing Post-Orientalist Histories of the Third World: Perspectives from Indian Historiography." *Comparative Studies in Society and History* 32.2 (1990): 383–408.

Prakash, Om. "Restrictive Trading Regimes: VOC and the Asian Spice Trade in the Seventeenth Century." In *Spices in the Indian Ocean World,* edited by M. N. Pearson, 317–36. Aldershot, U.K.: Ashgate, 1996.

Quétel, Claude. *History of Syphilis.* Baltimore: Johns Hopkins University Press, 1992.

Rajan, Balachandra. "Feminizing the Feminine: Early Women Writers on India." In *Romanticism, Race, and Imperial Culture, 1780–1834,* edited by Alan Richardson and Sonia Hofkosh, 149–72. Bloomington: Indiana University Press, 1996.

Raman, Shankar. *Framing "India": The Colonial Imaginary in Early Modern Culture.* Stanford: Stanford University Press, 2001.

Rashid, Salim. "The Policy of Laissez-Faire during Scarcities." *Economic Journal* 90.359 (September 1980): 493–503.

Raven, James. *Judging New Wealth: Popular Publishing and Responses to Commerce in England, 1750–1800.* Oxford: Clarendon Press, 1992.

Rawson, Claude. *Satire and Sentiment 1660–1830.* New York: Cambridge University Press, 1994.

Raynal, Abbé. *Histoire philosophique et politique des établissemens et du commerce des Européens dans les deux Indes.* 10 vols. Geneva: J.-L. Pellet, 1780–84.

———. *A Philosophical and Political History of the Settlements and Trade of the Europeans in the East and West Indies.* 10 vols. London: W. Strahan, 1783.

Rediker, Marcus. *Between the Devil and the Deep Blue Sea: Merchant Seamen, Pirates and the Anglo-American Maritime World, 1700–1750.* Cambridge: Cambridge University Press, 1989.

Refai, G. Z. "Sir George Oxinden and Bombay, 1662–1669." *English Historical Review* 92.364 (July 1977): 573–81.

Richards, John. "The Opium Industry in British India." In *Land, Politics and Trade in South Asia,* edited by Sanjay Subrahmanyam, 44–81. Oxford: Oxford University Press, 2004.

Richetti, John. *Defoe's Narratives: Situations and Structures.* Oxford: Clarendon Press, 1975.

———. *The English Novel in History 1700–1780.* New York: Routledge, 1999.

———. *The Life of Daniel Defoe: A Critical Biography.* Oxford: Blackwell, 2005.

———. *Popular Fiction before Richardson: Narrative Patterns, 1700–1739.* New York: Oxford University Press, 1969.

Rocher, Ludo. *Ezourvedam: A French Veda of the Eighteenth Century.* Philadelphia: John Benjamins, 1984.

Rocher, Rosane. "British Orientalism in the Eighteenth Century: The Dialectic of Knowledge and Government." In *Orientalism and the Postcolonial Predicament: Perspectives on South Asia,* edited by Carol Breckenridge and Peter van der Veer, 215–49. Philadelphia: University of Pennsylvania Press, 1993.

———. "Foreword." In *Sir William Jones: A Reader,* by William Jones. New York: Oxford University Press, 1993.

———. "Weaving Knowledge: Sir William Jones and Indian Pandits." In *Objects of Enquiry: The Life, Contributions, and Influences of Sir William Jones (1746–1794),* edited by Garland Cannon and Kevin Brine, 51–79. New York: New York University Press, 1995.

Rosecrance, Richard. *The Rise of the Trading State.* New York: Basic Books, 1986.

Rosen, Fred. "Elie Halévy and Bentham's Authoritarian Liberalism." In *Jeremy Bentham: Critical Assessments,* edited by Bhikhu Parekh. London: Routledge, 1993.

Rosenberg, Nathan. "Adam Smith on Profits—Paradox Lost and Regained." In *Essays on Adam Smith,* edited by Andrew Skinner and Thomas Wilson, 377–89. Oxford: Clarendon Press, 1975.

Ross, Ian. *The Life of Adam Smith.* Oxford: Oxford University Press, 1995.

Rothschild, Emma. *Economic Sentiments: Adam Smith, Condorcet, and the Enlightenment.* Cambridge, Mass.: Harvard University Press, 2001.

———. "Global Commerce and the Question of Sovereignty in the Eighteenth-Century Provinces." *Modern Intellectual History* 1.1 (2004): 3–25.

Rushdie, Salman. *The Moor's Last Sigh.* New York: Vintage Books, 1995.

Sahlins, Marshall. *Culture in Practice.* New York: Zone Books, 2000.

Said, Edward. *Culture and Imperialism.* New York: Alfred A. Knopf, 1993.

———. *Freud and the Non-European.* London: Verso, 2004.

———. *On Late Style: Music and Literature against the Grain.* New York: Vintage, 2007.

———. *Orientalism.* 25th anniversary ed. New York: Vintage, 2003.

Samet, Elizabeth. "A Prosecutor and a Gentleman: Edmund Burke's Idiom of Impeachment." *ELH* 68.2 (Summer 2001): 397–418.

Sarkar, Sumit. "Orientalism Revisited: Saidian Frameworks in the Writing of Modern Indian History." In *Mapping Subaltern Studies and the Postcolonial,* edited by Vinayak Chaturvedi, 239–55. London: Verso, 2000.

———. *Writing Social History.* Delhi: Oxford University Press, 1997.

Scammell, G. V. "European Exiles, Renegades and Outlaws and the Maritime Economy of Asia c. 1500–1750." *Modern Asian Studies* 26.4 (October 1992): 641–61.

Schille, Candy. "'With Honour Quit the Fort': Ambivalent Colonialism in Dryden's *Amboyna.*" *Early Modern Literary Studies* 12.1 (May 2006): 1–30.

Schmidt, James. "Introduction: What Is Enlightenment? A Question, Its Context, and Some Consequences." In *What Is Enlightenment?: Eighteenth-Century Answers and Twentieth-Century Questions,* edited by James Schmidt, 1–44. Berkeley: University of California Press, 1996.

Schnurmann, Claudia. "Wherever profit leads us, to every sea and shore . . .': The VOC, the WIC, and Dutch Methods of Globalization in the Seventeenth Century." *Renaissance Studies* 17.3 (September 2003): 474–93.

Schultz, Bart, and Georgios Varouxakis. "Introduction." In *Utilitarianism and Empire,* edited by Bart Schultz and Georgios Varouxakis, 1–32. New York: Rowman & Littlefield, 2005.

Schwab, Raymond. *Oriental Renaissance: Europe's Rediscovery of India and the East, 1680–1880.* New York: Columbia University Press, 1984.

Scott, David. *Conscripts of Modernity: The Tragedy of Colonial Enlightenment.* Durham, N.C.: Duke University Press, 2004.

Scott, Sarah. *The History of Sir George Ellison.* Lexington: University Press of Kentucky, 1996.

Scott, Walter. *Chronicles of Canongate.* New York: Penguin, 2003.

———. *Guy Mannering.* Edinburgh: Edinburgh University Press, 1999.

———. *Guy Mannering; or, The Astrologer.* Vols. 3 and 4 of *The Waverley Novels.* Boston: Parker, 1830.

Sekora, John. *Luxury: The Concept in Western Thought, Eden to Smollett.* Baltimore: Johns Hopkins University Press, 1977.

Sen, Sudipta. *Empire of Free Trade: The East India Company and the Making of the Colonial Marketplace.* Philadelphia: University of Pennsylvania Press, 1998.

Sencourt, Robert. *India in English Literature.* London: Simpkin Marshall, 1924.

Senior, C. M. *A Nation of Pirates: English Piracy in Its Heydey.* New York: Crane, Russak, 1976.

Shaw, Harry. *The Forms of Historical Fiction: Sir Walter Scott and His Successors.* Ithaca, N.Y.: Cornell University Press, 1983.

Sheridan, Richard Brinsley. *The Celebrated Speech of Richard Brinsley Sheridan, Esq; in Westminster-Hall, on the 3d, 6th, 10th, and 13th of June, 1788.* London: C. Foster, 1788.

———. *The Speech of R. B. Sheridan, Esq. on Summing Up the Second Charge against Warren Hastings.* London: J. Dicrie, 1788.

———. *The Speech of R. B. Sheridan, Esq. on Wednesday, the 7th of February, 1787.* London: J. French, 1787.

———. *Speeches of the Late Right Honourable Richard Brinsley Sheridan.* 2 vols. London: Patrick Martin, 1816.

Sherman, Stuart. "Dryden and the Theatrical Imagination." In *The Cambridge Companion to John Dryden*, edited by Steven Zwicker, 13–36. Cambridge: Cambridge University Press, 2004.

Sim, Stuart, and David Walker. *The Discourse of Sovereignty, Hobbes to Fielding: The State of Nature and the Nature of the State.* Aldershot, U.K.: Ashgate, 2003.

Simmons, Clare. *Reversing the Conquest: History and Myth in Nineteenth-Century British Literature.* New Brunswick, N.J.: Rutgers University Press, 1990.

Singh, K. S. *Birsa Munda and His Movement 1874–1901: A Study of a Millenarian Movement in Chotanagpur.* Calcutta: Oxford University Press, 1983.

Skinner, Andrew. "Adam Smith: An Economic Interpretation of History." In *Essays on Adam Smith*, edited by Andrew Skinner and Thomas Wilson, 154–78. Oxford: Clarendon Press, 1975.

Skinner, Gillian. *Sensibility and Economics in the Novel, 1740–1800: The Price of a Tear.* London: Macmillan, 1999.

Smith, Adam. *The Correspondence of Adam Smith.* Oxford: Clarendon Press, 1987.

———. *An Inquiry into the Nature and Causes of the Wealth of Nations.* 2 vols. Oxford: Clarendon Press, 1976.

———. *Lectures on Jurisprudence.* Oxford: Clarendon Press, 1976.

———. *Theory of Moral Sentiments.* Cambridge: Cambridge University Press, 2002.

Smith, David. "Orientalism and Hinduism." In *The Blackwell Companion to Hinduism*, edited by Gavin Flood, 45–63. Oxford: Blackwell, 2003.

Smith, Simon. *British Imperialism 1750–1970.* Cambridge: Cambridge University Press, 1998.

Sowell, Thomas. "Adam Smith in Theory and Practice." In *Adam Smith and Modern Political Economy*, edited by Gerald P. O'Driscoll Jr., 3–18. Ames: Iowa State University Press, 1979.

Spengeman, William. "The Earliest American Novel: Aphra Behn's *Oroonoko.*" *Nineteenth-Century Fiction* 38 (1984): 384–414.

Spivak, Gayatri Chakravorty. "'Breast-Giver': For Author, Reader, Teacher, Subaltern, Historian . . ." In *Breast Stories*, by Mahasweta Devi. Calcutta: Seagull Books, 1997.

———. *A Critique of Postcolonial Reason: Toward a History of the Vanishing Present.* Cambridge, Mass.: Harvard University Press, 1999.

———. *Death of a Discipline.* New York: Columbia University Press, 2003.

Starr, G. A. *Defoe & Spiritual Autobiography.* Princeton, N.J.: Princeton University Press, 1965.

Staves, Susan. "The Construction of the Public Interest in the Debates over Fox's India Bill." *Prose Studies: History, Theory, Criticism* 18.3 (December 1995): 175–98.

———. *Players' Scepters: Fictions of Authority in the Restoration.* Lincoln: University of Nebraska Press, 1979.

Steensgaard, Niels. *The Asian Trade Revolution of the Seventeenth Century: The East India Companies and the Decline of the Caravan Trade.* Chicago: University of Chicago Press, 1973.

———. "Violence and the Rise of Capitalism: F. C. Lane's Theory of Protection and Tribute," *Review* 5 (1981), 247–273.

Stein, Burton. *Thomas Munro: The Origins of the Colonial State and His Vision of Empire.* New York: Oxford University Press, 1989.

Steintrager, James. *Bentham.* New York: Routledge, 2004.

Stephen, Leslie. *English Literature and Society in the Eighteenth Century.* London: Methuen, 1966.

———. *English Utilitarians.* London: Duckworth, 1900.

Stern, Philip. "British Asia and British Atlantic: Comparisons and Connections." *William and Mary Quarterly* 63.4 (October 2006): 694–712.

Sterne, Laurence. *The Life and Opinions of Tristram Shandy, Gentleman.* New York: Penguin, 1997.

———. *A Sentimental Journey through France and Italy.* Berkeley: University of California Press, 1967.

Stokes, Eric. *The English Utilitarians and India.* Oxford: Clarendon Press, 1959.

Stone, Lawrence. *The Crisis of the Aristocracy 1558–1641.* Oxford: Clarendon Press, 1965.

Strugnell, Anthony. *Diderot's Politics: A Study of the Evolution of Diderot's Political Thought after the "Encyclopédie."* The Hague: Martinus Nijhoff, 1973.

Subrahmanyam, Sanjay. "Introduction." In *Merchants, Markets and the State in Early Modern India,* edited by Sanjay Subrahmanyam, 1–17. Oxford: Oxford University Press, 1990.

———. "A Note on the Rise of Surat in the Sixteenth Century." *Journal of the Economic and Social History of the Orient* 43.1 (2000): 23–33.

———. *The Portuguese Empire in Asia, 1500–1700: A Political and Economic History.* New York: Longman, 1993.

Suleri, Sara. *The Rhetoric of English India.* Chicago: University of Chicago Press, 1992.

Surat Factory Records. India Office Records. British Library. London.

Sutherland, John. *The Life of Walter Scott: A Critical Biography.* Cambridge: Blackwell, 1995.

Sutherland, Kathryn. "Introduction." In *An Inquiry into the Nature and Causes of the Wealth of Nations: A Selected Edition,* by Adam Smith. Oxford: Oxford University Press, 1998.

Taylor, George, ed. *Plays by Samuel Foote and Arthur Murphy.* New York: Cambridge University Press, 1984.

Teltscher, Kate. *India Inscribed: European and British Writing on India 1600–1800.* Delhi: Oxford University Press, 1995.

Thapar, Romila. "Communalism and the Writing of Ancient Indian History." In *Communalism and the Writing of Indian History,* by Romila Thapar, Harbans Mukhia, and Bipan Chandra, 1–21. Delhi: People's Publishing House, 1969.

———. "Imagined Religious Communities? Ancient History and the Modern Search for a Hindu Identity." *Modern Asian Studies* 23.2 (1989): 209–31.

Thompson, E. P. *Customs in Common.* New York: New Press, 1993.

Thompson, F. M. L. "Changing Perceptions of Land Tenures in Britain, 1750–1914." In *The Political Economy of British Historical Experience,* edited by Donald Winch and Patrick O'Brien, 119–38. Oxford: Oxford University Press, 2002.

Thompson, James. *Models of Value: Eighteenth-Century Political Economy and the Novel.* Durham, N.C.: Duke University Press, 1996.

Thomson, George. *Sir Francis Drake.* London: Future, 1976.

Thomson, Janice. *Mercenaries, Pirates, and Sovereigns: State-Building and Extraterritorial Violence in Early Modern Europe.* Princeton, N.J.: Princeton University Press, 1994.

Todd, Janet. *Sensibility: An Introduction.* New York: Methuen, 1986.

Touchstone, Timothy. *Tea and Sugar; or, The Nabob and the Creole.* London: J. Ridgway, 1772.

Trautmann, Thomas. *Aryans and British India.* Berkeley: University of California Press, 1997.

Travers, Robert. "British India as a Problem in Political Economy: Comparing James Steuart and Adam Smith." In *Lineages of Empire: The Historical Roots of British Imperial Thought,* edited by Duncan Kelly, 137–60. Oxford: Oxford University Press, 2009.

———. "Ideology and British Expansion in Bengal, 1757–72." *Journal of Imperial and Commonwealth History* 33.1 (January 2005): 7–27.

———. *Ideology and Empire in Eighteenth-Century India: The British in Bengal.* Cambridge: Cambridge University Press, 2007.

———. "'The Real Value of the Lands': The Nawabs, the British, and the Land Tax in Bengal." *Modern Asian Studies* 38.3 (2004): 517–58.

Trefman, Simon. *Sam. Foote, Comedian, 1720–1777.* New York: New York University Press, 1971.

Trevor-Roper, Hugh. "The Idea of the Decline and Fall of the Roman Empire." In *The Age of Enlightenment: Studies Presented to Theodore Besterman,* edited by W. H. Barber, J. H. Brumfitt, R. A. Leigh, R. Shackleton, and S. S. B. Tayler, 413–30. London: Oliver & Boyd, 1967.

———. "The Invention of Tradition: The Highland Tradition of Scotland." In *The Invention of Tradition,* edited by Eric Hobsbawm and Terence Ranger, 15–41. Cambridge: Cambridge University Press, 1983.

Trocki, Carl. *Opium, Empire, and the Global Political Economy: A Study of the Asian Opium Trade, 1750–1950.* London: Routledge, 1999.

Trotter, David. *Circulation: Defoe, Dickens, and the Economies of the Novel.* New York: St. Martin's Press, 1988.

Trumpener, Katie. *Bardic Nationalism: The Romantic Novel and the British Empire.* Princeton, N.J.: Princeton University Press, 1997.

———. "The Time of the Gypsies: A 'People without History.'" *Critical Inquiry* 18 (1992): 843–84.

Turley, Hans. "Piracy, Identity, and Desire in *Captain Singleton.*" *Eighteenth-Century Studies* 31 (1997–98): 199–214.

———. *Rum, Sodomy, and the Lash: Piracy, Sexuality, and Masculine Identity.* New York: New York University Press, 1999.

Turner, Jack. *Spice: The History of a Temptation.* New York: Vintage Books, 2004.

Turner, James Grantham. "From Revolution to Restoration in English Literary Culture." In *The Cambridge History of Early Modern English Literature,* edited by David Loewenstein and Janel Mueller, 790–833. Cambridge: Cambridge University Press, 2002.

Van Sant, Ann Jessie. *Eighteenth-Century Sensibility and the Novel: The Senses in Social Context.* New York: Cambridge University Press, 1993.

Veer, Peter van der. *Religious Nationalism: Hindus and Muslims in India.* Berkeley: University of California Press, 1994.

———. "Sati and Sanskrit: The Move from Orientalism to Hinduism." In *The Point of Theory: Practices of Cultural Analysis,* edited by Mieke Bal and Inge Boer, 251–59. Amsterdam: Amsterdam University Press, 1994.

Virilio, Paul. *Pure War*. New York: Semiotext(e), 1997.

Viswanathan, Gauri. "Colonialism and the Construction of Hinduism." In *The Blackwell Companion to Hinduism*, edited by Gavin Flood, 23–44. Oxford: Blackwell, 2003.

———. "The Naming of Yale College: British Imperialism and American Higher Education." In *Cultures of United States Imperialism*, edited by Amy Kaplan and Donald E. Pease, 85–108. Durham, N.C.: Duke University Press, 1993.

———. *Outside the Fold: Conversion, Modernity, and Belief*. Princeton, N.J.: Princeton University Press, 1998.

Voltaire. *The Complete Tales of Voltaire*. 3 vols. New York: H. Fertig, 1990.

———. *Essai sur les mœurs et l'esprit des nations*. 2 vols. Paris: Garnier frères, 1963.

———. *Les Lettres d'Amabed*. In *Les Lettres d'Amabed, de Voltaire*, by Alexandre Jovicevich. Paris: Éditions universitaires, 1961.

———. *Lettres sur l'origine des sciences, et sur celle des peoples de l'Asie*. Paris: De Bure, 1777.

———. *Œuvres complètes de Voltaire*. 40 vols. Paris: Hachette, 1860–66.

———. *Philosophical Dictionary*. New York: Penguin, 1972.

Wallerstein, Immanuel. "The Bourgeois(ie) as Concept and Reality." In *Race, Nation, Class: Ambiguous Identities*, by Étienne Balibar and Immanuel Wallerstein. London: Verso, 1991.

———. "Eurocentrism and Its Avatars: The Dilemmas of Social Science." *New Left Review* 226 (November/December 1997): 93–107.

———. *Historical Capitalism*. London: Verso, 1983.

———. *Historical Capitalism with Capitalist Civilization*. London: Verso, 1995.

———. *The Modern World-System I: Capitalist Agriculture and the Origins of the European World-Economy in the Sixteenth Century*. New York: Academic Press, 1974.

———. *The Modern World-System II: Mercantilism and the Consolidation of the European World-Economy, 1600–1750*. New York: Academic Press, 1980.

———. *Unthinking Social Science: The Limits of Nineteenth-Century Paradigms*. Philadelphia: Temple University Press, 1991.

Washbrook, David. "Economic Depression and the Making of 'Traditional' Society in Colonial India, 1820–1855." *Transactions of the Royal Historical Society* 3 (1993): 237–63.

———. "India, 1818–1860: The Two Faces of Colonialism." *The Oxford History of the British Empire*, edited by Andrew Porter, 3:395–421. Oxford: Oxford University Press, 1999.

———. "Progress and Problems: South Asian Economic and Social History, c. 1720–1860." *Modern Asian Studies* 22.1 (1988): 57–96.

———. "South India 1770–1840: The Colonial Transition." *Modern Asian Studies* 38.3 (2004): 479–516.

Watson, Ian. "Fortifications and the 'Idea' of Force in Early English East India Company Relations with India." *Past and Present* 88 (August 1980): 70–87.

———. *Foundation for Empire: English Private Trade in India 1659–1760*. New Delhi: Vikas Publishing House, 1980.

Watt, Ian. *The Rise of the Novel: Studies in Defoe, Richardson and Fielding*. Berkeley: University of California Press, 1962.

Watts, Carol. *The Cultural Work of Empire: The Seven Years' War and the Imagining of the Shandean State*. Edinburgh: Edinburgh University Press, 2007.

Weber, Max. *General Economic History*. Glencoe, Ill.: Free Press, 1927.

Wheeler, Roxann. *The Complexion of Race: Categories of Difference in Eighteenth-Century British Culture*. Philadelphia: University of Pennsylvania Press, 2000.

Whelan, Frederick. *Edmund Burke and India: Political Morality and Empire*. Pittsburgh: University of Pittsburgh Press, 1996.

Whitney, Lois. *Primitivism and the Idea of Progress in English Popular Literature of the Eighteenth Century*. New York: Octagon Books, 1965.

Williams, Raymond. *The Country and the City*. New York: Oxford University Press, 1973.

———. *Culture and Society 1780–1950*. New York: Columbia University Press, 1983.

Wilson, Charles. *Profit and Power: A Study of England and the Dutch Wars*. London: Longmans, Green, 1957.

Winch, Donald. "Adam Smith's 'Enduring Particular Result': A Political and Cosmopolitan Perspective." In *Wealth and Virtue: The Shaping of Political Economy in the Scottish Enlightenment*, edited by Istvan Hont and Michael Ignatieff, 253–69. London: Cambridge University Press, 1983.

———. *Adam Smith's Politics: An Essay in Historiographic Revision*. Cambridge: Cambridge University Press, 1978.

———. "Bentham on Colonies and Empire." *Utilitas* 9.1 (1997): 147–54.

———. *Classical Political Economy and Colonies*. Cambridge, Mass.: Harvard University Press, 1965.

Winn, James. *John Dryden and His World*. New Haven, Conn.: Yale University Press, 1987.

Wokler, Robert. "Diderot, Denis." In *Routledge Encyclopedia of Philosophy*, edited by Edward Craig, 3:63–69. London: Routledge, 1998.

Wolf, Eric. *Europe and the People without History*. Berkeley: University of California Press, 1997.

Wood, Allen. "Kant's Philosophy of History." In *Toward Perpetual Peace and Other Writings on Politics, Peace, and History*, by Immanuel Kant. New Haven, Conn.: Yale University Press, 2006.

Wood, Ellen Meiksins. *The Pristine Culture of Capitalism: A Historical Essay on Old Regimes and Modern States*. London: Verso, 1991.

Wright, Arnold, and William Sclater. *Sterne's Eliza, Some Account of Her Life in India: With Her Letters Written between 1757 and 1774*. London: W. Heinemann, 1922.

Young, Robert. *Colonial Desire: Hybridity in Theory, Culture, and Race*. New York: Routledge, 1995.

———. *White Mythologies: Writing History and the West*. New York: Routledge, 2004.

Zastoupil, Lynn. *John Stuart Mill and India*. Stanford: Stanford University Press, 1994.

Zwicker, Steven. "Dryden and the Poetic Career." In *The Cambridge History of English Literature, 1660–1770*, edited by John Richetti, 132–59. Cambridge: Cambridge University Press, 2005.

———. "Dryden and the Problem of Literary Modernity: Epilogue." In *The Cambridge Companion to John Dryden*, edited by Steven Zwicker, 280–85. Cambridge: Cambridge University Press, 2004.

———. "John Dryden." In *The Cambridge Companion to English Literature 1650–1740*, edited by Steven Zwicker, 185–203. Cambridge: Cambridge University Press, 1998.

INDEX